Poland From Partitions to EU Accession

Piotr Koryś

Poland From Partitions to EU Accession

A Modern Economic History,
1772–2004

palgrave
macmillan

Piotr Koryś
University of Warsaw
Warsaw, Poland

ISBN 978-3-319-97125-4   ISBN 978-3-319-97126-1   (eBook)
https://doi.org/10.1007/978-3-319-97126-1

Library of Congress Control Number: 2018956152

Cover illustration: Ageev Rostislav / Alamy Stock Photo

This Palgrave Macmillan imprint is published by the registered company Springer Nature Switzerland AG
The registered company address is: Gewerbestrasse 11, 6330 Cham, Switzerland

Acknowledgements

Unlike the political and social history of Poland presented in numerous books, most notably in Norman Davies' *Poland: God's Playground*, the economic history of modern Poland remains almost unknown to the contemporary Western reader. This book is the first systematic synthesis of the modern economic history of Polish lands published in English and offers the possibility of filling an important gap in the economic history of modern Europe.

It is not uncommon that the knowledge of Polish economic history among Western economists and historians is limited to very basic facts. Thus, information and data are often misused (as it is, e.g., in the case of the occupational structure of late-nineteenth-century Polish lands, that—according to some papers—is almost comparable to Britain). The aim of this book is to provide a more detailed view of the Polish economic history, the history of Polish development, its intellectual underpinning, and broader political and social context; this book contains new estimations of the Polish GDP and the occupational structure of Polish lands. It presents latest research of mine, my colleagues from Chair of Economic History in Faculty of Economic Sciences at Warsaw University, and researchers all over Poland and Europe.

While I'm purely responsible for all mistakes, omissions, and misinterpretations, obviously, I owe a great debt to my friends, colleagues, students, and last, but not least, family, support of whom was indispensable during the planning and writing of this book.

In particular, I would like to express my appreciation to my friends and colleagues from the Faculty of Economic Sciences at the University of Warsaw. Professor Jacek Kochanowicz (1946–2014) invited me to the world of economic history as my supervisor, head of the chair, and friend. His critique was always useful; discussions with him—always fruitful; and guidance, curious and patient. Jacek, thank you so much for everything. I am also entirely grateful for the co-operation and support given by Maciej Tymiński, Cecylia Leszczyńska, and Maciej Bukowski.

Discussion with Professors Janos M. Kovacs, Max S. Schulze, and Nikolaus Wolf drew my attention to some important problems of Polish economic history. Co-operation with Professor Marek Okólski, economist and demographer, was one of the most inspiring lessons on how to conduct research, how to infer from available data, and finally, how to use existing knowledge for a better understanding of Polish society and history. My great friends Paweł Dobrowolski and Adam Leszczyński spent a lot of time reading and commenting this book. Thank you! Tomasz Zarycki, Artur Wołek, Łukasz Hardt, and Jan Fałkowski also devoted their time for reading and discussing parts of the manuscript. I also thank the referees of the proposal and book. They offered me many fantastic and insightful critical comments. Ms. Małgorzata Matysik spent a lot of time patiently and attentively translating and editing subsequent versions of the manuscript. Without her, the final result would have been worse.

Institutional support also proved to be very important. My department at the University of Warsaw creates an extremely inspiring area for intellectual debate. University of Warsaw financially supported the translation and redaction of manuscript. The Institute for Human Sciences in Vienna offered me the perfect environment to work on this book during my stay there in the academic year 2016/2017. This book would not have been possible without the comfortable stay in Vienna. The generous support of research by the National Science Centre in the research projects "Economic Growth of The Polish territories in the Time of The First Globalization" (2012/07/B/HS4/00451) and "In pursuit of modernity.

Successes and failures of the politics of modernization in Poland since 1800" allowed me and my colleagues to focus on intellectual inquiries.

And last, but not least, my family was both extremely patient and helpful during the process of the creation of this book. I thank my parents, who supported me and believed in me for dozens of years. My beloved wife Izabela always gave me emotional and intellectual support while our incredible sons Jan, Krzysztof, and Stanisław assisted me all the time, deaf to my requests for a moment of peace. Maybe without them this book could have been written faster, but honestly speaking, it might have never been written. I love you!

Contents

1 Introduction: From the "Little Divergence" to Successful
   EU Integration: Towards Economic History of Modern
   Poland   1

2 The View from Afar: The Polish Economy Between the
   Golden Age and the Partitions (Sixteenth to Eighteenth
   Centuries)   35

3 The Age of Enlightenment Reforms and Partitions of
   Poland: Economy and Politics in the Late Eighteenth
   Century (1772–1795)   43

4 Between the Consolidation from Above and the
   Fragmentation of the State: Partitions, Duchy of
   Warsaw and Polish Lands After the Congress of Vienna
   (1795–1830)   77

5 On the Peripheries of the Modern Western World:
   Delayed Social Reforms and Unfinished Industrial
   Revolution (1830–1870)   115

6   The Dawn of Modern Economic Growth: Period of Late
    Industrialization (1870–1914)   151

7   The Window of Opportunity: Polish Lands During the
    Great War (1914–1921)   195

8   A Moment of Independence: Reconstruction and
    Economic Development of the Second Republic of Poland
    (1918/21–1939)   207

9   Under the Nazi and Soviet Rule: Polish Lands During
    World War II (1939–1945)   255

10 Communist Modernization? Economic Development of
    Poland Under State Socialism (1945–1989)   265

11 In Pursuit of the Western World: Poland Between the
    Transition and the EU Accession (1989–2004)   321

12 Conclusion: Two Centuries of Catching-up to the West   347

Annex   365

Bibliography   371

Index   373

List of Maps and Graphs

Map 3.1   Poland after the First Partition (1772) and Polish lands
            after the Third Partition 1795   53
Map 5.1   Polish lands after Vienna Congress. (Kingdom of Poland
            in purple colour, Grand Duchy of Posen in brighter green)   128
Map 8.1   Poland after WWI (1918–1939)   221
Graph 8.1   Value of industrial output (total and per capita), constant
            prices of 1928 (1928 = 100)   237
Map 10.1   Poland after 1945   281
Graph 12.1 GDP per capita of the territory of the Kingdom of Poland
            (Russian partition) in comparison to neighbouring
            countries and leaders of growth   359

List of Tables

Table 3.1	Population of Poland, 1775 and 1790 (thousands of people)	55
Table 3.2	Occupational structure of household heads in Radziwill estate towns, Sluck 1750 and Kopyl 1750	66
Table 3.3	Occupational structure of Kalisz, 1789	66
Table 3.4	Social and occupational structure of Warsaw, 1792 (number of people, excluding families)	67
Table 4.1a	Male occupational structure (PST), cameras of New Eastern Prussia, ca. 1800	99
Table 4.1b	Occupational structure (PST), Duchy of Warsaw 1810 by department	100
Table 4.1c	Structure of peasants' households (number of households and shares), 1810	101
Table 4.2	Occupational structure of Kingdom of Poland, 1828 (crude data)	103
Table 4.3	Regional (Voivodeship) occupational structure, Kingdom of Poland, 1828	104
Table 5.1a	Evolution of the ethnolinguistic structure of Greater Poland	133
Table 5.1b	Religious structure of Greater Poland (%)	133
Table 5.2	Industrial output (coal, pig iron) in the Kingdom of Poland and selected European countries in 1850 (in kg per capita)	139
Table 5.3	Regional occupational structure of Polish lands, 1859/61/69	142

Table 6.1   Religion and Polish language on Polish lands, early twentieth century (%)   163

Table 6.2   Primary education and literacy of Polish lands   171

Table 6.3   Occupational structure of Polish lands in the turn of the centuries (1895/97/1900)   175

Table 6.4   Roads and railways on Polish lands, 1911   176

Table 7.1   Buildings destroyed during war and share of buildings rebuilt by 1925, territory of interwar Poland   202

Table 8.1   Ethnolinguistic structure of Polish society, 1931—Share (%) of ethnolinguistic groups in total population   225

Table 8.2   Illiteracy levels in interwar Poland   228

Table 8.3   Voivodeships: economic, and demographic data   233

Table 9.1   Population balance of Poland 1939–1950   261

Table 9.2   Distribution of direct material losses by area and sector of economy (in comparison to September 1939)   262

Table A.1   Population of Poland (contemporary borders), thousands of people   365

Table A.2   Urbanization rates (populations of towns 5000+ as a share of total population)   366

Table A.3   Population of the largest cities and towns of Polish lands, 1810–1990. Thousands of people   367

Table A.4   Regional shares of GDP (contemporary borders)   368

Table A.5   Regional GDP per capita in Poland (contemporary borders, G-K dollars 2011)   368

Table A.6   Occupational structure   369

1

Introduction: From the "Little Divergence" to Successful EU Integration: Towards Economic History of Modern Poland

With all its peculiarities, Poland is an extremely interesting case of (partially) successful modernization in a hostile environment, as the changes of borders, states, society, policies, ideologies happened there in a much more dramatic way than in Western Europe. Therefore, I do believe that the story of Poland's development will satisfy the needs not only of economic historians and economists, but of all those interested in the case study of development paths and industrialization that differs from the typical Western experience of stability, continuity, and evolutionary changes. In addition, the reader is provided with the overview of crucial intellectual debates on modernization in Poland. Many of the formerly elaborated ideas and intellectual divisions are still reflected today; thus, it will be much easier for the reader to understand the contemporary political conflicts.

In this book, I analyse the process of the economic development of Polish lands and put it in the context of ideas of modernization and economic policies that aimed at catching up with the West and were organized by the Polish state (or political elites) or designed by the partitioning countries. The starting date of the analysis is the date of the first partition of Poland (the process of partitioning, started in 1772, was finished in the next 20 years and resulted in the collapse of Poland and its disappearance

© The Author(s) 2018
P. Koryś, *Poland From Partitions to EU Accession*,
https://doi.org/10.1007/978-3-319-97126-1_1

from European maps for the next 123 years); the closing date is the date of Poland's accession to the European Union.

Polish modernization attempts and modernization policies (i.e. performed by the Polish state and/or on territories inhabited by the Polish ethnic majority) in the last two centuries had a diverse character. They were statist or anti-statist; focused on just building factories or on establishing modern institutions; those which resulted in narrow-minded plans of political elites (to protect their social status); and those established as an indirect effect of social and political revolutions and transitions. Some of them may be interpreted as the emanation of a political will (of the nation or a social group), while others were simply the delayed imitation or application of external solutions. Some notable successes in convergence were/are observed as a result of implementing some of them, while others resulted in failures.

Derek Aldcroft entitled his book on the economic history of European peripheries during the interwar period *Europe's Third World* (Aldcroft 2013)—in the nineteenth and twentieth centuries, Poland perfectly fitted this description. Even the contemporary economic success of Poland (as well as many former partial successes and failures) seems to be a good demonstration of the dependency of Polish development in the last 200 years on external circumstances, such as external political and institutional stability. After 1989, the next wave of globalization, European integration, as well as the collapse of the Soviet empire and a long period of the internal and external weakness of Russia resulted in a long period of stability and continuity uncommon in modern Poland's economic history. The newly established institutions persisted for a relatively long time (at least from the Polish perspective), and Poland became a relatively safe place for FDIs (in fact, for the first time in the last two centuries). The reader interested in long-term growth patterns can pose numerous questions: what had happened before? Why were Polish lands underdeveloped in the last 200 years? Is this the first period of catching-up with the West? And how did discontinuity, fragmentation, and dislocation affect the economic development of Poland? This book provides the answers to these questions. It presents the economic (and social) history of Poland (1772–2004), supplemented with elements of political history and the history of ideas and extensive data.

1   Literature Review—Syntheses of Socio-Economic History of Poland at Glance

The economic history of Poland in the modern age is practically unknown to non-Polish-speaking readership, and there is not a monograph published in English comprising the whole period covered in this book. A certain exception is the collection of papers written by Jacek Kochanowicz (2006), which encompass—though not exhaustively—the whole period, and present many extremely important themes and narratives. The twentieth-century economic history of Poland up to the system transformation is presented in the book by Zbigniew Landau and Jan Tomaszewski (1985).

Recently, an ambitious attempt to analyse Poland's past was made by an economist, Marcin Piątkowski, who based his research on Daron Acemoglu and James Robinson's hypothesis on the negative impact of extractive institutions on economic development (Piatkowski 2018). In his interpretation, the Polish institutions up to WWII can be treated as extractive, and it was only after the system transformation that the conditions were conducive to the emergence of inclusive institutions in the egalitarian society (created during the communist period), which explains the nearly three decades of economic growth.

On the other hand, a valuable part of the body of literature on the subject are the comprehensive studies of the political history of Poland, such as the books published by Norman Davies (1986, 2005) and Adam Zamoyski (1987, 2009). An enormous resource of statistical data is a series of publications of the Polish Central Statistical Office History of Poland in Numbers (last editions in Polish includes Wyczański 2003; Kubiczek et al. 2006), including the part in English titled *Poland in Europe* (Kuklo et al. 2014).

An important addition to the field of Polish economic history is the economic history of the Central and Eastern European region, where Poland plays a significant role. There are few publications on this subject, including the work of Ivan Berend and Gyorgy Ránki, particularly the series of publications presenting the economic history of the region (Berend 1998a, b, 2006) and the research on the industrialization of the

European peripheries (Berend and Ránki 1982). The economic history of the region between 1815 and 1989 is also presented by David Turnock (2002, 2004). Derek Aldcroft and Steven Morewood (1995) focused on the twentieth-century economic history of the region. Finally, I need to mention the extremely interesting publication by Henryk Szlajfer, presenting the strategies of state-induced industrialization in Central Europe, particularly Poland, and in South America, from the Industrial Revolution to the outbreak of WWII (Szlajfer 2012). Recently, a synthesis of the political history of the region, including the economic aspect, was published by Wojciech Roszkowski (2015). Another recently published synthesis of the history of Central and Eastern Europe, which includes the socio-economic aspect, was edited by Irina Livezeanu and Arpad von Klimo (2017).

The research on the history of the Polish political and economic thought, including the debate on modernization, has not been presented in many publications, either. The interesting paper by James Pula and James Biskupski concerns the Polish democratic thought from the Renaissance to the Great Emigration after the November Uprising 1830–1831 (Biskupski and Pula 1990). The excellent synthesis by Jerzy Jedlicki presents the nineteenth-century discussions on modernization and the model of the Polish civilization (Jedlicki 1999), and Maciej Janowski outlines the tradition of the liberal thought in the nineteenth century (Janowski 2004). He is also involved in the work on the excellent book presenting the history of ideas in the region, with particular emphasis on the conceptions of modernization (Trencsényi et al. 2016). The history of Polish intelligentsia, the intellectual elite of the nation, is an important addition to intellectual history of Poland (Jedlicki et al. 2014). Until now, only Volume I has been published; it covers the nineteenth century and presents the intellectual trends prevailing in the Polish political thought, placing them in the Eastern European context. Andrew Janos (2000) in his monograph focused on the social, political, and intellectual history of the region. The extremely interesting book by Stefano Bianchini (2015) about the debate on modernization in Eastern Europe in the last two centuries focuses on the former USSR and the Balkans and hardly discusses the Polish intellectual traditions, but it is still valid for the present considerations because it brings up the problems which were a challenge also to the Polish thinkers and the various ways in which those problems were addressed all over the region.

Comprehensive studies published in Polish are far more numerous, including the works of Franciszek Bujak (1925, 1926), Jan Rutkowski (1950, 1953), and Andrzej Grodek and Irena Kostrowicka (1955) from the first half of the twentieth century and Władysław Rusiński (1961); however, here, I focus on the most recent work. The study by Wojciech Morawski (2011) synthesizes the economic history of Poland, and much of his research focuses on the period 1800–2004. The valuable study by Cecylia Leszczyńska and Andrzej Jezierski (2010) comprises the period up to 1989. The research of Janusz Kaliński resulted in a series of publications synthesizing the history of post-war Poland, but also a book co-authored with Zbigniew Landau on the twentieth century (Kaliński and Landau 2003). Short synthesis was also published by Janusz Skodlarski (2005). Moreover, the period up to 1989 is covered by the Encyclopaedia of the Economic History of Poland (Ajnenkiel, Dunin-Wąsowicz, et al. 1981; Ajnenkiel, Mączak, et al. 1981). The research of Anna and Grzegorz Wójtowicz is an attempt to reconstruct Poland's development path throughout history, from the beginning of the state to the present day (Wójtowicz and Wójtowicz 2009).

The comprehensive studies are supplemented by research in particular fields, like the history of the railways (Koziarski 1993a, b), the history of banking (Morawski 1998), or the history of industrial regions (Misztal 1970; Dwilewicz et al. 2015). An important resource is regional research, particularly the economic history of Greater Poland written by Czesław Łuczak (1973) and Jerzy Topolski (1973), the multi-volume history of Pomerania (Labuda et al. 1993; Salmonowicz et al. 2000; Andrzejewski et al. 2015), and the economic history of the Austro-Hungarian Galicia by Franciszek Bujak (1917). Recently, an interesting study of the economic history of Galicia was published by Klemans Kaps (2015). The research on the history of Galicia resulted in numerous papers, which were gathered in the two-volume book edited by Agnieszka Kawalec and Wacław Wierzbieniec (2011). Additionally, information concerning particular regions of Poland during the period of partition can be found in the research on the economic history of Germany, Austria, and Russia. As far as the demography of Poland is concerned, the body of literature includes the book by Andrzej Gawryszewski on the population of Poland in the twentieth century (2005), and Andrzej Jelonek's study presenting the statistics of the urban population in the Polish lands from the beginning of the nineteenth century to 1960 (Jelonek 1967). The data on the population and territory of Poland can also be found in the abovementioned series History of Poland in Numbers, in the part titled Population, Territory (Główny Urząd Statystyczny 1993). An excellent synthesis of Poland's social history, including the development of the social structure, from the beginning of the state to the outbreak of WWI, was prepared by Ireneusz Ihnatowicz and his collaborators (Ihnatowicz et al. 1979). The history of Jews in Poland is comprehensively presented, for example, in the encyclopaedia by Tomaszewski et al. (2001).

The noteworthy syntheses on the history of political thought and history of ideas are the ones by Rett Ludwikowski (2012) and Roman Wapiński (1997); however, both offer a very cursory view of the post-WWII period. Among the earlier research, I need to mention the seminal work by Wilhelm Feldman, comprising the Polish political thought in the nineteenth century (Feldman 1933). The eminent contemporary authors working on the synthesis of the intellectual history of the nineteenth century include Jerzy Jedlicki (1988), Tomasz Kizwalter (1999), and Tomasz Łepkowski (2003).

The Polish economic thought was comprehensively presented by Tadeusz Kowalik, whose research comprised the period up to 1965, and who very interestingly synthesized the debate on transformation (Kowalik 1992). Other scholars who conducted research on the Polish economic thought were Leszek Guzicki and Seweryn Żurawicki (1969, 1974) and Edwar Łukawer (1996). A recent study by Dariusz Grzybek (2012) presents the influence of the views of economists on the political ideas (up to 1939). Wojciech Musiał studied the subsequent state policies of the modernization of Poland between 1918 and 2004 (Musiał 2013).

Here, I have outlined the comprehensive works pertaining to the topic of the present monograph, that is, the last 200 years of the Polish economic, social, and intellectual history (the latter in the field of the debate on modernity), as well as a few books presenting the history of the region, that is, Central and Eastern Europe and Poland as its integral part. In the book, I also refer to numerous in-depth analytical studies, both books and research papers, concerning particular periods, persons, ideas, and processes. Anyway, the bibliography I include is by no means a complete list of the body of literature on the subject available in Polish, though I attempted to indicate the most important and most recent works. The English language literature on the subject is presented as exhaustively as possible.

2 Backwardness, Late Development, Labour-Intensive Industrialization, and the Culture of Capitalism: Theoretical Background

The analysis and interpretation of the economic development of the Polish lands throughout two centuries is certain to pose several problems, due to both the considerable length of the period under analysis and the particular course of the Polish history in this period. In economic history, 200 years is a period which can be studied, but not without difficulty, as over such a long time (*longue durée*), the changes do not only involve institutions, infrastructure, or the structure of production, but also the deep civilization structures described by Fernand Braudel (1995). The period under analysis featured a high pace of demographic changes and social restructuring—the population changed its size, age, structure, and social structure. Moreover, this was also the time of dramatic shifts of the dominant ideologies, concepts of development, and the countries perceived by political elites as points of reference or role models in modernization.

Additionally, Poland is particularly difficult to study in the *longue durée*. The period under analysis features territorial and political discontinuity, social structure changes far beyond the standard social modernization process, and wars. Analysing such a long period involves studying heterogeneous data and available sources, which practically enforces various analytical and statistical estimations, interpolations, and extrapolations. In order to understand the consequences of the experience of continual fragmentation, territorial and populational dislocation, and discontinuity, it is reasonable to refer to the debates concerning the historical factors determining economic development.

There has been an ongoing debate on the reasons and determining factors of industrialization, particularly the delayed one. The differences in the moment and pace of industrialization and the ensuing differences in the rate and level of development are described and explained in various ways. Many authors use the terms "early" and "late industrialization". Early industrialization, known as the Industrial Revolution, took place in Great Britain and more broadly in Western Europe, which was determined by several economic, demographic, institutional, geographical, and social factors. The question of backwardness is usually considered in the context of the exceptional development of Western Europe and the differences between it and the backward regions.

The idea of late industrialization—the imitative industrialization which took place later than that in Western Europe and sometimes followed a different path—is built on the analyses of Gerschenkron (1962) concerning backwardness. He indicated the features of the countries which were industrialized later than the leading economies of the West. In his view, the backward countries feature the faster pace of industrialization and bigger industrial enterprises than the developed countries, there is emphasis on capital-intensive rather than labour-intensive production and the lesser role of agriculture, and the state implements the industrial policy aiming to promote the development of the backward country to make it attain the status of a developed country.

Since Gerschenkron's research on late development, there has been a debate on the effectiveness of public policies, particularly the state ones, supporting development. Studying Russia, he identified the areas of the ineffectiveness of the pro-development interventions of the peripheral state, such as the premature development of heavy industry, the persistent backwardness of agriculture, the lack of incentives for entrepreneurship. Earlier, the problem of the efficiency of non-market allocation, crucial in the pro-development anti-market industrial policies based on fiscal expansion, was at the centre of the economic debate between Friedrich Hayek and Oskar Lange.

Debate on industrialization initiated the research concerning catching up and development convergence, particularly in terms of industrial output. The problem of identifying and measuring the development gap between the early and late industrialized countries and ways to bridge it has been discussed since Gerschenkron's times. One of the most important ideas concerning the possibility to catch up was formulated by Moses Abramovitz (1986). He indicated the possible channels through which the modernization of the backward countries and catching up can take place. Most important of them is the disparity between the human and social capital on the one hand and the institutions and technological advancement on the other. The high quality human and social capital can trigger development on the basis of the quick reception and implementation of cutting-edge institutional and technological solutions. This phenomenon allowed Japan (at the end of the nineteenth century and after WWII) and Western Europe (after WWII) to catch up very rapidly. The problem of the factors determining efficiency convergence and technological convergence has been researched by multiple scholars.

On the basis of Gerschenkron's insights, also Alice Amsden (1992, 2001), Amsden and Chu (2003) developed differentiation between early and late industrialization. The former involved the development of industry determined by technological innovation and individual ingenuity of entrepreneurs, who optimized the methods and organization of production, while the latter involved imitation and import of technology, at least in the initial period. The distinct models determined the differences in economic and trade policies. The early industrialized countries were generally inclined to conduct and promote free trade, whereas the late industrialized countries (including the countries industrialized at the end of the first wave of industrialization, such as Germany and the USA) promoted protectionism, at least periodically. One of the most important economic arguments in favour of protecting the internal market is the one of the infant industry: in the late industrialized countries, the possible (and often easily attainable) benefits can result from the lower labour cost, the transfer of technology, imitation, and so on, but the early industrialized countries may remain competitive due to the economic effects of scale of production. As the scale of production increases, the per-unit cost decreases, so there can be persistent considerable differences in production costs between the early and late industrialized countries within the particular branches of production.

In this context, it seems reasonable to look at the state-induced modernization and development policies implemented in South American countries after WWII—so-called import substitution industrialization.

Even though they were based mostly on the early ideas of developmental economics and the dependency theory, formulated in South America, they originated mostly in the Eastern European ideas of the economic policy based on the national investment programmes and import substitution, as well as the substitution of the capital by the state, as capital was expensive and difficult to obtain in the peripheral countries. These ideas were treated as the model of economic development strategies and recommended for backward countries (Love 1996). These theories are similar to the explanations offered by Marxists and neo-Marxists, stating that the source of backwardness is the deliberate policy of the countries of the developed centre towards the peripheries.

The other explanation of backwardness and consequently other development path that involved export-oriented industrialization and was adopted by Japan and other South-East Asian countries after WWII (Linnemann et al. 1987). Their aim was to use the local resources, particularly the practically limitless quantity of cheap skilled labour, to achieve the status of world-leading exporters of labour-intensive goods, and then build the human capital and modernize of the economy. This was to be achieved by means of the intense involvement of the public administration, whose role was to support export and the selected branches and entrepreneurs, and to develop education systems according to the needs of the labour market.

Import substitution industrialization and export-oriented industrialization can be regarded as two competing ideas for the development of peripheral countries. The former is based on the assumption that the exchange between the central and peripheral economies is not equivalent. The consequent belief is that the involvement of the state in industrialization, protectionist policies, and the self-exclusion from the global economic exchange will allow the country to develop its own industry. This can be supported by the aforementioned argument of infant industry, the Prebisch-Singer hypothesis indicating the decrease of the prices of natural resources relative to manufactured goods (which de-legitimized the policy of the development based on the export of resources), and the related hypothesis of the non-equivalence of the exchange between the centre and peripheries. In many countries, the moment when the local industry protection became unnecessary or even detrimental turned out to be impossible to determine, and in effect, the long-term protection supported the development of inefficient industry. On the other hand, export-oriented industrialization assumes that the profits from the trade on the globalizing market are also available for the developing countries. Thus, the state support of industrialization should primarily lead to the development of export potential and should be time-limited, as the enterprises must quickly become ready for global competition.

But in the historical (in opposition to theoretical) perspective, the success of late industrialization occurred to be related to combining both strategies in a favourable geopolitical environment. One of the latest examples is the East Asian export-oriented industrialization following the period of protecting the local industry. Its aim was to benefit from the (dynamically changing) competitive advantage of the countries of the region (first described by Akamatsu 1962), stemming from the low cost of the human capital, and build the sectors of industry which would be competitive on the global, not local, market. This allowed to achieve considerable advantage of scale. However, empirical research confirms that a period of widespread use of the import substitution strategy contributed to fast-paced industrialization of the peripheries (Williamson 2011; Bénétrix et al. 2012), but the greatest long-term benefit was gained by the countries that simultaneously managed to conduct the export-oriented industrialization policy as well. In the period 1920–1990 the absolute industrial catching-up was observed, defined as the situation when the industrial output per capita grew faster in the industrializing countries than in the early industrialized ones, and its greatest pace was in the years 1950–1973. Admittedly, however, it was the period when the West had begun de-industrialization, and it was the modern services sector which had started to become the basis for economic growth.

Effectiveness of state-induced development policies is another important problem in the context of the debate concerning the model of industrialization. According to some economists, the development experience of the South-East Asian countries proves that there are ways to conduct the state policy of development support in efficient way (i.e. to reduce development gap between peripheries and the centre of global economy), while others contest such an interpretation. This is reflected in the research on the new structural economics and in the arguments conducted within its framework, such as the debate between Justin Lin and Weying Zhang (Lin 2012, 2017; Zhang 2016, 2017). The former advocates the involvement of the state in the development process by means of an economic policy devised to provide a stimulus for the change in the branch structure and geographical distribution of production, in order to make optimum use of all the human, capital, and natural resources which the developing country has at its disposal. One of the important tools of such a policy would be picking winners, that is, the entrepreneurs and branches eligible for support. As he emphasizes, "Every developing country has the potential to grow dynamically for decades, and to become a middle income or high income country in one or two generations, as long as the government has the right industrial policy to facilitate the development of the private sector along the line of the country's comparative advantage and tap into the latecomer advantages" (Lin 2013) Thus, Lin is essentially a defender of the South-East Asian and Chinese model. His opponent in the dispute believes that better results are achieved by means of creating a safe institutional framework for individual entrepreneurship rather than through the direct control of economic development, because it is costly and its results are often the direct opposite of what was expected.

The question of early and late industrialization can be also considered from the cultural and institutional perspective, comprising another important economic history debate. An important element of the debate on proto-industrialization was Max Weber's theory, formulated over a century ago, on the role of religion in shaping the bourgeoisie values and, in particular, the influence of Calvinism on the development of the capitalist ethic. It was subsequently developed to explain the civilization success of the West, referring to the industrious revolution (entrepreneurship, ingenuity, and diligence), which created the cultural foundation for industrialization. Early industrialization in Europe was regarded as the effect of this revolution (De Vries 2008). The emergence of the set of virtues and values founding the capitalist culture (Hirschman 1977; Berger 1986; McCloskey 2010), the spreading of the Enlightenment ideas and rational decision making, and their practical implementation in the spirit of entrepreneurship and ingenuity (Mokyr 2009, 2017) gave rise to the changes which formed the modern Western industrial economy and can be the factors explaining the extraordinary success of the Atlantic civilization.

But according to some scholars, a different version of the industrious revolution took place in Japan (Saito 2010; Austin and Sugihara 2013), which determined the industrialization model characteristic of Asia, based on the low labour cost in relation to its quality and a relative persistence of the significant role of labour-intensive industries in the economy. This model can be connected with the processes of imitation and diffusion of technology indicated by Akamatsu (1962), Gerschenkron (1962), Amsden (1992) and others, and with the development policy model discussed by Lin (2013). As a result of these factors, Japan became the archetype of a peripheral state which achieved economic success. Labour-intensive industrialization prevails in South-East Asia, while other peripheral areas, such as the European peripheries and Latin America, have tried to imitate the Western European, capital- and resource-intensive model. It contributed to the emergence of highly productive but relatively small (especially in terms of employment) and non-innovative manufacturing sectors. This effect was even more pronounced in the Latin American countries adopting import substitution industrialization. In effect, the manufacturing sector developed there on a much smaller scale and at a slower rate than in South-East Asian countries.

An even more important role in determining different paths of industrialization and economic development is ascribed to the institutions. The research of Douglass C. North and Robert P. Thomas (1973) gave rise to the analysis of the institutional foundation of the capitalist economy. The institutional distinctiveness of the West was indicated by various authors, who defined its particularity in different ways, including the development of local markets, education, the rule of law, democracy, or the institutional framework of the market. To some extent, the conclusion of a certain stage of this debate are the analyses by Daron Acemoglu and James Robinson (2006, 2012), indicating two trajectories of the development of institutions—the one in which extractive institutions start to turn into inclusive institutions and promote the development of the society and economy, and the one in which they do not. The inclusiveness of institutions promotes ingenuity and contributes to the nation's economic success. Marcin Piatkowski (2018), in his study mentioned above, applied this model to explain the Polish transformation and its long-term sources. He showed that WWII, communism, and transformation resulted in the formation of modern, inclusive institutions in Poland.

Another approach is connected with the research of quality of institutional design. The scholars following this approach focus on the legal and fiscal capacity of the state (or state capacity), and its influence on development. Here, the problem of inclusiveness/extractiveness of institutions is replaced by the problem of the institutional conditions of high/low state capacity. Among the research in this field, we need to mention the analyses of Charles Tilly (1992), who indicated the role of the state capacity in war making. Lastly, Mark Dincecco (2018) continued the empirical research of this relation. The capacity to conduct effective fiscal policy has been studied in the research on fiscal states; the role of a responsible fiscal policy (both income and expenditure) was analysed, for example, by North and Barry R. Weingast (1989). Stephan R. Epstein (2000) studied the reasons for fiscal centralization in Europe, and indicated the weakening of the power of the local elites and the growing power of the kings. Among others, the research of Yun Casalilla and O'Brien (2012) shows the relation between the fiscal capacity and the development success of Great Britain. In his view, the success was due to the state's capacity to provide public goods (including national defence), particularly external security and protecting property rights (by means of the effective executing rule of law) and trade. The problem has also been studied by economists, for example, by Gunnar Myrdal (1968), who diagnosed the consequences of the weakness of institutions in the so-called soft states for economic development. Recently a comparative and theoretical analysis of the state capacity conducted by Besley and Persson (2007, 2011) and their conclusions are similar to the above: "The historical experience of today's rich nations hints that the creation of state capacity to collect taxes and enforce contracts are key aspects of development. Equally, the fortunes of many of today's poor countries indicate that state capacity cannot be taken for granted" (Besley and Persson 2007). This relation was empirically confirmed in the long term by the research of Marc Dincecco (2011), according to whom "the relationship between fiscally centralized and politically limited regimes and economic growth in European history is complex, and further research is required to establish clear causal links. Yet the findings suggest that sustained development was more likely in states where governments were able to solve two key political problems: fiscal fragmentation and absolutism. England possessed a centralized and limited regime before industrial takeoff during the middle of the eighteenth century. Likewise, most countries in continental Europe implemented modern fiscal systems before undergoing industrialization during the second half of the 1800s. The results thus point to the establishment of centralized and limited regimes as solid institutional foundations upon which European states could successfully pursue long-run growth" (p. 116).

Finally, the fourth important field of consideration on long-term development concerns the geographical location. The consequences of the central and peripheral location have been discussed in economy, philosophy, and history since the nineteenth century, and modern economic geography continues this debate. Basically, this research points out that the location at a big distance from the centres of development and innovations, and away from trade routes, is unfavourable and leads to development gaps. The empirical studies conducted by economic historians from Braudel (1995) and Marian Małowist (1973) to Kevin O'Rourke and Jeffrey G. Williamson (1999, 2017) show that, from the beginning of the capitalist revolution, in the Dutch Republic and Great Britain, the Commonwealth found itself on the remote periphery of European transformations.

3   Interpretation of the Economic History of Poland

The local and international discussions on the reasons for the backwardness of the Polish lands in Europe do not refer to many of these global debates. The interpretations of the long-term backwardness of Poland and the whole region indicate the institutional factors, shortages of capital, poorly educated population in the nineteenth century, unfavourable location, and other factors.

It is beyond doubt that the Commonwealth of the eighteenth century was a state with weak institutions, extractive or not, and low state capacity (which is discussed in Chap. 1). Certainly, the limited tax capacity of the state and prolonged fiscal fragmentation hindered or even blocked the provision of key public goods, including external security, contract enforcement, and ownership rights protection. Therefore, the benefit for the relatively modern political system, with the limited power of the king, decreased, and in the eighteenth century, practically disappeared. Additionally, with the growth of the importance of cities and townspeople, the relative power of the nobility in the political system started to work against development. A particular instance of this, though not the only one, was the "second serfdom".

The flaws of the political system and the social relations within the state, as well as the weaknesses of the state itself, have been discussed by Polish historians since the nineteenth century, when Michał Bobrzyński (1927) and other historians from the Cracow school indicated these factors as the possible causes of the collapse of the state, thus breaking the Romantic tradition in Polish historical studies, which focused on the external factors such as hostile neighbours (who hated Polish liberties). Since then, there is a long tradition of the discussion on the cultural and institutional barriers to development in Poland. The reasons for the weakness of the political, economic, social, and legal institutions of the Commonwealth has recurred multiple times, for example, in the studies of economic historians, particularly those of Witold Kula and his followers, including Jacek Kochanowicz (e.g. Kula and Kochanowicz 1993; Kochanowicz 2006). They pointed out the persistence of corvée as a barrier to development at the beginning of the modern age. The research of sociologists such as Janusz Hryniewicz (2004) or Jan Sowa (Sowa 2011) has led to the conclusion that the relations typical of serfdom have been preserved in multiple institutions forming the economic culture of the Polish society, which is reflected in the "culture of the estate" (Hryniewicz 2004) persisting in various areas of the social and economic life of present-day Poland, that is, the quasi-feudal relations in hierarchic organizations, such as enterprises or universities. The problem of corvée and its long-term effects has long been a point of interest of social scientists (Koryś 2016). Lastly, Marcin Piątkowski points out that until recently, the Polish institutions were extractive *par excellence* (Piatkowski 2018). In his opinion, it was only their transformation into inclusive institutions which made them conducive to development.

The recent discussions on the unsuccessful catching up with the West bring up these institutional and culturalist factors. The aforementioned analysis of Piątkowski, focusing mostly on the reasons for Poland's present-day economic success, indicates the key role of institutional factors, particularly the persistence of extractive institutions in the previous failures. Piątkowski, like Andrzej Leder (2014) earlier, points out the significance of the war and the formation of an egalitarian society in the communist system for social modernization. In this view, the war and the communist rule eliminated social divisions which had sustained the inefficient institutional solutions (Piątkowski) and enabled the upward mobility of the peasants, who took the urban jobs and social positions vacated as a result of the Holocaust and the disappearance of the large part of the elite (Leder).

Another important reason for the backwardness of the Polish lands mentioned in the discussion is under-urbanization and the consequent inexistence of the modern bourgeoisie until the mid-nineteenth century. The political dominance of the nobility, which did not safeguard the interests of the townspeople, and the dependency development model based on the export of unprocessed agricultural produce contributed to delaying the emergence of the urban middle class until the end of the eighteenth century. This resulted in the long-term shortage of capital in the nineteenth and twentieth centuries and the inability to finance economic development, particularly the emergence of the industrial economy. This capital could not be substituted by the policy of the state, because it collapsed and disappeared at the key moment of the Little Divergence in Europe (the barriers to development in this period are discussed in Chaps. 2, 3, 4 and 5). The problem has been studied for a long time, and the recent analyses of the consequences of the absence of the bourgeoisie and the excessive social and political influence of the intelligentsia, who had continued some of the traditions of the nobility, are conducted by Tomasz Zarycki and Rafał Smoczyński (2008; Smoczyński and Zarycki 2017).

Keeping much of the population as serfs and the lack of compulsory education systems on some of the Polish lands in the nineteenth century contributed to the low level of human capital throughout the nineteenth and part of the twentieth centuries (see Chaps. 5 and 7). In effect, despite the relatively limitless labour resources, there was limited access in cities to workers with relatively high human capital, particularly in the Austrian and Russian partitions. This led to the development of several strong industrial centres surrounded by poor agricultural regions, which blocked the possibility of adopting the Japanese-like development model, based on labour-intensive industrialization. It seems, however, that some of the Polish lands started to follow this path of development at the end of the nineteenth century (see Chap. 5).

Whenever it was possible, the state made attempts to implement pro-development industrial policies, which were described by Jerzy Jedlicki (1964), Jerzy Gołębiowski (1985), and others (see Chaps. 3, 7 and 9). They fit Gerschenkron's description—the focus was on the development of heavy industry, and the state tried to substitute and suppress market mechanisms (which was particularly pronounced in the period of state communism). In Poland, these attempts aimed at import substitution industrialization, and they were at most moderately effective, which was connected with the low fiscal and legal capacity of the state, persistent also in the twentieth century. Low tax income, relatively weak state institutions, and overwhelming problems with managing and controlling the territory rendered the catching-up efforts ineffectual. After WWII, the economy was based of the Soviet model and the communist anti-market catching-up strategy; its development was dynamic only in the short term, and its decline was preceded by several years of crises and social tensions (see Chaps. 7 and 9).

It needs to be emphasized that the strategies of the involvement of the state in promoting economic development practically never involved the support for the private sector. The idea of "picking the winners", supporting the branches and entrepreneurs who were potentially the springboard for development, was never taken into real consideration. The public policies in the nineteenth and twentieth centuries (except the development strategy created by Rajmund Rębieliński, discussed in Chap. 3, and the foundation for economic policy laid by Aleksander Wielopolski in the 1860s and by Władysław Grabski in the 1920s, see Chaps. 4 and 7) were all based on the direct investment of the state, which led to inefficiencies both in the short term, during the investment process, and in the long term, in the management of the economy.

The relatively slow economic development was also induced by the unfavourable location away from trade routes and—until Germany took the path of rapid development—away from the best-developed parts of Europe. The remoteness hindered the diffusion of innovation and institutions, hampered the development of the sectors of economy which had export potential, and left the Polish lands on the periphery of the modernization in Europe (cf. the chapters on the nineteenth century). It was not until 1989 that the transformation to capitalism, an open market economy, and export-oriented industrialization became possible, and the accession to the European Union fully included Poland into the European flow of income (see Chap. 10).

4   Ideas and Economic History

Important contexts of Poland's economic development were the debates on how to develop the country and catch up with the West, usually incorporating the imitation of the economic centre. To simplify, two dominant positions can be indicated: the "followers" took a dim view of the local institutions and social conditions and they acted towards sustaining the gap between Poland and the "better" development model; on the other hand, there was a group who defined their political goals in terms of the actual catching up with the economic centre, by means of using Poland's potential—social, national, people's, citizens', state, depending on the particular political option they represented. Apart from this division, or perhaps between these options, one can place all those who believed in the Polish unique, non-imitational path to economic success, either ignoring/questioning the problem of catching up with the West, or aiming at actually achieving that (or even overtaking the West), but by means of a different, unique path of development.

Every modernization policy is the result of the goals, the means proposed for achieving them, and the strategies selected for their implementation, but all the three levels are determined and influenced by the attitude to the local social institutions. In this respect, two lines of thought can be indicated. The first one is the (often unspoken) assumption that the society is capable of spontaneous modernization. Such modernizers believe that if the proper architecture of institutions is ensured (the ones which D.C. North calls the rules of the game), they will provide the framework for such spontaneous modernization. The other line of thought involves the belief that people have to be forced to modernize, for example, by means of relocating them to towns and cities, building factories for public money, and so on.

The Polish debate also involved two different views of the process of modernization itself. One position held that modernization had to involve the mobilization of the internal social energy, and only this kind of modernization could be successful. The opposite view involved external intervention, including even some justified limitation of sovereignty, as the only way to overcome the barriers resulting from the historical, institutional, or other factors which could not be removed from the inside. Finally, there was the middle way, whose proponents believed that some external intervention might be functional, but the modernization itself had to be based on the local social capital. The arguments concerning modernization have been presented very briefly here due to the shortage of space, but they may help to understand the political choices, industrialization policy strategies, or the geopolitical associations of particular political groups, sometimes determining the development trajectories.

5   Poland from Partitions to EU Accession: The Structure of the Book

During the last 200 years, Polish lands (and the whole CEE region) played the role of (close) peripheries of Western Europe—a poor and underdeveloped part of Europe. Moreover, the processes of fragmentation of territory and dislocation of both territory and population interfered with the process of economic development. These processes, not uncommon in the region, occurred in Poland with high frequency and intensity. But since 1990s, in the relatively stable and foreseeable geopolitical environment, Poland has enjoyed rapid economic growth and socio-economic development and from the Western perspective is an example of successful post-communist transition (according to Branko Milanovic (2014) and Marcin Piatkowski (2013), an exceptional one). Since 1991, Poland has been rapidly converging to developed Europe in terms of economic as well as social and political development. In effect, today's Poland is one of the largest members of the EU in terms of territory, population, and economy.

In my opinion, the prolonged backwardness of Poland (and the whole region) was a result of discontinuity more than any institutional, educational, or geographical reasons. The challenge of discontinuity is more common on the peripheries than in the centre of the global economy. In the last two centuries, the discontinuity negatively affected most of the modernization attempts which happened in Poland (except the contemporary one). They were suddenly terminated due to external/exogenous or internal/endogenous shocks. The economic history of Poland is also the story of fragmentation and dislocation of the state which disappeared in the nineteenth century and was consistently moved towards the West in the twentieth century. In that respect, the economic (and not only economic) history of Poland, particularly in the nineteenth century, is the history of the development of the remote peripheries of great European powers, the history of exogenous industrial and social policy, and the industrialization that was not related to the internal policy and internal dynamics of development, but which happened by chance. In turn, in the twentieth century, it is the history of the subsequent re-integrations of national territories, mass movements (dislocations) of population, and cruel wars, which led not only to the destruction of population and infrastructure, but also to the collapse of the social structure.

Therefore, the aim of this book is to present the economic history of Poland (and the Polish lands at the time when the state did not exist) in the nineteenth and twentieth centuries and to discuss the social, economic, and institutional consequences of political discontinuity, border changes, and dislocations of the population. I focus mostly on territories of Polish political units, territories inhabited by Polish majority in nineteenth century as well as on territories of contemporary Poland. Statistical data, unless stated otherwise, concern the contemporary territory of Poland. It should be noted that for the long time (until 1945) western part of this territory was part of Germany. The structure of the book is chronological. While the period I discuss starts in 1772, with the so-called First Partition of the Commonwealth of Poland and Lithuania, I start with a brief look of on the Polish economy between the Golden Age of Poland (the sixteenth century) and the period leading to the partitions. Then, the whole analysis is divided into nine chapters (from Chap. 2 to 10) and the final conclusion. Most of the chapters have a similar structure and include the parts which present:

- *The internal and international political context.* These parts (usually separate for the local and international level) outline the political context of economic development.
- *The ideas shared by political elites, translated into new and reformed institutions and policies.* I focus on the ideas of modernization and development and the different views on Polish modernity.
- *Demographic processes and territorial changes.* The aim is to present the spatial and demographic dimensions of discontinuity in the Polish history.
- *Social change.* Polish lands experienced the processes of dynamic social changes which affected economic modernization. Periods of the formation of nation-wide social movements demonstrated relatively high levels of social capital (still in the rather non-market form) while quite common corruption and nepotism were signs of the "backward society" structures.
- *Economic history.* It includes the macro-economic approach to economic development: economic growth and its factors as well as the institutional and microeconomic underpinning of growth. For deeper insight into this history, short case studies of firms and enterprises are presented.

The structure of the book is as follows:

Chapter 2: The View from Afar: The Polish Economy Between the Golden Age and the Partitions (Sixteenth to Eighteenth Centuries)

The sixteenth century is sometimes called the Golden Age of the Commonwealth of Poland and Lithuania (Piatkowski 2013). Then, due to inefficient institutions, resource-based economy, and continuous wars, the political and economic power of Poland declined. The chapter provides a concise overview of the factors which contributed to the decline of the Polish state between the sixteenth and eighteenth centuries and introduces the concepts applied by the author to the analysis of the crucial social and economic processes and to the formation of the modern Polish society, nation, and economy.

Chapter 3: The Age of Enlightenment Reforms and Partitions of Poland: Economy and Politics in the Late Eighteenth Century (1772–1795)

Between 1772 and 1795, in spite of the recently undertaken reforms, the Polish state gradually ceased to exist as a result of three partitions. The delayed reforms, the collapse of the state as well as the economic consequences of the partitions are presented in the context of the reception of the Enlightenment by the Polish elites.

Chapter 4: Between the Consolidation from Above and the Fragmentation of the State: Partitions, Duchy of Warsaw and Polish Lands After the Congress of Vienna (1795–1830)

After 1795, the Polish state ceased to exist as a separate entity. Subsequently, it was revived—on a significantly diminished territory— first by Napoleon, as the Duchy of Warsaw, and then, after the Congress of Vienna, as the Kingdom of Poland (known as Congress Poland) and the Free City of Cracow, both with relative autonomy (including their own constitutions). Within the Prussian state, some extent of autonomy was granted to the Grand Duchy of Posen. These quasi-states were abolished between 1831 (the defeat of the November Uprising) and 1848 (after the Revolutions of 1848). I present the economic consequences of the fragmentation of the Polish territory and the subsequent designs of modernization formulated by the Enlightenment reformers.

Chapter 5: On the Peripheries of the Modern Western World: Delayed Social Reforms and Unfinished Industrial Revolution (1830–1870)

The divergence among the formerly Polish regions continued in this period and was even strengthened by both the broader processes of the

"Little Divergence" in Europe and, locally, by the different timings and models of the agrarian reforms. I analyse the divergent paths of development of the fragmented Polish lands. I discuss the final collapse of the project of state-led industrialization in Congress Poland and the success of spontaneous industrialization there, but I particularly focus on the different paths of land reforms in partitioned Poland, and their consequences.

Chapter 6: The Dawn of Modern Economic Growth: Period of Late Industrialization (1870–1914)

The chapter covers the longest period of the inexistence of Polish formal institutions and the ongoing integration of the fragmented Polish lands and their societies into the partitioning countries. The processes of modern industrialization on the Polish territories started in the early 1870s, but the different timing and dynamics of industrialization resulted in the growing divergence of Polish lands. The German partition became a peripheral part of an industrial empire, Congress Poland started to industrialize and before WWI became one of the most modern provinces of Russia, and the Austrian partition remained a densely inhabited but mostly rural, poor, remote, and backward part of the Habsburg Empire.

Chapter 7: The Window of Opportunity: Polish Lands During the Great War (1914–1921)

In this chapter, I discuss the social and economic consequences of WWI and the subsequent conflicts (Silesian Uprisings, the Polish-Soviet War, the Polish-Lithuanian War, the Czechoslovak-Polish border conflict) on the Polish territories. I present the direct and indirect results of the war for the economy of the Polish lands, such as material damages, the outflow of capital, the breaking of trade and economic ties with the former empires, and so on. Finally, the process of the restoration of the Polish state is presented.

Chapter 8: A Moment of Independence: Reconstruction and Economic Development of the Second Republic of Poland (1918/21–1939)

The chapter presents the short interwar period (1921–1939). The economic history of this period is the history of re-integration (de-fragmentation) of the Polish lands, re-creation of the national market, and rebuilding the economy in very unfavourable geopolitical conditions. The chapter describes the challenges of hyperinflation (1920s), political and economic tensions with Germany and the Soviet Union, the crisis of parliamentarianism and the rise of authoritarianism (from 1926), and the Great Depression. It also presents a dispute between statists and economic liberals over the model of economic policy. Finally, the rise of state capitalism as a reaction to the Great Depression is presented.

Chapter 9: Under the Nazi and Soviet Rule: Polish Lands During World War II (1939–1945)

In this chapter, I analyse the consequences of WWII for Poland and the Polish society. I present the course of the German and Soviet occupations, the creation of the Polish Government-in-Exile, and the rise of the Polish Underground State. The economic, social, and demographic consequences of War are analysed, in particular, the scheduled extermination of the population of Poland (incl. the Holocaust). The debates on the political and economic architecture of post-war Poland are presented, as well as the new borders of Poland on the post-war map of Europe.

Chapter 10: Communist Modernization? Economic Development of Poland Under State Socialism (1945–1989)

The chapter concerns the period of state socialism. First, it deals with the rise and institutionalization of state socialism (1945–1970). The problem of the dislocation of the state (lost and "regained" lands) and resettlement of people (mass forced migrations in the 1940s–1950s, of both Polish and German citizens) is discussed, as well as the process of industrialization, along with the ensuing societal and economic structural changes. Then, the crisis and collapse of state socialism (1970–1989) are presented. I discuss the sources of the recurrent socio-economic crises, the workers' protests, and the role of the Solidarność movement in undermining the communist regime and in the transformation process. I also analyse the formation of the communist ruling class, the communist (under)urbanization, mass labour emigration, and the emergence of the grey and black markets. The impact of communism on social cohesion, class relations, and economic development is also in my focus. The idea of communist, non-market, state-led modernization and attempts at its implementation are discussed as well.

Chapter 11: In Pursuit of the Western World: Poland Between the Transition and the EU Accession (1989–2004)

Post-communist transformation is analysed both as a part of the story (social and economic challenges of transformation had their sources in the failed communist project of modernization) and as another (perhaps ultimate) attempt at Westernization. I analyse the successful process of catching up with the West, that is, the processes of democratization, the rise of market economy, rapid economic growth, and rapprochement with the West (EU) are presented simultaneously with the transformation of the Polish economy and society.

Chapter 12: Conclusion: Two Centuries of Catching-up to the West

The extended conclusion summarizes the short- and long-term economic and social consequences of partitions/fragmentation/discontinuity in the nineteenth century as well as the dislocations of the Polish state in the twentieth century. The comparative analysis of the Polish growth and catching-up history is included (I focus on the development of Central-Eastern Poland which used to be part of each Polish state or quasi-state since 1795).

References

Abramovitz, M. (1986). Catching up, forging ahead, and falling behind. *The Journal of Economic History, 46*, 385–406.

Acemoglu, D., & Robinson, J. A. (2006). *Economic origins of dictatorship and democracy*. Cambridge and New York: Cambridge University Press.

Acemoglu, D., & Robinson, J. A. (2012). *Why nations fail: The origins of power, prosperity and poverty* (1st ed.). New York: Crown Publishers.

Ajnenkiel, A., Dunin-Wąsowicz, A., Ciunowicz, M., & Mączak, A. (Eds.). (1981). *Encyklopedia historii gospodarczej Polski do 1945 roku. T. 1: A-N.* Warszawa: Wiedza Powszechna.

Ajnenkiel, A., Mączak, A., & Dunin-Wąsowicz, A. (Eds.). (1981). *Encyklopedia historii gospodarczej Polski do roku 1945. T. 2: O-Ż.* Warszawa: Wiedza Powszechna.

Akamatsu, K. (1962). A historical pattern of economic growth in developing countries. *The Developing Economies, 1,* 3–25. https://doi.org/10.1111/j.1746-1049.1962.tb01020.x

Aldcroft, D. H., & Morewood, S. (1955-) (1995). *Economic change in Eastern Europe since 1918.* Aldeshot: Edward Elgar Publishing, Incorporated.

Aldcroft, P. D. H. (2013). *Europe's third world: The European periphery in the interwar years.* Ashgate Publishing Ltd.

Amsden, A. H. (1992). *Asia's next giant: South Korea and late industrialization, 1. Issue as an Oxford University Press paperback.* New York: Oxford University Press.

Amsden, A. H. (2001). *The rise of "the rest": Challenges to the west from late-industrializing economies.* Oxford and New York: Oxford University Press.

Amsden, A. H., & Chu, W. (2003). *Beyond late development: Taiwan's upgrading policies.* Cambridge, MA: MIT Press.

Andrzejewski, M., Hajduk, B., Łaszkiewicz, T., et al. (Eds.). (2015). *Historia Pomorza. T. 5, Cz. 1: (1918–1939): województwo pomorskie i Wolne Miasto Gdańsk. Ustrój, gospodarka, społeczeństwo.* Toruń; [Warszawa]: Wydawnictwo Towarzystwa Naukowego w Toruniu; Narodowe Archiwum Cyfrowe.

Austin, G., & Sugihara, K. (Eds.). (2013). *Labour-intensive industrialization in global history.* New York: Routledge.

Bénétrix, A., O'Rourke, K., & Williamson, J. (2012). *The spread of manufacturing to the poor periphery 1870–2007.* Cambridge, MA: National Bureau of Economic Research.

Berend, T. I. (1998a). *Decades of crisis: Central and Eastern Europe before World War II.* Berkeley, CA: University of California Press.

Berend, T. I. (1998b). *Central and Eastern Europe, 1944–1993: Detour from the periphery to the periphery.* Reprinted. Cambridge: Cambridge University Press.

Berend, T. I. (2006). *History derailed: Central and Eastern Europe in the long nineteenth century.* Reprinted. Berkeley, CA: University of California Press.

Berend, T. I., & Ránki, G. (1982). *The European periphery and industrialization, 1780–1914.* Cambridge, New York, and Paris: Cambridge University Press; Editions de la Maison des Sciences de l'Homme.

Berger, P. L. (1986). *The capitalist revolution: Fifty propositions about prosperity, equality, and liberty.* New York: Basic Books.

Besley, T., & Persson, T. (2007). *The origins of state capacity: Property rights, taxation, and politics.* Cambridge, MA: National Bureau of Economic Research.

Besley, T., & Persson, T. (2011). *Pillars of prosperity: The political economics of development clusters.* Princeton, NJ: Princeton University Press.

Bianchini, S. (2015). *Eastern Europe and the challenges of modernity, 1800–2000.* Routledge.

Biskupski, M. B., & Pula, J. S. (1990). *Polish democratic thought from the renaissance to the great emigration: Essays and documents.* East European Monographs.

Bobrzyński, M. (1927). *Dzieje Polski w zarysie.* Warszawa: Nakładem Gebethnera i Wolffa.

Branko Milanovic. (2014). For whom the wall fell? A balance sheet of the transition to capitalism. *The Globalist.* Retrieved June 10, 2018, from https://www.theglobalist.com/for-whom-the-wall-fell-a-balance-sheet-of-the-transition-to-capitalism/.

Braudel, F. (1995). *The Mediterranean and the Mediterranean world in the age of Philip II.* Berkeley, CA: University of California Press.

Bujak, F. (1917). *Rozwój gospodarczy Galicyi (1772–1914).* Lwów: Księgarnia Polska B. Połoniecki.

Bujak, F. (1925). *Rozwój gospodarczy Polski w krótkim zarysie.* Kraków: Spółdzielczy Instytut Naukowy.

Bujak F (1926) Poland's economic development: A short sketch The man of action and the student. Publication for the Scientific Institute for Cooperation in Cracow by George Allen & Unwin, London.

Davies, N. (1986). *God's playground: A history of Poland. Vol. 2: To the present.* Oxford: Clarendon Press.

Davies, N. (2005). *God's playground: The origins to 1795.* Columbia University Press.

De Vries, J. (2008). *The industrious revolution: Consumer behavior and the household economy, 1650 to the present.* Cambridge and New York: Cambridge University Press.

Dincecco, M. (2011). *Political transformations and public finances: Europe, 1650–1913.* Cambridge and New York: Cambridge University Press.

Dincecco, M. (2018). *From warfare to wealth: The military origins of urban prosperity in Europe.* Cambridge, UK and New York: Cambridge University Press.

Dwilewicz, Ł., Morawski, W., & Polskie Towarzystwo Historii Gospodarczej (Eds.). (2015). *Historia polskich okręgów i regionów przemysłowych* (T. 1). Warszawa and Zalesie Górne: Pracownia Wydawnicza & Akant.

Epstein, S. R. (2000). *Freedom and growth: The rise of states and markets in Europe, 1300–1750/S. R. Epstein.* London: Routledge.

Feldman, W. (1933). *Dzieje polskiej myśli politycznej 1864–1914, Wyd. 2.* Warszawa: Instytut Badania Najnowszej Historji Polski.

Gawryszewski, A. (2005). *Ludność Polski w XX wieku.* Warszawa: Instytut Geografii i Przestrzennego Zagospodarowania im. Stanisława Leszczyckiego PAN.

Gerschenkron, A. (1962). *Economic backwardness in historical perspective a book of essays* (1st ed.). Cambridge, MA: Harvard University Press.

Główny Urząd Statystyczny. (1993). *Historia Polski w liczbach: ludność, terytorium.* Główny Urząd Statystyczny.

Gołębiowski, J. (1985). *Sektor państwowy w gospodarce Polski międzywojennej.* Warszawa and Kraków: Państwowe Wydawnictwo Naukowe.

Grodek, A., & Kostrowicka, I. (1955). *Historia gospodarcza Polski.* Warszawa: Szkoła Główna Planowania i Statystyki.

Grzybek, D. (2012). *Polityczne konsekwencje idei ekonomicznych w myśli polskiej 1869–1939.* Kraków: Księgarnia Akademicka.

Guzicki, L., & Żurawicki, S. (1969). *Historia polskiej myśli społeczno-ekonomicznej do roku 1914.* Państwowe Wydawnictwo Ekonomiczne.

Guzicki, L., & Żurawicki, S. (1974). *Historia polskiej myśli społeczno-ekonomicznej 1914–1945.* Warszawa: Państwowe Wydawnictwo Ekonomiczne.

Hirschman, A. O. (1977). *The passions and the interests: Political arguments for capitalism before its triumph.* Princeton, NJ: Princeton University Press.

Hryniewicz, J. T. (2004). *Polityczny i kulturowy kontekst rozwoju gospodarczego.* Warszawa: Scholar.

Ihnatowicz, I., Mączak, A., & Zientara, B. (1979). *Społeczeństwo polskie od X do XX wieku.* Książka i Wiedza.

Janos, A. C. (2000). *East central Europe in the modern world: The politics of the borderlands from pre- to post-communism.* Stanford, CA: Stanford University Press.

Janowski, M. (2004). *Polish liberal thought before 1918.* Budapest and New York: Central European University Press.

Jedlicki, J. (1964). *Nieudana próba kapitalistycznej industralizacji: analiza państwowego gospodarstwa przemysłowego w Królestwie Polskim XIX w.* Warszawa: Książka i Wiedza.

Jedlicki, J. (1988). *Jakiej cywilizacji Polacy potrzebują: studia z dziejów idei i wyobraźni XIX wieku*. Warszawa: Państwowe Wydawnictwo Naukowe.

Jedlicki, J. (1999). *A suburb of Europe: Nineteenth-century Polish approaches to Western civilization*. Budapest; Plymouth: Central European University Press; Distributed by Plymbridge Distributors.

Jedlicki, J., Janowski, M., Micińska, M., & Korecki, T. (2014). *A history of the Polish intelligentsia*. Peter Lang Edition.

Jelonek, A. (1967). *Ludność miast i osiedli typu miejskiego na ziemiach Polski od 1810 do 1960 r.* Warszawa: Instytut Geografii Polskiej Akademii Nauk.

Jezierski, A., & Leszczyńska, C. (2010). *Historia gospodarcza Polski*. Wydawnictwo Key Text.

Kaliński, J., & Landau, Z. (2003). *Gospodarka Polski w XX wieku* (Wyd. 2 zm). Warszawa: Polskie Wydawnictwo Ekonomiczne.

Kaps, K. (2015). *Ungleiche Entwicklung in Zentraleuropa: Galizien zwischen überregionaler Verflechtung und imperialer Politik (1772–1914)*. Böhlau Verlag Wien.

Kawalec, A., & Wierzbieniec, W. (2011). *Galicja 1772–1918: problemy metodologiczne, stan i potrzeby badań: praca zbiorowa*. Wydawnictwo Uniwersytetu Rzeszowskiego.

Kizwalter, T. (1999). *O nowoczesności narodu: przypadek Polski*. Semper.

Kochanowicz, J. (2006). *Backwardness and modernization: Poland and eastern Europe in the 16th–20th centuries*. Ashgate Variorum.

Koryś, P. (2016). Serfdom, feudal land tenure and their legacy in Poland. *Novoe Literaturnoe Obozrenie*, p. 141.

Kowalik, T. (1992). *Historia ekonomii w Polsce 1864–1950*. Wrocław; Warszawa: Zakład Narodowy im. Ossolińskich.

Koziarski, S. (1993a). *Sieć kolejowa Polski w latach 1918–1992*. Opole: Państwowy Instytut Naukowy.

Koziarski, S. M. (1993b). *Sieć kolejowa Polski w latach 1842–1918*. Opole: PIN-IŚ.

Kubiczek, F., Wyczański, A., & Zakład Wydawnictw Statystycznych (Eds.). (2006). *Historia Polski w liczbach. T. 2: Gospodarka*. Warszawa: Zakład Wydawnictw Statystycznych.

Kuklo, C., Łukasiewicz, J., & Leszczyńska, C. (2014). *Poland in Europe*. Warszawa: Zakład Wydawnictw Statystycznych.

Kula, W., & Kochanowicz, J. (1993). *Rozwój gospodarczy Polski XVI–XVIII w.* Wydawnictwo Naukowe PWN.

Labuda, G., Salmonowicz, S., Ślaski, K., & Wachowiak, B. (Eds.). (1993). *Historia Pomorza: opracowanie zbiorowe. T. 3, Cz. 1: (1815–1850)*.

Gospodarka, społeczeństwo, ustrój. Poznań: Poznańskie Towarzystwo Przyjaciół Nauk.

Landau, Z., & Tomaszewski, J. (1985). *The Polish economy in the twentieth century*. London and Sydney: Croom Helm.

Leder, A. (2014). *Prześniona rewolucja: ćwiczenie z logiki historycznej, Wydanie pierwsze*. Warszawa: Wydawnictwo Krytyki Politycznej.

Łepkowski, T. (2003). *Polska – narodziny nowoczesnego narodu 1764–1870* (Wyd. 2). Poznań: Wydawnictwo PTPN.

Lin, J. Y. (2012). *The quest for prosperity: How developing economies can take off*. Princeton, NJ: Princeton University Press.

Lin, J. Y. (2013). Industrial policy revisited: A new structural economics perspective. *Revue D'économie du Développement, 21*, 55–78. https://doi.org/10.3917/edd.272.0055

Lin, J. Y. (2017). Industrial policies for avoiding the middle-income trap: A new structural economics perspective. *Journal of Chinese Economics and Business Studies, 15*, 5–18. https://doi.org/10.1080/14765284.2017.1287539

Linnemann H., van Dijck P., Verbruggen H., & Council for Asian Manpower Studies (Eds). (1987). Export-oriented industrialization in developing countries. Published for Council for Asian Manpower Studies, Manila by Singapore University Press, Singapore.

Livezeanu, I., & Von Klimo, A. (2017). *The Routledge history of East Central Europe since 1700*. Florence: Taylor and Francis.

Love, J. L. (1996). *Crafting the third world: Theorizing underdevelopment in Rumania and Brazil*. Stanford, CA: Stanford University Press.

Łuczak, C. (1973). *Dzieje Wielkopolski: Lata 1793–1918*. Poznańskie: Wydawn.

Ludwikowski, R. R. (2012). *Historia polskiej myśli politycznej*. Warszawa: Wolters Kluwer Polska.

Łukawer, E. (1996). *Z historii polskiej myśli ekonomicznej: 1945–1995. "Olympus" Centrum Edukacji i Rozwoju Biznesu: Wyższa Szkoła Bankowości*. Warszawa: Finansów i Zarządzania.

Małowist, M. (1973). *Wschód a Zachód Europy w XIII-XVI wieku: konfrontacja struktur społeczno-gospodarczych* (Wyd. 1). Warszawa: Państwowe Wydawnictwo Naukowe.

McCloskey, D. N. (2010). *Bourgeois dignity: Why economics can't explain the modern world*. Chicago: University of Chicago Press.

Misztal, S. (1970). *Przemiany w strukturze przestrzennej przemysłu na ziemiach polskich w latach 1860–1965*. Warszawa: Państwowe Wydawnictwo Naukowe.

Mokyr, J. (2009). *The enlightened economy: An economic history of Britain, 1700–1850*. New Haven, CT: Yale University Press.

Mokyr, J. (2017). *A culture of growth: The origins of the modern economy.* Princeton, NJ: Princeton University Press.

Morawski, W. (1998). *Słownik historyczny bankowości polskiej do 1939 roku.* Muza SA.

Morawski, W. (2011). *Dzieje gospodarcze Polski* (Wyd. 2). Warszawa: Difin.

Musiał, W. (2013). *Modernizacja Polski: polityki rządowe w latach 1918–2004.* Toruń: Wydawnictwo Naukowe Uniwersytetu Mikołaja Kopernika.

Myrdal, G. (1968). *Asian drama: An inquiry into the poverty of nations.* New York: Pantheon.

North, D. C., & Thomas, R. P. (1973). *The rise of the Western world: A new economic history.* Cambridge: Cambridge University Press.

North, D. C., & Weingast, B. R. (1989). Constitutions and commitment: The evolution of institutions governing public choice in seventeenth-century England. *The Journal of Economic History, 49,* 803–832.

O'Rourke, K. H., & Williamson, J. G. (1999). *Globalization and history: The evolution of a nineteenth-century Atlantic economy.* Cambridge, MA: MIT Press.

O'Rourke, K. H., & Williamson, J. G. (Eds.). (2017). *The spread of modern industry to the periphery since 1871* (1st ed.). Oxford: Oxford University Press.

Piatkowski, M. (2018). *Europe's growth champion.* New York: Oxford University Press.

Piatkowski, M. M. (2013). *Poland's new golden age: Shifting from Europe's periphery to its center.* The World Bank.

Roszkowski, W. (2015). *East Central Europe: A concise history.* Warszawa: Instytut Studiów Politycznych Polskiej Akademii Nauk: Instytut Jagielloński.

Rusiński, W. (1961). *Historia gospodarcza Polski na tle dziejów gospodarczych powszechnych. Cz. 2: Od roku 1795.* Poznań: Wyższa Szkoła Ekonomiczna.

Rutkowski, J. (1950). *Historia gospodarcza Polski. T. 2: Czasy porozbiorowe do 1918 r.* Poznań: Księgarnia Akademicka.

Rutkowski, J. (1953). *Historia gospodarcza Polski: do 1864 r.* Warszawa: Książka i Wiedza.

Saito, O. (2010). An industrious revolution in an East Asian market economy? Tokugawa Japan and implications for the great divergence: Tokugawa Japan and an industrious revolution. *Australian Economic History Review, 50,* 240–261. https://doi.org/10.1111/j.1467-8446.2010.00304.x

Salmonowicz, S., Instytut Historii im. Tadeusza Manteuffla (Polska Akademia Nauk), Towarzystwo Naukowe w Toruniu, & Uniwersytet Szczeciński (Eds.). (2000). *Historia Pomorza. T. 4, Cz. 1: (1850–1918). Ustrój, gospodarka, społeczeństwo.* Toruń: Wydawnictwo TN.

Skodlarski, J. (2005). *Zarys historii gospodarczej Polski* (Wyd. 1, dodr. 2). Warszawa: Wydawnictwo Naukowe PWN.
Smoczyński, R., & Zarycki, T. (2017). *Totem inteligencki: arystokracja, szlachta i ziemiaństwo w polskiej przestrzeni społecznej.* Warszawa: Wydawnictwo Naukowe Scholar.
Sowa, J. (2011). *Fantomowe ciało króla: peryferyjne zmagania z nowoczesną formą.* Kraków: Towarzystwo Autorów i Wydawców Prac Naukowych "Universitas".
Szlajfer, H. (2012). *Economic nationalism and globalization: Lessons from Latin America and Central Europe.* Leiden and Boston, MA: Brill.
Tilly, C. (1992). *Coercion, capital, and European states, AD 990–1992* (Rev. pbk. ed.). Cambridge, MA: Blackwell.
Tomaszewski, J., Żbikowski, A., & Cała, A. (Eds.). (2001). *Żydzi w Polsce: dzieje i kultura: leksykon.* Warszawa: Cyklady.
Trencsényi, B., Janowski, M., Baár, M., et al. (2016). *A history of modern political thought in East Central Europe: Negotiating modernity in the "long nineteenth century".* Oxford: Oxford University Press.
Turnock, D. (2002). *Eastern Europe: An historical geography 1815–1945.* Routledge.
Turnock, D. (2004). *The economy of East Central Europe, 1815–1989: Stages of transformation in a peripheral region.* Routledge.
Wapiński, R. (1997). *Historia polskiej myśli politycznej XIX i XX wieku.* Gdańsk: Arche.
Williamson, J. (2011). *Industrial catching up in the poor periphery 1870–1975.* Cambridge, MA: National Bureau of Economic Research.
Wójtowicz, G., & Wójtowicz, A. (2009). *Dlaczego nie jesteśmy bogaci.* Warszawa: CeDeWu Warszawa Google Scholar.
Wyczański, A. (Ed.). (2003). *Historia Polski w liczbach. T. 1: Państwo, społeczeństwo.* Warszawa: Zakład Wydawnictw Statystycznych.
Yun Casalilla, B., & O'Brien, P. K. (Eds.). (2012). *The rise of fiscal states: A global history, 1500–1914.* New York: Cambridge University Press.
Zamoyski, A. (1987). *The Polish way: A thousand-year history of the Poles and their culture.* London: John Murray.
Zamoyski, A. (2009). *Poland: A history.* London: Harper Press.
Zarycki, T. (2008). *Kapitał kulturowy: inteligencja w Polsce i w Rosji* (Wyd. 1). Warszawa: Wydawnictwo Uniwersytetu Warszawskiego.
Zhang, W. (2016). *The road leading to the market.* Routledge, Taylor & Francis Group.
Zhang, W. (2017). China's future growth depends on innovation entrepreneurs. *Journal of Chinese Economics and Business Studies, 15,* 19–40. https://doi.org/10.1080/14765284.2017.1287540

2

The View from Afar: The Polish Economy Between the Golden Age and the Partitions (Sixteenth to Eighteenth Centuries)

At the beginning of the modern age, the Commonwealth reached the peak of its power, sometimes called the Golden Age, when it became a peripheral grain-producing empire and played a significant role both in the economy and in the political life of Europe (Rusiński 1960; Kula and Kochanowicz 1993; Davies 2005; Sosnowska and Kochanowicz 2011; Sowa 2011; Piatkowski 2013). It developed in regional power partly because of the relative weakness of its neighbours, Russia and fragmented Germany, and partly because of the effective dynastic policy of the kings from the Jagiellonian Dynasty. As a result, from the fifteenth century onwards, the Commonwealth existed for nearly two centuries without strong competitors or enemies in close proximity (Zamoyski 1987, 2009; Davies 2005).

Rapid territorial expansion ensued—at the end of the sixteenth century, the territory of the Commonwealth was almost 900,000 km², and at the beginning of the seventeenth century, it almost reached a million square kilometres. The Commonwealth was one of the most populous countries of Europe, though the density of population was very low (Główny Urząd Statystyczny 1993; Kuklo et al. 2014). It was traditionally multi-ethnic and—in comparison with the rest of Europe—the inhabitants enjoyed considerable religious freedom. However, most of

© The Author(s) 2018
P. Koryś, *Poland From Partitions to EU Accession*,
https://doi.org/10.1007/978-3-319-97126-1_2

the elite either originated from or were assimilated into the Polish nobility. In turn, a large part of population consisted of peasants. While during the Golden Age, the situation of peasants in the Commonwealth was comparable to the rest of Europe, then, the situation changed. Subsequently, the dependent development of Poland and the whole Central-Eastern Europe resulted in a so-called second serfdom and growing divergence between the legal status of peasants in the Eastern and Western parts of continent (Kamiński 1975). The number of towns was limited, and most of them were small. Townspeople played only a minor political role in a state dominated by the interests of the nobility. Such a social structure resulted in relatively high income and wealth inequalities, higher than in Western Europe (Malinowski and van Zanden 2017).

The state was the union of the two constituent countries—Poland and Lithuania—but in reality it was a relatively loose federation of lands gathered under one rule, with a parliament constituted of the nobility. Administration was poorly developed and the army was small—until the eighteenth century, the basic armed force was the Noble Host (*levee en masse*), the wartime mobilization of the nobility. The lack of a strong army and very low taxes controlled by the parliament vastly limited the king's power. The law was enforced by the nobility at the local level, as there was no central executive structure (Davies 2005).

The kings were elected by the nobility. The successive Jagiellonian kings were elected but, after that, no Polish family achieved the succession of the royal title, and the non-Polish dynasties achieved it only three times: the Vasa dynasty in the seventeenth century (twice) and the Wettin dynasty from Saxony. Such decisions of the nobility were designed to protect them from the excessive power of the monarch. The king's position was also weakened by the conditions which he had to accept before the coronation, each time enlarging the power of the nobility. The parliament (Sejm) almost exclusively represented the interests of the nobility, and the representation of the townspeople did not have substantial influence on the policy. Many solutions within the Sejm, such as the requirement of unanimity in making decisions (and the consequent *liberum veto*, when protest by even one person stopped the proceedings), slowly undermined the political system, even though they were functional at the beginning (Davies 2005).

The political structure of the state corresponded with the nature of its economy, based on the production and export of natural resources: grain, timber, forest products, cattle, and so on. Cities and towns were the centres of the grain trade and transhipment, so they developed in limited number primarily along trade routes, particularly rivers (Malinowski 2016). Some cities were administrative centres of the kingdom (e.g. Cracow, Warsaw, Vilnius, Piotrków Trybunalski) or of the magnate duchies; in the latter case, such centres, necessary to manage the huge estates (Kowalski 2013), played a role which was comparable to—or even more important than—that of the state administrative centres, particularly in the east of the country.

The model of the state in the Commonwealth was based on the idea of the state and its goals which was very different from the absolutist and Enlightenment ideas common in Western Europe at the time. The nobility controlled the law-making and executive bodies and wanted to minimize the cost of the state, particularly the taxes, even (or first of all) at the expense of the strength of the state and its ability to compete with its neighbours. For this reason, it is difficult to compare the standard of living in the Commonwealth and in the West. It was—within the respective social strata—probably comparable in some respects, but mostly because of the smaller burden of tax in the Commonwealth, both for the nobility and for the peasants. At the same time, the cities were not growing, and there was no transport infrastructure and administration, which could have built the unity of the state and help it to develop. At the end of the eighteenth century, when some of the elite saw the dangers of this way to manage the state, lasting changes were too difficult to implement (Rostworowski 1984).

The long-term political domination of the nobility meant that maximizing profits for the landowners always took precedence over the tax interests of the state. In effect, with lower productivity than in the West, limiting the size and the strength of the state was the only way for the nobility to maintain the standard of living comparable to that in the West (there are no data proving a higher average standard of living than in the West, even though the tax burden was much bigger there). That is the reason why the neighbouring countries at the same or lower economic level as the Commonwealth, but with different power relations (particularly with the stronger position of the king), in the long term spent much more money on public enterprises or on achieving state goals, even at the expense of a lower standard of living of the upper social strata. In effect, alongside war damage, that mechanism became the key factor determining the relative weakness of Poland in the second half of the eighteenth century. It seems that the low tax income may be interpreted as another indicator (alongside the poor urbanization and no industry) of the relatively low level of development of the Polish lands in that period.

The source of income for the nobility was agriculture, animal husbandry, and forest management; the production was extensive and used corvée labour. The efficiency in this sector was low because of both low capital investment and labour relations, as the peasants were obliged to work the lord's fields for an appointed time in return for the right to use the house and land. Anyway, the agricultural estate (*folwark*) had a capitalist character, with large-scale production determined by the large-scale grain trade (and, to lesser degree, cattle trade). Grain export played a key role in the balance of trade of the Commonwealth, and the main trade centre was Danzig, so the principal grain production took place near the big rivers, particularly the Vistula (Jezierski and Leszczyńska 2010; Morawski 2011). The richest landowners possessed huge estates through exclusive and shared titles, particularly in eastern Poland. In central Poland, most of the estates were smaller, but some of them were owned by the great landowners. The landowners' policy involved the preference for bigger peasant plots/households, because then the corvée could be served with draught horses or oxen. Thus, the landowners supported the more complex social structure, with status differences between the peasants (Wyczański 1960).

Apart from the large-scale production, the other kind of agriculture in the Commonwealth was peasants' farming. The Polish model was no different from that in other countries (though in the seventeenth and eighteenth centuries, the legal and economic status of peasants in Western Europe started to differentiate). In terms of political status, peasants had practically no rights and did not play any role in the society. Some scholars compare their situation to that of American slaves. The main feature of peasants' farming was the focus on subsistence, not maximum production, that is, it fulfilled the needs of the peasants and was mostly moneyless. With the limited access to the market, the peasants were mostly self-sufficient and produced little or no surplus, and poor flow of information and limited resources were the reason why peasant farming was conservative in the choices of produce, methods, and so on (Wyczański 1969; Kochanowicz 2006).

The research of Wyczański shows that the nobility had no short-term incentives to change the economic system. In his opinion, in the sixteenth and seventeenth centuries, the cost of running the estate in the hypothetical situation when the landowner paid for labour would have increased by one-third. Therefore, the nobility had no interest in introducing any changes and modernizing the agriculture. The weakness of the cities and urban economy meant that it was only the interest of the nobility which was taken into consideration (Wyczański 1960).

In the late seventeenth century, the agricultural innovations in the West and low prices of grain as well as low foreign demand worsened the situation of agricultural producers in the Commonwealth, despite cheap labour. This was mostly due to the agricultural revolution in Western Europe, which changed the terms of trade for the Polish grain trade. War damage was also an important factor. The worsening condition of estates is described by travellers and reflected in inventories. As the common response of landowners to economic difficulty was increasing the peasants' workload, the peasants had very less free time—the time away from labour services for the landowner was spent tending their own plots. This made life worse for them, to which they responded with growing resentment and resistance towards the lords. At the same time, the landowners tried to diminish their own responsibilities towards the peasants. All this led to peasants' revolts in the first half of the eighteenth century and resulted in declining productivity in the eighteenth century (Kula 1976; Topolski 1977; Kula and Kochanowicz 1993).

In terms of technological development, the economic model prevailing in the Commonwealth dominated by low-productive, extensive grain production gradually became obsolete in relation to the West. With the emergence of economic powers in Europe (like England) and in the region (like Prussia, or even Austria), the lowering productivity and the obsolete management methods put the Commonwealth's economy in a particularly disadvantageous position (Topolski 1977; Ajnenkiel et al. 1981a, b; Rostworowski 1984).

From the geo-political perspective, in the eighteenth century, the Commonwealth lost its ability to compete with the neighbouring countries, mostly because of the institutional barriers restricting its ability to mobilize resources in times of crisis. The economy became backward and incompetitive. In effect, in the mid-eighteenth century, the Commonwealth was a state which was very big and relatively populous, but weak in terms of its economic, political, institutional and military power. With the emergence of new economic and political powers in Europe (like England) and in the region (like Prussia, or even Austria), the lowering productivity and the obsolete management methods put the Commonwealth's economy in a particularly disadvantageous position. Prolonged recession in the agrarian economy caused the growing backwardness as well as the lack of resources to finance the economic and institutional reforms. Additionally, the relative impoverishment of the country, and persistently disadvantageous terms of trade resulted in the relative decline of tax income, made the military potential of the state significantly lower than that of the neighbouring countries.

References

Ajnenkiel, A., Dunin-Wąsowicz, A., Ciunowicz, M., & Mączak, A. (Eds.). (1981a). *Encyklopedia historii gospodarczej Polski do 1945 roku. T. 1: A-N.* Warszawa: Wiedza Powszechna.

Ajnenkiel, A., Mączak, A., & Dunin-Wąsowicz, A. (Eds.). (1981b). *Encyklopedia historii gospodarczej Polski do roku 1945. T. 2: O-Ż.* Warszawa: Wiedza Powszechna.

Davies, N. (2005). *God's playground: The origins to 1795.* Columbia University Press.

Główny Urząd Statystyczny. (1993). *Historia Polski w liczbach: ludność, terytorium.* Główny Urząd Statystyczny.

Jezierski, A., & Leszczyńska, C. (2010). *Historia gospodarcza Polski.* Wydawnictwo Key Text.

Kamiński, A. (1975). Neo-Serfdom in Poland-Lithuania. *Slavic Review, 34,* 253–268. https://doi.org/10.2307/2495187

Kochanowicz, J. (2006). *Backwardness and modernization: Poland and Eastern Europe in the 16th–20th centuries.* Ashgate Variorum.

Kowalski, M. (2013). *Księstwa Rzeczpospolitej: państwo magnackie jako region polityczny.* Instytut Geografii i Przestrzennego Zagospodarowania im. Stanisława Leszczyckiego PAN.

Kuklo, C., Łukasiewicz, J., & Leszczyńska, C. (2014). *Poland in Europe.* Warszawa: Zakład Wydawnictw Statystycznych.

Kula, W. (1976). *An economic theory of the feudal system: Towards a model of the Polish economy, 1500–1800* (New ed.). London: N.L.B.

Kula, W., & Kochanowicz, J. (1993). *Rozwój gospodarczy Polski XVI–XVIII w.* Wydawnictwo Naukowe PWN.

Malinowski, M. (2016). Serfs and the city: Market conditions, surplus extraction institutions, and urban growth in early modern Poland. *European Review of Economic History, 20*, 123–146. https://doi.org/10.1093/ereh/hew002

Malinowski, M., & van Zanden, J. L. (2017). Income and its distribution in preindustrial Poland. *Cliometrica, 11*, 375–404. https://doi.org/10.1007/s11698-016-0154-5

Morawski, W. (2011). *Dzieje gospodarcze Polski* (Wyd. 2). Warszawa: Difin.

Piatkowski, M. M. (2013). *Poland's new golden age: Shifting from Europe's periphery to its center.* The World Bank.

Rostworowski, E. (1984). *Historia powszechna: wiek XVIII.* Państwowe Wydawnictwo Naukowe.

Rusiński, W. (1960). Historia gospodarcza Polski na tle dziejów gospodarczych powszechnych (Cz. 1). Poznań: Wyższa Szkoła Ekonomiczna.

Sosnowska, A., & Kochanowicz, J. (2011). Economic history of pre-industrial Poland: An obsolete subject? In *Dove va la storia economica?: Metodi e prospettive: secc. XIII–XVIII [Where is economic history going?: Methods and prospects from the 13th to the 18th centuries/A cura di Francesco Ammannati].* Italy: Firenze University Press.

Sowa, J. (2011). *Fantomowe ciało króla: peryferyjne zmagania z nowoczesną formą.* Kraków: Towarzystwo Autorów i Wydawców Prac Naukowych "Universitas".

Topolski, J. (1977). *Gospodarka polska a europejska w XVI–XVIII wieku.* Wydawnictwo Poznańskie.

Wyczański, A. (1960). *Studia nad folwarkiem szlacheckim w Polsce w latach 1500–1580.* Warszawa: Państwowe Wydawnictwo Naukowe.

Wyczański, A. (1969). *Wieś polskiego Odrodzenia.* Warszawa: Książka i Wiedza.

Zamoyski, A. (1987). *The Polish way: A thousand-year history of the Poles and their culture.* London: John Murray.

Zamoyski, A. (2009). *Poland: A history.* London: Harper Press.

3

The Age of Enlightenment Reforms and Partitions of Poland: Economy and Politics in the Late Eighteenth Century (1772–1795)

The reign of the last king of Poland, Stanislaw August Poniatowski, is the period of the decline of the Polish state, the Polish-Lithuanian Commonwealth. It was the time of the growing influence of the neighbouring powers on internal politics and the decline of the state capacity of the Commonwealth. But it was also the period of the reception of Western ideas, particularly the thought of the French and German Enlightenment, by the elites, and the growing sense of backwardness resulting from this reception; this resulted in the early concepts of social, political, legal, and economic reforms, which were expected to help to rebuild the state. Also, the first attempts at financing manufacturing industry by the government took place in the late eighteenth century, as well as early plans of social reforms.

1   Internal Politics

In the mid-eighteen century, after the reign of the two kings from the Saxon House of Wettin, Augustus II and Augustus III, Poland was a state with weak central authority, ineffective government, and a small group of powerful magnate families who had a lot of political influence and ruled

© The Author(s) 2018
P. Koryś, *Poland From Partitions to EU Accession*,
https://doi.org/10.1007/978-3-319-97126-1_3

their demesnes as independent territories. The state was additionally weakened by the conflicts inside the elite, such as the one between the proponents of the modern nation state and the conservative traditionalists, concerning the political and economic system, or the one between Catholics and members of other denominations, concerning the scope of religious freedom (Butterwick 2001). The rival factions were often supported by neighbouring countries, Russia, Prussia and Austria. During the reign of Augustus III a strong reform-oriented faction emerged, postulating modelling the state on the Western nation states, which would limit some of the privileges of the Polish nobility (Michalski 1956; Zielińska 1983). The aim of the projected reform was to augment the central power, strengthen the government, increase the treasury income, create a modern army, and weaken the power of the magnate families. This idea was the result of the fact that some members of the elite were really convinced that building the nation state is necessary, but on the other hand, it was part of the game between the opposite factions among the magnates, aiming to weaken the opponents.

Attempts at reforms in this direction were made throughout the reign of King Stanisław August Poniatowski, who supported the progressive faction (Zamoyski 1992). This aggravated the conflict, finally resulting in the Bar Confederation in the years 1768–1772 and the Targowica Confederation in 1793 (Wąsicki 1952). Initially, the reforms were supported by Empress Catherine the Great of Russia, but later, Russia supported also the anti-reform faction. The internal conflict, the growing power of the magnate families, and the corruption among the elite created the situation where the neighbouring powers increased their influence on the Polish political life, which resulted in the partitions and finally in the collapse of the state. It is worth noting that these foreign interventions were not perceived as a serious problem by any of the factions—for a long time, they were seen as an additional mechanism useful in achieving internal goals (Butterwick 2001, 2012).

The Enlightenment reform faction, known as the Familia (literally 'the Family'), which started to form at the beginning of the 1750s around the Czartoryski and Poniatowski magnate families, wanted a radical restructuring of the state. They wanted to modernize the state, but they also expected benefits for Familia. Their programme was first formulated at the time of the royal election of Stanisław August Poniatowski, and the first attempt at a radical reform, or even a revolution of the public institutions, was conducted during his reign (Michalski 1956; Zielińska 1983). However, as a result of a Russian intervention and some internal tensions (non-Catholic confederations, the Bar Confederation), its impact was considerably limited. The reformers seem to have ignored the specific conditions in Poland that hampered the reform. The key factor in that failure was the conservative faction among the nobility, who—by means of the Bar Confederation—took action against Russia and at the same time against Familia, and against strengthening the central power of the state and the government. During this period, Russia became the protector of the Commonwealth, guaranteeing its political stability and, to some extent, supporting the reform (Stanek 1991; Stone et al. 2001; Szczygielski 2015).

The suppression of the Bar Confederation, mostly by Russian military forces (which formally supported Polish king, Poniatowski) was followed by the First Partition of Poland. Prussia and Russia internationally presented the annexation of the Polish lands as the result of Poland's inability to manage its big territory. Parts of the territory were divided among Russia, Prussia, and Austria, and the two latter states took over some of the best developed Polish lands. The period after the First Partition was fraught with internal conflict and the weakness of the state, but at the same time there were attempts at a gradual reform, focused mostly on education. The key achievement was the creation of a modern system of education, the first step of which was the opening in 1765 of The Corps of Cadets, the first state school in the Commonwealth, which soon became the forge of the Enlightenment elite. In 1773, the system of education was partially centralized, when the newly created Commission of National Education took over the property and the school system of the Jesuit Order. The Commission partly continued the reform outlined by the king's faction. Although the Polish education system was poorer than that in the more developed countries, it was more successful than those in the other countries in the region. However, education was only available to the nobility, which was a natural consequence of the fact that the social reform had not yet been conducted (Korzon 1898; Lukowski 2010).

This period also witnessed other reforms, such as those of the treasury and taxes. Gradually, the central power increased and the government was strengthened; however, the attempt to codify the law was unsuccessful, as the Sejm of 1780 rejected the collection of unified court laws of the

Commonwealth, called the Zamoyski Code, because the majority of the nobility saw it as an attempt at robbing them of their privileges and freedoms. The scope of the reforms was also unacceptable for Russia, who slowed down their implementation. However, when Russia was weakened as a result of its war effort (it was involved in the wars against Sweden and Turkey), the Sejm of 1788, called the Great Sejm, decided to continue the reform, that were temporally accepted by Russia in return for Poland's neutrality or even support in these wars. In that brief period, Poland once again became an important player on the European arena— trying to stop the excessive growth of Russian power, Great Britain allied with Prussia and used it to separate Poland from Russia. That changed the power play within the Polish Sejm, and in the new political situation, it was possible for the Sejm to introduce the reforms, resulting in emancipating Poland from the status of *de facto* Russian protectorate in 1789, organizing the first census of Poland (1789), creating a modern army, and finally, reforming the political system. The successful implementation of the reforms was to be guaranteed by the alliance with Prussia (Wąsicki 1952; Kądziela 1991; Butterwick 1998, 2001; Lukowski 2010; Szczygielski 2015).

The final expression of the reforms was the Constitution announced on the 3 May 1791, creating strong central power, strengthening the government, and weakening the power of the Sejm, turning the monarchy from elected to hereditary; there was also a plan for the full codification of the law, but it was not carried out before the state collapsed. A year later, the defenders of the old system based on the ties with Russia created a confederation at Targowica, which later became the epitome of treason. However, it should also be treated as part of the internal political play, in which the leaders of factions of nobility tried to use the foreign powers regardless of the real goals of the latter. The Confederation was approved by Catherine II, now unequivocally opposing the activity of the Enlightenment faction still gathered around the king. Russia sent troops and a war developed to protect the Constitution. Finally, the king joined the Targowica Confederation, which confirmed the defeat of the reform faction. The Sejm in Grodno, in 1793, nullified all the decisions of the Great Sejm, including the Constitution, and confirmed the Second Partition of Poland, which had been Prussia's objective. Poland was suffering from a deep economic crisis, which ultimately destabilized the state. Following the Sejm in Grodno, the power fell into the hands of the confederates from Targowica, but in the situation of economic crisis—that is, the collapse of the banking system and the bankruptcy of the state—they could not govern effectively (Korzon 1898; Kornatowski 1937; Morawski 1998).

The growing influence of the faction opposing Targowica and the partitions, the spreading of social unrest, the widespread knowledge about the corruption of the political elites, and the bribing of some Polish politicians by Russia as well as—or maybe first of all—the French Revolution, and the growth of revolutionary and progressive factions contributed to the outbreak (in the spring of 1794) of an insurrection against Russia, which practically controlled the remaining part of Poland after the Second Partition. The leader of this uprising was Tadeusz Kościuszko, a general and a veteran of the American War of Independence. The immediate cause for the uprising was the Russian demand to reduce the Polish army, which was interpreted as a step towards depriving Poland of independence. The insurrection lasted until the end of the year, and its defeat finally resulted in the Third Partition and the ultimate extinction of the Polish state (Wąsicki 1957a; Zahorski 1985; Szyndler 1994; Storozynski 2009).

2   International Situation

The close ties of Commonwealth with France and Austria, started to lose their importance in the eighteenth century. The last attempt of France to intervene in Poland was the royal election of Stanislaw Leszczyński and the War of the Polish Succession in the years 1733–1735, which ended with the defeat of the French faction as a result of the Saxon-Russian alliance and the election of Augustus III Wettin. Throughout the eighteenth century, Poland was in a precarious political situation. The potential allies, like France or the Dutch Republic, and even Great Britain, were far away and their involvement in the Polish affairs was decreasing. In the second half of the eighteenth century, Poland was left without reliable allies or a vision of any foreign policy (Fedorowicz et al. 1982; Rostworowski 1984; Davies 2005; Sutton 2015).

The former allies also withdrew their financial support, and Poland's lack of military potential resulted in not obtaining the funding that European powers directed to, for example, Sweden. However, the wars fought by regional powers in the first half of the eighteenth century were conducted in part on the Polish territory, deepening the economic and political crisis. After the Great Northern War, the dominant position in the region was held by Russia, though in the direct vicinity of Poland, Habsburg Austria and the growing power of Hohenzollern Prussia emerged as a potential threat. The fight between Austria and Prussia weakened the former and moved it away from the Polish border, but Prussia, with its territorial expansion, remained a dangerous neighbour.

The Commonwealth tried to build relations with Saxony, an element of which was electing two prince-electors of Saxony as kings of Poland. Then, Poland got closer to Russia, which was supported by part of the nobility's elite, particularly those in favour of the Enlightenment reform of the state (including the Czartoryski family). This closeness was also the result of the growing power of Russia and indicated Poland's gradual loss of sovereignty, as it had been slowly becoming, from the time of the Silent Sejm in 1717 onwards, an informal Russian protectorate, like Sweden in the same period. The last Polish king was a Russian protégé for most of his reign, and in the previous half a century Russia had performed military interventions on the Polish territory several times. They took place during the 7-Years' War (1756–1763), during the royal election of Stanisław August Poniatowski in 1764 (also supported by Prussia), in 1767–1768 to support the anti-reform confederations of the nobility, protecting the religious freedom and the old political system threatened by the royal faction, in 1771–1775, while suppressing the Bar Confederation and guarding the Partition Sejm, and in 1792, during the Confederation of Targowica and the War of the Constitution. Formally, between 1775 and 1788, the Commonwealth was a Russian protectorate jointly governed by the king and the Russian ambassador (Michalski 1956; Butterwick 1998; Davies 2005).

The treaty against Russia, signed in the late 1780s by the Commonwealth and Prussia—who had cooled its relations with Russia—did not bring the results Poland had expected. In the 1790s, Prussia chose the more advantageous option of dividing the Commonwealth together with

Russia instead of coming into conflict with it. Similarly, the weakening of Russia during its wars against Turkey and Sweden in the late 1780s and early 1790s did not improve the situation of the Commonwealth in the long term, and the attempts to reform the state undertaken in that period ultimately led to the collapse of the Polish state.

3 Ideas

Later than in other European countries, the eighteenth century was the time of intense reception of the thought of the Age of Enlightenment in Poland. In particular, the revolutionary ideas of the French Enlightenment became influential among factions of the modernizers of the state. Also, the conceptions of the cameralist economic policy of Prussia and the successes of Austrian-Enlightened absolutism were carefully disputed. In effect, the idea of progress and the concept of backwardness became present in the Polish political discourse. These debates on human progress, the European economic and political development, and the local, Polish backwardness were followed by the discussion on the need and the scope of political and social reforms. This debate referred both to the heritage of the Polish political philosophy and—increasingly—to foreign models and ideas. In the neighbouring countries, Prussia introduced absolutist reforms, while Austria (particularly Joseph II) tried more liberal ones. However, the Polish reformers looked for inspiration in more distant countries, that is, Great Britain as an emerging modern economic power, France on the threshold of a bourgeois revolution, and the still prosperous Dutch Republic. Still, it is worth noting that the reception of the Scottish Enlightenment and the liberal ideas of Adam Smith were delayed in Poland by dozens of years, and started only in the early nineteenth century (Konopczyński 1966; Trencsényi et al. 2016).

From at least the mid-1700s, an important form of expression for the Polish intellectuals was a variety of warnings and admonitions directed at the government and Poland. In 1733–1734, the treatise *Free Voice to Make Freedom Safe* was published as a work of the king of Poland Stanisław Leszczyński (1733) (though he was probably not the author). At the same time, another work was disseminated—*A Brotherly*

Admonition, also written by Leszczyński, or someone from his entourage. Both these works outlined a reform program with considerable attention paid to the socioeconomic aspect. The most important postulate was the emancipation of peasants and replacing serfdom with tax. The economy based on serfdom was seen not only as leading to the increasing poverty of the peasants (incapable of any form of self-reliance or entrepreneurship), but also as creating a barrier to the further development of the country. The author of *Free Voice to Make Freedom Safe* pointed out the importance of the selection of talents for the economic growth, and indicated serfdom as its key obstacle. He wrote:

> What is the condition to which we have reduced the people of our kingdom? Reduced by misery to the state of brutes, they drag out their days in a lazy stupidity, which one would almost mistake for a total want of sentiment: they love no art, they value themselves on no industry; they labour no longer than the dread of chastisement forces them; convinced that they cannot enjoy the fruit of their ingenuity, they stifle their talents, and make no essays to discover them. Hence that frightful scarcity in which we find ourselves of the most common artisans! Should we wonder that we are in want of things the most necessary, when those who ought to furnish them, cannot hope for the smallest profit from their cares to furnish us! It is only where liberty is found, that emulation can exist. (Adams 1787, 90)

He also emphasized the vital role of the good condition of cities and industry for the development of the country, and he called for stronger central power, the improvement of the tax system, and creating a strong army. These works can be treated as one of the first voices in favour of the modernization of Poland according to the Western model.

Less than a decade later, first in 1742 in Berlin, then in 1750 in Warsaw, a nobleman from Greater Poland, Stefan Garczyński (1753; Wegner 1871), published a treatise titled *The Anatomy of the Commonwealth*, in which he thoroughly analysed the condition of the state and ways to mend it. Like Leszczyński, he saw the problem in the excessive power of the nobility, the serfdom, and the poor condition of cities and industry. He warned against the growing social inequalities, lack of education, and the results of the weakness of the central government. He postulated the development of education, particularly among the peasants, strengthening the manufacturing industry and creating the market for its products, for example, by means of public procurement, and the effective taxation of the nobility. He also wanted the public positions to be given only to those citizens who had gained experience on their own estates, and who were effective managers and treated their subordinates well. He advised the readers to look for models in England and Holland, but also in Prussia.

The years 1760–1763 brought probably the most important publication before the reign of Stanisław August Poniatowski, *On an effective way of councils* by Stanislaw Konarski (1760). The author pointed out that the economic reforms must be preceded by political reforms, because, in the existing institutional framework, the interests of the nobility will always prevail over the interests of the state. Hence, he postulated the reform of the Polish parliamentary system, including the abolition of the *liberum veto*. That reform would be the starting point for other reforms, including—again—strengthening the central power, improving the condition of the treasury, introducing equal rights, and building a modern system of education. Within the idea of the centrally governed state, Konarski postulated creating a central bank, modelled on the English solution, which could use estates owned by the nobility to secure the parity of paper money. This could limit the outflow of precious metals from Poland, caused by the long-term negative balance of trade (Konopczyński 1966; Trencsényi et al. 2016).

During the reign of Stanisław August Poniatowski, the ideas of the Enlightenment reforms found increasing numbers of proponents, which can be seen in the growing influence of the Familia, supporting the king in his intention to reform the state. The most important writers of that period are Józef Wybicki (who later wrote the lyrics of the Polish national anthem), Hugo Kollontaj (Pol: *Kołłątaj*), Stanislaw Staszic,, and Franciszek Salezy Jezierski. They all emphasized the need to strengthen the central government and introduce equal rights for peasants. Kollontaj, Jezierski, and other writers from so-called Kollontaj's Forge during the Great Sejm propagated the ideas of the French Revolution, and their thinking was close to that of the French Jacobins. They radically opposed any class and feudal privileges (Biskupski and Pula 1990; Zielińska 1991; Grześkowiak-Krwawicz 2000, 2012).

Stanislaw Staszic, a statesman during the Great Sejm and also politically active later, during the partitions and the Duchy of Warsaw, in his
Remarks upon the Life of Jan Zamoyski (Staszic 1785), published in 1787,
formulated the ideas that shaped the reform thinking of the time of the
Great Sejm. He was influenced by Rousseau and the French Enlightenment,
but his views were less radical than those of Kollontaj's Forge. He thoroughly analysed the economic aspects of the difficult situation of the
peasants, which he saw as the reason for the lower birth rate than in the
neighbouring countries. In his opinion, serfdom was not only unjust, but
also detrimental to the development of the country. He also saw the need
to increase taxes, which would strengthen the state and enable it to create
an army. He also recommended reforms to improve the political and
economic situation of the townsfolk, including granting them access to
public offices and to the Sejm (equal representation) and the right to
acquire landed property (Szacka 1966).

The main reforms brought up in practically each publication were the
emancipation and possibly change of feudal labour rent into land rent for
peasants, or at least some checks on the amount of labour required from
them, the improvement of the political status of townspeople, and
strengthening the economy of the cities, augmenting the central power,
increasing taxes, and creating a strong regular army. Another question
under discussion was Konarski's idea of the central bank. Such ideas,
rooted in mercantilism, were present in the debates during the Great Sejm
and in the writings published at the time, and some of these ideas were
included in the Constitution, which was to be the basis and the starting
point for the reforms. With regard to cities and townsfolk, the reforms
were included in the Law on the Cities, and with regard to peasants in the
last important legal act of the Polish-Lithuanian Commonwealth, the
Proclamation of Połaniec (also known as the Polaniec Manifesto). Towards
the end of the existence of the Commonwealth, the Polish Jacobin ideas
gained more proponents, for example, Kollontaj's Forge. Polish Jacobins
expressed the growing criticism of monarchy in general and demanded a
radical change of social relations, as well as equality and freedom for all
(Biskupski and Pula 1990; Trencsényi et al. 2016).

The problems resulting from the negative balance of trade (i.e. the lack
of mercantilist policy) were more and more clearly seen. Thus, the reforms
were often oriented on increasing the export of not only raw materials,

but also manufactured products. Even though it was relatively rarely that anybody postulated the direct state involvement in building the manufacturing industry (such ideas appeared in the writings of some thinkers, including Garczyński), the royal faction made some attempts of state investments (particularly made by Tyzenhaus in the royal demesnes near Grodno) (Kościałkowski 1971; Lipiński 1975).

Most of the debated problems never turned into political plans. The real reforms were relatively limited until 1790. In the last years of sovereignty, the radical ideas became more and more common, but the reforms actually implemented were cancelled by the Targowica and the Russians before any visible results could be obtained.

4   The Territory and Population

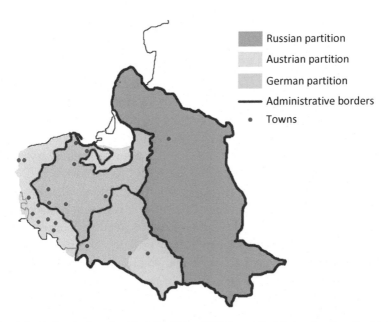

Map 3.1 Poland after the First Partition (1772) and Polish lands after the Third Partition 1795. Note: Territory of contemporary Poland shaded. Borders of Poland and borders of partition—thick line. Proximate location of towns and cities enumerated in column 1810 of Table A.3 in Annex. Source: Own elaboration on the basis of various historical maps

In the eighteenth century, the territory of the Commonwealth underwent rapid changes. In the mid-century, it was one of the biggest European countries, divided into two autonomous units—the Polish Crown and the Great Duchy of Lithuania. Its territory gradually diminished as a result of the partitions in 1772 and 1793, and finally, the state disappeared. Until 1793, Poland was one of the biggest and most populated countries in Europe, though much of the best developed and urbanized land was taken over by Prussia and Austria during the First Partition. After the First Partition, the internal market was considerably diminished, and, as a result of the partitions and the fall of the state, it became fragmented and practically collapsed.

In the middle of the eighteenth century, the territory of the Commonwealth was approximately 734,000 km². In the First Partition, the territory taken over by Austria was 83,000 km², by Prussia—36,000 km², and by Russia—92,000 km² (211,000 km² in total). The Commonwealth lost the salt mines in Wieliczka and Bochnia near Kraków (Cracow), which had brought considerable income to the Polish treasury and which were taken over by Austria, and the lower reaches and the estuary of the Vistula River were taken over by Prussia, inhibiting foreign trade via Gdańsk (Danzig). Austria took Lwów (Lvov), the third biggest city of the Commonwealth. Gdańsk and Toruń (Thorn) were formally the Commonwealth enclaves on the Prussian territory, but their ties to Poland were loosened. The territory taken by Russia was a remote sparsely populated periphery (Wandycz 1975; Główny Urząd Statystyczny 1993; Lukowski 2014).

The Second Partition meant the cession of 250,000 km² to Russia and of 57,000 km² to Prussia. In the last partition, Austria took 47,000 km², Prussia took 48,000 km² and Russia—120,000 km². A major part of the former Crown of Poland was taken over by Prussia and Austria, and most of the former Grand Duchy of Lithuania—by Russia. Austria took Lesser Poland, and Prussia took Greater Poland, Pomerania and Masovia, as well as some territory adjoining Silesia.

The Commonwealth was inhabited by about 12 million people. By the end of the eighteenth century, the loss of territory resulted in the loss of population. The lands lost in the First Partition were inhabited by over a third of the Commonwealth population, and further population loss ensued from the second and third partition soon afterwards. After all the partitions, the lands ceded to Austria constituted 18% of the territory of the former Commonwealth with 32% of its population, the Prussian gains were 20% of the territory with 23% of the population, and Russian—62% of the land with 45% of the people (Vielrose 1957; Główny Urząd Statystyczny 1993), cf. Table 3.1.

The cities on the territory of the Commonwealth were few and far between. There were only a handful (6–9) of towns with more than 10,000 inhabitants—in the mid-eighteenth century, their total population was 140,000 people, that is, 1.5% of the total population. At that time there were no big cities, and the only medium-size cities were Warszawa (Warsaw) and Gdańsk (Danzig). At the beginning of the eighteenth century, Gdańsk, with its population of 64,000 people, was one of the 30 biggest cities in Europe, but by the middle of the century, it was affected by the diminishing trade as a result of the economic and political weakness of the Commonwealth, and its population fell to 55,000 inhabitants and then to 37,000 at the end of century (Preuß 1835; Śliwiński 2012). On the other hand, Warszawa grew in importance and, by the end of

Table 3.1 Population of Poland, 1775 and 1790 (thousands of people)

Population	1775–1776, proxy from number of households	1790 census	1790, proxy from number of households
Greater Poland	930	1020	979
Lesser Poland	3831	3778	4399
Masovia	610	519	695
Great Duchy of Lithuania		2344	2537
Crown of the Kingdom of Poland	5371	5317	6072
Polish-Lithuanian Commonwealth		*7661*	*8609*
Estimations of population of the territory of contemporary Poland			
Part of Great Duchy of Lithuania			150
Part of Lesser Poland			1330
Greater Poland and Masovia			1674
Austrian partition			905
Prussian partition and Prussian state in contemporary border			4576
Population of contemporary territory of Poland			8635

Source: Own calculations (Wyczański 2003; Kaps 2015)

the eighteenth century, its population increased to over 100,000 people, a number similar to that in Hamburg, Marseilles, Barcelona, or Copenhagen, which made Warszawa one of the major cities in Europe. In most of the Polish territory, big or medium-size towns were not easily accessible because of the distances and the poorly developed transport. This meant that most of the population had poor access to town economy and markets, but also that the urban economy could not get enough talent from the outside to develop modern enterprises. Small towns were inhabited by 10–15% of the population, but most were very loosely connected with the urban functions. Often, the largest professional group were farmers, and the population of many towns (i.e. municipalities with a town or city charter) was below 1000 people. The most urbanized areas were in Greater Poland, which was ceded to Prussia, and in Lesser Poland, ceded to Austria (Gieysztorowa 1976; Bogucka and Samsonowicz 1986; Główny Urząd Statystyczny 1993; Kuklo 2009).

After the partitions, most of the big cities were on the lands acquired by Prussia (Warszawa, Gdańsk, Poznań, and the smaller ones: Elbląg, Bydgoszcz, and Toruń), and Austria (Kraków, Lwów and Lublin, Sandomierz, Przemyśl). As regards the territory taken by Russia, the only city of considerable size was Wilno (Vilnius), with about 20,000 people; the other towns were few and small.

Mid- to late-eighteenth-century-Poland was a large country with a relatively big, albeit scattered population, living mostly in rural areas. The big distances between towns, the limited number of roads (of poor quality) and small urban population became major barriers to further development. Thus, the possibility of rapid reforms was limited by geographical and demographic factors.

5   The Society

In the eighteenth century, the society of the Commonwealth was divided into three estates of the realm. The most numerous and the weakest politically were the peasants, most of whom were burdened with feudal dues—mainly in the form of the corvée. The influence of the townspeople was small—both because of the low urbanization and because of the limitations on their political and economic rights (most importantly, they did not have the right to acquire landed property). Many towns did not perform urban functions, and the townsfolk had taken to farming. In the central and eastern parts of the Commonwealth, a considerable portion of the urban population were Jews, in the western part— Protestants. The strongest estate of the realm, the one with the power to decide about the state policy, was the nobility. Within it, the most important role was played by a small group of extremely rich families owning the so-called magnate duchies.

The society of the Commonwealth was also diversified in terms of ethnicity. Apart from the Poles, there was a considerable number of Jews, but also Rusyns, Lithuanians, Armenians, and Germans. As to religion, on the basis of the census from 1790 to 1791, Tadeusz Korzon (1898) gave the numbers of below 60% Catholics and Protestants, about 30% Greek Catholics, about 10% Jews, and about 3% Russian Orthodox (Kądziela 1993; Latuch 2005).

The most numerous social group were the peasants, and within this group—the serfs, even though there were differences between regions as to the structure of this group. From the seventeenth century onwards, the number of free tenants was growing, particularly in the western regions, following the modernization of the economy of the agricultural estate (*folwark*). In some parts of Greater Poland, up to 50% of the peasants paid rent. However, the more to the east, the more traditional the economy, with greater prevalence of the corvée (except in very sparsely populated or remote regions, like in the land now belonging to Belarus, where instead of labour, peasants paid rent in the form of produce). According to the census conducted in the Duchy of Warsaw a few decades later (1808, 1810), in the Posen Department, 18% of the peasant households paid rent, and almost 30% were landless. In the Bygdoszcz Department, the percentage of landless households was similar, but there were fewer households that paid rent. In the Calisia Department, 10% of the peasant households paid rent and 36% were landless. In the whole Greater Poland the percentage of the peasants who were obliged to do labour services was lower than 60% (this number includes some landless peasants). In the eastern departments of Warsaw, Radom, and Lublin, that number was over 85%, and in the centrally located Cracow

Department—75%. Most probably the occupational structure until 1810 was relatively stable, and during the partitions period, the situation was very similar (Grossmann 1925).

As the above data shows, there were numerous groups of landless peasants (cottagers) and landless labourers. Many of them turned into vagabonds without any connection to a particular place. They were usually escaped serfs, landless peasants looking for paid work, and urban paupers. The way this group functioned was similar to their counterparts in the Western countries. The real size of this group and the scale of this phenomenon cannot be estimated. Landless peasants and unlanded labourers were the poorest part of the population, and they survived by working for both richer peasants and landowners. Undoubtedly, the very low pace of development of the urban and pre-industrial economy did not allow to incorporate these labourers into a stable social structure. Because of the weakness of the paid labour market, they could not find work outside agriculture, as the labour demand in the modern sectors of the economy was even lower than the labour supply, scarce as it was within the economic system of that period (Assorodobraj-Kula 1946).

At that time, towns and cities were losing importance and townspeople did not play any political role, but they had personal freedom, and towns had the right to create self-government institutions. There were differences between the status of royal towns and the ones within private demesnes, and the reforms usually applied to the former. The social structure of towns and cities was complex, including ethnic, religious, and financial status differences. In many of them, the ethnic and religious groups functioned separately, for example, the groups of Christians and Jews (Teller 2016). The number of Jews in the Commonwealth in 1764 was 565,000 (Wyczański 2003). In some towns, particularly in the west, Protestants constituted a significant minority within the Christian group. Towns and cities were regulated by obsolete rules, giving precedence to artisan guilds and supporting the old, post-medieval model of the social structure. Craftsmen were a dominant group in towns and cities, but the group of merchants and tradesmen was also populous. This sector of the urban economy was dominated by Jews, just like the sector of alcohol trade. Many cities were small and did not perform urban functions, which was discovered by the Prussian government after 1795 and resulted in regulations turning many towns into villages and cities into market towns. Sometimes, such towns had a population of 200–300 people (Wąsicki 1957b; Jelonek 1967; Wandycz 1975; Fedorowicz et al. 1982).

In fact, the urban function was performed by a small number of medium-size and big towns. The social and economic structure of the city of Grodno may give a picture of a town at the end of the existence of the Commonwealth (Poniat 2015). The city, situated in the west of the Great Duchy of Lithuania, played an important role in Poland, both politically and economically. It was one of the bigger cities in this part of the Commonwealth and it was the central node of the royal manufacturing system created by Antoni Tyzenhaus (Kościałkowski 1971), and the centre of one of the most important royal demesnes (the estates bringing income to the royal treasury), which makes it a good example of the urbanization process and the formation of the social structure in cities at that time. It had a population of about 10,000, two-fifths of which were Jews. On the basis of the study of taxpayers' lists, the financial structure was varied, with the Gini coefficient indicating high income inequality (0.77), but it did not differ much from the western cities of that time. The number of paupers was big (over 90% of the households paid very low taxes), and the financial elite was small—10% of the richest Christian households contributed almost 80% of the wealth tax of Christian population, while 20% of the richest Jewish households—to 70% of the wealth tax of Jewish population.

Warszawa—by far the largest Polish city in the late eighteenth century, as the political, administration, economic, banking, and cultural centre of the state, had a social structure not unlike that of European capitals such as Vienna or London. Many influential aristocratic families had their permanent or temporary residences there, and the nobility from all over the Commonwealth would go there to conduct business or engage in politics. The regular political events in Warszawa, like elections and Sejms, created a demand for services—in the second half of the eighteenth century, Warszawa was practically the only place in the state where banking services were available, so the nobility from all over the country applied there for funding for their enterprises (Ihnatowicz 1972; Grochulska 1980, 1988).

The top of the social structure in the Commonwealth was the nobility. Formally, each noble was eligible for voting by relatively complicated electoral law. This meant that only 10%, or in some areas about 20% of the population, had political rights. The nobility was divided by huge wealth and status differences, just like the other social strata. There were big numbers of the poor nobility, sometimes without their own estates, and a small number of extremely rich magnates, owning huge areas of land with their own, private towns (magnate lordships) as well as property in the cities and abroad. The process of building an oligarchy in the Commonwealth, completed in the eighteenth century, was based on the activity of the small group of enterprising noblemen and aristocrats who accumulated huge estates to the east of the Commonwealth. On the other hand, the gradual impoverishment of the mid- and low-rank nobility, resulting from civil and foreign wars, the bad situation on the foreign markets, and an economic crisis in the Commonwealth, made the poor nobility prone to corruption, which resulted in the growing influence of the magnate families (Ihnatowicz et al. 1979; Fedorowicz et al. 1982; Pawłowski et al. 1994).

The social structure of the country was backward, with a large, poor peasant stratum and a small urban stratum. The political and economic power was concentrated in the hands of a limited number of extremely rich aristocratic families. As a result, the state was *de facto* divided into magnate lordships and its political system had turned into oligarchy.

6   The Economy

In the eighteenth century, the Commonwealth was a poorly developed agricultural country. The state was poor, its income was smaller than that of the neighbouring countries. The level of economic development was considerably lower than the European average, which was due to the agriculture-dominated economy. The interests of the nobility, the class structure, and the comparative dominance of agriculture slowed down the economic change. Additionally, the low supply of labour and the low demand for industrial products hampered the development of cities.

The level of economic development of the Commonwealth in the eighteenth century is not well studied. The research of Robert Allen (2001) shows the growing difference between the wages in the cities of the European centre and those on the peripheries, including Kraków. When he studied agricultural output in Europe, he showed (on the basis of rather unrealistic assumptions concerning the dynamics of population and urbanization) that dynamic growth in the Commonwealth in the eighteenth century was one of the fastest in Europe at that time. It is contrary to the opinion of Polish historians, for example, Jerzy Topolski (1977), Antoni Mączak (1995), and Witold Kula (Kula and Kochanowicz 1993). Also Mikołaj Malinowski and Jan L. van Zanden (2017) studied GDP per capita in the Cracow Voivodship in the long term and showed stagnation in the eighteenth century and the growing divergence between this area and western Europe. This region had lost its political and economic importance, so it may have been developing more slowly than other parts of the Commonwealth, but it was still one of the best developed areas. The estimates seem to be more realistic for the Crown than for the whole state, whose eastern regions were significantly less urbanized and more sparsely populated.

Attempts to estimate the rate of development in this period were made by the Polish historians Witold Kula (Kula and Kochanowicz 1993) and Jerzy Topolski (1977). Kula showed the growing income differentiation in the Commonwealth, analysing the consumption basket of various social strata in the long term. Topolski estimated the rates of development in the Commonwealth in different periods, including the years 1750 and 1800. In his opinion, at the end of the Commonwealth, the level of development was comparable to that before the first Northern War (about 1655), and the agricultural output was even lower than that due to depopulation and poorer efficiency. On the basis of Topolski's estimates, Grzegorz and Anna Wójtowicz (Wójtowicz and Wójtowicz 2009) made their estimates of GDP per capita in the Commonwealth. In their opinion, the level of development in the Commonwealth in the second half of the eighteenth century was approximately half as high as that of the developed economies in the West, and the difference grew throughout the eighteenth century.

According to Malinowski and van Zanden, the whole of the eighteenth century is a time of stagnation. Consequently, the gap between the economies of the Commonwealth and Western Europe widened, particularly in the second half of the century. This view does not seem completely true, as in the last decades of the century there is an acceleration in the process of urbanization, visible in the dynamic growth of the population in the capital. This urbanization was the consequence of the restructuring that—albeit slowly—did take place in the Polish economy. Malinowski and van Zanden focused on the region which in the mid-seventeenth century started to lose its political and economic importance (the Cracow Voivodship), so its rate of development was probably lower than that in the whole country. This process continued in the nineteenth century.

From the beginning of the nineteenth century onwards, there exist reliable data on the basis of which the levels of urbanization can be estimated. On this basis, it is possible to estimate the levels of Polish GDP on a regional level (Bukowski et al. 2018) (cf. Tables A.1 and A.2 in Annex).

All these estimations show that in terms of economic development in the second half of the eighteenth century, Poland, with its small cities, poor transport, weak banking system, and practically non-existent industry, was on the remote economic peripheries of Europe. This is the picture of Poland preserved in the memoirs of travellers (Zawadzki 1963; Wolff 1994) and reflected in the words of European thinkers and economists at the time, who appreciated the Polish freedoms, like Edmund Burke or Voltaire, but also saw the weakness and ineffectiveness of the state, like Adam Smith, who mentioned Poland in his book *An Inquiry into the Nature and Causes of the Wealth of Nations*, writing "in Poland there are said to be scarce any manufactures of any kind, a few of those coarser household manufactures excepted, without which no country can well subsist" (Smith 1843, 4). The Polish elites also increasingly realized the backwardness of the state, which triggered the discussion on the reforms within the framework of the ideas of the Age of Enlightenment, described above.

The low rate of development was connected with the obsolete structure of the economy. In the whole period of our analysis the dominant form of economic activity was post-feudal agricultural enterprise. The basic economic unit was the agricultural estate (*folwark*) based on serf labour (the corvée). The relations between the landowner and the serfs were determined, on the one hand, by the land ownership structure and, on the other hand, by the legal dependence of serfs. The serfs cultivated the land partially owned by the landowner and he had the power to decide as to who could cultivate or inherit the land. However, the agricultural output depended on the efficiency of the peasants. The estimates of land productivity show that throughout the eighteenth century it gradually diminished, as a result of depopulation (war damage), the growing amount of labour services, and the obsolete development model; as the impoverishment of landowners made them less inclined to invest, the peasants worked less efficiently, and the land grew less productive (Zamorski 1987; Chirot 1989; Pawłowski et al. 1994; Kochanowicz 2006).

Until the end of its existence, the Commonwealth was a royal demesne state (as opposed to the modern state with its income from taxes). The king's income was from Crown land, so there was no need for an elaborate tax collection administration. The tax system involved the fixed tax on all households, regardless of the social status of the members of the household (introduced in 1775). It was the houses that were taxed or, more precisely, the hearths; hence the Polish name of this tax—*podymne* ("smoke tax"). Jews paid the poll tax. There were separate taxes for the maintenance of the army. Additionally, after the loss of salt mines in the First Partition, a salt tax was introduced to supplement the income of the king. Most taxes were purposeful and temporary and had to be imposed by the nobility-dominated Sejm, which was unwilling to accept any taxes, particularly permanent ones, including those on peasants, who were dependent on the nobility (Rybarski 1937; Jezierski and Leszczyńska 2010).

Throughout its existence, the Commonwealth had relatively weak state institutions and a very limited state capacity, as shown in the introductory chapter. Apart from the uncodified law or the decentralization and privatization of the government, an important symptom of the weakness was the ineffective taxation—not only the low rate of taxation, but also the inability to collect the taxes, which became very clear towards the end of statehood, with the ineffectual attempts to increase the tax revenue. This weakness is indicated by the state income, which is available for use in achieving the goals established in the political process. The total income of the Crown Treasury from Poland and Lithuania throughout the eighteenth century was not only lower than that of the best developed countries (30–40 times lower than in France, 20–30 times lower than in England), but also lower than in the countries at a similar or lower level of development (in 1700, 2.5 times lower than in Russia and Prussia, in 1788, 15 times lower than in Russia, and 7 times lower than in Prussia). Most of the income came from the royal demesne, not taxes (Rostworowski 1984).

With the low income and scarce financing from foreign banks (resulting from the precarious situation of Poland after the First Partition), the state budget was very low, which hampered the development of some institutions whose goal was to safeguard the state, particularly the army. The growing threat of conflict, however, and the increasing influence of the reform faction were the direct reasons for the introduction of extraordinary taxes financing the army (imposed on the nobility and clergy), but the income from these taxes was much smaller than expected. The state also obtained, very expensively, partial financing from internal and foreign loans (Koryś and Tymiński 2013).

The agricultural labour force was almost unlimited and very cheap (actually, usually costless). Serfs (i.e. the vast majority of peasants) are obliged to provide labour only in exchange for the right to use the house and cultivate a plot of land. It was the serfs who provided the tools to cultivate the lord's land. In this way, the landowner had no incentives to check the cost or intensify the production; the only direct incentive for optimization was to support the richer peasants whose responsibility was to provide the draught horses or oxen. A short-term drop in profitability was not a problem, until the situation became difficult or impossible to mend. The landowners responded to problems by limiting investment rather than consumption, and by increasing the peasants' workload and duties; this was observable in the eighteenth century, probably as a response to depopulation and shortage of labour and as a means to maintain productivity rather than increase it. Or they leased out some land in exchange for rent and, in this way, they increased the income. At the state level, this kind of thinking made the nobility reduce all taxes.

With regard to manufactured goods and services, the estates, particularly those of very rich landowners, were practically self-sufficient (or they used imported goods), which was understandable with the poorly developed market and transport. The needs of the big estates (demesnes) were fulfilled by local manufacturing enterprises, which—small and scattered as they were—became at least as important as similar enterprises set up in cities in building the pre-industrial manufacturing sector. These plants were created to meet the current needs of the estates, for example, they produced bricks or glass during the construction of a residence (such brickyards or glassworks were later either closed down or leased out), or manufactured consumer goods, for example, cloth. The best-documented example of such an enterprise was the silk belt factory in Nieśwież in the Radziwiłł demesne. The factory operated for several years and its production mostly covered the needs of the Radziwiłł court, while only a small portion of the production was sold to cover the variable costs. The cost of labour in such operations was very low because serf labour was used. A greater challenge was to find qualified workers—the poor development of cities caused the scarcity of craftsmen and specialists, so sometimes, they were brought from abroad (Kula 1956a, b).

A different type of an aristocratic estate manufacturing operation used the putting-out system. The first phases of manufacturing, usually preparing materials, for example, spinning the linen thread, were performed off site, at people's homes, and the production itself—for example, weaving, processing, and dyeing the fabric—was conducted on site, in the factory. Often, the factory had a school for training peasants, for example, to become spinners. Such manufacturing enterprises were most effective in the densely populated central regions of the country. The last king's brother, bishop Michał Poniatowski, tried to build a system of such factories near Warszawa, for example, in Łowicz (Józefecki 1997). Like other aristocratic enterprises, they suffered from the scarcity of qualified workers, which affected the quality, quantity, and stability of production. Poniatowski's factories were a commercial enterprise, and they also performed services to other manufacturers, for example, dyeing, as they had limited possibility to manufacture their own products. The magnates' estates also developed the food processing industry: their distilleries, breweries, cheese factories, bakeries worked for the estates, but also did outside trade. Sadly, the activities of these operations are poorly documented, as the archives have been destroyed.

Using serf labour in factories and employing expensive specialists from the outside resulted in relatively high production costs. The efficiency was low and the cost of materials relatively high, with a lot of wastage, so—as transport was expensive—these products could only be sold locally, where there was no competition.

Urban economy—a term applying to a relatively small number of towns and cities actually performing urban functions—was based on a few factors. Many towns held markets and provided services connected with trade (for the occupational structure of selected towns, see Tables 3.2, 3.3 and 3.4). In big towns and cities, trade developed in more sophisticated forms, that is, specialized stores. They were the supply base for rural areas, though some craftsmen, such as blacksmiths or millers, worked in villages. Some services were only available in towns, particularly big ones, with better developed job markets. Towns were also the

Table 3.2 Occupational structure of household heads in Radziwill estate towns, Sluck 1750 and Kopyl 1750

	Heads of households	Share (%)	Number of persons	Share (%)
Agriculture	14	1	1	0
Crafts	783	61	273	74
Of which propinacja	74	6	30	8
Services	243	19	33	9
Trade	182	14	28	8
Indigents/beggars	65	5	16	4
Not listed			16	4
Total heads of household	1287	100	367	100
Total population	4888		1086	

Source: Teller (2016)

Table 3.3 Occupational structure of Kalisz, 1789

	Number of persons	Share (%)
Agriculture	213	9.9
Crafts	691	32.1
Of which propinacja	106	4.9
Services	429	19.9
Trade	71	3.3
Indigents/beggars	748	34.8
Total heads of household	2152	

Source: Wyczański (2003)

Table 3.4 Social and occupational structure of Warsaw, 1792 (number of people, excluding families)

	Total	Clergy	Nobility	Bourgeoisie	Jews	Total	Domestic service
Public service	18,195	772	12,533	4828	62	*18,195*	7387
Freelancers	10,431		1380	8564	487	*10,431*	4387
Agriculture	1257		209	1048	0	*1257*	503
Trade	7828		440	5594	1794	*7828*	3826
Crafts/ industry	23,108		611	20,221	2276	*23,108*	12,047
Total	60,819	772	15,173	40,255	4619	*60,819*	28,150

Source: Drzażdżyńska (1931)

sites of new factories, some privately owned, for example, the carriage factories like Dangle's in Warszawa or Leszczyński's in Leszno, some set up by the king or the government (e.g. manufacturing weapons). Besides that, there was a relatively well-developed food processing industry in towns and cities, particularly breweries. The biggest manufacturing enterprises in big cities employed several hundred people, the biggest craftsmen's workshops—several dozen. Finally, the bigger cities provided some financial and banking services; this sector was best developed in Warszawa. Some cities, particularly Warszawa, had some administrative functions, which influenced their social structure. Warszawa also became the place of residence of the magnates, and a considerable portion of the city's population was their entourage (Grochulska 1980).

In the second half of the eighteenth century there were the first attempts to create the basis for the public sector in the economy, financed usually by the money from the royal demesne or loans taken out by the king. Royal factories were built in Warszawa and near Kielce—at the time, it was one of the most industrialized regions in Europe. But the best organized and focused attempt was the project conducted by Antoni Tyzenhaus near the town of Grodno. He created a network of factories manufacturing various goods, mostly textile. The development of the Grodno project lasted for several years and it employed over 1000 people. However, the economic results were not satisfactory, most of the time, it was not profitable. The project was part of Poniatowski's political campaign, as the local nobility, benefiting from the enterprise, helped the royal supporters to achieve the majority in the local assemblies in Grodno. At the same time, Tyzenhaus built his personal fortune while working on the factory project. This investment model, coupled with the bad condition of the royal treasury, brought about the fall of the factories and their maker (Kościałkowski 1971). It is obvious that the royal and state investments were still in the interest of a small group of the nobility getting direct or indirect benefits rather than a new public policy aiming at centrally controlled industrialization, for example, according to the Prussian model (Kula 1956a).

In the 1770s and 1780s, there was economic growth, with increased economic activity of the nobility, growth of the money lending market, accelerated urbanization, growth of public and private investment, particularly in cities, and an attempt to build a standing army. However, as it lacked a strong financial basis, it did not have a significant impact on the modernization of the economy of the Commonwealth. A particular threat to the economic stability was the banking system, which was poorly regulated and developed spontaneously as a handful of Warszawa banks constituting the backbone of the financial system of the Commonwealth. Warszawa banks financed numerous investments of the nobility in the urban housing market and the industrial sector that rapidly developed in peripheral, rural regions (in quite an inefficient way). The loans were secured on the nobility's property (Grochulska 1980, 1988).

To a large extent, Warszawa banks relied on foreign (mostly Dutch) loans, and thus, the system was unstable, particularly in such an unstable political period of European history. But, on the other hand, they offered easy access to cash for the nobility. The growing dependence of the king and the nobility on their loans resulted in the dangerously excessive political influence of bankers, additionally strengthened by their informal connections with the foreign powers. They became a vital element of the institutionalized corruption system which checked the king's policy. A considerable portion of the income of banks came from their half-illegal services in political transactions. The king, many state officials, and many members of the elite got regular or temporary payments, mostly from Russia, which was revealed in 1793: when the banks collapsed, the documents found in the residence of Piotr Tepper, the most important banker in Warsaw, proved that the king and his entourage had received regular allowances from the Russian ambassador (Kornatowski 1937; Morawski 1998).

The total assets of the these banks in Warszawa were many times bigger than the Crown (state) budget. The debts of the state, the king, and the most important officials made the banks vulnerable to the international situation. The banking crisis of 1793 stemmed from the drop in the provision of foreign capital in Poland after the Second Partition, and the public institutions did not have enough fiscal and financial capacity to maintain the stability of the system. With no instruments to secure the loans, the system collapsed. The ones who lost were the noblemen who had financed the banks and who had put up property as collateral for investment loans, which—after the investment mania of the late 1780s—resulted in the growing distrust towards modern economic structures and investing outside agriculture (Kowalczyk 2010). In this way, the collapse of the banking system not only contributed to the fall of the state, but also slowed down the change of attitudes towards the modernization of the state among economic elites and, consequently, delayed the actual economic change. For the next decades, the state remained the only possible agent of large-scale economic modernization.

The collapse of the state was the result of not only political, but also economic crisis. Inefficient public institutions, large-scale bribery, clientelism and nepotism (Mączak 1995; Korys and Tyminski 2016), a puny tax system, the importance of grain export for the economic situation of the nobility, and the reliance of the bank system on foreign loans made the economic system of the Commonwealth particularly vulnerable to the impact of external economic factors. The outflow of western capital from the Polish banking system triggered the banking and economic crisis, which undermined the foundation of the state and contributed to its final collapse.

7   Conclusion

Just before the partitions, the Commonwealth was a country on the periphery of the European economy, with poorly developed cities, practically non-existent transport, weak and ineffectual government, poor circulation of money, and the dominant role of agriculture. Some elements of this sector, landowners' estates, conducted large-scale production aimed at foreign markets, and the staple export were unprocessed agricultural and forest products (mainly wheat, rye, and wood). The dependence of the economy on the export of raw materials, where the competitiveness was the result of moneyless labour, limited its potential for development and industrialization. This contributed to the so-called Dutch disease—any non-agricultural economic activity was practically not profitable, except for the small-scale locally operating enterprises. The industrial sector was dispersed and used obsolete technologies.

Additionally, the oligarchic political system maintained the power of the nobility (in particular, the power of a group of the richest families), suppressing the interests of other social groups, particularly the townspeople, who were crucial for the contemporary reforms in numerous European countries; ironically, even the ideas of the French Revolution were disseminated mostly by noblemen. The political elites were corrupted, mostly by the neighbouring powers.

In the middle of the eighteenth century, there was some activity in the pre-industrial sector, both in the form of royal and state investments, and in the growing involvement of the nobility in creating manufacturing enterprises. This was mostly financed from foreign loans, with the Warsaw banks working as intermediaries. The banks' collapse in 1793 shook the economy of the Commonwealth, vastly contributing to its extinction. The economic problems of the Commonwealth were also aggravated by the partitions, in which the Commonwealth lost lands of key economic importance, particularly to Prussia and Austria (e.g. the salt mines, ceded to Austria and the low reaches of the Vistula, ceded to Prussia).

Still, in macroeconomic terms, the economy of the Commonwealth was not much less developed than that of many other countries of the region, including Austria and Prussia. However, due to better administration, more efficient tax systems, and higher urbanization, these countries were better prepared for the change brought about by the Industrial Revolution. The political system of the Commonwealth, mythologized by Polish historiography, also turned out to be less efficient than those of its neighbours. Moreover, with their greater state capacity and the resulting military power, they caused the collapse of the Commonwealth at the end of the century.

References

Adams, J. (1787). *A defence of the constitutions of government of the United States of America*. C. Dilly.

Allen, R. (2001). The great divergence in European wages and prices from the middle ages to the first world war. *Explorations in Economic History, 38,* 411–447.

Assorodobraj-Kula, N. (1946). *Początki klasy robotniczej: problem rąk roboczych w przemyśle polskim epoki Stanisławowskiej*. Czytelnik.

Biskupski, M. B., & Pula, J. S. (1990). *Polish democratic thought from the renaissance to the great emigration: Essays and documents*. East European Monographs.

Bogucka, M., & Samsonowicz, H. (1986). *Dzieje miast i mieszczaństwa w Polsce przedrozbiorowej*. Zakład Narodowy im. Ossolińskich.

Bukowski, M., Koryś, P., Leszczyńska, C., et al. (2018). Urban population and economic development: Urbanization and approximation of GDP per capita in history—The case of the Polish lands in the 19th century. Mimeo.

Butterwick, R. (1998). *Poland's last king and English culture: Stanisław August Poniatowski, 1732–1798*. Clarendon Press.

Butterwick, R. (2001). *The Polish-Lithuanian monarchy in European context, C. 1500–1795*. Palgrave Macmillan.

Butterwick, R. (2012). *The Polish revolution and the Catholic Church, 1788–1792: A political history*. Oxford: Oxford University Press.

Chirot, D. (1989). *The origins of backwardness in Eastern Europe: Economics and politics from the middle ages until the early twentieth century*. University of California Press.

Davies, N. (2005). *God's Playground: The origins to 1795*. Columbia University Press.

Drzażdżyńska, H. (1931). Ludność Warszawy w roku 1792. *Kwart Stat, VIII,* 45–66.

Fedorowicz, J. K., Bogucka, M., & Samsonowicz, H. (1982). *A republic of nobles: Studies in Polish history to 1864*. Cambridge University Press.

Garczyński, S. (1753). Anatomia rzeczypospolitey-polskiey. [Wrocław]. Digitalized version https://jbc.bj.uj.edu.pl/dlibra/doccontent?id=87423.

Gieysztorowa, I. (1976). *Wstęp do demografii staropolskiej*. Państwowe Wydawnictwo Naukowe.

Główny Urząd Statystyczny. (1993). *Historia Polski w liczbach: ludność, terytorium*. Główny Urząd Statystyczny.

Grochulska, B. (1980). *Warszawa na mapie Polski stanisławowskiej: podstawy gospodarcze rozwoju miasta*. Wydawnictwa Uniwersytetu Warszawskiego.

Grochulska, B. (1988). Wielcy bankierzy Warszawy. *Elity Poliyczne W Polsce, 5*, 69–90.

Grossmann, H. (1925). *Struktura społeczna i gospodarcza Księstwa Warszawskiego na podstawie spisów ludności 1808–1810*. Warszawa: Główny Urząd Statystyczny.

Grześkowiak-Krwawicz, A. (2000). *O formę rządu czy o rząd dusz?: publicystyka polityczna Sejmu Czteroletniego*. IBL.

Grześkowiak-Krwawicz, A. (2012). *Queen liberty: The concept of freedom in the Polish-Lithuanian commonwealth*. Brill.

Ihnatowicz, I. (1972). *Burżuazja warszawska*. Państwowe Wydawnictwo Naukowe.

Ihnatowicz, I., Mączak, A., & Zientara, B. (1979). *Społeczeństwo polskie od X do XX wieku*. Książka i Wiedza.

Jelonek, A. (1967). *Ludność miast i osiedli typu miejskiego na ziemiach Polski od 1810 do 1960 r*. Instytut Geografii Polskiej Akademii Nauk.

Jezierski, A., & Leszczyńska, C. (2010). *Historia gospodarcza Polski*. Wydawnictwo Key Text.

Józefecki, J. (1997). Manufaktura sukiennicza w Skierniewicach w latach 1786–1795. *Mazowieckie Studia Humanistyczne, 3*, 225–244.

Kądziela, Ł. (1991). *Narodziny Konstytucji trzeciego maja*. Agencja Omnipress.

Kądziela, Ł. (1993). *Między zdradą a służbą Rzeczypospolitej: Fryderyk Moszyński w latach 1792–1793*. Oficyna Wydawnicza Volumen.

Kaps, K. (2015). *Ungleiche Entwicklung in Zentraleuropa: Galizien zwischen überregionaler Verflechtung und imperialer Politik (1772–1914)*. Böhlau Verlag Wien.

Kochanowicz, J. (2006). *Backwardness and modernization: Poland and Eastern Europe in the 16th–20th centuries*. Ashgate Variorum.

Konarski, S. (1760). *O skutecznym rad sposobie albo o utrzymywaniu ordynaryjnych seymów*. Warszawa: Drukarnia Pijarów.

Konopczyński, W. (1966). *Polscy pisarze polityczni XVIII wieku (do Sejmu Czteroletniego)*. Państwowe Wydawnictwo Naukowe.

Kornatowski, W. (1937). *Kryzys bankowy w Polsce 1793 roku: upadłość Teppera, Szulca, Kabryta, Prota Potockiego, Łyszkiewicza i Heyzlera*. Drukarnia Samorzad, Instytutu Wydawnictwo.

Koryś, P., & Tymiński, M. (2013). Polish and Swedish fiscal policy in the years 1772–1792. A short-run analysis. *Central European Economy Journal, 33*, 79–99.

Korys, P., & Tyminski, M. (2016). The unwanted legacy. In search of historical roots of corruption in Poland. *Sociologija, 58*, 203–219.

Korzon, T. (1898). *Wewnętrzne dzieje Polski za Stanisława Augusta, 1764–1794: Badania historyczne ze stanowiska ekonomicznego i administracyjnego.* L. Zwoliński.

Kościałkowski, S. (1971). *Antoni Tyzenhauz: podskarbi nadworny litewski.* Stefan Batory University (London Community).

Kowalczyk, R. (2010). *Polityka gospodarcza i finansowa Księstwa Warszawskiego w latach 1807–1812* (Wyd. 1). Łódź: Wydawnictwo Uniwersytet Łódzkiego.

Kuklo, C. (2009). *Demografia Rzeczypospolitej przedrozbiorowej.* Wydawnictwo DiG.

Kula, W. (1956a). *Szkice o manufakturach w Polsce XVIII wieku: 1780–1795.* Państwowe Wydawnictwo Naukowe.

Kula, W. (1956b). *Szkice o manufakturach w Polsce XVIII wieku.* Państwowe Wydawnictwo Naukowe.

Kula, W., & Kochanowicz, J. (1993). *Rozwój gospodarczy Polski XVI–XVIII w.* Państwowe Wydawnictwo Naukowe.

Latuch, K. (2005). *Pierwszy spis domów i ludności Rzeczypospolitej Polskiej 1789 r: wybrane pisma historyczno-demograficzne.* Polskie Towarzystwo Demograficzne.

Leszczyński, S. (1733). Głos Wolny Wolność Ubespieczaiący. s.n. Digitalized version: https://polona.pl/item/glos-wolny-wolnosc-ubezpieczajacy,MTE1N jE2Njg/4/#info:metadata.

Lipiński, E. (1975). *Historia polskiej myśli społeczno-ekonomicznej do końca XVIII [i.e. osiemnastego] wieku.* Ossolineum.

Lukowski, J. (2010). *Disorderly liberty: The political culture of the Polish-Lithuanian commonwealth in the eighteenth century.* Bloomsbury Publishing.

Lukowski, J. (2014). *The partitions of Poland 1772, 1793, 1795.* Taylor & Francis.

Mączak, A. (1995). Development levels in early-modern Europe. In A. Mączak (Ed.), *Money prices power Poland.* Norfolk: Variorum.

Malinowski, M., & van Zanden, J. L. (2017). Income and its distribution in preindustrial Poland. *Cliometrica, 11*, 375–404. https://doi.org/10.1007/s11698-016-0154-5

Michalski, J. (1956). *Plan Czartoryskich naprawy Rzeczypospolitej.* Instytut Historii PAN.

Morawski, W. (1998). *Słownik historyczny bankowości polskiej do 1939 roku.* Muza SA.

Pawłowski, F., Ślusarek, K., & Turek, W. P. (1994). *Drobna szlachta w Galicji, 1772–1848*. Księgarnia Akademicka.

Poniat, R. (2015). Zróżnicowanie majątkowe mieszkańców Grodna w 1794 roku. *Klio, 32*, 83–109.

Preuß, A. E. (1835). *Preußische Landes- und Volkskunde: oder Beschreibung von Preußen: Ein Handbuch für die Volksschullehrer der Provinz Preußen.* Koenigsberg: Borntrager.

Rostworowski, E. (1984). *Historia powszechna: wiek XVIII.* Państwowe Wydawnictwo Naukowe.

Rybarski, R. (1937). *Skarbowość Polski w dobie rozbiorów.* Nakładem Polskiej Akademii Umiejętności.

Śliwiński, B. (Ed.). (2012). *Encyklopedia Gdańska.* Gdańsk: Fundacja Gdańska.

Smith, A. (1843). *An inquiry into the nature and causes of the wealth of nations with a life of the author: Also a view of the doctrine of Smith, compared with that of the French economists, with a method of facilitating the study of his works, from the French of M. Jariner.* Thomas Nelson.

Stanek, W. (1991). *Konfederacje generalne koronne w XVIII wieku.* Wydawnictwo Adam Marszałek.

Staszic, S. (1785). *Uwagi nad życiem Jana Zamoyskiego Kanclerza i Hetmana W. K.: do dzisieyszego stanu Rzeczypospolitey Polskiey przystosowane.* [Warszawa].

Stone, D., Sugar, P. F., & Treadgold, D. W. (2001). *The Polish-Lithuanian state, 1386–1795.* University of Washington Press.

Storozynski, A. (2009). *The peasant prince: And the age of revolution.* St. Martin's Press.

Sutton, J. L. (2015). *The king's honor and the king's cardinal: The war of the Polish succession.* University Press of Kentucky.

Szacka, B. (1966). *Stanisław Staszic.* Państwowy Instytut Wydawniczy.

Szczygielski, W. (2015). *Sejm Wielki (1788–1792): studium z dziejów łagodnej rewolucji.* Łódzkie Towarzystwo Naukowe.

Szyndler, B. (1994). *Powstanie kościuszkowskie 1794.* Ancher.

Teller, A. (2016). *Money, power, and influence in eighteenth-century Lithuania: The Jews on the Radziwill estates.* Stanford, CA: Stanford University Press.

Topolski, J. (1977). *Gospodarka polska a europejska w XVI–XVIII wieku.* Wydawnictwo Poznańskie.

Trencsényi, B., Janowski, M., Baár, M., et al. (2016). *A history of modern political thought in East Central Europe: Negotiating modernity in the "long nineteenth century".* Oxford: Oxford University Press.

Vielrose, E. (1957). Ludność Polski od X do XVIII wieku. *Kwartalnik Historii KulturyMaterialnej, vol. 5, 1*, 3–49.

Wandycz, P. S. (1975). *The lands of partitioned Poland, 1795–1918.* University of Washington Press.

Wąsicki, J. (1952). *Konfederacja Targowicka i ostatni Sejm Rzeczypospolitej z 1793 roku: studium historyczno-prawne.* Nakładem Poznańskiego Towarzystwo Przyjaciół Nauk.

Wąsicki, J. (1957a). *Powstanie kościuszkowskie w Wielkopolsce.* Wydawnictwo Poznańskie.

Wąsicki, J. (1957b). *Ziemie polskie pod zaborem pruskim: Prusy południowe, 1793–1806: studium historycznoprawne.* Zakład im. Ossolińskich.

Wegner, L. (1871). *Stefan Garczyński wojewoda poznański i dzieło jego Anatomia Rzeczypospolitéj polskiéj: (1706–1755).* Nakładem Towarzystwa [Przyjaciół Nauk].

Wójtowicz, G., & Wójtowicz, A. (2009). *Dlaczego nie jesteśmy bogaci.* Warszawa: CeDeWu.

Wolff, L. (1994). *Inventing Eastern Europe: The map of civilization on the mind of the enlightenment.* Stanford, CA: Stanford University Press.

Wyczański, A. (Ed.). (2003). *Historia Polski w liczbach. T. 1: Państwo, społeczeństwo.* Warszawa: Zakład Wydawnictw Statystycznych.

Zahorski, A. (1985). Powstanie Kościuszkowskie w świetle najnowszych badań. *Przegląd Humanistyczny, vol. 29, 11–12,* 65–73.

Zamorski, K. (1987). *Folwark i wieś: gospodarka dworska i społeczność chłopska Tenczynka w latach 1705–1845.* Wrocław and Kraków: Zakład Narodowy im. Ossolińskich.

Zamoyski, A. (1992). *The last king of Poland.* London: Jonathan Cape.

Zawadzki, W. ed. (1963). Polska Stanisławowska W Oczach Cudzoziemców. Warszawa: PIW.

Zielińska, Z. (1983). *Walka "Familii" o reformę Rzeczypospolitej 1743–1752.* Warszawa: PWN.

Zielińska, Z. (1991). *Kołłątaj i orientacja pruska u progu Sejmu Czteroletniego.* Instytut Wydawniczy Pax.

4

Between the Consolidation from Above and the Fragmentation of the State: Partitions, Duchy of Warsaw and Polish Lands After the Congress of Vienna (1795–1830)

This chapter focuses on the period of slow decline of any form of Polish sovereignty after the collapse of the Commonwealth in 1795. Thus, three sub-periods are discussed: the partitions period, the Duchy of Warsaw (the Napoleonic era), and the period after the Congress of Vienna (1815–1830). Between 1772 and 1795, in spite of the reforms, the Polish state ceased to exist as a result of three partitions. Subsequently, it was revived—on a significantly diminished territory—first by Napoleon, as the Duchy of Warsaw. The new order after the Congress of Vienna redefined the distribution of the Polish lands and moved the Russian border far to the west, to the Warta River. The post-Congress political entities on the Polish lands were the Kingdom of Poland (known as Congress Poland), established on most of the territory of the Duchy of Warsaw as a Russian protectorate, and the Free City of Kraków (Cracow), under the control of three partitioning states, both with relative autonomy (including their own constitutions). Within the Prussian state, some extent of autonomy was granted to the Grand Duchy of Posen. These quasi-states came to a decline between 1831 (the defeat of the November Uprising) and 1848 (after the Revolutions of 1848).

© The Author(s) 2018
P. Koryś, *Poland From Partitions to EU Accession*,
https://doi.org/10.1007/978-3-319-97126-1_4

The period of partitions and Enlightenment reforms after the Congress of Vienna brought—apart from the collapse of the state—a profound institutional change, as the modern institutions were created and the society began to assume the modern form. The state tried to conduct a mercantilist policy in order to lay the foundation for an industrial economy. The locally written economic history usually emphasizes the importance of early industrialization, particularly of the emergence of the state-funded heavy industry in the Świętokrzyskie Mountains and along the border with Upper Silesia. However, the actual influence of these projects on the economy was indeed small, even at the regional level and in the short term. The weakly developed internal market, underdeveloped infrastructure, unfavourable geopolitical situation, and the briefness of successive political entities were not suitable conditions for development and introducing an industrial revolution on the Polish territory.

1   Internal Politics

During the partitions period, the states that participated in the division of the Polish territory tried to integrate the newly acquired lands with their other regions. It was particularly easy in the case of Prussia—the new territories were close and easily accessible from the other parts of the country and from the main cities such as Berlin, Breslau, and Stettin. In Austria, the new lands were much less favourably located, as they were remote and separated from the capital by mountain ranges. In Russia, the Polish lands were the remote peripheries of the empire, but unlike the rest of Empire of Tsars, geographically close to the West.

In Prussia, the new public investment projects, including Friedrich Wilhelm von Reden's project in the eastern part of Upper Silesia and the territories of the former Duchy of Siewierz (Schmidt-Rutsch and Reden 2008), contributed to the acceleration of economic growth. The new legal regulations improved—after an initial crisis—the situation in towns and cities, where the old post-feudal laws were nullified. The Prussian state conducted vast modernization of the economy, particularly during the reign of Frederic II (until his death in 1786), including the modernization of agriculture and the army as well as the development of industry and trade, and the economy of the Polish lands incorporated into Prussia benefitted from these reforms. According to the guidelines of the Prussian economic policy, the new lands quickly obtained modern centralized administrational structures (Schieder et al. 2016). The new institutions soon removed the vestiges of the old uncodified legal and administrational system of the Commonwealth. The scope and the thoroughness of the reform came as a surprise to the Poles, as reflected in the contemporary memoirs. At the same time, German became the dominant official language. The tax solutions gave preference to the Lutherans, most of whom were German-speaking. The key administrational institutions were the Chambers, like in the rest of Prussia. The administration was extremely efficient (in comparison to the public institutions of the Commonwealth), as proved by the new investment projects, discussed below, the implementation of new regulations and the whole new legal system, the new administrative division and the census, immediately conducted on the territories acquired in the Second and Third Partitions (one of the first censuses on the Polish lands) (Wąsicki 1957; Kowalczyk 2010).

Austria also made an effort to integrate the new lands. The lands acquired in the First Partition were included in the Josephine reforms (Magocsi 2010, 416; Korobowicz and Witkowski 2012, 26–34), including the one abolishing serfdom, limiting the corvée and ensuring that the peasant could not be evicted from his land as long as he performed his duties. The changes were repealed after the death of Joseph II Habsburg by his successor, Leopold II, which hampered the modernization of the economy of this part of Poland, already declining throughout the eighteenth century. Galicia was also incorporated into the Austrian customs territory in 1784, and the protectionist policy introduced in Austria at the same time resulted in loosening the economic ties between the Austrian lands and the remainder of the Commonwealth (which caused the economic decline of the best developed parts of Western Galicia) (Wandycz 1975; Lukowski 2014; Kaps 2015).

In Russia, the scope of the integration was smaller, though there were some reforms of law and administration unifying the new lands with the rest of the state. The city that benefitted was Wilno (Vilnius), because it gained importance in comparison with the final period of the Commonwealth, as it was the only university city and most important administrative centre within the part of the Commonwealth taken over by Russia in the partitions. The local university also flourished. However, in the long term, the consequences of the partitions for the Russian part were similar to those in Austria—the long-term stagnation of the former peripheries of the Commonwealth, which were sparsely populated, poorly urbanized, and economically only loosely connected with Russia (Serejski 1970; Wandycz 1975; Korobowicz and Witkowski 2012; Lukowski 2014). In 1791, the former territories of the Commonwealth (Russia's western provinces. Later, since the Congress of Vienna, when borders changed, it started to comprise the Kingdom of Poland established in 1815), as well as some territories formerly governed by the Ottoman Empire and the Cossack Hetmanate, became the Pale of Settlement, the only territory of Russia where the permanent settlement of Jews inside Russia was accepted (Pipes 1985).

This process of incorporating the Polish lands into the new states lasted a decade and was interrupted by the Napoleonic Wars. In 1806, the Duchy of Warsaw was created, mostly on the lands ceded to Prussia and Austria in the Third Partition. The Duchy of Warsaw, created in the Napoleonic era, was expected to be the first step to the reconstruction of the Polish state, but it was small and remained politically dependent on France. The policy that was implemented there was a mixture of the French political and legal institutions and the Prussian administrational structure, inherited from the period of the Prussian government (most of its territory comprised the lands taken over by Prussia in the three partitions) (Czubaty 2011).

The Duchy lasted until 1815. At the time of its creation, its lands were largely destroyed by war. The prefect of the Płock Department, Rajmund Rembieliński, reported war damage of up to 80% of the physical capital, though probably only locally. This condition of the Duchy rendered tax collection or organizing administration ineffective. The situation was worsened by Napoleon's army stationed in the Duchy. With the army constantly translocating, the protection of borders and efficient custom policy was virtually impossible.

The administration of the Duchy of Warsaw was modelled on Prussian solutions rather than French ones. Tax administration was preserved, as well as most of the taxes introduced by the Prussian government. The system was gradually enlarged, which was connected with the need to keep a standing army and with the so-called sums of Bayonne, the credit owed by the Polish nobility to the Prussian government and taken over by Napoleon. These two factors and the imitation of the Prussian and French institutions contributed to the rise of the modern tax state, for the first time on Polish lands. The authorities of the Duchy made a conscious decision not to follow the old rules or introduce the French model (Kowalczyk 2010; Korobowicz and Witkowski 2012).

However, the legal system imposed by Napoleon followed the French model very closely. Its foundation was the constitution, conferred by Napoleon in Dresden in 1807 (Dziadzio 2007, 2008), and the Napoleonic Code of Civil Law. In effect, all the social inequalities in the Duchy were nullified and equal rights for all were introduced. The corvée was abolished, but all the land remained the property of the landowners. This, like in other countries in Europe, led to the evictions of peasants and the accumulation of land, as well as—because of the technological and systemic backwardness—the gradual return to labour services, which was legal under the Code. On the other hand, the nobility gained new opportunities for investment and enterprise, no longer limited by class membership. In this way, Poland found itself among the many European countries in which the French Revolution was a catalyst for social and economic change.

Apart from the Duchy of Warsaw, on the formerly Prussian land, Napoleon created the Free City of Gdańsk (Danzig), which existed in the years 1807–1814 (formally it was nullified in 1815) (Cieślak and Biernat 1988). Napoleon's Code was implemented there, but the work on the constitution was never completed. Gdańsk was suffering from an economic crisis at the time, in the long term resulting from the diminishment of the Baltic trade (which lasted throughout the eighteenth century) and in the short term caused by the collapse of trade because of the war and the continental blockade. Before the blockade, the trade with England constituted about 90% of the grain export from Gdańsk. Additionally, the Prussian tariffs on the Vistula River hampered the grain import to Gdańsk. In effect, many old merchant houses went bankrupt. Moreover, the growing French garrison and the administration costs used most of the city's income, which brought to a halt any public investment.

The Congress of Vienna finished the Napoleonic era and brought considerable political changes on the Polish lands. Most of the Duchy of Warsaw was turned into the Kingdom of Poland (Congress Poland), in the real union with Russia. Gdańsk came back to Prussia. Also, most of Greater Poland was incorporated into Prussia (its eastern part remained in the Kingdom of Poland), but it retained some autonomy as the Grand Duchy of Posen (Topolski 1973). The Free City of Kraków had a good deal of autonomy, though formally it was supervised by all the three states which had partitioned the Commonwealth, and was regarded as one of the most liberal states in Europe (Bartel 1976; Korobowicz and Witkowski 2012). The autonomy of these territories lasted until 1831. The defeat of the November Uprising in 1831 can be seen as the definitive end of autonomy on the Polish territories.

The Kingdom of Poland was a constitutional monarchy, and the monarch was the emperor of Russia. The constitution, prepared by the Polish aristocracy, ensured a relatively wide range of civil rights. While in the real union with Russia (Wojas 2017), the state obtained political freedom in many respects—it had its own parliament, army, language, education system with a university in Warsaw, its own money and, importantly, its own economic policy. It was only foreign policy which was conducted uniformly by the Russian Tsar and the King of Poland, Alexander I. The law was largely based on the regulations from the time of the Duchy of Warsaw (Korobowicz and Witkowski 2012; Mażewski 2013). The solutions based on the Napoleonic Code regarding property continued ceaselessly till WWI and longer, which made the legal status of the Kingdom of Poland unique within Russia. In the future, this uniqueness (and favourable location) was reflected in the Kingdom's greater attractiveness for investors than Russia's.

Until 1830 the Kingdom of Poland had a large scope of real political autonomy. In matters of internal policy, the parliament and the government ("the Administrative Council", part of "the Council of the State") had a power of decision (Izdebski 1978). In the years 1815–1830, the key political factions continued the traditions of the political differences of the Commonwealth, that is, aristocratic liberals against the proponents of the protectionist and interventionist policy of the state—only the proportions changed (Bortnowski 1976; Kizwalter 1999; Szczepański 2008).

The views of the former are connected with the interests of the big landowners, those of the latter—with the growing townsfolk and the gentry. In 1830, the November Uprising broke out (sometimes called the Polish-Russian War of 1830–1831) and, as a result of its defeat, the Kingdom of Poland lost its autonomy and long-term martial law was introduced (Łojek 1986).

The Grand Duchy of Posen had much less autonomy. It was ruled by the King of Prussia, and, unlike the Kingdom of Poland, it was not a fully autonomous administrative region. Its political autonomy, confirmed by the existence of a separate parliament, was actually very limited. The parliament was only an advisory body, and the legal system was the same as in the rest of Prussia. The Great Duchy was a peripheral, agricultural province of Prussia, and until 1830, the local policy was dominated by the interests of big landowners. Between 1815 and 1830, the Great Duchy of Posen implemented the same land ownership laws as the rest of Prussia, which resulted in the partial enfranchisement of peasants. The other territories of the Commonwealth seized by Prussia were incorporated into the Prussian state. Although the November Uprising did not spread to Prussia, the autonomy of the Grand Duchy of Posen was also taken away. The rest of the Polish territories included into Prussia was rapidly integrated and the language, cultural, and educational rights were ignored (Topolski 1973).

In Austria, Galicia found itself on the remote peripheries of the monarchy. The Josephine reforms failed to change the status of the peasants, so—like in the Kingdom of Poland—their economic situation and legal status fostered neither the development of agriculture, nor urbanization. The political and public rights of the Polish majority were limited: German became the only language used in public institutions and the majority of school education was conducted in German. However, there was an effective policy of incorporating the Polish upper and middle classes into the imperial administration institutions. Galicia, now without the northern, industrial part of the Cracow Voivodship and without Kraków (Cracow) itself (as it had become a Free City), situated away from trade routes and from the capital, was entering a time of stagnation, which would last for several decades (Kawalec and Wierzbieniec 2011; Kaps 2015).

On the other hand, the Free City of Kraków remained an enclave of liberal policy, and a supply base for the Polish conspiracy and independence movement. It did not have a big population or territory, but it played a vital role in the trade between the now-separated parts of the former Commonwealth, because it had trade privileges from all the states that had partitioned the Commonwealth (on Tsar Alexander's initiative, all the partitioning states were involved in creating the Free City). Low taxes, a modern constitution (which abolished the corvée) and liberal economic institutions positioned Kraków for two decades as an enclave of political and economic liberalism in Central Europe. This contributed to quick urbanization both within the city and across the border (the development of Podgórze in Galicia), indicating the dynamic economic growth based on trade (Bartel 1976; Korobowicz and Witkowski 2012).

The Napoleonic period and the Congress of Vienna resulted in regaining partial political autonomy by Poles. It opened the possibility of sovereign (autonomous) public policies, including economic policy there. But the defeat of the November Uprising and the decline of Polish autonomic quasi-states can be regarded as the end of the attempts at the Enlightenment reforms in the Polish politics and economy.

2   The International Situation

Between the Third Partition and the Duchy of Warsaw, the conditions for recreating at least partial independence of the Polish state became increasingly favourable. At the end of the Commonwealth, part of the Polish elite was attracted to the ideas of the French Revolution and saw the success of the revolutionary army, and later Napoleon's army, as the key to rebuilding the statehood. This led to the direct involvement of Polish emigrants in military activity, like that of the Polish Legions formed by general Jan Henryk Dąbrowski. Another option considered by Polish politicians was connected with Russia. Its supporters were active throughout the Napoleonic period, and it is because of their efforts (particularly Adam Czartoryski's) that after Napoleon's defeat most of the territory of the Duchy of Warsaw was turned into the Kingdom of Poland (in real union with Russia).

Until the beginning of the nineteenth century, the situation on the Polish lands was stable, but Napoleon's military success undermined the political power of Prussia and Austria, and Poland's position was temporarily improved. This finally allowed the creation of a French protectorate, the Duchy of Warsaw, on some of the territories formerly seized by Prussia and Austria. The Duchy was unfavourably located and was the theatre of war throughout its existence (1807–1815). Napoleon created the dependent quasi-state as an outpost of his empire in order to obtain recruits and create a supply base for the army, particularly during the Russian campaign. However, he made the new state economically weak, as Gdańsk and Pomerania were not included in its territory and it had no access to the sea. The Duchy of Łowicz, presented to one of Napoleon's marshals, was exempted from paying taxes. Another prosperous area not included into the Duchy of Warsaw was the newly created Duchy of Siewierz and Olkusz, comprising the industrial areas recently created by Prussia (Czubaty 2011).

As a result of Napoleon's defeat in Russia, the Russian army captured the territory of the Duchy. The new order after the Congress of Vienna redefined the distribution of the Polish lands and moved the Russian border far to the west, to the Warta River. Now Russia had much more of the territory of the former Commonwealth than before, as the new Kingdom of Poland, in real union with Russia, comprised part of the lands seized by Prussia and Austria in the partitions, as well as a considerable part of the Duchy of Warsaw. This territorial division was in place for several decades, as the geopolitical situation in the region, based on good relations between Russia, Prussia, and Austria, did not change until the end of the century (Wandycz 1975; Lukowski 2014).

The Western European countries stopped focusing on Poland and the Poles. It changed for some time during and after the November Uprising (or the Polish-Russian War of 1830–1831), as this war reduced the risk of the planned Russian intervention in Belgium and France against the bourgeois revolutions (Zajewski 2012). The wave of Polish political emigrants after the defeat of the Uprising (the so-called Great Emigration) played an important role in shaping the Polish political and cultural ideas (mostly from France), and maintaining the awareness among Western European elites of the Polish problem and Polish history (which was only partially successful).

3   Ideas

The partitions period witnessed a great discussion on the question of economic development, as many intellectuals and politicians perceived the Commonwealth's economy as the main source of the collapse of the state. The debates focused on three approaches to economic growth: the implementation of the liberal economic policy, protectionism and interventionism supporting the private sector outside agriculture, and the development of the public sector in the economy.

The proponents of the liberal model were influenced by the ideas of classical economy, with the growing reception of the Scottish Enlightenment with Adam Smith and early nineteenth-century liberal economists, from David Ricardo to Jean-Baptiste Say. Initially, they also looked for inspiration in the tradition of physiocratic economic thought. The most important members of this group in Poland were Dominik Krysiński and Fryderyk Skarbek, who represented the aristocratic liberalism traditionally connected with the interests of the big landowners. Neither of them was in favour of the industrialization policy of the state. Krysiński (1956), while discussing the theory of development stages, expressed the idea that the spontaneous development of industry and trade should be a direct result of achieving a certain level in the development of agriculture. He thought that forcing premature development of industry would result in the outflow of capital from agriculture but would not improve the condition of the state. Hence, he criticized protectionist tariffs, the state support for the development of industry, and the direct involvement of the state in the economy (Górski 1963).

This criticism of the state-funded industrialization efforts of the time was continued by Skarbek. He stated that the development of industry should be connected with the existing demand for its products, particularly the demand on the internal market. He admonished the proponents of the hurried industrialization: "They want to introduce all sorts of manufactured products immediately and by force, regardless of the wealth and the needs of the land", and added that "they build the prosperity of crafts solely on the trade with Russia" (Górski 1963; Lityńska 2000; Skarbek and Szymaniec 2013).

It should be stressed that neither Skarbek nor Krysiński actually represented the interests of big landowners; they simply thought that agriculture, as the core economic activity, should reform first of all. According to Krysiński, it was necessary to enfranchise the peasants, which would increase the consumption of agricultural produce, and consequently, create the demand for industrial products, the *sine qua non* of the natural, unforced and spontaneous, that is, proper, industrialization.

Another careful reader of Smith's economy and philosophy was Wawrzyniec Surowiecki (Surowiecki and Szymaniec 2014), whose main writings were created at the time of the Duchy of Warsaw. He recognized the difference between the well-developed and modern British economy and the underdeveloped Polish one. Then, he made an attempt to adapt Smith's ideas to Polish circumstances. In effect, he offered a less critical approach to active industrialization. His way of thinking about economic reform was a continuation of the ideas of the Enlightenment. He thought that it was the market that should determine the value of work. Within his paternalistic attitude to peasants, he advocated urgent abolition of serfdom and gradual enfranchisement. He thought that the faster changes should be made in the areas with bigger demand for labour outside agriculture. He proposed partial legal rights for peasants, particularly the freedom of movement (with the lord's consent) and the capacity to enter legally binding contracts. In his extensive programme of agricultural reform, based on the constitution of the Duchy of Warsaw, he demanded that the peasants' farms and plots should become the property of the tenants, hereditary and transferable, though still partially retaining the features of a long-term lease, bringing profits to the landowner. He thought that the lord should have the power of decision concerning the peasants and their farms, including the peasants' mobility and child-rearing, as well as the right to repossess poorly tended farms.

In his seminal work published in 1810 *On the Collapse of Industry and Cities in Poland* (which is sometimes called the last moral treatise of the Polish Enlightenment) Surowiecki (Górski 1963; Surowiecki and Szymaniec 2014) returned to the discussion on the sources of the economic crisis on Polish lands. He continued, in stronger terms than ever before, the criticism of serfdom (formally abolished by the constitution of the Duchy) as the main source of the political, moral, and economic collapse of the Commonwealth. He believed that the key to the development of the country was the towns and cities, with their trade and industry. He thought that trade, both internal and—particularly—international, was even more important than industry, so he saw the greatest chance for economic development in free trade and exporting cheaper manufactured goods. He saw export as the main stimulus for entrepreneurship and manufacturing leading to economic success. For him, other countries were exchange partners rather than fierce competitors. This exchange, however, should be conducted between partners at similar economic levels—without its own industry, a country selling only agricultural produce was doomed to failure, not only developmentally, but also politically.

This approach to international relations recognized the role of the state in the economy. Surowiecki noticed the dangers of import, but he did not consider protectionist tariffs or state monopolies to be a good solution. He approved of some interventionist measures, for example, tax relief for the branches of production that were not competitive on foreign markets, or direct help in particular cases. The state was also responsible for creating and maintaining the good quality of transport infrastructure, such as roads and canals. Another responsibility of the state was the development of education. Surowiecki defined backwardness as the lack of industriousness and industries, including market-oriented agricultural production. In his view, backward nations only work to satisfy their basic needs, while in the modern nations, the drive to achieve comfort and to fulfil new needs breeds entrepreneurship and opens the path to affluence. Hence, he thought that abolishing serfdom, creating conditions to improve the economic situation of peasants, and their enrichment were the springboard for development.

After the Prussian and Napoleonic period, the proponents of state investments became strong and influential. The Kingdom's political life of that time was dominated by the protectionists and supporters of the direct involvement of the state in the country's economy, like in the cameralist model. The two men who had the greatest influence on the economic policy were Xawery Drucki-Lubecki and Stanislaw Staszic. Staszic created the idea of using public money to build an industrial area in the Świętokrzyskie Mountains, near Kielce. Drucki-Lubecki favoured the idea of the reform of the treasury, and he saw the solution for industry in supporting private investment. This model came into being in the industrial area that started to develop along the Kalisz (Calisia) Road, joining Warsaw with Kalisz and then Prussia (Jedlicki 1999; Kizwalter 1999; Jedlicki et al. 2014).

Staszic and Drucki-Lubecki were proponents of state-induced industrialization. In their opinion, the scope of the involvement of the state in the economic development should be significantly larger than that suggested by Surowiecki, and the period after the Congress of Vienna created favourable conditions for implementing these ideas. At the time, both Staszic and Drucki-Lubecki were practitioners rather than theorists of economic policy, and the views and opinions formulated in their letters can be seen in the context of their activity (Jedlicki 1964). The goal of the industrialization policy was to replace imported goods with local production, that is, import substitution *avant la lettre*, implemented by means of policy instruments modelled on Prussian cameralism (Schieder et al. 2016).

This meant, on the one hand, the policy of capital accumulation by means of fiscal instruments, implemented by Drucki-Lubecki, and, on the other hand, the accelerated state-induced industrialization funded from public resources. Industrial development was not expected to be funded only from private sources—on the contrary, the state had a key role to play, like in the period of the Prussian government, which became the model of successful industrialization (Szlajfer 2012).

In the Duchy of Warsaw, the most influential faction among the intellectuals were the proponents of moderate modernization and limited state involvement in the economy, while in the Kingdom of Poland, the advocates of state-induced industrialization became more influential and found favourable conditions for implementing their ideas. The liberals developed their theory, while the practice focused on finding ways to catch up with the West using public resources. Nevertheless, both groups were impressed by successes of Prussian economic policy after the Third Partition.

The successes of the Prussian state economic policy impressed part of the Polish elite, and from this moment state-led accelerated industrialization became perceived as one of the best tools of economic policy, particularly by active politicians. According to the supporters of accelerated industrialization, building industry from scratch was to become an instrument of social change working exactly the opposite way to that expected by thinkers like Krysiński. The new lifestyle induced by industry, burdening the agriculture with the cost of industrialization and involving the state, which reduced the problem of efficiency (in the name of achieving macroeconomic goals) were to modernize the society "from above" and transform the Polish economy into industrial and capitalist by means of a public policy.

4   Territory and Population

The borders established in 1795, during the last partition, remained unchanged until the creation of the Duchy of Warsaw by Napoleon in 1807. At first, its territory comprised the lands seized by Prussia in the Second and Third Partitions. In 1809, after the Austrian campaign, it was enlarged with the part of Western Galicia incorporated into Austria after the Third Partition. As a result of the new territorial division established during the Congress of Vienna, Russia obtained the majority of the former Commonwealth, moving its borders to the Warta River. Even though the autonomous Kingdom of Poland was extracted from Russia, it was joined to it by a real union (Wandycz 1975; Czubaty and Phillips 2016).

The territorial division of the Commonwealth in 1795 was relatively easily accepted by the international community (though the public opinion in countries like the Dutch Republic, England, and France appreciated Poland's reformatory effort, Libiszowska 1973)—their only concern was the increasing power of Russia and Prussia after the partitions. In total, about two-thirds of the territory and 45% of the population of the Commonwealth was incorporated into Russia, 20% of the territory and 22% of the population—into Prussia, and 17% of the territory and 33% of the population—into Austria. The majority of the regions inhabited by ethnic Poles found themselves in Prussia and Austria.

According to the census, the population of the Duchy of Warsaw in 1810 was 4.3 million people, and that on the territories of the later Kingdom of Poland was 3.3 million (Grossmann 1925). According to the census conducted at the beginning of the existence of the Kingdom, these lands were inhabited by 2.8 million people, which might indicate a considerable population drop. The data from the mid-1820s show the number of inhabitants at a little below 3.5 million (Rodecki et al. 1830; Janczak 1983). Actually, the former data seem to have been underestimated, and probably the number of inhabitants was relatively stable. The population of Western Galicia reached 1.1 million in 1810 and 1.4 million in 1825, what was equal to one-third of total population of Galicia (Główny Urząd Statystyczny 1993), while Prussian partition in new borders counted 1.4 million of people in 1816, and over 1.8 million in 1831 (Kumor 1978, 1984). The other Prussian lands in contemporary Polish borders were inhabited by 4 million people in 1816 and 5.1 million in 1831 (Hohorst 1977).

As a result of the war, population growth slowed down. The erstwhile Commonwealth lands were still poorly developed, as indicated by the weakness of the urban economy and the small number of towns. The wars and changing borders also slowed down urbanization, which did not revive until 1815, when geopolitical stability was achieved. Urbanization slowed down in all the lands of the Prussian Partition and in Galicia. The dynamic growth of Warszawa from the end of the Commonwealth stopped, as the city had lost its capital status and was severely affected by the crisis of 1793. In effect, it was significantly depopulated. The cities of Greater Poland did not fare well in the competition with Silesian and Saxon ones—the disappearance of the customs border resulted in the collapse of the textile and weaving industry, steadily developing up to that period. The situation of craftsmen was also badly affected by the abolition of guild privileges. The most dynamic urbanization took place on the territories incorporated into the Polish state after 1945, particularly Lower Silesia and Upper Silesia (at that time inhabited mostly by ethnic Germans) but, in the nineteenth century, the Polish-speaking population in that region was very small (Jelonek 1967; Główny Urząd Statystyczny 1993).

The biggest cities of the Duchy of Warsaw, apart from the depopulated Warszawa (Warsaw) (77,700 inhabitants), were Kraków (Cracow) (since 1809, with 23,600 inhabitants) and Poznań (16,000 inhabitants). The population of towns bigger than 5000 people amounted to 160,000 people, that is, about 4% of the total population. In the Kingdom of Poland, the population of Warszawa came back to the level from before the partitions as, in the 1820s, Warszawa regained the status of a major administrational and economic centre (that process had already started at the time of the Duchy of Warsaw). In the mid-1820s, the population of Warszawa was over 120,000 people, and there were two cities with populations of over 10,000 people: Lublin (13,000) and Kalisz (Calisia) (11,500). The only major city within the Russian partition outside the Kingdom of Poland was Wilno (Vilnius), with about 25,000 inhabitants (Karpineć 1932; Jelonek 1967).

On the territories of the former Commonwealth governed by Prussia after 1815, the biggest city was Gdańsk, with the population of 37,000 in 1810 and about 50,000 in the late 1820s. Besides that, two cities exceeded the population of 10,000: Elbląg (Elbing) (17,000 in 1810) and Poznań (Posen). Inside the borders of present-day Poland, another two cities were relatively big: Breslau (Wrocław) in Silesia (68,000 people at the beginning of the nineteenth century) and Stettin (Szczecin) in Pomerania (21,000 people), as well as a few Silesian towns with populations of about 10,000 at the time, such as Brieg (Brzeg), Schweidnitz (Świdnica), Liegnitz (Legnica). In the Austrian Galicia, the only big cities were Kraków (Cracow) and Lwów (Lvov) (about 41,000–42,000 in 1808 and 1817, 49,000 in 1835) (Jelonek 1967).

On the basis of the existing data, some information about the religious structure of at least some of the regions of Poland in this period may be presented. According to the census conducted in the Duchy of Warsaw, the majority of the population was Polish and Roman-Catholic, and about 7% of its inhabitants were Jewish. The greatest percentages of Jews in Duchy were in the Łomża Department (about 10%), Warszawa (Warsaw) Department (9%), Siedlce Department (8%), and Lublin Department (7%). In the western departments, these percentages were lower (5% and less). In the whole of the Duchy, the Protestants, that is, Lutherans and Calvinists, constituted 8.6% of the population (of which Calvinists were 0.3%), but Western departments had higher percentages of Protestants (i.e. 24% in Posen Department, 32% in Bydgoszcz Department). Jews also constituted about 7–8% of the Austrian population of Western Galicia at the time and similar share of the population of the remaining part Russian partition (Grossmann 1925).

5 The Society

The legal barriers enforcing the rigid system of the landowner's estates of the realm began to weaken, and slowly permitted social mobility; the boundaries between the classes sanctioned by law started to disintegrate in the second half of the eighteenth century. The process of the creation of modern social structures was accelerated by the partitions, and even more by Napoleon's policy. By the end of the eighteenth century, most post-feudal regulations of the former Commonwealth were nullified on the lands of the Prussian and Austrian partitions. One of the very few exceptions was the corvée—the failure of the Josephine reform in Austria brought back labour services and, in Prussia, it was not abolished until the creation of the Duchy of Warsaw. However, the division of the country had a negative influence on spontaneous social processes such as urbanization.

The economic, social, and political position of some of the nobility deteriorated after the partitions due to the division of the territory and the emergence of new customs borders. The biggest demesnes suffered, because, according to the agreement between Austria, Prussia, and Russia, the demesnes could only be located within one country, and the parts abroad had to be sold. The new tax policy also affected the nobility under Prussian rule. With the changing economic circumstances, the decreased demand for Polish grain (caused by the continental blockade and the emergence of customs borders) undermined the economic situation of many agricultural estates. Additionally, the situation was aggravated by the crisis of 1793 and the new tax systems. What was economically viable in a country, and with virtually no taxation, turned out unprofitable in the new situation. A short-term solution was the cheap and easily available state loans, like in the other Prussian provinces. However, most of the money was used for consumption, and the debt to the Prussian state led to the growing number of bankruptcies and evictions (Topolski 1973).

Formally, the nobility retained their status in the partitions period, at the time of the Duchy, during the constitutional period of the Kingdom of Poland, and in the Prussian and Austrian partitions after the Congress of Vienna. Prussia and Austria lifted the limitations on the economic activity allowed to the nobility (in particular, they were now permitted to deal in trade), as a result of which some of them turned into the bour-geoisie. After the Congress of Vienna, the internally differentiated nobil-ity was still a sizeable and influential social group, particularly in the Kingdom of Poland, where their status was ensured by the constitution. In Austria and Prussia, the position of the Polish nobility was slowly dete-riorating. Similarly, the growing taxes and debts undermined the eco-nomic situation of the nobility in the Duchy of Warsaw and then in the Kingdom of Poland. After the November Uprising, Russia started the reform of the nobility aimed to verify the rights to nobility and down-grade those who were not able to prove their titles. In effect, the number of the legally confirmed Polish nobility diminished, and it was slowly transformed into the Russian state nobility (Jedlicki 1968; Pawłowski et al. 1994; Sikorska-Kulesza 1995; Janowski and Jedlicki 2008; Kaps 2015).

While cities were undergoing economic crisis, a new class of modern bourgeoisie started to emerge. The fortunes of this group were made in new enterprises: army supplies, banking services, state salt and tobacco monopolies. The important factor was the good relations with the state authorities, and some of the enterprises were based on political rent-seeking rather than individual managerial competitions and entrepre-neurship of the owners. The rising new class of bourgeoisie (urban middle and upper middle class) acquired some of the property of the old aristoc-racy, particularly in Warszawa (Czubaty 1997), purchasing town houses and palaces sold by the families who had no business living in Warszawa any more, but also acquiring the parts of the big demesnes which had to be sold as a result of the abovementioned agreement concerning property in other countries (Kołodziejczyk 1957, 1979; Ihnatowicz 1972).

The most favourable conditions for the development of the middle class were in the two relatively liberal constitutional states created after the collapse of the Duchy of Warsaw, that is, the Kingdom of Poland and the Free City of Cracow (Kraków). In the Kingdom of Poland, the ben-eficial factors were the protectionist policy, state interventionism, and the scope of public investment in industry. In Kraków, it was its importance as a trade centre for this part of Europe, enhanced by the favourable duty agreements with the neighbouring states, which promoted the develop-ment of new sectors of the economy (Bartel 1976). Relatively good conditions for the development of cities and the bourgeoisie also existed in the Prussian partition after Congress of Vienna (after decades of crisis), with its traditionally more developed and better urbanized lands. In the lands under the Austrian rule, particularly Galicia, and in the rest of the Russian partition, cities suffered stagnation or even decline (Miodunka 2014).

The most numerous social class, and one with the lowest economic status, were the peasants, still constituting about 80% or more of the population on the territories inhabited by Poles. The peasants' social and financial status was diversified, and new regulations aggravated the stratification. In the eighteenth century, a group of wealthier farms emerged, providing labour services with draught horses or oxen, and their development was supported by the landowners. On the other hand, the number of landless or almost landless peasants was growing. The regulations implemented in the Duchy of Warsaw, that is, granting the peasants personal freedom without granting them the title to the land, aggravated the evictions and enlarged the number of landless peasants. Another result was peasants' voluntary return to the corvée in return for tenancy. In Prussia agrarian reforms granted personal freedom for peasants as well and abolished serfdom, but the state policy implemented in the early 1820s contributed to the emergence of wealthy independent peasant farms (and a large group of landless agricultural workers). The differences in the legal regulations resulted in the growing discrepancies in the socioeconomic situation of peasants in different partitions (Kochanowicz 1981, 2006; Zamorski 1987; Fryda 2002; Ślusarek 2017).

Apart from peasants, another large social group was the mobile labourers and vagabonds looking for paid work. They were landless peasants, impoverished nobility, and townspeople, and they were mobile, looking for jobs all over the country. The slow development of industry made it difficult for the economy to incorporate these people as industrial workers. In the period of partitions and the Duchy of Warsaw, mobile labourers found work mostly in agriculture. In later periods, the economic change sent this group in various directions. In Prussia, the modernization of agriculture and the development of the cities turned this group (and a large part of former serfs) into the urban and rural proletariat. In the Kingdom of Poland, such transition happened only locally, in the regions where the state built industrial areas. In the other parts of the Kingdom of Poland, in the Austrian partition, and in the rest of the Russian partition, the changes were much slower.

6   The Economy

The partitions and the banking crisis in late eighteenth century resulted in economic recession all over the land of the former Commonwealth, because of the disintegration of the internal market and some economic ties (e.g. between the weaving factories in Greater Poland and their markets in the eastern regions). The emergence of customs borders and tariffs was particularly detrimental for agriculture. The central and southern parts of Poland lost access to the sea, as Gdańsk (Danzig) and the lower reaches of the Vistula were incorporated into Prussia. This undermined the economic situation of agricultural estates in the Russian and Austrian partitions and slowed down the modernization of these regions.

Partitions (until 1806) resulted in the formation of considerable differences between regions. The public investments of the Prussian state contributed to the intense development of the public sector on the Commonwealth lands incorporated into Prussia. With the successive changes of borders resulting from the successive partitions of the Commonwealth, the range of Polish territory under the Prussian cameralist policy increased and finally comprised a considerable part of present-day Poland. The scope of Prussian investment was significant, comprising the construction of roads and water routes, networks of salt warehouses and modern factories, built mostly in the south, in the province of New Silesia. The Prussian success of industry and infrastructure development became the benchmark for politicians trying to modernize the Polish economy. Many Prussian solutions were imitated in the Duchy of Warsaw and the Kingdom of Poland in the first, constitutional period of its existence. A number of Polish officials and economic policymakers, like Rajmund Rembielinski, acquired experience through periods of work in the Prussian administration and then continued their activity in the Duchy of Warsaw and the Kingdom of

Poland (Kociszewski 1982). The experiences of the failed reforms of late Commonwealth and the extremely efficient Prussian administration were a lesson that the Warsaw elite duly learnt. Contrary to Prussian experience, the Austrian lands, after the initial development impulse of the Josephine reform, went into stagnation. The situation was similar in the Russian partition.

In the partitions period (until 1807), there was no independent fiscal and monetary policy on the territories of the former Commonwealth. They were incorporated into the new states, which soon—in Prussia, and to some extent in Austria—resulted in the increase of the tax burden and, consequently, of the tax revenue. The Duchy of Warsaw preserved the Prussian tax system, and it also became the model for the relatively efficient tax system of the Kingdom of Poland (Czubaty and Phillips 2016).

But on the other side, the partitions period marked the beginning of the modern policy of state-induced industry and infrastructure development on the Polish lands. This policy was implemented in the regions incorporated into Prussia, but then there were attempts at a similar policy in the Duchy of Warsaw and the Kingdom of Poland. Particularly in the case of the Kingdom of Poland, the industrialization policy was invented as a means to catch up with the West and create the modern social structure. Between 1815 and 1830, the state tried to implement the policy imitating the solutions typical of the Prussian eighteenth-century cameralism (Jedlicki 1964).

In the period under analysis, the only political entities with some independence as regards the economic, fiscal, monetary, and tax policy were the Duchy of Warsaw, the Kingdom of Poland, and the Free City of Cracow. The analysis of the foreign trade of the Duchy of Warsaw shows that after the partitions the national market of the Commonwealth disintegrated much more slowly than its institutions (Grochulska 1967). The export of manufactured goods was directed mostly towards the east—it was the export of the goods produced by the textile industry in Greater Poland to the former Commonwealth lands, then in Russia. Austria became an important foreign supplier of salt—from the former royal salt mines in Wieliczka near Kraków. The final loss of Gdańsk and the lower reaches of the Vistula, as well as the continental blockade, led to the decline of grain export and the deterioration of the situation of agriculture (Cieślak and Biernat 1993).

The Duchy of Warsaw (1807–1815) was constantly under financial pressure because of the low revenue and high expenses of the state budget. As a result of the policy in previous decades of the partitioning powers as well as political decisions of Napoleon, the state had lost traditional source of income of the Polish state, the king's demesne, and it had not developed the necessary tax base. The low revenue resulted not only from the low efficiency of the collection of taxes and monopoly revenues, but also from the exemption of large, well-developed regions from taxation (these are particularly the two duchies that Napoleon donated to French army marshals: the Duchy of Łowicz, donated to Marchal Davout, and the Duchy of Siewierz, to Marchal Lannes). The loss of the latter region was particularly unfortunate, as before Napoleon's invasion it was the site of Prussian industrial investment, which was ruined under the management of Marchal Lannes and his widow. This moved the region backwards by a few decades, and the effort made later, in the 1820s, by the Kingdom of Poland, to rebuild the industrial centre in that part of the country, was very costly and brought the state little profit (Kowalczyk 2010).

Napoleon took the control over the territory of former Poland along with an unpaid private debt to the Prussian government, which Napoleon acquired and sold to the Duchy for half the value (the so-called sums of Bayonne). The budget expenses involved servicing this debt, but the Duchy was not able to collect the debt from the debtors, the impoverished Polish nobility. It became a long-term burden on the budget of the Duchy, which then was passed on to the Kingdom of Poland. The Duchy also had to maintain a standing army of 25,000–100,000 soldiers (about 1812). The fiscal revenue of the state was stable, but did not grow because of the geopolitical situation—in the *de facto* frontier state, in the contest between Napoleon and the other European powers, the conditions for economic growth were limited, so the tax revenue could not grow.

Napoleon's quasi-state existed so briefly that it is difficult to discuss its economic situation. The ongoing war prevented effective investment policy, and most of the revenue was spent on the army. With Napoleon's decisions depriving the Duchy of the access to the sea and of some richer regions, and with constant dependence on France, it was impossible to

conduct an independent economic policy. However, it is worth empha-
sizing that the development ideas were maintained and elaborated on.
Despite the unfavourable circumstances, the government made attempts
to stimulate economy—by means of regulations (e.g. they introduced the
rule of minimum capital in the exchange of bills, which contributed to
the concentration of capital in the banking sector), protection in international exchange, and building the policy of the state intervention in the
economy. In many cases, the economic policy of the Kingdom of Poland
can be seen as the implementation of the ideas formulated in the Duchy
of Warsaw in the new geopolitical context.

A certain picture of the economic evolution in the centrally located Polish
lands emerges from the censuses conducted at the end of the eighteenth
century in the newly acquired Prussian territories, and in 1808 and 1810 in
the Duchy of Warsaw (Grossmann 1925) and censuses in other former
Polish lands. They show the structure of the population by occupation and
show the slow urbanization in Poland. In turn, in Tables 4.1a, 4.1b and
4.1c, the occupational structure of Prussian Partition (ca. 1800) and the
Duchy of Warsaw (1810) is presented. To make the picture of economy
even more complex, data concerning international trade in the Duchy of
Warsaw should be discussed (Grossmann 1925; Grochulska 1967). Partial
data (from Vistula trade and Greater Poland trade only) shows that a large
part of export consisted of raw materials, grain (mostly wheat) in particular.
In terms of the value of export, also manufacturing products, particularly
textiles from Greater Poland were important. Data from trade via Vistula
and Greater Poland trade show that at least one-third of the total value of

Table 4.1a Male occupational structure (PST[a]), cameras of New Eastern Prussia, ca. 1800

Male LF	Marienwerde (%)	Bromberg (%)	Posen (%)	Warschau (%)
P	80	83	79	77
S	7	6	6	8
T	13	11	14	15

Source: Own calculation (Holsche 1800, 1804, 1807)
[a]PST represents three-sectoral structure of the economy, with the primary sector (mostly agriculture), secondary (manufacturing and mining), and tertiary (services), according to the methodology that is developed by The Cambridge Group for the History of Population and Social Structure

Table 4.1b Occupational structure (PST), Duchy of Warsaw 1810 by department

1810	Warszawski (%)	Krakowski (%)	Kaliski (%)	Radomski (%)	Poznański (%)	Bydgoski (%)	Płocki (%)	Lubelski (%)	Total (%)
P	68	78	76	78	63	62	75	79	72
S	14	9	12	11	18	14	11	9	13
T	19	12	12	11	19	24	14	12	15

Source: Own calculation (Grossmann 1925)

Table 4.1c Structure of peasants' households (number of households and shares), 1810

	Number of households	Shares (%)
Non-serfs (free peasants)/niepańszyźniani	17,488	3
Of which townspeople	4886	
Serfs/pańszczyźniani	206,083	40
Landless peasants (cottagers)/chałupnicy	66,432	13
Landless (in service sector)/Bezrolni	220,643	43
Of which farmhands	140,269	
And maids	80,374	
	510,646	100

Source: Own calculations (Grossmann 1925). Households were unequal in size, for example, landless peasants who served as domestic/agricultural service often represented single-person households

exports was the export of grain, while half of the total value of exports was the export of textiles. Economy of Polish lands still relied almost only on agriculture, dominated by folwarks. At that time, the process of economic modernization, if any, was still very slow.

Being a frontier state did not create good conditions for building economic stability, but it did foster a suitable ground for developing speculative capital. The presence of the state's big standing army and the translocations of foreign armies contributed to building the fortunes of war profiteers or army and government suppliers. Many of these fortunes outlived the Duchy, but few of their owners decided to invest in other branches of economy than those connected with consumption and speculation. In particular, the banking sector was revived, modelled on the solutions adopted in France, and regulated by the laws allowing the circulation of bills of exchange. Consequently, the new financial bourgeoisie emerged in Warsaw in the Kingdom of Poland, and the fortunes accumulated in the years of the Duchy and the first years of the Kingdom played an important role in financing industrialization in Poland with the support of the state (Kołodziejczyk 1979).

The Kingdom of Poland inherited the budget problems from the Duchy of Warsaw. The main factors were the Duchy's debts, including the sums of Bayonne, and the disintegration of the Duchy's tax system and administration. The situation was not much improved by the successful negotiations that were conducted by a representative of the Duchy of Warsaw Liquidation Commission, Xawery Drucki-Lubecki, and which limited the Duchy's obligations to the neighbouring states. It was not until the early 1820s that Drucki-Lubecki,as a minister of finance, rebuilt the tax system and the state revenue. His policy was based on the efficiency of tax collection and increasing the tax rates (particularly through increasing the franchising fees for the government-granted monopolies including a tobacco monopoly and a salt monopoly, raising the price of salt, etc.) (Smolka and Kołodziejczyk 1984).

The efficient collection of taxes and overdue payments negatively affected the economic situation of many agricultural estates and further discouraged landowners from spontaneous reforms and investing in modernization. At the same time, the burden on the lower classes was retained, and even increased throughout the partitions period. As a result, the fiscal success and the ensuing state-funded growth of the industrial sector were not accompanied by the successful development in the agricultural sector. In 1825, the response to the crisis was the creation of The Land Credit Society, a public institution whose goal was to help to solve the problem of debt, which was widespread among landowners (Majer 2015). From the pre-partition period, Warsaw had a mint, which minted zloty coins in the Duchy of Warsaw and in the Kingdom of Poland until 1841. But a new age started in 1828, when the Bank of Poland was created as a central state bank with the right to issue money. It played a vital role in financing the infrastructure and mining in the Kingdom of Poland (Morawski 1998; Leszczyńska 2006, 2010).

Importance on non-agricultural sector of economy of the Kingdom slowly grew. Nonetheless, it was still dominated by agriculture (cf. Tables 4.2 and 4.3), much less efficient than that in the Western Europe and based on the increasingly backward landowner estate economy. Anyway, attempts of modernization of estates were undertaken by landowners, particularly when access to credit became easier. Simultaneously, peasant agriculture had been slowly modernizing (Kochanowicz 1981). Nonetheless, ultimately Polish lands ceased to be European granary (Jezierski 1967).

At that time and in later periods, numerous public institutions, including the central bank, did not act on the basis of credible business calculations; they just served as an instrument of quick industrialization. In effect, they were also a means to transfer public funds into private hands (Jedlicki 1964). There were also attempts to develop the urban economy and industry based on state-induced and state-funded development, but also on supporting the private sector. The former approach was adopted

Table 4.2 Occupational structure of Kingdom of Poland, 1828 (crude data)

	Total	Warsaw	Share, total (%)	Share, Warsaw (%)
Construction	12,347	2114	1	4
Capitalists and owners of factories	4086	1928	0	3
Craftsmen	68,590	9054	6	16
Workers	52,048	7255	5	13
Domestic service	310,163	20,164	28	35
Agriculture/peasants	522,376	70	48	0
Landowners	40,806	0	4	0
Communication and transport	3611	760	0	1
Private service sector	72,057	13,337	7	23
Public services	10,164	2971	1	5
	1,096,248	57,653		

Source: Own calculation (Rodecki et al. 1830)

in the state-led industrialization strategy created by Stanisław Staszic, and an example of the industrial policy that strengthened private entrepreneurs with state support is that of Rajmund Rembielinski, which he created when he was the director of the Płock Department in the Duchy, and implemented in the Masovia Department of the Kingdom of Poland.

Stanislaw Staszic formulated the tenets of the state-induced industrialization and decided on the regions and sectors where the state interventions were to be implemented. His goal was to revive the Old Polish Industrial Area in the Świętokrzyskie Mountains, as the partition of the state divided Lesser Poland (in particular the Cracow voivodship). As a result, the region near Kielce, industrialized at the beginning of the eighteenth century, now lost its importance, and the local industry, including ironworks, suffered crisis. Staszic tried to use the state to avert that crisis.

The new investment comprised building a chain of ironworks, along the rivers Kamienna and Bobrza (modelled on well-known industrial areas in England, like Coalbrookdale). A serious drawback was the lack of access to coal deposits, which forced the factories to use obsolete technologies involving the use of charcoal. Other obstacles to the development of the project were the unfavourable location far from the centre of the Kingdom and near the border with Galicia, which was suffering stagnation, poor quality of the local ores, obsolete technologies, and low

Table 4.3 Regional (Voivodeship) occupational structure, Kingdom of Poland, 1828

LF	Krakowskie (%)	Sandomierskie (%)	Kaliskie (%)	Lubelskie (%)	Płockie (%)	Mazowieckie (%)	Podlaskie (%)	Augustowskie (%)	Total (%)
P	71	73	72	80	77	62	81	80	73
S	8	11	9	8	8	12	7	6	9
T	20	16	19	12	16	25	11	15	18

Source: Own calculation (Rodecki et al. 1830)

supply of cheap labour. In addition, the state administration of the project was inefficient. In effect, the production costs were high and uncompetitive, the products (iron, iron industry products) were low quality, and the demand was limited. The whole enterprise was not profitable (Kowalska et al. 1958; Jedlicki 1964).

The response to the problems of the old industrial area was to create a new one, the Western Industrial Area, near the present-day town of Dąbrowa Górnicza. Some of the Prussian investments in the Duchy of Siewierz (ironworks and mines) were used, and new investments aimed at developing coal mining (in Dąbrowa, Niemce, and Niwka) and iron industry (foundries in Niwka and Panki, in present-day Dąbrowa Górnicza).

The public industrial sector faced fundamental development barriers. They resulted from the limited demand for the manufactured products, the lack of transport infrastructure, bad management structure, and the lack of specialists—managers, engineers, and qualified workers. As there was no stable job market for workers, this group remained fluid and consisted of vagabonds—"mobile labourers" taking temporary jobs and often moving from one place to another. The effort to improve the workers' qualifications by creating technical education was moderately successful, and the problem of the demand for the products of the newly created industry was not yet solved at the time of the November Uprising in 1830, which became a significant check to its development.

The strategy of the development of the public industrial sector, which was expected to become the springboard for further economic development, was connected not only with the proponents of industrialization described above, playing the key role in the economic policy at the time, but also, or maybe first of all, with the experience of the Prussian cameralist policy during the partitions period, extremely effective from the Polish perspective. However, after the defeat in the Napoleonic war, the Prussian state put a stop to its policy of state-funded manufacturing industry and developed strategies to support private entrepreneurship and building the industrial bourgeoisie.

As mentioned above similar strategy was also implemented in the western part of the Masovia Voivodeship (and even at the time of the Duchy of Warsaw) by Rajmund Rembielinski, who was responsible for the regional economic policy (Puś 1987; Badziak et al. 1998; Woźniak 2016). This was the time when the textile industry in Greater Poland, across the border from the western parts of the Kingdom, was in decline, because it had to compete with the better developed textile industry in Saxony and Silesia, and it had lost the Commonwealth market. Many cities were badly affected, and the workers and craftsmen moved to the east, to the Kingdom. That stimulated the industrialization of the region between Kalisz, Łęczyca, and Piotrków, particularly along the road joining Kalisz and Warszawa (Warsaw). Rembielinski supported these processes by means of organizing the financing of the enterprises and creating good conditions for the development of industrial settlements such as Łódź. As a result of his activity, light industry, particularly textile, started to develop with the help of a system of incentives for the private sector, such as easily available loans, development of infrastructure in response to the needs of entrepreneurs, the protection of the internal market, and keeping the Russian market accessible.

The data published by Franciszek Rodecki in 1828 (Rodecki et al. 1830) shows the contemporary occupational structure, as presented in Table 4.2. The employment outside agriculture was still very low. The occupations of the people working outside agriculture comprised mostly manufacturing and providing services for agriculture (blacksmiths, cart wrights, inn keepers, coopers), food processing (millers, bakers, butchers, alcohol producers), and some textile industry (shoemakers, tailors, weavers, cloth makers)—the relatively big groups of people in the latter trades may indicate the beginnings of textile industry at this time, particularly along the Warszawa-Kalisz (Calisia) road. A small percentage of employees were qualified construction workers (masons, carpenters), probably because construction work was usually conducted by unqualified workers, and in villages people built by themselves. A large proportion of the labour force counted by Rodecki as "domestic service" were actually agricultural workers (cf. Table 4.3 with adjusted data), while a part of "workers" and "craftmen" were employed in contemporary services.

While the government of the Kingdom of Poland tried to implement an Enlightenment mercantilist policy, the other two main Polish regions suffered development crisis—Galicia under the Austrian rule, and the Prussian lands, particularly Greater Poland. Galicia was a remote periphery from the very start of the Austrian rule; the loss of the industrial supply base, the extraction of Kraków, and the loss of the ties with the rest of the country caused long-term stagnation.

The decades after the Congress of Vienna brought period of slow development to the Prussian partition territories as well, despite the positive effects of the agrarian reform and—after decades of decline— improvement in the cities. After implementing the regulations already existing in the rest of Prussia, most post-feudal obligations were abolished, and the structure of ownership changed. The subsistence peasant farms, still common in the Duchy of Warsaw (according to the census data), started to disappear in Prussian part, and modern agriculture was developed in the modernized estates as well as in bigger peasant farms emerging as a result of the agrarian reform. In effect, efficiency started to grow and even peasant farms started to produce increasing amounts of surplus. The growth of the number of landless peasants, on the one hand, turned them into the village proletariat, and on the other hand, began the population outflow to other Prussian provinces or abroad. During the periods of the partitions, cities in Greater Poland suffered crises resulting from the disappearance of the customs borders between Greater Poland and the rest of Prussia—with the competition from the Saxon and Silesian industry, the quite well-developed textile industry in Greater Poland practically ceased to exist, and most craftsmen moved to the Kingdom of Poland or other provinces of Prussia. After the Congress of Vienna, the cities started to develop again, but mostly as trade centres for agricultural production and the supply base for agriculture.

7   Summary and Conclusions

The division of Polish lands and long periods of war resulted in an economic crisis followed by stagnation. After 1800, the Prussian industrial and infrastructural policy initiated the modernization process, but it was stopped after a few years by the Napoleonic wars. The new state created by the French emperor—the Duchy of Warsaw—underwent rapid institutional change, but its economy stagnated due to the unfavourable geopolitical situation and the costs of maintaining a large army. New borders inside the Polish lands were established once again after the collapse of Napoleon in 1815, this time separating Greater Poland from the Kingdom of Poland with a customs border, which contributed to the decline of textile industry in that region. Many craftsmen and workers moved to the Russian side of the border (i.e. to the Kingdom of Poland), beginning the process of creating industrial areas near Łęczyca, Kalisz, and Łódź. A similar crisis affected another important industrial area of the Commonwealth, the Old Polish Industrial Area near Kielce. Separated from its traditional market by the new Austrian-Russian border, it went into a decline that was not averted even by the state investments in mining and iron production. It was only the growing importance of Warszawa as a local administrative centre as well as the inflow of craftsmen from Greater Poland, which created a relatively stable environment for the development of the western parts of the Kingdom of Poland. Also, other Prussian lands (which became Polish after 1918 and 1945), particularly Silesia, started to industrialize in this period.

Since the early nineteenth century, modern quasi-states—the Duchy of Warsaw, the Kingdom of Poland (less sovereign than the former but still Polish)—gained enough state capacity to introduce the policy of modernization based on fiscal expansion. The obvious aim of the government of the Kingdom was to create the strong local bourgeoisie involved in the modern manufacturing industry, which was either state-funded or private, but supported by state protectionism. But this policy relied on political autonomy and institutional continuity, which ended up in 1830. The Kingdom of Poland in the years 1815–1830 turned out to be the last Enlightenment political project on Polish lands. Even though at the time there were two other Polish quasi-states, the Grand Duchy of Posen and the Free City of Cracow, their political and economic role was insignificant, due to the minuscule size of the latter and the Prussian policy in the former.

The era of the Enlightenment reforms actually ended with the outbreak of a major rebellion in Russian Poland, the November Uprising. The efforts of early modernizers to strengthen the economy and enhance the state's capacity in a complex geopolitical situation had to be abandoned. The period of partitions and the Enlightenment reforms after the Congress of Vienna brought—apart from the collapse of the state and the first period of the displacement of the territory—deep institutional changes. The institutions and the administration's infrastructure created at the time, both under the governance of the partitioning powers and in the ephemeral quasi-states, were modern, comparable to those in the West. However, it was not accompanied by structural change in the economy.

For the first time, the really important factor which started to hinder economic changes was the institutional and geographical discontinuity of the Polish state. The briefness of successive political entities and the loss of the access to the sea (which meant that the Polish agriculture from Masovia and the upper reaches of the Vistula was separated from the ports and its traditional foreign markets) were not suitable conditions for introducing industrialization on the Polish territory. Moreover, due to conservative legal regulations and poverty the labour force remained immobile (in geographical and social terms), with the exception of the Prussian lands starting from the 1820s. In effect, neither the market demand nor the supply of cheap labour fostered industrialization. The development gap between the Polish lands and the West began to widen.

References

Badziak, K., Woźniak, K., & Wydawnictwo Uniwersytetu Łódzkiego (Eds.). (1998). *Materiały do dziejów uprzemysłowienia Królestwa Polskiego: raporty prezesów komisji województwa kaliskiego*. Łódź: Wydawnictwo Uniwersytetu Łódzkiego.

Bartel, W. M. (1976). *Ustrój i prawo Wolnego Miasta Krakowa: (1815–1846)*. Wydawnictwo Literackie.

Bortnowski, W. (1976). *Kaliszanie: kartki z dziejów Królestwa Polskiego*. Książka i Wiedza.

Cieślak, E., & Biernat, C. (1988). *History of Gdańsk*. Wydawnictwo.

Cieślak, E., & Biernat, C. (Eds.). (1993). *Historia Gdańska: opracowanie zbiorowe. T. 3 [cz.] 2: 1793–1815*. Gdańsk: Wydawnictwo Morskie.

Czubaty, J. (1997). *Warszawa 1806–1815 – miasto i ludzie*. Neriton.

Czubaty, J. (2011). *Księstwo Warszawskie (1807–1815)*. Wydawnictwa Uniwersytetu Warszawskiego.

Czubaty, J., & Phillips, U. (2016). *The Duchy of Warsaw, 1807–1815: A Napoleonic outpost in Central Europe*. Bloomsbury Publishing.

Dziadzio, A. (2007). Konstytucja Księstwa Warszawskiego 1807: polska odmiana bonapartyzmu. *Państwo Społecz Półrocznik Krak Wyższej Szk Im Andrzeja Frycza Modrzewskiego, 7*, 113–122.

Dziadzio, A. (2008). The constitution of the Duchy of Warsaw 1807. Some remarks on occasion of 200 year anniversary of its adoption. *Krakowskie Studia z Historii Państwa i Prawa, 2*, 163–174.

Fryda, M. (2002). *Wieś pomorska w pierwszym okresie panowania pruskiego na przykładzie klucza gemelskiego w powiecie człuchowskim (1772–1830)*. Gdańsk: Instytut Kaszubski.

Główny Urząd Statystyczny. (1993). *Historia Polski w liczbach: ludność, terytorium*. Główny Urząd Statystyczny.

Górski, J. (1963). *Polska myśl ekonomiczna a rozwój gospodarczy, 1807–1830: studia nad początkami teorii zacofania gospodarczego*. Państwowe Wydawnictwo Naukowe.

Grochulska, B. (1967). *Handel zagraniczny Księstwa Warszawskiego: z badań nad strukturą gospodarczą*. Warszawa: Państwowe Wydawnictwo Naukowe.

Grossmann, H. (1925). *Struktura społeczna i gospodarcza Księstwa Warszawskiego na podstawie spisów ludności 1808–1810*. Warszawa: Główny Urząd Statystyczny.

Hohorst, G. (1977). *Wirtschaftswachstum und Bevölkerungsentwicklung in Preussen, 1816 bis 1914*. Arno Press.

Holsche, A. K. (1800). *Geographie und Statistik von West- Süd- und Neu-Ostpreußen: Nebst einer kurzen Geschichte des Königreichs Polen bis zu dessen Zertheilung*. Maurer.

Holsche, A. K. (1804). *Geographie und Statistik von West- Süd- und Neu-Ostpreußen: Nebst einer kurzen Geschichte des Königreichs Polen bis zu dessen Zertheilung*. Maurer.

Holsche, A. K. (1807). *Geographie und Statistik von West- Süd- und Neu-Ostpreußen: Nebst einer kurzen Geschichte des Königreichs Polen bis zu dessen Zertheilung*. Maurer.

Ihnatowicz, I. (1972). *Burżuazja warszawska*. Warszawa: Państwowe Wydawnictwo Naukowe.

Izdebski, H. (1978). *Rada Administracyjna Królestwa Polskiego w latach 1815–1830*. Wydawnictwa Uniwersytetu Warszawskiego.

Janczak, J. K. (1983). Statystyka ludności Królestwa Polskiego 1815–1830. *Przeszłość Demograficzna Polski, 14*, 17–23.

Janowski, M., & Jedlicki, J. (2008). *Narodziny inteligencji 1750–1831*. Warszawa: Instytut Historii PAN: Wydawnictwo Neriton.

Jedlicki, J. (1964). *Nieudana próba kapitalistycznej industralizacji: analiza państwowego gospodarstwa przemysłowego w Królestwie Polskim XIX w.* Warszawa: Książka i Wiedza.

Jedlicki, J. (1968). *Klejnot i bariery społeczne: przeobrażenia szlachectwa polskiego w schyłkowym okresie feudalizmu.* Warszawa: Państwowe Wydawnictwo Naukowe.

Jedlicki, J. (1999). *A suburb of Europe: Nineteenth-century Polish approaches to Western civilization.* Budapest; Plymouth: Central European University Press; Distributed by Plymbridge Distributors.

Jedlicki, J., Jedlicki, J., & Korecki, T. (2014). *The vicious circle: 1832–1864.* Frankfurt am Main: Peter Lang Edition.

Jelonek, A. (1967). *Ludność miast i osiedli typu miejskiego na ziemiach Polski od 1810 do 1960 r.* Instytut Geografii Polskiej Akademii Nauk.

Jezierski, A. (1967). *Handel zagraniczny Królewstwa Polskiego 1815–1914.* Państwowe Wydawnictwo Naukowe.

Kaps, K. (2015). *Ungleiche Entwicklung in Zentraleuropa: Galizien zwischen überregionaler Verflechtung und imperialer Politik (1772–1914).* Böhlau Verlag Wien.

Karpineć, Ì. (1932). *Ilość osad miejskich byłej Galicji i podział ich na miasta i miasteczka.* Lwów: sgł. Kasa im. J. Mianowskiego, Instytut Popierania Polskiej Twórczości Naukowej.

Kawalec, A., & Wierzbieniec, W. (2011). *Galicja 1772–1918: problemy metodologiczne, stan i potrzeby badań: praca zbiorowa.* Wydawnictwo Uniwersytetu Rzeszowskiego.

Kizwalter, T. (1999). *O nowoczesności narodu: przypadek Polski.* Semper.

Kochanowicz, J. (1981). *Pańszczyźniane gospodarstwo chłopskie w Królestwie Polskim w I połowie XIX w.* Warszawa: Wydawnictwa Uniwersytetu Warszawskiego.

Kochanowicz, J. (2006). *Backwardness and modernization: Poland and Eastern Europe in the 16th–20th centuries.* Ashgate Variorum.

Kociszewski, A. (1982). *Rajmund Rembieliński jako prefekt departamentu płockiego.* Ciechanów: Ciechanowskie Towarzystwo Naukowe: Zakład Naukowy MOBN.

Kołodziejczyk, R. (1957). *Kształtowanie się burżuazji w Królestwie Polskim 1815–1850.* Warszawa: Państwowe Wydawnictwo Naukowe.

Kołodziejczyk, R. (1979). *Miasta, mieszczaństwo, burżuazja w Polsce w XIX w: szkice i rozprawy historyczne.* Warszawa: Państwowe Wydawnictwo Naukowe.

Korobowicz, A., & Witkowski, W. (2012). *Historia ustroju i prawa polskiego (1772–1918)*. Warszawa: Państwowe Wydawnictwo Naukowe.

Kowalczyk, R. (2010). *Polityka gospodarcza i finansowa Księstwa Warszawskiego w latach 1807–1812* (Wyd. 1). Łódź: Wydawnictwo Uniwersytet Łódzkiego.

Kowalska, S., Jedlicki, J., & Jezierski, A. (1958). *Ekonomika górnictwa i hutnictwa w Królestwie Polskim 1831–1864*. Warszawa: Państwowe Wydawnictwo Naukowe.

Krysiński, D. (1956). *Wybór pism*. Państwowe Wydawnictwo Naukowe.

Kumor, B. (1978). Spis wojskowy ludności Galicji z 1808 r. *Przeszłość Demograficzna Polski, 10*, 39–134.

Kumor, B. (1984). Spis wojskowy ludności Galicji z 1808 r. (uzupełnienie). *Przeszłość Demograficzna Polski, 15*, 95–113.

Leszczyńska, C. (2006). Polska bankowość centralna 1828–1989: Bank Polski, Polska Krajowa Kasa Pożyczkowa, Bank Polski SA, Narodowy Bank Polski. *Bank i Kredyt*, Wyd Pol 43, no. 2.

Leszczyńska, C. (2010). *Zarys historii polskiej bankowości centralnej*. Warszawa: Narodowy Bank Polski. Departament Edukacji i Wydawnictw.

Libiszowska, Z. (1973). Prasa i publicystyka angielska wobec drugiego rozbioru Polski. *Rocznik Historii Czasopiśmiennictwa Polskiego, XII*, 299–325.

Lityńska, A. (2000). Fryderyk Skarbek – twórca polskiej szkoły narodowej w ekonomii. *Zeszyty Naukowe – Akademia Ekonomiczna w Krakowie, 555*, 87–94.

Łojek, J. (1986). *Szanse powstania listopadowego: rozważania historyczne*. Instytut Wydawniczy Pax.

Lukowski, J. (2014). *The partitions of Poland 1772, 1793, 1795*. Taylor & Francis.

Magocsi, P. R. (2010). *A history of Ukraine: The land and its peoples*. University of Toronto Press.

Majer, T. (2015). Kredyt ziemski w Królestwie Polskim przed i po 1832 r. In *Królestwo Polskie w okresie namiestnictwa Iwana Paskiewicza 1832–1856. System polityczny, prawo i statut organiczny z 26 lutego 1832r* (pp. 247–258). Radzymin: Wydawnictwo von borowiecky.

Mażewski, L. (2013). *System polityczny, prawo i konstytucja Królestwa Polskiego 1815–1830: w przededniu dwusetnej rocznicy powstania unii rosyjsko-polskiej*. Wydawnictwo "von borowiecky".

Miodunka, P. (2014). Wybrane problemy rozwoju małych miast galicyjskich w okresie przedautonomicznym (1772–1866). *Zeszyty Naukowe Uniwersytetu Ekonomicznego w Krakowie*, 23–43. https://doi.org/10.15678/ZNUEK.2014.0935.1102

Morawski, W. (1998). *Słownik historyczny bankowości polskiej do 1939 roku.* Warszawa: Muza.

Pawłowski, F., Ślusarek, K., & Turek, W. P. (1994). *Drobna szlachta w Galicji, 1772–1848.* Księgarnia Akademicka.

Pipes, R. (1985). *Catherine II and the Jews: The origin of the pale of settlement.* Institute of Jewish Studies.

Puś, W. (1987). *Dzieje Łodzi przemysłowej: zarys historii. Muzeum Historii Miasta Łodzi.* Łódź: Centrum Informacji Kulturalnej.

Rodecki, F. B., Gałęzowski, A., Oleszczyński, S., & Dayczer, K. S. (1830). *Obraz geograficzno-statystyczny Królestwa Polskiego. Mappa polityczna Królestwa Polskiego.* Warszawa: Drukarnia Gałęzowskiego.

Schieder, T., Scott, H. R., & Krause, S. (2016). *Frederick the great.* Taylor & Francis.

Schmidt-Rutsch, O., & Reden, F. W. von. (Eds). (2008). Friedrich Wilhelm Graf von Reden (1752–1815): Beiträge zur Frühindustrialisierung in Oberschlesien und an der Ruhr; [Begleitband zur Sonderausstellung des LWL-Industriemuseums "Im Auftrag Seiner Majestät." Die Reise des Oberbergrats Friedrich Wihelm von Reden von Oberschlesien ins Ruhrtal]. Essen: Klartext.

Serejski, M. H. (1970). *Europa a rozbiory Polski: studium historiograficzne.* Państwowe Wydawnictwo Naukowe.

Sikorska-Kulesza, J. (1995). *Deklasacja drobnej szlachty na Litwie i Białorusi w XIX wieku.* Pruszków: Ajaks.

Skarbek, F., & Szymaniec, P. (2013). *Gospodarstwo narodowe: wybór pism.* Kraków: Ośrodek Myśli Politycznej: Wydział Studiów Międzynarodowych i Politycznych Uniwersytetu Jagiellońskiego.

Ślusarek, K. (2017). Wieś galicyjska 1772–1914: stagnacja czy rozwój? *Rocznik Łódzki,* Wydawnictwo Poświęcone Dziejom Łodzi Ziem Województwa Łódzkiego, 66, 151–165.

Smolka, S., & Kołodziejczyk, R. (1984). *Polityka Lubeckiego przed powstaniem listopadowym* (Wyd. 2). Warszawa: Państwowe Instytut Wydawniczy.

Surowiecki, W., & Szymaniec, P. (2014). *O upadku przemysłu i miast w Polsce: wybór pism.* Kraków: Ośrodek Myśli Politycznej: Wydział Studiów Międzynarodowych i Politycznych Uniwersytetu Jagiellońskiego.

Szczepański, J. (2008). *Książę Ksawery Drucki-Lubecki: 1778–1846.* DiG.

Szlajfer, H. (2012). *Economic nationalism and globalization: Lessons from Latin America and Central Europe.* Leiden and Boston: Brill.

Topolski, J. (1973). *Dzieje Wielkopolski: Lata 1793–1918.* Wydawnictwo Poznańskie.

Wandycz, P. S. (1975). *The lands of partitioned Poland, 1795–1918*. University of Washington Press.

Wąsicki, J. (1957). *Ziemie polskie pod zaborem pruskim: Prusy południowe, 1793–1806: studium historycznoprawne*. Zakład im. Ossolińskich.

Wojas, J. (2017). Unia polsko-rosyjska z 1815 r. na tle unii lubelskiej i projektów unii Rzeczypospolitej i Rosji z XVI i XVII w. *Studia Prawa Publicznego, 1*, 123–140.

Woźniak, K. (2016). *Rajmund Rembieliński: wizjoner i menedżer Łodzi przemysłowej: raporty z lat 1824–1830*. Łódź: Wydawnictwo Uniwersytetu Łódzkiego.

Zajewski, W. (2012). *Powstanie listopadowe 1830–1831*. Warszawa: Bellona.

Zamorski, K. (1987). *Folwark i wieś: gospodarka dworska i społeczność chłopska Tenczynka w latach 1705–1845*. Wrocław and Kraków [etc.]: Zakład Narodowy im. Ossolińskich.

5

On the Peripheries of the Modern Western World: Delayed Social Reforms and Unfinished Industrial Revolution (1830–1870)

The defeat of the November Uprising (1830–1831) was followed by the abolishment of the more or less autonomous remnants of the Polish state, the Kingdom of Poland and the Grand Duchy of Posen. For a time, they kept their names (though very soon, the latter was officially renamed Provinz Posen), but the autonomy was practically annulled, and martial law was introduced in the Kingdom of Poland, to be maintained for a few decades.

This was the time when the Polish lands were nearly integrated into the partitioning states. After the July Revolution (1830), which had briefly rekindled Poland's hopes for regaining independence, the geopolitical situation was not favourable for the Polish. Some hopes were aroused at the time of the Spring of Nations (1848), particularly in the Austrian and Prussian partitions, but the democratic movements were soon suppressed.

In economic terms, it was the period of early signs of spontaneous industrialization, particularly in the Prussian partition and the Kingdom of Poland. Also, transport infrastructure started to emerge, with the development of the road system and then the railways. With new infrastructure and different institutional arrangements, the paths of development and the dynamics of industrialization and urbanization in different parts

© The Author(s) 2018
P. Koryś, *Poland From Partitions to EU Accession*,
https://doi.org/10.1007/978-3-319-97126-1_5

of Poland started to diverge, and they became integral parts of their national economies. This process was the fastest in the Prussian part.

At the same time, agrarian reforms, which started in Prussia in the first decades of the nineteenth century and ended with the enfranchisement of the peasants in the Kingdom of Poland, changed the social, political, and economic structure of society. A stable political situation, the end of serfdom, the enfranchisement of peasants, and the decline of landowners' estates resulted in creating relatively favourable conditions for initiating modern growth (even though these circumstances were unfavourable for Poles as a nation).

1   Internal Politics and the Role of Political Emigration

The period 1830–1870 is the time when practically the only option for Polish political expression was that of rebellion. The Polish political institutions within the partitioning states were abolished, and thus the Poles lost any means to conduct autonomous policy, however limited. Therefore, all the key social reforms of that period, particularly the emancipation and enfranchisement of peasants and granting them full legal rights, were introduced by Austrian, Prussian, and Russian state authorities (Groniowski 1976).

Autonomous Polish quasi states finally disappeared until the 1840s and were integrated into the institutional frameworks and economies of Austria, Prussia, and Russia. Because of an uprising in 1846 (the Cracow Uprising), the Free City of Kraków was abolished and incorporated into Austria. The Grand Duchy of Posen was renamed into the Prussian province of Posen, without any special legal status in comparison with other Prussian provinces. Some hopes for regaining independence were aroused at the time of the Spring of Nations and the outbreak of rebellions in the Austrian and Prussian partitions, but they were soon suppressed. After that, the only distinct legal entity was the Kingdom of Poland, but it was under martial law. It was lifted for some time after Crimea War, but after the January Uprising, since 1864, it underwent intense unification with the Russian state.

Since the collapse of the November Uprising, the Kingdom of Poland was governed by military leader, Russian Viceroy, Marshal Ivan Paskevich. It was the period of martial law, the political repression of the Poles and the first wave of Russification. The liberal institutional design that distinguished the Kingdom for the rest of Russia was removed to a large extent (but some remnants of this system persisted, e.g. the Bank of Poland, which was absorbed by State Bank of Russian Empire only in 1885, and elements of the Napoleonic Civil Code) and gradually replaced by Russian institutions (Węgrzynowicz 2014; Mażewski 2015a, b).

The situation of peasants in the Kingdom of Poland was gradually changing. Initially, in the aftermath of the November Uprising (1830–1831), all the debate on the emancipation was suspended. There was a spontaneous movement among the nobility, and growing numbers of peasants were being emancipated by their lords, particularly in the western provinces of the Kingdom. However, the growing resentment among the peasants in the 1840s posed a threat of a revolt, similar to that in Galicia. In 1846, the Russian Tsar responded with a decree allowing state intervention into the relations between the lords and the peasants. The regulations protected peasants from evictions from bigger farms, abolished many non-labour duties, and required listing all the duties and obligations of each household, which later was the basis for the scrutiny of the scopes of obligations and the terms of tenure and for taking the legal measures to abolish some of them. When this law was introduced, the process of spontaneous emancipation and enfranchisement of peasants stopped. It was not until after the Crimean War that the peasant emancipation reform was prepared for the whole of Russia, and separately for the Kingdom of Poland.

The situation on the international arena created a favourable moment for the Polish struggle for independence during the Crimean War (1853–1856). Poland's fight briefly appeared on the European agenda because a possible rebellion making matters difficult for Russia was one of the options considered by the European powers. Russia, involved in the Crimean War and subsequently weakened by the defeat, was inclined to make some concessions to avoid such a rebellion. Additionally, the war was followed by a radical change of internal policy in Russia, followed by reforms (e.g. the abolition of serfdom), so the situation at the end of the 1850s created conditions for first lifting the martial law and then for the partial restitution of autonomy in Poland. This was the only exception to the general rule of the lack of the autonomy of the Polish lands and their complete integration into the partitioning states.

The leader of the attempt to restore the autonomy of the Kingdom of Poland at the beginning of the 1860s was a conservative politician from Galicia, Margrave Aleksander Wielopolski. He managed to recreate some institutions of the Kingdom, including the State Council and the Government Commission for Religious Denominations and Public Enlightenment, and to create Poland's Civil Administration as a chief governing institution. In 1861, an administration reform was started, creating province and county councils as advisory bodies with some judiciary power (especially, county councils obtained a wide scope of authority), which could exercise influence on the local economic and social policy, including the charity activity. Apart from these, city councils were created as the executive bodies of the municipal authorities. These new bodies replaced the nobility deputations, the previous local self-government institutions with very limited power. The reform process was interrupted by the January Uprising (1863–1864) (Rosevaere 1969; Mażewski 2012).

Wielopolski's government introduced a series of reforms resulting in the abolition of serfdom and enfranchisement of peasants in the years 1861–1862, but the problem of land ownership remained unsolved, as ownership still had the joint, that is, feudal, character. There were plans to transfer the ownership onto the peasants, with full compensation for the landowners. The implementation of Wielopolski's conservative reform was hampered by the growing social tension and the independence movement. The tensions and dissatisfaction with Wielopolski's government resulted in the outbreak of the January Uprising mentioned above, replacing the conservative programme of gradual changes offered by Wielopolski with a radical social and agricultural reform programme reflecting the views of the Polish radical and left-wing formations active both in Poland and abroad. Serfdom was to be abolished everywhere instantaneously, the peasants were to be enfranchised, and the landowners were to be compensated from public money, which would finally break the chain of dependence hampering the development of agriculture (Kieniewicz 1953, 1963).

However, the Uprising and its ideas were not very popular among peasants. Even though some guerrilla troops consisted of up to 50% of the peasants, the Uprising has to be seen as the last political act of the Polish nobility and the first political act of the new emerging social group—the intelligentsia. The industrial bourgeoisie were engaged to varying extents—in Warsaw, even members of the richest merchant and banker families either organized the Uprising (like Leopold Kronenberg, businessman of Jewish origins, one of the richest people in Europe of that time) or took part in it (e.g. the Wawelbergs, a family of entrepreneurs and bankers of Jewish origins), while the poorly integrated, mostly immigrant bourgeoisie of Łódź got involved to a much lesser extent, and some immigrants, like Ludwik Geyer, a textile manufacturer, even supported the Russian state. Unlike the uprising in 1830, the January Uprising never evolved into an open war, it was, rather, a series of battles, skirmishes, and terrorist attacks typical of guerrillas fighting for independence (Kieniewicz 1963, 1964, 1972).

Finally, the Tsar's decree abolishing serfdom and enfranchising the peasants, which terminated the existence of the corvée on the Polish lands, was issued in 1864. It basically followed the reform outlined by the Uprising government. The Uprising itself was defeated soon afterwards. Immediately the lands of the Kingdom of Poland were completely integrated into the structure of the Romanov Empire: in 1866, a new administrative division was conducted, and in 1867 the autonomy of political and administrative institutions of the Kingdom was abolished, including the State Council and Poland's Civil Administration. However, the separate legal system was partially preserved, including the use of Napoleon's Civil Code (Leskiewicz 1961).

At the same time, the Austrian Galicia had hardly any autonomy and Poles had restricted access to many offices of importance. The body representing Polish interests was the Estates of Galicia, a parliamentary advisory organ with very limited power, based in Lwów (Lvov), the capital of Eastern Galicia, selected by Austria as the capital of the whole province instead of Kraków (Cracow), which used to be the capital of the Free City of Kraków until 1848 (Wolff 2012; Kaps 2015; Vushko 2015). However, there were attempts at bottom-up policymaking through social organizations and institutions, such as the Land Credit Society, established in 1841, savings banks created from the mid-1840s, or the Galician

Economic Society, founded in 1845. In the 1830s, the Free City of Kraków was the main centre of Polish politics for the former Commonwealth lands. In 1846, the left-wing independence leaders instigated the Cracow Uprising, which was expected to spread to the rest of the Polish lands. However, it ended after nine days and was the direct reason for incorporating Kraków into Galicia (i.e. Austria) (Daszyk et al. 2016).

In 1846, there was also the peasants' revolt in Galicia, the so-called Galician Slaughter, which preceded the Cracow Uprising. It resulted from a difficult economic situation, exacerbated by the potato blight, but also from the activity of the Austrian authorities trying to turn the peasants against the Polish nobility in order to hamper the Cracow Uprising. A few hundred estate manors were destroyed, about 1000 nobles were killed, and the scale and dynamics of the revolt clearly demonstrated to the Polish elites and to the partition states administration how important the peasant problem had become—until its final resolution, it constituted the key issue of Polish politics and political debates. Two years later, at the time of the Spring of Nations, Austria enfranchised the peasants with compensations from the state, financed from a special tax introduced for the period of 30 years. The peasants became the owners of the land which they had so far cultivated. However, the estate owners' propination monopolies, that is, monopolies on the production and trade of alcohol, established already in the Commonwealth, were not abolished until four decades later (Pawłowski et al. 1994; Ślusarek 2002, 2017).

In 1861, Galicia gained autonomy within the Austrian monarchy as the Kingdom of Galicia and Lodomeria. The legislative power rested in the assembly called the Diet of the Kingdom of Galicia and Lodomeria, and the executive body was the Province Department, both headed by a marshal. The electoral system based on curiae (assemblies representing social classes, which elected the deputies) and the high tax status eligibility for voting and for standing for election caused the dominance of the Diet by the big Polish landowners and rich bourgeoisie, leaving the other social and ethnic groups underrepresented. The emperor's power was represented by the governor, a position which in the years 1848–1859 and later, from the mid-1860s, was held by Polish aristocrats and bourgeois, including the eminent Austrian politicians Agenor Gołuchowski and Kazimierz Badeni (Grzybowski 1959; Buszko 1989; Kosicka-Pajewska 2002).

In the Prussian part, Poles played a relatively important political and economic role in the Grand Duchy of Posen, which ceased to exist in 1848, and was replaced by the Prussian Province of Posen after the Spring of Nations. In 1848, the Polish rebellion organized there became part of the Spring of Nations, but it was unsuccessful. The last remnants of the autonomy of Poles in the Prussian state disappeared.

Anyway, the Poles had a representation in the Prussian parliament from 1848, when it was first established. The noteworthy Polish activists and influential politicians of that time were August Cieszkowski (landowner and Romantic philosopher), and Tytus Działyński, one of the inventors of the new, Positivist political strategy called organic work (Topolski 1973; Łuczak 1973; Trzeciakowski 2003).

The question of Polish independence was present both in Poland and on the European arena, where it was brought up whenever possible by the elite of the political emigration after the November Uprising (the so-called Great Emigration). The most influential of these groups was the conservative-liberal Hotel Lambert, led by the Czartoryski family. The left-wing emigration groups were the Polish Democratic Society (*Towarzystwo Demokratyczne Polskie—TDP*) and the revolutionary Communes of Polish People (*Gromady Ludu Polskiego*), focusing on the emancipation of the peasants. In Europe, the only Polish group with any recognizable influence, albeit small, was the Hotel Lambert, whereas in Poland, it was the radical ideas which gain the greatest popularity. The leaders of the successive uprisings and protests (the Cracow Uprising of 1846, the Spring of Nations in Greater Poland in 1848) as well as some of the leaders of the January Uprising (1863–1864) co-operated with the left-wing and democratic organizations (Borejsza 1966; Kalembka 2003; Żurawski vel Grajewski 2014).

2   Ideas

In the 1830s, new economic ideas of development emerged in Germany and laid the foundation for the future development of the country. In the 1840s, Friedrich List formulated the concept of economic development. In his opinion, the state should be able to use protectionist measures to strengthen its own entrepreneurs and industry. He often referred to Poland as a negative example. He wrote:

> Without a system of protection, and under a system of free trade with further advanced nations, even if Poland had retained her independence up to the present time, she could never have carried on anything more than a crippled agriculture; she could never have become rich, powerful, and outwardly influential. (List 1856, 303)

And explained:

> Let us compare Poland with England: both nations at one time were in the same stage of culture; and now what a difference. Manufactories and manufactures are the mothers and children of municipal liberty, of intelligence, of the arts and sciences, of internal and external commerce, of navigation and improvements in transport, of civilisation and political power. They are the chief means of liberating agriculture from its chains, and of elevating it to a commercial character and to a degree of art and science, by which the rents, farming profits, and wages are increased, and greater value is given to landed property. (List 1856, 219)

But List's *National System of Political Economy* (first published in 1841) never became obligatory reading for Polish modernizers. Similarly, the reception of other prominent economists of that time, debating on development and economic and social progress, such as Karl Marx, John Stuart Mill, or Jean de Sismondi, was delayed. One can say that the development gap existed not only in the "real economy", but also in the economic ideas that remained underdeveloped. The economic concepts and solutions were of marginal interest among Polish intellectuals, and it turned out that this attitude lasted much longer than the partitions.

Much later, the historical school of economics would become the point of reference for Polish modernizers (e.g. Władysław and Stanisław Grabski), but in the mid-nineteenth century the German experience did not seem to be the proper solution of Polish problems. The Polish debates did not refer to List's ideas—it was pointless when there was no Polish influence on the state policies, other than through rebellion. Actually, the ideas of Romanticism, the defeat of the November Uprising, and the

ensuing Great Emigration influenced the way Poland and its development was seen during the period between the uprisings of 1830 and 1864
much more than the foreign debates on development. The faith in the
possibility of regaining independence was replaced by the sense of the
relative inevitability of Poland's situation (Walicki 1994; Kloczkowski
2004; Trencsényi et al. 2016). In effect, the intellectuals lost contact with
the main current of Western European economic debates on economic
development, and focused either on Romantic mirages or searching for
more pragmatic, microlevel local solutions.

At first, the Romantic streak dominating in the Polish political thinking involved the belief in a revolution bringing back independence; over
time, it acquired a left-wing, radical character and generated social ideas
whose goal was a deep social reform. The manifestoes of the Polish
Democratic Society expressed the need to combine the fight for independence and the social reform, without which it was difficult to involve the
peasants in the fight. Thus, the emancipation of the nation had to be
paralleled by social emancipation, which in particular involved the agrarian reforms and enfranchisement of the peasants, as Poland had a predominantly rural and peasant society. More radical views were expressed
by the Communes of Polish People, a faction of émigrés that offered a
concept of radical social revolution close to some utopian socialist views
(Dzięciołowski 1989; Janowski 2004; Walicki et al. 2009).

These ideas were founded on the belief that everybody was equally
entitled to use the land and its produce. Over time, this conviction led to
more radical conclusions, widespread in the left-wing faction of the Great
Emigration at least up to the Spring of Nations (1848). Some of the left-
wing politicians of the time, for example, Stanislaw Worcell, a co-founder
of the Communes of Polish People, or the leader of the Cracow Uprising
Stanislaw Dembowski, promoted abolishing private property in the name
of progress. These ideas were increasingly connected with the post-
Romantic belief that Poland could be the spearhead of world advancement, be it national emancipation or equal rights. However, these were
the grand designs of intellectuals, which had little or no bearing on the
socioeconomic situation and class relations on the Polish lands
(Temkinowa 1962; Kizwalter 1999; Sykulski 2007).

Many of the Polish radical ideas drifted towards the utopian visions of the future society. Such were the ideas included in the writings of the abovementioned Worcell, Dembowski or the Polish Democratic Society. In this vein, Dembowski formulated the philosophy of history, where history was seen as continuous progress from lower to higher forms of social organization; the final stage was the fully democratic society, where everybody would have time for work and for learning, and common property would replace the unnatural private property. This escape from reality seemed to be the result of the reception of Western European ideas, but might also be the response to the sense of the inability to influence that reality.

Other political factions increasingly accepted the ideas of the emancipation of the peasants and abolishing the corvée as a way to modernize the society and build the nation, and a prerequisite to continuing the fight for independence. Even though the concept of social change formulated by liberal and conservative circles (such as the Hotel Lambert, created by Prince Adam Czartoryski but also conservatives in Poland) was much narrower, its key component was the gradual enfranchisement of the peasants (Ludwikowski 1976, 1991). However, the radicals combined the fight for independence and the social revolution, whereas Czartoryski considered these two matters separately and differently. As to the former, he thought that independence could be regained by means of diplomatic methods; as to the latter, he thought the reforms were to be gradual and should not harm the economic interests of the nobility (Żaliński 1990; Żurawski vel Grajewski 2014; Trencsényi et al. 2016).

This difference of opinion was reflected in the political activity during the January Uprising of 1863–1864, where the Whites, the more conciliatory faction, wanted moderate and gradual social reforms, and the Reds, the radical faction, wanted to fight both for independence and for the rights of the exploited classes. As a result, the success of the Red faction in underground politics led to an attempt at full enfranchisement of peasants. Uprising government dominated by Reds' faction issued an edict enfranchising the peasants and abolishing all feudal obligations. In reality, it was only the Tsar's decree of 1864, mostly repeating that edict, which implemented the reform in a legally binding way (Ludwikowski 2012).

Apart from the ideas of the future society and the endless post mortem of the defeat of the November Uprising (which we do not discuss here), the problem extensively discussed in the period was the causes of the backwardness of the Polish lands. Again, the Romantic narrative dominated, in which Poland was an innocent victim of the predatory policy of its neighbours. Walerian Kalinka was one of the first to question this interpretation. According to him, the real culprit had been the Polish elite and the system which it sustained. He also pointed out the discriminatory treatment of Galicia by Austria, calling the former "a colony of Austrian factories" (Król 1985).

Apart from the independence movement, both on the Polish lands and abroad, there was a considerable circle of proponents of the policy of conciliation or even assimilation. One such case was Henryk Rzewuski, more a writer than a political thinker, who believed that Poland was a redundant entity. Another case was the programme of unconditional agreement with Russia which was formulated in *Letter of a Polish Nobleman to Prince Metternich* by Aleksander Wielopolski in 1846 (Lisicki 1879; Mażewski 2012), after the Galician Slaughter, a peasant uprising against the Polish nobility. He thought that the restoration of the Polish state would not be supported by the West, and the experience of the Galician Slaughter undermined the trust towards the government in Vienna. Therefore, he decided that the best option for Poland was to be connected with Russia. He thought that a reasonable set of reforms should be conducted with the help of Russia to prevent a social revolution. In 1861, Wielopolski had an opportunity to implement his ideas as the leader of the Polish Civil Administration. However, his reasonable policy aiming to ensure development and to retain part of the autonomy, as well as a set of well-advised reforms, met with an unexpected lack of social support. He failed to stop the social process leading to the outbreak of the January Uprising in 1863.

A similar conciliatory process started in Kraków after the emergence and rise in importance of the so-called Stańczyk party (co-created by Kalinka), representing the ideology of the conservative-liberal bourgeoisie of Kraków. It was possible because of the liberalization of the Austrian policy towards the remote peripheries of the empire, which took place at the end of the 1860s. The politicians involved in the Stańczyk movement decided that in the existing political situation the best chance to preserve the Polish identity was supporting Galicia's autonomy and a loyalist policy. They also got involved in the criticism of the political system and the institutions of the Polish Commonwealth and of the policy of national uprisings. Earlier, a similar loyalist policy was attempted by the conservative faction of the Polish nobility in the Kingdom of Poland (Król 1982; Trencsényi et al. 2016).

In the Prussian part of the Polish lands, the revolutionary tendencies culminated during the Spring of Nations, with the outbreak of an unsuccessful uprising in Greater Poland. Afterwards, the ideas of organic work started to develop there—an attempt to create bottom-up economic and social structures ensuring the preservation of the Polish identity and aiming to retain the material possessions of the Polish nation. These concepts laid the foundation of the Positivist doctrine, which became widespread on the Polish lands, particularly in the Kingdom of Poland, after the January Uprising. Its main economic theoretician was Józef Supiński.

Supiński was the most interesting economic theoretician in Poland at that time. He took part in the November Uprising and had to emigrate, and after his return he lived in Lvov in Galicia. He developed his political-economic system in separation from the political arguments of the time, and his views were rooted in the Enlightenment tradition. He studied the development of capitalism and he created a considerably original theory of social economics. In his opinion, because of Poland's historical situation, its development path should be different from that of other countries. He also stated that there were no economic rules that apply to all situations (i.e. unconditionally), except a handful of general laws (Ossowski 2007; Supiński et al. 2010).

He did not criticize the Western European models, but he thought that excessive imitation may threaten the Polish identity. Thus he was sceptical about rapid state-funded industrialization. Instead, he saw the greater potential for development in modern large-scale agriculture, based on the capitalist principles. He did not believe that the partitioning states' economic policy, including industrialization, could serve the Polish interests. For this reason, he thought that bottom-up modernization was necessary, that is, one involving individual people in protecting local industry and, first of all, agriculture, without the protection of the state. He promoted using

Polish capital, and using it wisely, as it was in short supply. These views provided an important theoretical background to the practical solutions, and the Positivist activity and organic work developed in Greater Poland.

The ideas of Supiński led to concept of organic work. It was based on the assumption that the peasants were a vital part of the nation, but as long as they suffered poverty, their connection with the rest of the nation remained only potential. What was needed to make it real, and to actually include the peasants into the life of the nation, was education, empowerment, and some assistance in the development of their households to turn them into productive market enterprises. Thus, the elite—the nobility and intelligentsia—should engage in organic work aimed at the improvement of the economic situation of the peasants, bringing about the bottom-up development that would strengthen the nation and make it capable of using the sudden opportunities to rebuild sovereignty. In such a way, the idea of social reform aimed to empower the lower strata of the society, similar to ideas expressed in the German historical school of economics, impossible to achieve without a sovereign state, was replaced with the idea of microchanges from the bottom up. Finally, this new, pragmatic concept replaced Romantic beliefs in successful rebellion (Kizwalter and Skowronek 1988).

Why Poland was backward and collapsed, why the strategies already implemented, including the Enlightenment state industrialization projects, were unsuccessful, how to catch up with the West—these were the basic questions concerning the development of Poland, but they were not answered during the period between the uprisings. As a result of the loss of the influence on the future of the state and the society, the question of economic development became of secondary importance to that of regaining independence. Moreover, whatever discussion took place was far removed from the European debates on development, which focused on the role of the nation state in promoting the development of the market, industry, and modern society. However, the discussion concerning the Polish economic development started to involve the following important elements: (1) the necessity to emancipate the peasants, whether radically or gradually, (2) taking into account not only the external causes of the decline of the state, but also internal, (3) considering the conciliatory policy towards the partitioning states, which would ensure economic and social development and avert the risk of social revolution, and (4) the Positivist ideas of bottom-up development. Simultaneously, some utopian socialists became proponents of social revolution and establishing the new, communist social order.

3   The Territory and Population

In the years 1831–1864, there was only one border change on the Polish lands—the abolishment of the Free City of Kraków and incorporating it to the lands under the Austrian rule. The Kingdom of Poland underwent several changes of its internal administrative structure. In 1837, the voivodeships were replaced by provinces (*gubernyas*), which had two

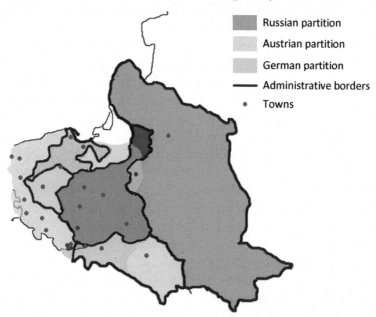

Map 5.1 Polish lands after Vienna Congress. (Kingdom of Poland in purple colour, Grand Duchy of Posen in brighter green). Note: Territory of contemporary Poland shaded. Borders of partition and borders of Poland after 1772—thick line. Proximate location of towns and cities enumerated in column 1868 and 1910 of Table A.3 in Annex. Blue dots represent towns enumerated only in column 1910. Source: Own elaboration on the basis of various historical maps

main consequences—the administrative structure became the same as in the rest of Russia, and the Polish local administration was eliminated. The province borders were subsequently changed in 1845 and again in 1867 (Główny Urząd Statystyczny 1993).

The population on the Polish lands grew relatively quickly. The only factor that hampered this growth was the potato blight in the 1840s, which affected the Prussian and Austrian partitions more than the Kingdom of Poland, where potatoes were less commonly grown and their loss was less severely felt. It is important to note, however, that the consequences of the potato famine involved a lower birth rate and higher mortality among the elderly, rather than mass starvation (Szewczuk and Bujak 1939; Kwak 1987).

In the years 1830–1865, there was the growing differentiation of the demographic processes between the partitions. In the Russian partition, in the Kingdom of Poland, there was a rapid population growth, with similar rates in rural and urban populations (Janczak 1995). The population of Warszawa grew quickly (Kazimierski 1977), the industrial region around Łódź urbanized intensely, and Łódź (Janczak 1982) found itself among the biggest cities of the Kingdom, but in other places urbanization was slow, even in the state-owned industrial complexes near Kielce and in the Dabrowa basin. The largest town in the formerly Polish western provinces of Russia was Wilno.

In Greater Poland and West Prussia, the changes were determined by the agricultural reform, the growing outflow of the population to the richer and better developed Prussian provinces, and by the development of roads and railways. Consequently, the population growth was slow in comparison both to the other Polish lands, and to the other Prussian provinces. However, the proportion of the population of urban areas grew, which was a continuation of the process of the differentiation of levels of urbanization between the partitions already visible in the previous decades. This tendency was also observable in the provinces of Pomerania and East Prussia. Silesia, on the other hand, underwent rapid industrialization, intense urbanization, and quick population growth. It was to Upper Silesia that the labourers migrated from the neighbouring lands of the Austrian and Russian partitions and from the poorer provinces of Prussia. Breslau was one of the largest towns in Prussia. Other important towns in contemporary Polish borders were Gdańsk, Stettin, Poznań. Upper Silesian towns, however densely distributed and rapidly growing, remained relatively small in this period (Jelonek 1967; Główny Urząd Statystyczny 1993).

In Austria, population change was slower than in the Kingdom of Poland, with a similarly slow development of towns and cities. Apart from two or three medium-size cities, Lwów, Kraków, and the much smaller Przemyśl, there were hardly any urban centres. Even though the network of villages was dense, much denser than in Greater Poland as well as most of Russian Poland, the stagnant towns were losing their function as educational, economic, and sometimes even administrative centres (Karpineć 1932; Jelonek 1967).

4   The Society

The social reform within the partitions and the ensuing social change in the partitioning states influenced the social structure on the Polish lands. Prussia and to a smaller extent Austria were experiencing rapid social modernization and the emergence of an industrial society. Its symptom was the scale of social unrest in both countries during the Spring of Nations. These changes affected the situation in the Polish provinces, both through spontaneous adjustments and as the evolution of institutions. In Russia, the Tsar conducted conservative policy, based on the nobility and the supposedly conservative peasantry. The changes were introduced no sooner than after the Crimean War, partly because of the change on the throne, as Nicholas II was succeeded by Alexander II. However, in the Kingdom of Poland, the scope and rate of changes were different than in Russia proper. After the November Uprising the position of the nobility was weakened as a result of the deliberate action conducted against it by the Russian authorities, as the nobility was considered the main source of the Polish national identity.

Still, the powerful tool to weaken the position of the nobility was the obligatory verification, that is, proving one's nobility (Sikorska-Kulesza 1995). It resulted in diminishing the numbers of the privileged nobility and—through the introduction of new forms of obtaining the titles—in changing the nature and the social structure of this class. It effectively finished the history of the Polish nobility, which either turned into the landed gentry in the country and the intelligentsia in the city or was downgraded to the level of peasantry or urban proletariat (Jedlicki et al. 2014). Part of the nobility obtained a status equal to that of the Russian state nobility.

While the nobility was losing their social and economic status, the bourgeoisie was growing, both in numbers and position, as a result of industrialization and of the metropolitan character that Warszawa, but later also Łódź and the neighbouring cities, started to assume. Many of the townspeople were members of the Jewish minority, dealing in banking, trade, and inn-keeping, but also in industrial entrepreneurship, often of foreign origin (e.g. Steinkeller or Geyer), and sometimes acquiring great wealth and high status (families such as Epstein, Wawelbergs, Kronenberg in Warszawa, and Poznański in Łódź). The position of merchants and bankers, with their fortunes and influences, had been increasing from the end of the eighteenth century, and even more so from the beginning of the industrial civilization in the Kingdom of Poland, but the real take-off was later in the second half of the nineteenth century, after the January Uprising and the full economic integration with Russia. In the Western provinces of Russia, due to lack of large cities, the process of development of the bourgeoisie was much slower. Many small towns were inhabited mostly by Jews and Poles, sometimes with a Jewish majority.

In the 1850s, the interests of the landowners and of the rich bourgeoisie gradually started to converge. During the period of post-Crimean War reforms, this alliance obtained considerable political power, particularly when Aleksander Wielopolski was at the helm of the country. During the January Uprising, the interests of the conservative bourgeoisie and the landed gentry were represented by the Whites' faction (Kołodziejczyk 1968; Żor 2011; Mażewski 2012).

The poorest and the most populated social group was the peasantry, a lot of peasants were landless, but burdened with feudal duties in the form of labour and other obligations. The scope of these duties and the way they were enforced was the source of constant tension and resentment between the landowners and the peasants. In the Kingdom of Poland and the rest of Russian partition, the final resolution to the problem did not come until the 1860s. The enfranchisement catalysed the process of spontaneous social mobility (usually connected with rural-urban migrations) in Polish lands, additionally supported by improving quality and range of basic education. The dynamic of the development of mass education was different in three partitions (Groniowski 1976; Borkowski and Inglot 1995).

For the whole period, the education system of the Kingdom of Poland was very poorly developed. It hampered the processes of social modernization, particularly in peripheral rural areas. There was no compulsory education, and, since the 1830s, schools and the whole education system became a tool for Russification. Schools were not obligatory, and peasants did not have access to education (apart from informal schools organized by the nobility after 1864 as part of organic work). The Russian state was not interested in any education policy in Russian Poland. In effect, illiteracy was very high, particularly outside bigger cities. Since the 1860s, the Polish intelligentsia and nobility started to make efforts to offer informal Polish education for peasants (in forms of Sunday or evening schools). This model of informal education reached a momentum few decades later (Karłowska-Grenda and Nawrot-Borowska 2004; Jedlicki et al. 2014; Galek 2015).

In the Kingdom of Prussia, the Polish lands were the agricultural supply base for the rapidly urbanizing state, therefore, the big landowners played a significant role. Some of them took part in the modernization of agricultural production, like Dezydery Chłapowski in Greater Poland, but also in creating conditions for the development of the Polish bourgeoisie (thanks to institutions like *Bazar*, a Polish department store and hotel in the centre of Poznań, co-founded by Polish noblemen and aimed at strengthening Polish entrepreneurs) and of the Polish economic institutions in general. The Polish nobility in Prussia got involved in this kind of activity earlier than in the other partitions, which was their response to the intense colonization of the Polish lands under the Prussian rule and to the growing importance of the German population in this region (Topolski 1973; Łuczak 1973). The ethnolinguistic structure of the population of Greater Poland as well as the vanishing of bilingual population during the colonization period is shown in Tables 5.1a and 5.1b.

As a result of the agrarian reforms from the first decades of the nineteenth century, the peasantry quickly turned into either wealthy farmers or

Table 5.1a Evolution of the ethnolinguistic structure of Greater Poland

Year	Polish-speaking population	Polish- and German- speaking population	German-speaking population
1846	49.7% (690,000)	22.1%	28.2% (391,000)
1890	59.9% (1,048,000)	0.6%	39.5% (692,000)

Source: Łuczak (1973)
Note: Shares of the Polish- and German-speaking populations

Table 5.1b Religious structure of Greater Poland (%)

Year	Roman-Catholics	Protestants	Jews
1816	65.8	27.8	6.4
1831	64.4	28.9	6.7
1849	63.5	30.7	5.8
1858	62.7	32.4	5.1

Source: Łuczak (1973)
Note: Germany promoted the settlement of Protestant Germans in Polish
provinces, thus, dynamics of changes in the religious structure of the province
may be treated as an (unprecise) proxy of ethnic structure. Most of the Jews
declared themselves as German-speaking population in censuses from the
second half of the nineteenth century

the rural proletariat. This accelerated the modernization and social change
in the country. In the 1860s, the countryside in the Prussian Greater
Poland differed greatly from that in the Kingdom of Poland or Galicia, as
the modernization process resulted first in the diminishing and later in
the gradual disappearance of the peasantry (as social class). From today's
perspective, the lands under the Prussian rule were the only part of Poland
where this phenomenon took place. In the other partitions, the successive
exogenous development shocks in the nineteenth and twentieth centuries—
uprisings, two world wars, the Great Depression, state socialism—delayed
the completion of this process until several generations later.

The lands under the Prussian rule were also unique with respect to
education. Compulsory education was introduced in 1825 in Greater
Poland and Pomerania; on the one hand, it was perceived as a tool for
Germanization, but on the other hand, it created conditions for social
mobility and the modernization of the economy, including the development of the industrial economy. In response to Germanization, the Polish
inhabitants of Greater Poland strove to limit the impact of the Prussian
public institutions and developed a set of actions and strategies such as

scholarships for the talented youth, periodicals, and so on, to build and maintain the Polish national identity (Galek 2016).

In Galicia, a backward rural province of Austria, the key social class was the nobility and landowners. Unlike in Prussia and Russia, their influence on the Polish culture and institutions was limited at that time. The emergence of the bourgeoisie was restricted to the limited number of bigger urban centres, that is, Kraków and Lwów. The Free City Cracow until 1848, developed particularly quickly, and its limited territory made the bourgeoisie strong in relation to the landed gentry. The Galician countryside did not change, except for the fact that the growing population density and the enforcement of feudal duties by landowners, along with the tax and conscription duties towards the Austrian state (also enforced by the landowners), generated tension and resentment, as a result of which, in 1846, the peasants' revolt broke out in the western part of the region. The Cracow Uprising, on the other hand, can be treated as the first political act where the key factors were the new social groups emerging at the time, the intelligentsia, and the bourgeoisie (Buszko 1989; Pawłowski et al. 1994; Ślusarek 2012; Miodunka 2014; Daszyk et al. 2016).

In Galicia, growing social tensions between the peasantry and the nobility led to the aforementioned peasants' rebellion, called the Galician Slaughter, which catalysed legal changes—the Emperor's decree from 7 June 1846 improved the peasants' situation and relieved the tension by limiting the non-labour obligations. In 1848, after the enfranchisement of the peasants and the abolishment of feudal duties, the process of social change began in Galicia, though its rate was low and its scope was narrow, particularly in the countryside, due to the low development level of the region and the relatively slow implementation of the new regulations. The regulations themselves were not conducive to radical change, as they did not support the development of big farms. Quite the opposite—the lack of proper regulations concerning inheritance contributed to the gradual fragmentation of the lands owned by the peasants in the next decades, which impoverished the Galician countryside and significantly slowed down the modernization process (Ślusarek 2002, 2017).

The quality of education in Galicia was higher than in the Russian partition but much lower than in Prussia. What is important is, since

Galician autonomy, the education was partially polonized, and also, the environment for the development of Polish cultural and educational institutions became much better than elsewhere in Polish lands. Since autonomy, Jagiellonian University slowly turned into a single Polish institution of higher education (Dybiec et al. 2015).

At the end of the period, emigration emerged as a noteworthy new phenomenon. Its reason was no longer political, like in the case of the Great Emigration after the November Uprising (1831) or the Small Emigration after the January Uprising (1863–1864), but economic, that is, seeking employment. Labourers emigrated either for the short term or permanently, within the partitioning state (mostly in Prussia, partly also in Austria) or internationally (initially between the partitioning states). However, emigration did not become a mass phenomenon until the final decades of the nineteenth century (Borejsza 1966; Pilch 1984; Kalembka 2003).

With the notable exception of the lands under the Prussian rule, the social change on the Polish lands was relatively slow until the 1860s. The key factor accelerating this process was the resolution of the problem of serfdom. In Austria and Russia, the authorities tried to play it against the Polish majority by maintaining the conflict between the Polish elite and the peasantry. However, within a generation, it turned out that the state regulations eliminated the basic sources of conflict, that is, the feudal duties and the obligations towards the state which before the regulations had had to be enforced by the landowners. Eventually, because of the development of a network of Polish educational and cultural institutions in the rural communities, modelled on the solutions from Prussia, that is, Greater Poland, Pomerania, and to some extent, Silesia, the Polish national identity was formed among the rural community in the final decades of the nineteenth century.

5   The Economy

The division of the territory, the disappearance of the former connections, the peripheral location of the Polish lands within the partitioning states, and—in the case of Russia—an unfavourable customs policy hampered development and caused a shift in development centres within the Polish lands. This process is best exemplified by the crisis in the formerly prosperous economic regions of Poland divided between the partitioning states, that is, Greater Poland (divided between Prussia and Russia) and Lesser Poland (divided between Russia and Austria), described in the previous chapter, as the division led to the decline of the textile industry in Greater Poland and to the decline of the industrial region near Kielce in Lesser Poland. In the Russian part of Greater Poland, a certain developmental impulse was the migration of craftsmen from the Prussian part in the first decades of the nineteenth century and then the creation of the road between Warszawa and Kalisz. However, soon, the economic centre shifted to the east, towards Łódź, and both sides of the border suffered stagnation. A similar crisis, even more acute, affected Lesser Poland.

Gradually, the initial similarities lost their importance and, in the 1830s, the development paths of the different Polish regions started to diverge. By that time, all the distinctness of the formerly Polish lands had practically disappeared in the Prussian and Austrian partitions. The Kingdom of Poland retained remnants of its distinct legal status, and some autonomous institutions, like the Polish-controlled Bank of Poland, emitting the money (it is noteworthy that at that time its lending policy indicated the growing conflict between the interests of its managers, including the Łubieński family, and the public interest. Corruption and nepotism became common in the Bank in the 1830s and 1840s) (Leszczyńska 2006, 2010).

In Prussia, the region which started to develop very quickly was Silesia, traditionally well developed. The development was stimulated by the increased demand for coal and the growth of heavy industry in the middle of the century. Its development level on pair with the western provinces of Prussia, but significantly higher than that of the other eastern provinces, which retained their agricultural character, except for the seaside towns with ports and shipyards (Gdańsk, Stettin, Elbing), whose economy was stimulated by the industrialization in Prussia.

At that time, Greater Poland and Pomerania increasingly benefitted from the integration with Prussia, which was undergoing rapid development. The changes in technology entailed the development of small and medium-scale mechanical engineering enterprises providing services to agriculture and transport infrastructure, but also created conditions for the rapid development of the agroindustry: breweries, distilleries, sugar mills, and mills. The crisis and collapse of the textile industry in Greater Poland, which started at the beginning of the nineteenth century, turned out to be irreversible. The peripheral position of the Polish lands and their specialization within the Prussian state were not conducive to creating big factories—in the Prussian partition, industrial enterprises were few and far between (Misztal 1970; Topolski 1973; Łuczak 1973).

The majority of the industrial bourgeoisie in the urban areas of Greater Poland and Pomerania were German and most industrial enterprises created in these regions were German-owned. The Polish and German bourgeoisie found themselves in competition, particularly in Greater Poland. The landed gentry supported the development of Polish industry and trade and, as a result, the Polish bourgeoisie was relatively strong. In the Polish tradition the epitome of success in industry is the life of Hipolit Cegielski (Rezler 2000), a teacher who, having lost his job because of his involvement in the independence movement, set up a tool shop in *Bazar* in Poznań. Soon, he added a workshop, and then in the 1850s he created a factory employing several dozen workers, producing agricultural tools and successfully competing with the German-owned factories from Poznań and Greater Poland. In the subsequent decades, it became one of the biggest factories in Greater Poland and was one of the biggest factories in sovereign Poland after 1918.

Most of the former Polish lands under Prussian rule remained remote agricultural peripheries, which became a barrier to development, but the growth of the transport infrastructure—roads, canals, also the railway from the mid-1800s—and the growing internal demand stimulated development very quickly. The development of the railway network was particularly impressive, both its rate and its extent. Since that period, the railway network in the formerly Prussian provinces has remained much denser than elsewhere in Poland (Koziarski 1993; Mielcarek 2000; Myszczyszyn et al. 2013; Myszczyszyn 2016). The increasing demand for labour in the industrialized areas—the Ruhr region, Silesia, and the growing biggest cities—contributed to the internal emigration of a large part of the population, solving the problem of labour surplus and leading to increased efficiency, particularly in agriculture.

Anyway, agricultural production developed rapidly. The ongoing social and demographic changes of peasantry reflected the economic development—the abolishment of post-feudal duties, institutional support for the creation of farms, and the growing internal demand were conducive to restructuring and modernizing the agricultural sector. Productivity increased, new crops were introduced (potatoes, sugar beets), modern tools and efficient technologies were implemented, and oxen were replaced by horses. This rapid modernization of agriculture and the growth of productivity and specialization (including rapid growth of potato production) also had unexpected disadvantages—among all the Polish lands, it was the Prussian partition lands that were most severely affected by the potato blight. The temporary food shortage was particularly acute in Silesia, but the whole region suffered, which was visible in the demographic data (Kwak 1987).

In the Kingdom of Poland, the unprofitable state industry was in recession after the defeat of the November Uprising. Lower financing, particularly in the 1840s, revealed the cost-ineffectiveness of the state investments in heavy industry, and the obsolete technologies made the products uncompetitive with imported goods. The last big investment in this sector was the construction of the *Huta Bankowa*, a big ironworks in Dąbrowa Górnicza. When it achieved its full production capacity in 1842, the power of the steam engines in the plant comprised over 30% of the power of the steam engines in the entire Kingdom and exceeded the power of the steam engines in the Warszawa industrial area. However, the production capacity of the plant was only fractionally used because of the limited demand and technological problems, such as the shortage of coking coal (Kowalska et al. 1958; Jedlicki 1964; Pietrzak-Pawłowska 1970; Puś 1987).

Private enterprises developed more dynamically, particularly in the Łódź and Warszawa regions (Pruss 1977; Rosin et al. 1989). It resulted from the inflow of entrepreneurs, investment capital, and technologies, mostly from Germany, but also from France (like in the case of the linen factory in Żyrardów) and the other European countries (e.g. Karol Scheibler, one of the greatest entrepreneurs in Łódź, originally came from North Rhine-Westphalia, but his experience was connected with Belgian and Austrian industry). Gradually, the private investments started to dominate, financed by bank loans, state loans, the capital of the landed gentry, and the growing fortunes of entrepreneurs and industrialists (Kołodziejczyk 1957, 1979; Ihnatowicz 1972; Skrzydło 2000; Stefański 2014).

In the 1850s, manufacturing involved mostly craft production, but the factories in Łódź and Warszawa started to become quite sizeable. Around 1850, Ludwik Geyer's cotton factory employed over 600 workers. The slightly smaller wool factories, the Repphan Brothers' factory in Kalisz and Fiedler's factory in Opatówek, also employed several hundred workers each. The Evans Brothers' metal factory in Warszawa (from 1854 called Evans, Lilpop, and Rau's) employed 500 people in the 1850s. In 1863, the linen factory in Żyrardów employed 800 workers. Altogether, in the 1850s, the manufacturing industry in the Kingdom of Poland employed approximately 50,000 workers, with about 50% in the textile industry (about 2000 in modern factories and the rest in workshops and in the cottage industry), and just before the January Uprising, approximately 70,000 workers (employment in traditional crafts was still much higher). At the time, the modern branches of industry were clustered around Warszawa (metal works and mechanical engineering, but also modern agroindustry), Łódź (textile industry) and Kalisz; the state-owned heavy industry was falling into decline in the Dabrowa basin and near Kielce. However, there was still the dominance of small industry based on hand labour, workshops, and small plants. It was inefficient, based on old technologies, and scattered as a result of poor transport infrastructure (Załęski 1876; Łukasiewicz 1963; Misztal 1970; Pruss 1977; Kołodziejczyk 1981; Grochulska and Pruss 1983; Puś 1987). The comparison of coal and pig iron production in the Kingdom and selected European countries in 1850, which indicates the developmental distance between Polish lands and Western Europe, is presented in Table 5.2.

Table 5.2 Industrial output (coal, pig iron) in the Kingdom of Poland and selected European countries in 1850 (in kg per capita)

	Coal (kg per capita)	Pig iron (kg per capita)
Kingdom of Poland	28	4
France	87	17
Germany	112	8.4
Great Britain	1635	105
Russia	1	3.7

Source: Jezierski (1967)

Transport infrastructure was developing, however. Public investments resulted in building roads from Warszawa to most province centres. The first railway line joining Warszawa with the Prussian border in Upper Silesia, that is, with the Prussian and Austrian railway networks, was built in the years 1845–1848. The subsequent railway lines, from Warszawa to Toruń (Thorn) in Prussia via Aleksandrow Kujawski and to St. Petersburg via Białystok, were not built until the early 1860s. However, in spite of these investments, in the mid-century, the network density and the quality of the transport infrastructure in the Kingdom of Poland compared unfavourably with those in the Prussian partition, and the subsequent years widened the gap with respect to all types of infrastructure—roads, railways, canals, and navigable rivers (Koziarski 1993).

The Kingdom of Poland was located between Russia and Prussia, near the European trade routes, and for that reason it started to become an attractive investment region. Labour costs were significantly lower than in Prussia (despite the limited supply before the peasants' emancipation), and the land was cheaper, which made investing in older and labour-intensive technologies economically viable. Additionally, the investments in the Kingdom gave access to the huge Russian market, particularly after the customs border between the Kingdom and Russia, introduced after the November Uprising, had been lifted in 1851. In effect, the Kingdom of Poland became one of the fastest-growing industrial regions of Russia (Łukasiewicz 1963; Jezierski 1967).

In turn, the main barrier to the development of the rural economy in the Kingdom of Poland was serfdom, which remained unsolved longest—until 1864. As a result, the agriculture was inefficient and the inflow of people into urban areas was relatively slow. The evolution of the economic structures in agriculture was uneven—in the western provinces of the Kingdom, there was spontaneous change of peasant duties from labour to cash rent (actually, similar evolution started a few decades earlier in Greater Poland, before the Prussian agrarian reform), while in the eastern provinces (and in the western provinces of Russia), the changes were slower. The emergence of the textile industry contributed to the development of animal husbandry, with a particularly quick increase in the number of sheep. The development of the agroindustry involved increasing the size of enterprises—like in the case of breweries and distilleries, now becoming industrial-scale—but also the emergence of new enterprises, like big sugar mills from the late 1830s. The plants that remained small and scattered longer were the mills, mostly due to the lack of efficient transport infrastructure required for the concentration of grain processing. The modernization of agriculture was slower than in Prussia; therefore, the potato blight affected the agricultural production less severely.

The Polish lands incorporated into Russia developed much more slowly than the Kingdom of Poland. There were few urban centres, transport infrastructure was still almost non-existent, and modern industry did not develop except in Białystok, a textile industry centre. Białystok for some time profited from the customs border between the Kingdom of Poland and the rest of Russia, but its abolishment resulted in the stagnation of the local industry—investing in Łódź was much more attractive because of its location. Agriculture was prevailingly inefficient as obsolete production methods were still in use (Werwicki 1957; Joka 1972; Kaczyńska 1974; Kalabiński and Kaczyńska 1986).

In the Austrian partition, development was slow. The peripheral position and slow urbanization hampered the emergence of modern industry, with the notable exception of mining. Salt was excavated in the mines in Wieliczka and Bochnia, coal and calamine in Chrzanów, crude oil started to be excavated in 1854, at first, near Krosno. A small textile industry centre emerged near Biała. Agroindustry was scattered and small-scale, and its most important element was a huge number of small distilleries (up to 5000 in the 1830s), which profited from propination and an underdeveloped transport infrastructure (much of this industry collapsed in the subsequent decades). With low demand, the high population density, and the relatively difficult terrain, agriculture was still based on traditional methods of production, with some slight changes in the organization and technology (Burzyński and Madurowicz-Urbańska 1982; Kaps 2015).

The low level of development of the transport infrastructure was another factor hampering economic growth. The network density and the quality of roads were comparable to those in the Kingdom of Poland and considerably poorer than in most other provinces of Cisleithania. The railway started to develop in the 1850s thanks to state investments. The first line joined Kraków and Upper Silesia (1847), then the connection between Cracow and Lvov was built (completed in 1861).

The lands under the Prussian rule were much better developed than most other Polish territories. Data on occupational structure in the late

Table 5.3 Regional occupational structure of Polish lands, 1859/61/69

	Posen	Pomerania	East/ West Prussia	Upper Silesia (Oppeln)	Silesia (excl. Oppeln)	Total, Prussian part	Congress Kingdom	Galicia
	1861 (%)	1861 (%)	1861 (%)	1861 (%)	1861 (%)	1861 (%)	1859 (%)	1869 (%)
Primary	70	63	70	66	53	64	76	86
Secondary	13	19	13	21	28	19	11	4
Tertiary	17	18	17	14	19	17	13	9

Source: Own calculations (Sobieszczański 1860; Statistischen Central-Commission 1874; Tipton 1976)

1860s/1870 are shown beneath (Table 5.3), and they clearly present the differences in development between regions—particularly the greater importance of the manufacturing sector in the economy of the Prussian part compared to other Polish lands.

Until the mid-1860s, it was difficult to indicate the processes which could unequivocally prove that the Polish lands underwent a technological breakthrough and started to industrialize. The conspicuous exception was the Prussian province of Silesia. However, there were increasing development differences between the regions. The lands governed by Prussia took advantage of infrastructure investments and modern institutions. The Kingdom of Poland started to benefit from its geographical position within the Russian Empire. Galicia remained a peripheral agricultural province of Austria, and within a century it turned from one of the best developed regions of Poland into one of the poorest.

6   Conclusion

Although it is difficult to prove the opinion, quite common among Polish economic historians, that the period between 1830 and 1870 was the time of the transition into the industrial economy on the Polish lands—though in my opinion it happened later—it is beyond doubt that the abolition of serfdom (conducted between 1821 and 1864) and the ensuing social change was of key importance for the further modernization process. The period between the uprisings was also the time of the emergence of the modern industrial bourgeoisie, who played the key role in the industrialization of Poland in the subsequent decades.

At the same time, the process of the disintegration of the Polish national market continued. The disintegration of the Polish regions was quickened by the different timing of agrarian reforms, and the different dynamics of urbanization, industrialization, and infrastructure development in the three partitioning states. The resulting fragmentation of the nation and the possible remedies appeared in the centre of the political discourse and—whenever possible—the political activity, including organic work.

Industrialization, which was the focal point of the Polish discussions concerning further development in the final period of the Commonwealth and political efforts in the early nineteenth century at the time of the partitions and the Napoleonic Wars as well as in the period afterwards, after the November Uprising was overshadowed by the questions of the emancipation of the peasants. The Polish thinkers and politicians, both inside the country and abroad, saw them as the *sine qua non* of social, economic, and political change. However, the problem was not resolved as a result of Polish discussions and actions, but as exogenous decisions of the authorities of the partitioning states.

Another problem in the centre of attention of the Polish leaders was protecting the national identity. The intention of the authorities of Russia, Austria, and Prussia was the disruption of the peasants' sense of national identity and their quick, effective assimilation; however, within a generation the Polish identity was forged across state borders not only among the elite, but also among the lower classes—the main intents of both the Romantic ideals and the Positivist organic work were met in achieving this goal. In the long term, it constituted the key factor in the reintegration of the Polish lands.

References

Borejsza, J. W. (1966). *Emigracja polska po powstaniu styczniowym*. Warszawa: Państwowe Wydawnictwo Naukowe.

Borkowski, J., Inglot, S. (Eds.). (1995). *Historia chłopów polskich* (Wyd. 2). Wrocław: Wydawnictwo Uniwersytetu Wrocławskiego.

Burzyński, A., & Madurowicz-Urbańska, H. (1982). *Informator statystyczny do dziejów przemysłu w Galicji: górnictwo, hutnictwo i przemysł rafineryjny (struktura zatrudnienia na tle wartości produkcji)*. Kraków: UJ.

Buszko, J. (1989). *Galicja 1859–1914: polski Piemont?* Warszawa: Krajowa Agencja Wydawnicza.

Daszyk, K. K., Kargol, T., Szubert, T., & Towarzystwo Wydawnicze "Historia Iagellonica" (Eds.). (2016). *Rok 1846 w Krakowie i Galicji: odniesienia, interpretacje, pamięć*. Kraków: Towarzystwo Wydawnicze "Historia Iagellonica".

Dybiec, J., Krawczyk, J., Meissner, A., et al. (Eds.). (2015). *Szkolnictwo i oświata w Galicji 1772–1918*. Rzeszów: Wydawnictwo Uniwersytetu Rzeszowskiego.

Dzięciołowski, S. (Ed.). (1989). *Towarzystwo Demokratyczne Polskie: akt założenia, Manifest Wielki*. Warszawa: Epoka.

Galek, C. (2015). *Obraz szkoły w II połowie XIX wieku w zaborze rosyjskim w świetle pamiętników i literatury pięknej*. Zamość: Wyższa Szkoła Zarządzania i Administracji.

Galek, C. (2016). *Szkoła polska drugiej połowy XIX wieku w zaborze pruskim w świetle pamiętników i literatury pięknej*. Zamość: Wyższa Szkoła Zarządzania i Administracji.

Grochulska, B., & Pruss, W. (Eds.). (1983). *Z dziejów rzemiosła warszawskiego*. Warszawa: Państwowe Wydawnictwo Naukowe.

Groniowski, K. (1976). *Uwłaszczenie chłopów w Polsce: geneza-realizacja-skutki*. Warszawa: Wiedza Powszechna.

Grzybowski, K. (1959). *Galicja 1848–1914: historia ustroju politycznego na tle ustroju politycznego Austrii*. Zakład Narodowy im. Ossolińskich.

Ihnatowicz, I. (1972). *Burżuazja warszawska*. Państwowe Wydawnictwo Naukowe.

Janczak, J. (1982). *Ludność Łodzi Przemysłowej 1820–1914*. Łódź: Acta Universitatis Lodziensis. Folia Historica.

Janczak, J. K. (1995). Statistics of population and demographic development of the Congress Kingdom of Poland 1815–1900. *Polish Population Review, 6*, 44–81.

Janowski, M. (2004). *Polish liberal thought before 1918*. Budapest and New York: Central European University Press.

Jedlicki, J. (1964). *Nieudana próba kapitalistycznej industralizacji: analiza państwowego gospodarstwa przemysłowego w Królestwie Polskim XIX w.* Warszawa: Książka i Wiedza.

Jedlicki, J., Janowski, M., Micińska, M., & Korecki, T. (2014). *A history of the Polish intelligentsia*. Peter Lang Edition.

Jelonek, A. (1967). *Ludność miast i osiedli typu miejskiego na ziemiach Polski od 1810 do 1960 r.* Instytut Geografii Polskiej Akademii Nauk.

Jezierski, A. (1967). *Handel zagraniczny Królewstwa Polskiego 1815–1914.* Państwowe Wydawnictwo Naukowe.

Joka, J. (Ed.). (1972). *Studia i materiały do dziejów miasta Białegostoku: praca zbiorowa. T. 3.* Białystok: Państwowe Wydawnictwo Naukowe.

Kaczyńska, E. (1974). *Społeczeństwo i gospodarka północno-wschodnich ziem Królewstwa Polskiego w okresie rozkwitu kapitalizmu.* Wydawnictwo Uniwersytetu Warszawskiego.

Kalabiński, S., & Kaczyńska, E. (1986). *Pierwszy okres przemysłu i klasy robotniczej Białostocczyzny: 1807–1870.* Warszawa: Państwowe Wydawnictwo Naukowe.

Kalembka, S. (2003). *Wielka Emigracja 1831–1863.* Toruń: Wydawnictwo Adam Marszałek.

Kaps, K. (2015). *Ungleiche Entwicklung in Zentraleuropa: Galizien zwischen überregionaler Verflechtung und imperialer Politik (1772–1914).* Böhlau Verlag Wien.

Karłowska-Grenda, G., & Nawrot-Borowska, M. (2004). Metody nauczania domowego w rodzinie polskiej w zaborze rosyjskim w XIX i na początku XX wieku. *Acta Elbingensia Rocz Nauk Elbląskiej Uczel Humanist-Ekon, 119–133.*

Karpineć, Ì. (1932). *Ilość osad miejskich byłej Galicji i podział ich na miasta i miasteczka.* Lwów: sgł. Kasa im. J. Mianowskiego, Instytut Popierania Polskiej Twórczości Naukowej.

Kazimierski, J. (Ed.). (1977). *Społeczeństwo Warszawy w rozwoju historycznym.* Warszawa: Państwowe Wydawnictwo Naukowe.

Kieniewicz, S. (1953). *Sprawa włościańska w powstaniu styczniowym.* Zakład im. Ossslińskich.

Kieniewicz, S. (1963). *Powstanie styczniowe 1863.* Polskie Towarzystwo Historyczne.

Kieniewicz, S. (1964). *Powstanie styczniowe 1863.* Polskie Towarzystwo Historyczne.

Kieniewicz, S. (1972). *Powstanie styczniowe.* Państwowe Wydawnictwo Naukowe.

Kizwalter, T. (1999). *O nowoczesności narodu: przypadek Polski.* Semper.

Kizwalter, T., & Skowronek, J. (Eds.). (1988). *Droga do niepodległości czy program defensywny? praca organiczna – programy i motywy.* Warszawa: Pax.

Kloczkowski, J. (Ed.). (2004). *Póki my żyjemy: tradycje insurekcyjne w myśli polskiej.* Warszawa: Muzeum Powstania Warszawskiego.

Kołodziejczyk, R. (1957). *Kształtowanie się burżuazji w Królestwie Polskim 1815–1850.* Warszawa: Państwowe Wydawnictwo Naukowe.

Kołodziejczyk, R. (1968). *Portret warszawskiego milionera*. Warszawa: Książka i Wiedza.

Kołodziejczyk, R. (1979). *Burżuazja polska w XIX i XX wieku: szkice historyczne*. Warszawa: Państwowy Instytut Wydawniczy.

Kołodziejczyk, R. (Ed.). (1981). *Klasa robotnicza i ruch robotniczy na zachodnim Mazowszu 1878–1948: materiały z sesji popularnonaukowej, Żyrardów, 5–6 grudnia 1978 r.* Książka i Wiedza, Warszawa.

Kosicka-Pajewska, A. (2002). *Zachowawcza myśl polityczna w Galicji w latach 1864–1914*. Poznań: Wydawnictwo Uniwersytetu Adama Mickiewicza.

Kowalska, S., Jedlicki, J., & Jezierski, A. (1958). *Ekonomika górnictwa i hutnictwa w Królestwie Polskim 1831–1864*. Warszawa: Państwowe Wydawnictwo Naukowe.

Koziarski, S. M. (1993). *Sieć kolejowa Polski w latach 1842–1918*. Opole: PIN-IŚ.

Król, M. (Ed.). (1982). *Stańczycy: antologia myśli społecznej i politycznej konserwatystów krakowskich*. Warszawa: Pax.

Król, M. (1985). *Konserwatyści a niepodległość: studia nad polską myślą konserwatywną XIX wieku*. Warszawa: Pax.

Kwak, J. (1987). *Klęski elementarne w miastach górnośląskich (w XVIII i w pierwszej połowie XIX w.)*. Opole: Wydawnictwo IŚ.

Leskiewicz, J. (1961). *Warszawa i jej inteligencja po powstaniu styczniowym, 1864–1870*. Państwowe Wydawnictwo Naukowe.

Leszczyńska, C. (2006). Polska bankowość centralna 1828–1989: Bank Polski, Polska Krajowa Kasa Pożyczkowa, Bank Polski SA, Narodowy Bank Polski. *Bank Kredyt*, Wyd Pol no. 2, 43.

Leszczyńska, C. (2010). *Zarys historii polskiej bankowości centralnej*. Warszawa: Narodowy Bank Polski. Departament Edukacji i Wydawnictw.

Lisicki, H. (1879). Aleksander Wielopolski: 1803–1877. 4: Przyczyny powstania r. 1830–1831; Papiery z misyi do Londynu; List szlachcica polskiego do ks. Metternicha; Dokumenta z r. 1862. Drukarnia "Czasu", Kraków.

List, F. (1856). *The national system of political economy*. J. B. Lippincott & Company.

Łuczak, C. (1973). *Dzieje Wielkopolski: Lata 1793–1918*. Poznańskie: Wydawnictwo Poznańskie.

Ludwikowski, R. R. (1976). *Konserwatyzm Królestwa Polskiego w okresie międzypowstaniowym =: (z rozważań na ideologią i polityką) = De conservatismo Regni Polaniae tempore inter duas insurrectiones: (meditationes de ideologia et politica)*. Kraków: UJ: Państwowe Wydawnictwo Naukowe.

Ludwikowski, R. R. (1991). *Continuity and change in Poland: Conservatism in Polish political thought*. Washington, DC: The Catholic University of America Press.

Ludwikowski, R. R. (2012). *Historia polskiej myśli politycznej*. Warszawa: Wolters Kluwer Polska.

Łukasiewicz, J. (1963). *Przewrót techniczny w przemyśle Królestwa Polskiego 1852–1886*. Warszawa: Państwowe Wydawnictwo Naukowe.

Mażewski, L. (2012). *Aleksander Wielopolski: Próba ustrojowej rekonstrukcji Królestwa Polskiego w latach 1861–1862*. Pracownia Wydawnicza Elset.

Mażewski, L. (2015a). Namiestnictwo Iwana Paskiewicza: kształtowanie się nowego systemy politycznego w Królestwie Polskim w latach 1830–1832. In *Królestwo Polskie w okresie namiestnictwa Iwana Paskiewicza 1832–1856. System polityczny, prawo i statut organiczny z 26 lutego 1832r* (pp. 163–174). Radzymin: Wydawnictwo von borowiecky.

Mażewski, L. (Ed.). (2015b). *Królestwo Polskie w okresie namiestnictwa Iwana Paskiewicza (1832–1856): system polityczny, prawo i statut organiczny z 26 lutego 1832 r*. Radzymin: Wydawnictwo von borowiecky.

Mielcarek, A. (2000). *Transport drogowy, wodny i kolejowy w gospodarce prowincji pomorskiej w latach 1815–1914* (Wyd. 1). Szczecin: Wydawnictwo Naukowe Uniwersytetu Szczecińskiego.

Miodunka, P. (2014). Wybrane problemy rozwoju małych miast galicyjskich w okresie przedautonomicznym (1772–1866). *Zeszyty Naukowe Uniwersytetu Ekonomicznego w Krakowie*, 23–43. https://doi.org/10.15678/ZNUEK. 2014.0935.1102

Misztal, S. (1970). *Przemiany w strukturze przestrzennej przemysłu na ziemiach polskich w latach 1860–1965*. Warszawa: Państwowe Wydawnictwo Naukowe.

Myszczyszyn, J. (2016). Powstanie i rozwój kolei żelaznych w prowincji Pomorze jako wyraz aktywności lokalnych środowisk i sektora publicznego. *Studia z Historii Społeczno-Gospodarczej XIX i XX wieku, 16*. https://doi. org/10.18778/2080-8313.16.06

Myszczyszyn, J., Uniwersytet Łódzki, & Wydawnictwo. (2013). *Wpływ kolei żelaznych na wzrost gospodarczy Niemiec (1840–1913)*. Łódź: Wydawnictwo Uniwersytetu Łódzkiego.

Ossowski, J. (2007). Józef Supiński: pionier polskiej socjologii i ekonomii społecznej. *Pieniądze i Więź, 4*, 28.

Pawłowski, F., Ślusarek, K., & Turek, W. P. (1994). *Drobna szlachta w Galicji, 1772–1848*. Księgarnia Akademicka.

Pietrzak-Pawłowska, I. (Ed.). (1970). *Uprzemysłowienie ziem polskich w XIX i XX wieku: studia i materiały.* Wrocław: Zakład Narodowy im. Ossolińskich Wydawnictwo PAN.

Pilch, A. (Ed.). (1984). *Emigracja z ziem polskich w czasach nowożytnych i najnowszych (XVIII-XX w.).* Warszawa: Państwowe Wydawnictwo Naukowe.

Pruss, W. (1977). *Rozwój przemysłu warszawskiego w latach 1864–1914.* Warszawa: Państwowe Wydawnictwo Naukowe.

Puś, W. (1987). *Dzieje Łodzi przemysłowej: zarys historii.* Łódź: Muzeum Historii Miasta Łodzi. Centrum Informacji Kulturalnej.

Rezler, M. (2000). *Hipolit Cegielski: 1813–1868.* Poznań: Wydawnictwo WBP.

Rosevaere, I. M. (1969). From reform to rebellion: A. Wielopolski and the Polish question, 1861–1863. *Canadian-American Slavic Studies, 3,* 263–285. https://doi.org/10.1163/221023969X00394b

Rosin, R., Baranowski, B., Fijałek, J., & Badziak, K. (Eds.). (1989). *Łódź: dzieje miasta. T. 1: Do 1918 r[oku]* (Wyd. 2). Warszawa and Łódź: Państwowe Wydawnictwo Naukowe.

Sikorska-Kulesza, J. (1995). *Deklasacja drobnej szlachty na Litwie i Białorusi w XIX wieku.* Pruszków: Ajaks.

Skrzydło, L. (2000). *Rody fabrykanckie* (Wyd. 2). Łódź: Oficyna Bibliofilów.

Ślusarek, K. (2002). *Uwłaszczenie chłopów w Galicji zachodniej.* Kraków: Historia Iagellonica.

Ślusarek, K. (2012). Austria wobec polskiej szlachty z Galicji w latach 1772–1861. *Studia Historyczne.,* Kraków, *55,* 185–200.

Ślusarek, K. (2017). Wieś galicyjska 1772–1914: stagnacja czy rozwój? *Rocznik Łódzki.,* Wydawnictwo Poświęcone Dziejom Łodzi Ziem Województwa Łódzkiego, *66,* 151–165.

Sobieszczański, F. M. (1860). *Kalendarz wydawany przez Obserwatoryum Astronomiczne Warszawskie na rok zwyczajny 1861.* Warszawa: Obserwatoryum Astronomiczne Warszawskie.

Statistischen Central-Commission. (1874). *Orts-Repertorium des Königreiches Galizien und Lodomerien mit dem Grossherzogthume Krakau: auf Grund d. Volkszählung vom Jahre 1869.* Berlin: Carl Gerold's Sohn.

Stefański, K. (2014). *Wielkie rody fabrykanckie Łodzi i ich rola w ukształtowaniu oblicza miasta: Geyerowie, Scheiblerowie, Poznańscy, Heinzlowie, Kindermannowie.* Łódź: Księży Młyn Dom Wydawniczy Michał Koliński.

Supiński, J., Bernacki, W., & Kuczkiewicz-Fraś, A. (2010). *Szkoła polska gospodarki społecznej: wybór pism.* Kraków: Ośrodek Myśli Politycznej.

Sykulski, L. (2007). *Edward Dembowski (1822–1846): biografia polityczna.* Toruń: Wydawnictwo Naukowe Grado.

Szewczuk, J., & Bujak, F. (1939). *Kronika klęsk elementarnych w Galicji w latach 1772–1848: z wykresami.* Lwów: skł. gł. Kasa im. J. Mianowskiego. Instytut Popierania Polskiej Twórczości Naukowej.

Temkinowa, H. (1962). *Gromady Ludu Polskiego: zarys ideologii.* Warszawa: Książka i Wiedza.

Tipton, F. B. (1976). *Regional variations in the economic development of Germany during the nineteenth century.* Wesleyan University Press.

Topolski, J. (1973). *Dzieje Wielkopolski: Lata 1793–1918.* Poznańskie: Wydawnictwo Poznańskie.

Trencsényi, B., Janowski, M., Baár, M., et al. (2016). *A history of modern political thought in East Central Europe: Negotiating modernity in the "long nineteenth century".* Oxford: Oxford University Press.

Trzeciakowski, L. (2003). *Posłowie polscy w Berlinie 1848–1928.* Warszawa: Wydawnictwo Sejmowe: Kancelaria Sejmu.

Vushko, I. (2015). *The politics of cultural retreat: Imperial bureaucracy in Austrian Galicia, 1772–1867.* Yale University Press.

Walicki, A. (1994). *Philosophy and romantic nationalism: The case of Poland.* Notre Dame, IN: University of Notre Dame Press.

Walicki, A., Mencwel, A., & Walicki, A. (2009). *Filozofia polskiego romantyzmu.* Kraków: Towarzystwo Autorów i Wydawców Prac Naukowych Universitas.

Węgrzynowicz, S. (2014). *Patrioci i zdrajcy: społeczeństwo Królestwa Polskiego wobec mikołajowskiej polityki Rosji w latach 1846–1856.* Kraków: Wydawnictwo Arcana.

Werwicki, A. (1957). *Białostocki okręg przemysłu włókienniczego do 1945 roku: czynniki rozwoju i zagadnienia lokalizacyjne.* Warszawa: Państwowe Wydawnictwo Naukowe.

Wolff, L. (2012). *The idea of Galicia: History and fantasy in Habsburg political culture.* Stanford, CA: Stanford University Press.

Załęski, W. (1876). *Statystyka porównawcza Królestwa Polskiego: ludność i stosunki ekonomiczne.* Warszawa: Gebethner i Wolff.

Żaliński, H. (1990). *Poglądy Hotelu Lambert na kształt powstania zbrojnego 1832–1846.* Kraków: Wydawnictwo Naukowe WSP.

Żor, A. (2011). *Kronenberg: dzieje fortuny.* Warszawa: Wydawnictwo Naukowe PWN.

Żurawski vel Grajewski, R. P. (Ed.). (2014). *Rządy bez ziemi: struktury władzy na uchodźstwie.* Warszawa: Wydawnictwo DiG.

6

The Dawn of Modern Economic Growth: Period of Late Industrialization (1870–1914)

1 Politics

The period between 1870 and 1914 is the time of the emergence of modern political movements on the Polish lands. Directly after the January Uprising, the political scene in all the partitions was dominated by the conciliatory faction, holding conservative and liberal views. In Galicia, they started to play an active role in the political life of the monarchy as early as in the 1870s—representatives of conservative groups from Kraków and Eastern Galicia became the ministers for Galicia and the governors of Galicia (Agenor Gołuchowski Jun, Kazimierz Badeni, Julian Dunajewski, Michal Bobrzyński), but they also held important cabinet positions in Vienna, including the positions of the minister of the treasury (Dunajewski and Leon Biliński), the minister of home affairs (Badeni), and diplomacy (Gołuchowski Jun). There was a Polish representation in the parliament in Vienna, active until 1918. Galicia was also the birthplace of the Polish peasant movement; the first peasants' parties created there included the Union of the Peasants' Party, one of the first people's parties in Europe (1893). Moreover, the two phenomena which developed among the peasants in all the partitions in the decades after

© The Author(s) 2018
P. Koryś, *Poland From Partitions to EU Accession*,
https://doi.org/10.1007/978-3-319-97126-1_6

1870 were the co-operative movement and the gradual process of the creation and strengthening of the national identity (Jachymek et al. 1996; Wapiński 1997). Co-operatives organized often with the help of landowners focused on the improvement of agricultural production, as well as organizing the trade of agricultural products, combating illiteracy among peasants, and developing Raiffeisen-style credit unions. Newly organized peasant parties and Catholic Church promoted a Polish identity among peasants.

In Prussian Greater Poland and the Kingdom of Poland, it is more difficult to follow the political influences within the Polish community, as a political career was impossible for the Poles until the beginning of the twentieth century, but there, too, the faction which gained importance was the conciliatory one, representing the Positivist ideas of organic work—building the modern nation by means of supporting the economic and cultural development of the rural and urban lower classes, including factory workers. According to the proponents of organic work, the construction of the strong foundations of development required peace and stability, the enrichment of the society, and avoidance of subsequent ill-advised rebellions. Throughout the period under consideration, the Polish under the Prussian rule was represented in the Prussian parliament (later, German and Prussian). From 1848, there was a Polish group in the Prussian parliament in Berlin (its numbers varied from just over 10 to 20-odd representatives); after 1871, it acted in the Reichstag, but it had hardly any influence on the decisions concerning the Polish districts. It was active until 1918. Over time, the right wing of Polish politics in the Prussian partition, traditionally filled by liberal and conservative members of the bourgeoisie and the landed gentry, was taken over by representatives holding national-democratic views (Trzeciakowski 2003).

The phenomenon which turned out to be very important in the long term was the emergence of new political movements, mostly illegal as a result of the bans and restrictions imposed on Polish political organizations in the Prussian and Russian partitions. Political movements, from conservative to radical, developed with particular intensity in the Kingdom of Poland, where, in spite of the restrictions, the final decades of the nineteenth century witnessed the creation of most of the organizations, which later became major actors on the political scene of the restored Poland, including the Polish Socialist Party (*PPS*) and National Democracy. The Kingdom of Poland was also the birthplace of the Polish workers' and communist movement, in which an important role was played by Rosa Luxemburg (who soon emigrated to Germany and as a naturalized German became one of the leaders of the socialist movement there). Some of these political movements were radical, like the Polish Socialist Party, which divided in 1905 and one part of it got involved in urban guerrilla fight and conducted numerous attacks and assaults, or early National Democracy, but some were conciliatory, like some conservative groups, for example, the Real Politics Party. At the beginning of the twentieth century, the law changed, and they were able to conduct legal activity. Another group that began legal activity after 1905 was National Democracy, which also introduced a few representatives to the newly created Russian parliament, the Duma. The Polish group in the Duma existed for three terms, until 1915. It was dominated by the members of National Democracy, and increasingly represented the interests of the bourgeoisie and landowners, and so did the whole Duma, as the electoral system promoted these particular groups.

This was the period when Prussia and Russia implemented liberalization policy on the Polish lands incorporated into their states. In Greater Poland and West Prussia, the German state conducted a large-scale operation of supporting the immigration and settlement of Germans. The key role was played by the Colonization Commission (Königlich Preußische Ansiedlungskommission in den Provinzen Westpreußen und Posen), created in 1886, and by Deutscher Ostmarkenverein, active in Greater Poland and West Prussia (Pragier 1920). The German state also supported buying up land; by WWI, the Colonization Commission was involved in buying up about 8% of the agricultural land of Greater Poland and West Prussia. As a result of German settlement by 1906, the German population increased by 150,000 people. Germany created anti-Polish regulations (like the prohibition to use Polish language in public in the towns where the Polish population was under 60%) or used the existing regulations against the Polish (e.g. by rejecting their building permit applications). Between 1885 and 1890, the Polish and Jewish citizens of Russia and Austria (i.e. non-Prussian citizens), migrating in search of work and employed in agriculture and industry (mostly in Upper Silesia), were brutally expelled from Prussia, even if they had lived in Prussia for many years. In Polish history, this event, which affected 30,000 people, is remembered as the Prussian Deportations and has become a symbol of the anti-Polish policy of the government in Berlin. The pressure of employers, the shortage of labour, and the public outcry in Germany led to softening the expulsion policy after 1890. The Poles were allowed to come to Prussia and be employed, but only as seasonal workers.

Germany conducted intense Germanization by means of the legal measures introduced between 1871 and 1878, during Kulturkampf (Zieliński 2011). On the Polish lands, it involved increasing the control over the Roman Catholic Church and limiting its rights and autonomy. Some of the regulations also pertained to the Lutheran Church, most of them comprised all Prussia and later all Germany. However, because of the particular role of the Roman Catholic Church in preserving the Polish identity, and because of its great influence on the Polish majority in the Polish lands, these regulations were particularly distressing for the Polish. The Germanization of schools had a similar effect—by the mid-1870s, the Polish language was practically eradicated from education and, after 1894, Germanization became particularly strong (Galek 2016).

Russia intensified the Russification of the Polish lands after the January Uprising. The state introduced martial law in the Congress Kingdom, abolished the Unitarian Church (the Chelm Diocese), confiscated some of the property of the Roman Catholic Church, and fully Russified education from primary to university level. The administration reform conducted at the time resulted in the full integration of the Polish lands with Russia and the disappearance of the last remnants of Polish autonomy. In 1885, the Bank of Poland was liquidated. There were also harsh measures taken against the insurgents and, later, against the people involved in illegal political activity: they were banished to Siberia for many years, without the possibility of returning to Poland. Banishment to Siberia had already been used after the Bar Confederation in the eighteenth century and after the November Uprising (1830–1831) but, after the January Uprising (1863–1864), it affected the greatest so far number of people— about 17,000 (Korobowicz and Witkowski 2012).

At the beginning of the twentieth century, Russia's defeat in the war against Japan (1905), its internal problems (1905 Russian revolution) and the revolts, strikes, and tension on the Polish lands (Revolution in the Kingdom of Poland, 1905–1907) resulted in the softening of the Russification policy. The new regulations after 1905 allowed for Polish private education and the development of the co-operative movement and brought back the use of the Polish language in administration at the level of the commune.

The period of the first globalization was the time of the emergence of modern mass political movements in the Polish lands. Simultaneously, elements of parliamentarian democracy were introduced in the partitioning states. Over time, the Poles became represented in their parliaments, including the representatives of both the traditional conservative and liberal political factions and the new, nationalist, peasant, and socialist movements. Some parts of Poland, particularly Galicia, obtained increasing autonomy in conducting its internal policy. The political factions created at the time continued after the war and continued their existence in the first parliaments of the restored Poland.

2   Ideas

After 1850, economic and social sciences started to institutionalize in Poland, and political thinkers were joined by professional economists both in the political debate and on public positions (e.g. Leon Biliński and Julian Dunajewski held prominent offices in Austria). It is worth noting that, unlike in the earlier periods, the Polish political thought got closer to the Western European ideas. The process of the institutionalization of the social sciences, including economics and sociology, which started in this period, resulted in the growing reception and application of Western ideas by Polish intellectuals and thinkers. The impact of the conservative and liberal tradition may be observed particularly among older generations and in some new academic schools. The best example is the Cracow school of economics, founded by academics related to the conservative circles of the Cracow historical school. It represented the classical tradition, and had some intellectual as well as institutional ties with the Austrian school of economics (Król 1982, 1985; Jaskólski 2014).

The ideas that gained popularity among the younger generation of social critics included socialist and communist thought. It was particularly the Marxist philosophy that influenced numerous intellectuals, activists, and politicians, who were later involved in different political movements, such as the Communist Party, the Socialist Party (e.g. Józef Piłsudski, Ignacy Daszyński), and the Nationalist Party (e.g. Stanisław and Władysław Grabski). Some concepts derived from the Positivist tradition, applied to social sciences and international relations, including Darwinism and Spencerism, were also widely used in the debates (e.g. Aleksander Świętochowski, Roman Dmowski, Zygmunt Balicki). Moreover, the German economic tradition, particularly the historical school of economics, attracted some interest and influenced some development ideas (Brykalska 1987; Wójcik 1995; Bończa-Tomaszewski 2001; Balicki 2008; Koryś 2008; Popławski 2012).

One of the most interesting ideas formulated by professional economists was the one created by Biliński, who advocated public infrastructural investments as well as the public funding of culture and education. Economists also saw the agrarian reform as an important issue. Józef Milewski, Adam Krzyżanowski, and Stanisław Grabski wanted to stop the process of the fragmentation of peasant households, but they differed in their opinions on parcelling out the big agricultural estates into peasant plots. Milewski considered it ill-advised, while the conservative Adam Krzyżanowski's policy for the Austrian partition involved parcelling out inefficient estates and supporting emigration. Stanisław Grabski, connected with the National Democracy, formulated a policy for the Congress Kingdom, where the key element for the development of Poland was the modernization of agriculture. He wanted to parcel out the estates, and he promoted mutual help and co-operatives, supported by the elites. Generally, however, the economists' discussion was mostly academic and did not become practice-oriented until the restoration of the state in 1918 (Guzicki and Żurawicki 1969; Grzybek 2005, 2012). In last decades of nineteenth century, an increasing amount of statistical data was published, and Lwów and Warszawa became important centres for statistics, with Tadeusz Piłat (in Lwów) and Witold Załęski (in Warszawa), who was interested both in the statistical science itself and in its application in the studies of industrialization and economic development. The data collected were the basis for the discussion on the development of the particular regions (Berger 2010; Grzybek 2012).

The period was also the time of the formation of modern political movements, and the main participants of the discussions were their ideologists. In the aftermath of the defeat of the January Uprising, the policy of a radical fight for independence was superseded by the activity aiming to ensure the greatest possible autonomy within the political reality of the time. The Positivist circles in Galicia and the Congress Kingdom criticized the fight for independence and advocated the solutions already implemented in the Prussian Greater Poland and theorized by Józef Supiński, that is, organic work, aiming to support the economic development of rural and peripheral regions, and educating the lower classes with a view to enabling upward mobility. It was to be a bottom-up movement, which would release social transfer and help to reconstruct the national identity, but also create conditions for the economic success of the Polish community. The group of the new theorists of the Positivist movement included Aleksander Świętochowski and Ludwik Gumplowicz, who later became one of the founders of European sociology (Śliwa 1995).

The Positivist movement developed two important schools of thought involved in the critical analysis of the Polish history. The Cracow school (Józef Szujski, Walerian Kalinka, Michał Bobrzyński) looked for internal reasons for the decline of the Commonwealth and indicated the archaic political and social institutions. The Warsaw school (Tadeusz Korzon, Władysław Smoleński) presented a more optimistic view of the Polish history and looked for the development potential, particularly during the Enlightenment, which they treated as a moment when there was a change of the mindset and reforms that brought Poland closer to the West. The Cracow historians were involved in politics, and their views on Polish history justified their loyalist attitude towards Austria. The success of the conciliatory loyalist attitude and the involvement in the political life of the monarchy resulted in the flourishing of Polish culture in Kraków and became perceived by part of the elite as a (temporary or permanent) way to protect the Polish national identity. In effect, the new politically realistic approach involving conciliation in order to create conditions for social and economic development gained some popularity among the elite in the Russian and Prussian partitions (Łepkowski 1960; Kizwalter 1999; Janowski 2004; Trencsényi et al. 2016).

The Positivist, liberal, and conservative social thought involved social criticism which extended beyond the political debate and the dichotomy between the rebellious and the loyalist. Apart from the views of Józef Supiński, which were discussed in the previous chapter, an example of a critical analysis of the reality are the writings of Stanisław Szczepanowski, an entrepreneur and social thinker, who wrote the pamphlet *The Poverty in Galicia in Numbers* (Szczepanowski 1888), where he discussed the situation of the Polish peasants in Galicia and presented them as Poland's greatest potential for the future. For this reason, according to him, investing in compulsory education in the country and supporting the modernization would help to eliminate poverty and would become the springboard for future development. Szczepanowski used the poverty in Galicia as the narrative structure for his analysis, but his description of the poverty was clearly exaggerated. The contemporary statistical publications, such as the ones prepared by Tadeusz Piłat (who critically reviewed Szczepanowski's pamphlet), help to create a more realistic picture of the actual socioeconomic situation in the region (Grzybek 2012).

Social criticism was also reflected in literature, which often described the economic situation of the Poles, which was the concern of authors such as Bolesław Prus and Eliza Orzeszkowa, or the Nobel Prize winners Władysław Reymont and Henryk Sienkiewicz. Their descriptions of villages and workers' districts, of the lifestyle of the middle and upper classes, and of the social disparities sometimes took on the character of an anthropological study. They gave insight into the process of the emergence of industrial cities (Warszawa, Łódź), the transformations in the country, or the lifestyle changes of the elite adjusting to the European standards. Simultaneously, these authors included considerable political and economic criticism. Prus focused on the Positivist view that economic development should precede the further fight for independence. On the other hand, in his novel about Łódź, *The Promised Land*, Władysław Reymont warned against the expansion of foreign capital and its potentially exploitative character, and it is the topic which has been recurring in the Polish debate up to the modern times.

Modernists connected with so-called Young Poland in the late nineteenth and early twentieth centuries offered another view in their social critique. They criticized the Positivists, bourgeoisie, and civilization and praised locality, rurality, and the Polish tradition, to some extent reviving the Romantic tradition. From this perspective, at the beginning of the twentieth century, Stefan Żeromski, a member of this literary movement, criticized the conciliatory policy of the growing numbers of the elite. Żeromski's social critique was close to the socioeconomic ideas of the socialist movement and of the Polish Socialist Party (*PPS*) in particular (Cywiński 1985; Mencwel 1997, 2009).

The socialist movement itself was torn by internal conflict concerning their goals, that is, whether they should aim at restoring Poland or at creating a pan-European workers' republic (Snyder 1997). Some members regarded themselves as responsible for the continuation of the Polish independence and revolutionary tradition, and the Poland they wanted to restore was to be a modern, socially just republic of the people, who were all equal. Others questioned this approach and engaged in the international socialist movement. The former group included Józef Piłsudski (Król and Karpiński 1997; Snyder et al. 2015), the future military leader against the Bolsheviks in the victorious Battle of Warsaw in 1920, and some of his entourage, the latter group included Rosa Luxemburg and Feliks Dzierżyński (Blobaum 1984; Ślęzak and Śliwa 2004; Marzec 2016).

The major competitor of the socialists as a mass political movement was National Democracy, which emerged after 1880 and in the first decades of its activity was one of the radical political movements. Its ideological foundation was created by Zygmunt Miłkowski (Jeż 2009), a writer and political activist working on emigration. He formulated the concept of active defence, a third path to regaining independence, going beyond organic work and uprisings, and aiming to create the modern national identity among the masses. The programme of the emancipation of the Polish nation formulated by the nationalists at the time became the foundation of the political programme of National Democracy in the Second Republic of Poland. The ideologists emphasized the modernization imitating the West while preserving the Polish national identity (Roman Dmowski) and the precedence of national over individual interests in the social and economic development (Dmowski, Zygmunt Balicki). In a broader perspective, they saw the functioning of nations in terms of social Darwinism (or Spencerism) and competition rather than co-operation. According to them, the key factor of internal policy was national rather than class solidarity. At the beginning of the twentieth century, the national democratic movement got involved in the legal political activity and their programme got closer to that of the conciliatory circles (Wapiński 1980; Porter 2000; Bończa-Tomaszewski 2001; Snyder et al. 2015; Marzec 2016).

In the period after the January Uprising, the debate on economic development was vastly limited. Instead of the arguments about the role of the state in stimulating development, the debate started to focus on the improvement of the standard of living on the micro-economic scale. The participants of the discussions could not have missed the relation between the standard of living and the popularity of the political ideas (particularly nationalist) among the masses. However, the loss of influence on the economic policy resulted in changing the perception of where the potential for development was to be found.

3   Territory and Population

The geopolitical shape of the Polish lands remained stable throughout the period of the first globalization. After the January Uprising, practically until WWI, there were only very slight changes of both internal and external borders. There were some alterations of the provincial borders in the Kingdom of Poland, and the only important one was the creation of the Chelm province out of the lands of the provinces of Siedlce and Lublin, and the decision to exclude it from the territory of the Vistula Country—former Kingdom of Poland (which reduced its territory by 13%) and incorporate it into Russia, with the view to intensifying the Russification of the Unitarian Catholics, who started to convert to Roman Catholicism after the abolishment of their church. However, this decision was made in 1915 and was not implemented, because the whole territory of the Kingdom was occupied by the German and Austrian armies.

The final decades of the nineteenth century was the time of rapid population growth (resulting from high birth rate and decreasing mortality rate), quick urbanization, and big migration, both internally and abroad (Główny Urząd Statystyczny 1993). These processes are documented by the growing numbers of statistical data being collected, especially the regular censuses. Russia was an exception, as only one census was conducted there in 1897, and the preparations for the next one were interrupted by the war (Łukasiewicz 2009).

A particularly high rate of population growth can be observed in the Congress Kingdom. The rapid population increase was accompanied by the growth of urban population and a notable development of several municipal centres. At the beginning of the twentieth century Warszawa became one of the biggest cities in Europe, and Łódź (Janczak 1982) developed at an impressive rate. Łódź and Warszawa were among the ten biggest cities of the Russian Empire. In the south, near the border with Silesia, there was rapid development of the urban areas of Będzin, Siewierz and the mining villages of the former Southern Industrial Area created by Staszic in the first decades of the nineteenth century. The two towns which developed at the time were Sosnowiec, which obtained the municipal charter in 1902, with over 60,000 inhabitants and reaching almost 100,000 at the beginning of WWI, and Dąbrowa Górnicza, which already had almost 30,000 inhabitants when it obtained the municipal charter from Austria in 1916 (Jelonek 1967). The urban population grew very rapidly: in 1910, 15% of the population of the Kingdom lived in its five biggest cities (including the industrial towns Łódź, Sosnowiec, and Częstochowa) and almost 30% in towns over 5000 people, while 85 years earlier, it was only 5%.

Apart from Warszawa, the only metropolitan area on the territory of present-day Poland was Wrocław (Breslau), the capital of the German province of Silesia (both Breslau and most of Silesia, excluding Upper Silesia with growing Polish speaking population, were inhabited by small Polish minority; cf. table 6.1). In Upper Silesia, the urban population grew rapidly, thanks to which the area gradually acquired a metropolitan character. The bigger cities on the territories were Poznań (Posen) and Gdańsk (Danzig) in the Prussian partition, Kraków and Lwów in the Austrian partition, and Wilno (Vilnius), the present-day capital of Lithuania, then on the territory of Russia.

The rapid population growth on the Polish lands was accompanied by the internal migration (connected with urbanization), as well as international migration on a scale unprecedented in the Polish history. Internal migration was directed from the country to the bigger towns and cities and was related with the changing structure of the economy of the Polish regions within the partitioning states. It was also directed from the poorer to the richer regions of the partitioning states, particularly from Galicia to Austria proper and towards the industrial regions of Germany. The biggest waves of short-term migration came from the poorer lands of Austria and Russia (Kingdom of Poland) and headed for Germany. They found seasonal employment in agriculture in eastern and central Germany and in industry, mainly in Silesia. The impact of the internal migration to non-Polish areas of the partitioning states on the population of Polish lands was the same as that of international migration (Krzyżanowski and Kumaniecki 1915; Grabski 1916; Główny Urząd Statystyczny 1993).

Apart from the political emigration after the November Uprising (1830–1831), January Uprising (1863–1864), Cracow Uprising (1846), and the Spring of Nations (1848), and the emigration and labour emigration to neighbouring countries, large-scale international migration towards remote regions of Europe and Americas in search of employment, both short-term and long-term, began in the late nineteenth century. Over the four decades preceding WWI, about 5 million people emigrated from Poland (Krzyżanowski and Kumaniecki 1915; Grabski 1916), mostly from Austrian and Russian parts.

On the other hand, the reconfiguration of the borders of the Pale of Settlement and opening the Kingdom of Poland for the Jewish migration from Russia (1868) resulted in the large inflow of the Jewish population (up to 600,000 people between 1890 and 1907, as a result of which the Jewish immigrants constituted up to 15% of the total population of the Kingdom). The rapid growth and structural change of the Jewish population in Russian Poland (immigrants from Russia and their descendants constituted the majority of Jews in the Kingdom of Poland in the early twentieth century) resulted in growing economic and social tensions between Jews and the Polish majority, and the rise of modern anti-Semitism, which occasionally resulted in anti-Semitic tumults (such as the one in Warszawa in 1881). Waves of anti-Semitism occurred also

Table 6.1 Religion and Polish language on Polish lands, early twentieth century (%)

	Roman-Catholics	Protestants	Orthodox and Greek Catholics	Jews	Use of Polish language or Polish nationality
Russian part					
– Kingdom	76	4	5	15	72
– Ruthenia[a]	6	2	79	13	4
– Lithuania and Belarus	31	1	54	14	6
Prussian part					
– Posen	68	31		1	61
– Silesia	42	56		1	26
– Western Prussia	52	47		1	35
– Eastern Prussia	15	83		1	5
Austrian part					
– Galicia	47		42	11	59
– Austrian Silesia	76	21		3	55

Source: Königlich Preussischen Statistischen Bureaus (1913), Romer and Weinfeld (1917), Wyczański (2003)

[a]Western provinces of Russia (Ruthenia, Lithuania and Belarus) include Grodno, Kowno (Kaunas), Minsk, Mohylew, Vitebsk and Wilno (Vilnius) provinces in the Lithuanian and Belorussian parts, while Kiev, Podole (Podolia), and Wołyń (Volynia) provinces in the Ruthenian part. This territory is larger than eastern part of interwar Poland and covers territories (or parts of territories) of contemporary Lithuania, Latvia, Belarus, and Ukraine

in the Russian Pale of Settlement, including the formerly Polish territories (ethnic structure of Polish lands is presented in Table 6.1).

The rapid growth of the urban population and mass internal and international migration shaped the Polish population in the late nineteenth and early twentieth centuries. Before WWI, Russian Poland, the Prussian partition, and the western portion of Galicia were densely populated by Poles, and the Polish nation (or the Polish-speaking population) became by far the largest nation in Europe without its own state. In the remaining parts of the former Commonwealth, Poles (particularly in Eastern Galicia and western provinces of Russia) were a minority who inhabited towns (like Lwów or Wilno) and were big landowners, while the majority consisted of Ukrainians, Belarusians, or Lithuanians, who were mostly peasants; in this way, the social differences paralleled the ethnic ones. The relatively large Jewish minority, which grew rapidly, particularly in Russian Poland (but also in Galicia), played an important economic and social role, especially in towns. On the other hand, the Jewish minority in the Prussian part was relatively small in numbers.

4   Society

After 1864, there was considerable acceleration of the processes of social modernization resulting from the growing urbanization, relatively quick industrialization, and the disappearance of the main barriers to social mobility.

On the Polish territory within Germany, the regulations that were discussed in the previous chapters resulted in the development of the most modern model of agricultural economy. The effective, well conducted division of the estates and support for bigger peasant farms caused the emergence of the class of richer farmers and a relatively numerous group of farm workers. As a result of intense internal migration to the fastest-growing provinces, the agricultural provinces—Greater Poland, Pomerania, West and East Prussia—suffered the shortage of labour already in the 1870s, and perhaps even earlier. There were also big agricultural estates, now based on paid labour. However, Polish landowners never achieved a status equal to that of the Prussian Junkers, and the Germanization policy, including the buying up of the Polish land, weakened their position even further. Simultaneously, industrialization and the development of a transport infrastructure (i.e. the railway), as well as public investments of the German state, contributed to the urbanization and the development of towns and cities, but also to the diversification of the urban economy.

In Greater Poland, part of West Prussia, and part of Upper Silesia, the German population was in the minority, but their numbers were growing as a result of support from the German state. It encouraged migration of Germans to Polish provinces. The German state also financially supported the development of social organizations of the Germans. There was often economic competition between the Polish and German bourgeoisie in these regions. The state support for the German entrepreneurship was counterbalanced by the involvement of the richer strata of the Polish society, both the bourgeoisie and the landed gentry, resulting in creating, for example, institutions like the *Hotel Bazar* in Poznań, which became the base and the site of numerous socioeconomic enterprises in Greater Poland, such as Polish economic, scientific, and popular education societies and Polish periodicals.

The conflict between the growing German minority and the Polish majority was visible both in towns and in rural regions. It became particularly bitter in that period, apparently overshadowing class conflicts. It was exemplified by the experience of a Polish peasant, Wojciech Drzymała, who was refused a building permit by the German authorities and tried to solve the problem by living in a wagon that he stationed on his land (1904–1909), but also by the school strike in Września (Wreschen) (1901–1902) and mass school strikes in Greater Poland (1906), where Polish children struggled against conducting religion lessons in German, as well as by the many bottom-up initiatives aiming to empower the Polish communities, such as agricultural co-operatives and saving co-operatives, informal schools for peasant children and so on (Miller 2001). The greatest achievement was the development of the co-operative movement, supported by the landowners and contributing to the development of agriculture in Greater Poland and Pomerania, and—later—also in the Kingdom of Poland and Galicia. It helped to modernize peasant agriculture by joint investments in agricultural machines, promoting modern techniques of cultivation and so on. At the end of the nineteenth and the beginning of the twentieth centuries there was dynamic growth of competing Polish and German co-operatives and associations of co-operatives.

At the end of the nineteenth century, there was development of the workers' movement in towns and cities, particularly in Upper Silesia, but also in Greater Poland and Pomerania. It also reflected the ethnic conflict between Poles and Germans, as Polish workers often got involved in the activity of separate Polish trade unions and workers organizations. This phenomenon did not occur in the other partitions, where the colonization was less strongly enforced and the dominance of the Polish majority in the Congress Kingdom and West Galicia remained unchanged throughout the nineteenth century (Kaczyńska 1970).

In the Russian partition fundamental social changes took place both in the rural and urban communities. The enfranchisement of the peasants altered their economic and legal status, but the particular regulations did not contribute to the emergence of modern farm agriculture. The division of land into small plots to include the greatest possible number of peasants, no limitations on the division of property (until the end of the nineteenth century), the still slow and patchy urbanization and industrialization and the quick growth of the rural population contributed to perpetuating the traditional model of poor, small, and mostly subsistent peasant farms. Apart from these, there were still the estates of the big landowners, over time playing an increasingly important role in introducing the new production methods and the co-operative movement. This kind of involvement of the landowners into organic work was modelled on the successful practices of the landed gentry in Greater Poland (Kula 1966; Kula and Leskiewiczowa 1971, 1972; Kochanowicz 2006).

The cities that started to develop into modern industrial centres were Warszawa and Łódź, and the urbanized area of Dabrowa basin near German Upper Silesia with the number of suburban crowded districts and makeshifts such as (up to 100,000 inhabitants in 1915) or much smaller Widzew in Łódź, some villages around Warszawa (e.g. Bródno), or the fast-growing industrial towns such as Sosnowiec and Dąbrowa Górnicza. One of the interesting examples of newly established industrial towns is one of the first factory towns in the Kingdom of Poland, Żyrardów near Warszawa, built around a single large textile factory of Hille and Dittrich. These rapidly growing urban areas were the birthplace of the modern working class. If we consider the present-day Poland, actually, the only places where there were conditions for the development of the modern working class and the bourgeoisie were these few areas in the Congress Kingdom, the big cities and metropolitan areas of Eastern part of Germany and the Polish sliver of the Austrian province of Silesia (and, to some extent, also oil fields of Austria Galicia—but prevailing part of them were located outside the contemporary Eastern border of Poland).

In the Congress Kingdom, the modern industrial conflict appeared relatively early. The growing political power of workers as a new social class was reflected in numerous protests and strikes. The first large-scale strike in the Kingdom broke out in 1883 in Żyrardów, with all the workers of the Hille and Dittrich factory taking part (8000 people). It had the character of a general strike, lasted for several days, and ended in police intervention and the first fatalities in the fights against the Russian police since 1864. In 1892, in Łódź, the strike was even bigger (tens of thousands of workers took part, and the production was stopped for a few days in many factories), just like the strikes connected with the Revolution of 1905 (Kaczyńska 1970; Marzec 2016).

In 1905, workers' protests broke out in the bigger industrial centres of the Kingdom of Poland: Łódź, Warszawa, and the area near Kielce. The revolution started at the same time as the one in Russia (or even earlier, as there were some protests on the Polish territories in 1904), but it had different goals and was not only anti-Tsar, but also called for a fight for independence. In 1905 and 1906, the strikes in Congress Poland involved 1,300,000 workers, and about 400,000 participated in the general strike on 28 January 1905.

The strikes originated in economic problems, but—as a result of the involvement of the Polish intelligentsia—they were increasingly focused on the fight for independence, so the economic conflict was turned into a political one, at least partly. Turning workers into citizens was made easier by the fact that most of the industrial bourgeoisie were of German or Jewish origin, and the state, protecting the interests of the middle class, became associated with the policy which was both anti-worker and anti-Polish, so the new parties of the intelligentsia (the Polish Socialist Party, National Democracy) could interpret the economic conflict as ethnic and/or national. The process of building the national identity of the workers, although faster, was similar to that among the peasants (particularly in the Russian and Austrian partitions)—the key roles were played by the Polish intelligentsia and the Catholic Church. However, among the ideas that were popular with the workers were those of communist groups questioning the need for nation states. At the beginning of her career, Rosa Luxemburg conducted political activity among the workers in Kraków.

In the Austrian partition, like in the former Congress Kingdom, the conflict between the peasants and landowners had subsided. Within a generation from the Galician Slaughter (1846), the peasants of Western Galicia had developed the sense of their Polish identity. This process was supported by the nobility, who conducted education groups and supported the co-operative and mutual help movement. On the other hand, the peasants of Eastern Galicia, in opposition to the cultural identity of the Polish elite, started to create the Ukraininan/Rusyn identity, by means of language and religion. Both in Galicia and in the Russian Vistula Country, the state authorities' expectations remained unfulfilled—the agrarian reforms were supposed to bring about the peasants' loyalty and love for the state, that is, Austria and Russia, respectively. However, as a result of the inefficiency of school systems, but also of the active involvement of the Polish upper classes and the Catholic Church, the peasants developed a Polish identity instead. Apparently, another factor in that process was the fact that the reforms had reduced the economic tension between the landowners, representing Polish culture, and the peasants. It was replaced by the new industrial conflict but, due to the slowness of industrialization in the region, it was much less sharp than in the other partitions (Łuczewski 2012).

It is important to note that the shaping of the modern Polish identity and modern cultural nationalism took place in disconnection from the political institutions and the administration of the partitioning states (partly with the exception of Galicia). Moreover, the political and spiritual leaders of the Polish community had practically no influence on the process of social and economic modernization (discussed in the next section), which depended solely on the policies and decisions of the partitioning states and led to the growing differentiation of the attitudes and lifestyles of the Polish community within the three partitions. It was the state authorities that created the institutional framework for the restructuring of agriculture, decided on the development of infrastructure (Polish lands within the partitioning states constituted remote peripheries which affected the scale, structure, and location of investments in infrastructure and urbanization), on the education policy, on the quality of the judicial system, or on public investment. The governments in Vienna, Berlin, and St. Petersburg made the decisions (usually pertaining to their whole countries) determining the process of removing social barriers (such as class privileges) and creating an open society, but also lifting the economic barriers to the development of the market.

The emergence of the modern social classes in all the partitions involved the emergence of the new social groups unique to Eastern Europe—the intelligentsia and the local version of landed gentry (*ziemianstwo*), who played an important role in the modernization process. They first started to emerge at the beginning of the nineteenth century, but it was in the second half of the nineteenth century when they became really important. The intelligentsia is a group of highly educated people, functioning as professionals, that is, lawyers, doctors, managers, and so on, who have a high position in the structure of the Western European societies. On the Polish lands, however, particularly in the Russian and Austrian partitions, the demand for their expertise was small, which negatively affected their economic status, and created a group with a considerable amount of cultural capital but low income. This group came mainly from the impoverished and downgraded nobility, and they fostered the Polish identity and got involved in the fight for independence and in the bottom-up activity aiming to educate the peasants and workers (organic work). The post-nobility and bourgeoisie intelligentsia originated many politicians whose activities contributed to the restoration of the Polish state, such as Józef Piłsudski and Roman Dmowski. The new Polish political parties and movements, including the socialist Polish Socialist Party and the nationalist National Democracy, were created by the intelligentsia.

The landed gentry can be defined by their source of income: they were landowners. Most of them came from the non-downgraded nobility, but over time, this group started to include enriched members of the middle class—the bourgeoisie and businessmen. The landed gentry retained the status of one of the richest social classes and—as a result of the Polish history and tradition—they were perceived as superior to the industrial bourgeoisie. Some members of the landed gentry played an important role in the modernization of agriculture after the enfranchisement of the peasants, particularly in the final decades of the nineteenth century and the beginning of the twentieth century, supporting the institutions and investments such as co-operatives, agricultural industry, and local transport networks contributing to the restructuring of the peasant economy. The richest landed gentry invested their capital in new industrial and infrastructural enterprises (e.g. the railway) (Ihnatowicz 1972; Kołodziejczyk 1979; Żor 2011, 2015).

The end of the nineteenth century is the time of the development of education systems. In Germany, the system was very modern, and German schools played an important cultural role. Elementary school was compulsory, with effective enforcement mechanisms, and after 1854, the curricula were unified. There is no doubt that starting from the mid-century, the Polish population within the Prussian partition were practically fully literate. However, school also became an important tool of the Germanization (assimilation) policy towards the Polish majority on the lands formerly belonging to the Polish state. This led to numerous social conflicts, including the protests against the Germanization of schools (which started in the 1830, first increased slowly, then was intensified in the 1870s), such as the school strikes discussed above at the beginning of the twentieth century. On the other hand, the intensification of Germanization in schools was an impulse for the bottom-up development of Polish social educational institutions, aiming to counter the effects of the German national policy. In the 1870s, the Society of People's Education was created, but it was dissolved within a decade by a German court order claiming its engagement in activities contravening the statute of the society. Its activities were continued by the Society of People's Schools, aiming to teach and promote the Polish language among the peasants (Galek 2016).

In the Russian and, to a lesser extent, Austrian partitions, the low standard of education systems were an important factor impeding social mobility and fossilizing the social structure, particularly in the country. In the Russian partition, education was never compulsory or available to all, so at the beginning of the twentieth century, two-thirds of the grown-up population were illiterate. In the Austrian partition, compulsory education for children between 6 and 12 was introduced in 1873, but it was not effectively enforced in the subsequent decades. The higher levels of education were even less available to most of the society. Secondary schools were private, and located primarily in bigger towns and cities, which made them inaccessible to all but the most privileged. There were two universities in the Austrian partition, in Kraków and in Lwów, but the only university in Russian Poland was the Imperial University in Warszawa, which provided very low-quality education. Therefore, many young Poles from the Russian partition studied in St. Petersburg, Moscow, and Kiev, but also at the universities in Austria and Germany. The German universities located closest to the Polish lands were those in Berlin and Breslau, and they attracted numerous Polish people from Greater Poland and from the Russian partition. Since the first decades of the nineteenth century, the differentiation of the quality and coverage of education systems translated into the differences in the quality of the human capital, determining the long-term economic development potential in the Polish lands. In the Austrian and Prussian parts, the basic educational coverage of the generation born in the early twentieth century was close to 100%, while in the Russian part it was still low. The number of pupils in schools and literacy in the Polish lands in early twentieth century is shown in Table 6.2 (the age structures of Polish lands presented in table were relatively similar).

Germany was the most modern of the three partitioning states and, as a result of the effort it was making in the second half of the nineteenth century to become one of the European economic powers, its infrastructure—both material and institutional—developed rapidly, creating good conditions for social modernization. However, the increasing Polish-German conflict and the peripheral location of the Polish lands (excluding Upper Silesia, rich of natural resources, where industrialization was rapid) did not support their economic development, and the growing demand for labour in the new industrial centres led to dynamic internal migration. In the Russian partition, martial law was maintained for a long time, which resulted in the Polish-Russian conflict and the oppressive character of the Russian administration in the aftermath of the January Uprising; however, as noted in former chapters the location of the Polish lands within the Russian empire was exceptionally favourable for economic development, as they were the

Table 6.2 Primary education and literacy of Polish lands

	Pupils in primary schools per 1000 of inhabitants	Illiterates per 1000 inhabitants
Russian part	36	680
– Kingdom	28	590
– Western provinces of Russia[a]	39	720
Prussian part	185	3
– Posen	201	5
– Silesia	182	1
– Western Prussia	186	5
– Eastern Prussia	171	3
Austrian part	168	375
– Galicia	165	408
– Austrian Silesia	180	37

Source: Romer and Weinfeld (1917), Weinfeld (1922, 1925), Wyczański (2003)
[a]For territorial coverage, see note on Ruthenia, Lithuania and Belarus (i.e. territory of Western provinces of Russia) in Table 6.1

lands closest to Western Europe, along the Russian-German border. This created good conditions for dynamic economic development and urbanization, particularly after the enfranchisement of the peasants, and the rapid industrialization became the springboard for social modernization, which quickly led to class warfare. The Germanization and Russification policy implemented in schools additionally contributed to the tensions between the Polish majority and the state administration. A different situation could be observed in Galicia, where the favourable political situation compensated, at least to some extent, for relatively slow development and the obsolete economic structure, as Galicia remained the backward agricultural periphery unable to compete with the economic centres of the Austrian empire. The poverty of the region resulted in large-scale emigration to Germany, Western Europe and—increasingly—to North America.

As can be seen, institutional changes, particularly the enfranchisement of the peasants, urbanization, and the modernization of the economy resulted in rapid social changes. The position of the nobility as the most important social group ultimately declined, peasants slowly became an important social and political power and new classes—industrial workers and the intelligentsia—started to play a vital role in Polish society. However, these processes followed a different course in each partitioning state, due to the differences in the legal and institutional models and the diversity of the infrastructure development levels. However, modernization of Polish lands took on very different paths in each of the partitions.

5   Economy

The first globalization is the period of the differentiation of the paths of development of the Polish lands within the partitions, particularly in terms of industrialization and the development of infrastructure, but also in terms of the dynamics of the modernization of agriculture. The best developed lands were those within the Prussian partition, the poorest were Galicia within the Austrian partition and the territories incorporated directly into Russia. The development of the Congress Kingdom was uneven, with the rapid development of the western provinces, particularly the areas around Warszawa and Łódź and along the Silesian border.

In spite of their peripheral location, the Polish lands within Prussia, when comparing to other Polish lands, benefitted quite early from the industrialization and the infrastructure development policy of the Prussian state. German economic development also created favourable conditions for the development of industry, with mostly small and medium-size enterprises in Greater Poland, Pomerania, and East Prussia, and bigger ones in the more industrialized West Prussia, especially near Gdańsk (Danzig). The modernization of agriculture stimulated the development of agroindustry and machine engineering. At the end of the nineteenth century, Cegielski's enterprise in Poznań, producing agricultural machinery for the local market and expanding onto the markets of the other Polish lands, became one of the biggest enterprises based on Polish capital; just before WWI, as a joint-stock company, it developed quickly, employing several hundred workers. There was also rapid industrial development in the towns on the Baltic Sea, Gdańsk, and Elbląg (Elbing). The military shipyards, Schihau (which had a branch in Elbląg as well), and Kaiserliche Werft Danzig played the key role in building the German navy before WWI.

Upper Silesia developed even more dynamically and became one of the main centres of mining and industry in Germany, with very well-developed metallurgy and steel production. The industry in Upper Silesia was never as modern as that in the industrial areas located in the west of Germany, particularly the Ruhr area, but this region became the biggest industrial area of the formerly Polish lands, and attracted numerous workers from the other Polish regions (Misztal 1970).

The German lands that were incorporated into Poland after WWII also developed dynamically. At the end of the nineteenth century, smaller industrial centres started to emerge in Lower Silesia, at the foot of the Sudetes, in the Hirschbereger Valley and in and around Waldenburg. The economy of Breslau also flourished, stimulated by the railway connection created between Breslau and Berlin and Vienna in the late 1840s, making Breslau one of the biggest and richest cities on the territory of present-day Poland. It was the site of the Linke-Hoffmann carriage and railway engine factory, not only the biggest industrial plant in Breslau but also one of the biggest producers of rolling stock in Europe. Silesian industry was dominated by industrial conglomerates, employing tens of thousands of workers throughout Germany and controlled by the richest Prussian families, such as the Hohenlohes, the Donnersmarcks, and the Schaffgotsches. In turn, in the capital of Pommern province, Stettin, located on the estuary of the Oder, shipbuilding developed; the Vulcan shipyard was the first non-military shipyard in Prussia, and one of the biggest industrial plants in the city.

At the time when German agriculture was recovering after the crisis caused by the potato blight, Greater Poland, Pomerania, and East Prussia became an important supplier of grain and livestock to other German provinces. The agriculture in Greater Poland was as efficient as that in Western Europe, and much more efficient than that in other Polish territories. New crops were introduced relatively fast and the mechanization of agriculture started growing in the last decades of the nineteenth century. The structure of agriculture was modern; it was based on big agricultural estates, a considerable number of big, market-oriented, efficient farms and relatively few traditional subsistence peasant farms; there were also numerous groups of landless farm workers. Some of the land was owned by the Polish landed gentry. Outside Greater Poland, the land ownership structure was similar, with a greater share of big landowners' estates. In East and West Prussia and Pomerania, the big estates were owned by the Junkers, an influential group of the Prussian nobility, and in Silesia, much of the land was owned by the same Prussian aristocratic families that controlled the industry (Topolski 1973; Łuczak 1973; Jezierski 1984; Jezierski and Leszczyńska 2010).

The development of services is difficult to grasp in the statistical data of the period, because a significant part of that sector remained within the grey economy in all the partitions. However, the Prussian partition shows a well-documented dynamic development of transport services, connected with the development of roads, railways, and navigable rivers and canals. Moreover, the modern and efficient German banking system supported industrialization. In agriculture, there was the development of co-operatives and social economy, or, in fact, two competing systems, Polish and German, and mutual assistance societies developed, along national lines, with a separate set of Polish and German institutions. Public services also developed dynamically, including the modern, well-developed system of education (see Table 6.1). The data on the structure of employment within sectors are provided in Table 6.3.

Table 6.3 Occupational structure of Polish lands in the turn of the centuries (1895/97/1900)

Administrative unit (province/chamber of commerce/Austria*l*)	Posen	Pomerania	East/West Prussia	Upper Silesia (Oppeln)	Silesia (excl. Oppeln)	Total Prussian part	Lwów	Kraków	Brody	Total Galicia
Year of census	1895	1895	1895	1895	1895	1895	1900	1900	1900	1900
Primary (%)	64.4	55.5	61.4	48.2	45.2	54.9	80	82	86	81.9
Secondary (%)	18.0	24.3	17.9	36.4	35.4	26.1	7	8	5	6.8
Tertiary (%)	17.6	20.2	20.7	15.4	19.4	19.1	13	10	9	11.3

Administrative unit (province)	Kalisz	Kielce	Lublin	Łomża	Piotrków	Płock	Radom	Siedlce	Suwałki	Warszawa	Total Kingdom of Poland	Western provinces of Russia
Year of census	1897	1897	1897	1897	1897	1897	1897	1897	1897	1897	1897	1897
Primary (%)	72	79	71	68	46	66	74	74	76	41	62.6	80
Secondary (%)	10	6	8	7	31	8	9	8	6	20	13.5	5
Tertiary (%)[a]	17	15	21	24	24	26	17	18	18	40	23.9	15

Source: Romer and Weinfeld (1917) and Koryś and Tymiński (2015)

[a]Part of agricultural workers in Russian statistics was counted as a domestic service. Data presented in table are corrected, but anyway, the size of service sector in rural provinces might be overestimated slightly. For methodology, see Koryś and Tymiński (2015)

The development of transport infrastructure was an important element of economic growth. The Prussian government developed waterways, and the first construction on the Polish lands was the Bromberger Canal, joining the Vistula and the Oder, built as early as in the second half of the eighteenth century. The development of industry in Upper Silesia stimulated the development of transport on the Oder and the growth of the importance of the port in Stettin. On the other hand, as a result of the border dividing the Vistula, Gdańsk lost its importance and never regained the position it had had in the times of the Commonwealth, despite the dynamic growth that it and the nearby Elbląg achieved in the second half of the nineteenth century. Throughout the nineteenth century, the dense network of paved roads was created, and the railway started to develop in mid-century. At the end of the century, most urban areas were served by a railway, and its network was denser and of better quality than in the other Polish territories. This contributed to the emergence of a relatively dense network of small- and medium-size towns, functioning as administration, market, and trade centres, but also as food processing and often industrial centres. The development of transport infrastructure and the lowering of the cost of transport contributed to the development of the region, but it may also be a factor causing the early labour migrations from the lands of the partition. Table 6.4 shows the dynamics of the development of roads and railways (Krzyżanowski and Kumaniecki 1915; Koziarski 1993; Mielcarek 2000).

Table 6.4 Roads and railways on Polish lands, 1911

	Railroads per 100 km²	Paved roads per 100 km²
Russian part		
– Kingdom	2.7	6.9
– Ruthenia	2.3	1.4
– Lithuania and Belarus	2.1	1.4
Prussian part		
– Posen	12.1	24.8
– Silesia	13.6	36.3
– Western Prussia	11.3	28
– Eastern Prussia	10.5	25.4
Austrian part		
– Galicia	5.3	19.5
– Austrian Silesia	13.4	78.7

Source: Krzyżanowski and Kumaniecki (1915) and Romer and Weinfeld (1917)

The change of the land ownership structure resulting from agrarian reforms and quick industrialization consolidated the economic disparities between the lands under the Prussian rule, that is, Greater Poland, West Prussia, and Pomerania, on the one hand, and the Polish territories within the other partitions on the other. As a result of the development in the second half of the nineteenth century, just before WWI, the Prussian partition was better developed than the other Polish regions. It also had the highest standard of living, and its poorest districts achieved the GDP per capita much higher than underdeveloped areas of the other partitions. The quality of life was also the highest (except for the few prosperous enclaves, such as Warszawa), as a result of the high level of urbanization and well-developed infrastructure (particularly the railway), but also because of the wide range and high quality of public services—the quality and credibility of the Prussian Rechtsstaat. It is also important to note that the income disparities were relatively low in the Prussian partition, due to factors like the agrarian reforms facilitating relatively high incomes in agriculture, and the outflow of the surplus labour force through internal migration.

The source of the disparities is an important question—why did the Prussian partition belong to the richest and best developed districts of Poland at the end of the partitions period? Was it the result of the dynamic development of Prussia? The hypothesis that the disparities between Greater Poland and the other regions originate in the partitions or, to be exact, are the direct result of the policy and economic culture of Prussia is quite widespread (Hryniewicz 2001, 2004, 2007, 2015; Wysokińska 2016) and at least partly justified. However, as shown in former chapters, the regional differences started earlier, and considerable economic disparities between various regions of Poland were visible already in the eighteenth century (Korzon 1898; Zawadzki 1963), with the high level of development of the western part of the Crown of Poland, particularly Greater Poland (Topolski 1973). Its main indicators were the high level of urbanization, the early transition from the corvée to land rent in agriculture, the structure of agricultural production, and the size of the peasant households. The influence of these initial differences has not been well researched. Besides, it is important to note that, within the Prussian state, Greater Poland was a periphery for the whole nineteenth century, both as a result of political decisions and in terms of its location; the same applied to West Prussia and Pomerania, where the Polish minority was relatively small. The marginalization resulted in the lower level of development of these regions than that in the rest of Prussia and then Germany. This process can be clearly seen in Gdańsk, which lost importance in the eighteenth century and in the nineteenth century became a peripheral town and port within the Reich (Cieślak and Biernat 1988).

In the Austrian partition, the area developing heavy industry and mining was the Austrian part of Silesia, with the towns of Ostrava and Bielsko, along the border with the German Upper Silesia. Another area that started to industrialize at the turn of the nineteenth century was the westernmost part of Galicia, between Kraków and the Prussian-Silesian border. The area near Kraków, in the Chrzanow district, traditionally a lead and silver mining region, now developed coal and zinc mining and zinc metallurgy. There were also salt mines near Kraków in Bochnia and Wieliczka, and near the Silesian border (e.g. in and around the town of Biała) textile industry developed, based on cheaper labour (Buszko 1989; Kaps 2015).

The eastern end of Galicia developed the excavation and refining of petroleum and ozokerite (mineral wax) in the Boryslav-Drohobycz area and Gorlice area. The oil industry started at the beginning of the nineteenth century in that region, but the dynamic development took place in the second half of the nineteenth century; in 1892 and 1893, there were 400 enterprises mining petroleum and mineral wax employing about 8000 people. At the beginning of the twentieth century, the Galician oil industry constituted 5% of the world's oil production (most of which was in the Boryslav-Drohobycz area). However, in 1908, the oil prices slumped as a result of the problems with storing the raw material and with the efficiency of the refineries, the development was slowed down, particularly near Borysław, and the whole region lost its leading position among the world's oil producing areas (it was the third most productive region in the world). The oil industry was an important sector of the economy of eastern Galicia and contributed to fast and chaotic urbanization and the emergence of slums interspersed with industrial facilities, quite like the industrial areas in the Congress Kingdom (Burzyński and Madurowicz-Urbańska 1982).

However, the development of urban areas and industry was rather slow. In fact, apart from the areas discussed above and the bigger cities (Kraków, Lwów, Przemyśl), it is difficult to indicate modern industrial centres in Galicia even at the beginning of the twentieth century. The biggest companies did not employ more than a few hundred people. One of the biggest Galician enterprises was Ludwik Zieleniewski's company from Kraków, which just before WWI became a conglomerate of rolling stock factories and metal works operating in Lwów, Sanok, and other towns. Collectively, it employed about 600–700 workers, which makes it rather a medium-size than large company. The oil industry was scattered and the enterprises were on an even smaller scale. The only branch of industry that developed was the agroindustry, though it remained quite backward. Cottage industry was still widespread, providing the small and poor peasant households with additional income (Burzyński and Madurowicz-Urbańska 1982; Kwiatek 1994; Gąsowski 1997; Kawalec and Wierzbieniec 2011).

The dominant sector of the economy of the region was agriculture. By 1848, the peasants had obtained freedom, civil rights, and their own plots of land; however, because of the ill-advised regulations adopted by the reform and considerable population growth, the fragmentation of peasants' land became very rapid, and was not alleviated by internal migration or growing emigration. Local industry developed slowly and could not absorb the surplus of labour. An additional obstacle to the modernization of agriculture was the mountainous terrain, but also the conflict appearing in eastern Galicia between the predominantly Ukrainian/Rusyn peasants and the mostly Polish or Jewish townspeople and the Polish landed gentry. The big agricultural estates had a more modern, commercial character, and developed food processing and agro-industry, including distilleries, breweries, and mills. The efficiency of agriculture was much lower than in Greater Poland and slightly lower (due to the difficult terrain) than in the Congress Kingdom. Even just before WWI, agriculture employed about 80% of the labour force of the region (K.K. Statistischen Zentralkommision 1916; Vnenchak and Mandurowicz-Urbańska 1983).

Like in many backward economies, the service sector was dominated by cheap, personal services and traditional trade (pedlars, fairs and markets etc.). Modern services, including banking, trade, medical care, insurance, and transport developed in bigger towns and cities. At the beginning of the twentieth century, a network of co-operative financial institutions developed in Galicia, modelled on the Raiffeisen system. One of the creators of this system was Franciszek Stefczyk (Zagóra-Jonszta 2013).

The development of hotel and transport services was stimulated by the construction of the railway, particularly the Karl Ludwig line between Kraków and Lwów, started in the late 1850s and developed into about 800 km at the beginning of the twentieth century, but also the Galizische Transversalbahn, the 700 km railway line linking Żywiec, Nowy Sącz, Krosno, and Stanisławów across the Carpatian Mountains, and the trans-Carpatian line linking Przemyśl (and Lwów) and Budapest. The two former lines had an east-west orientation and were connected with the Austrian and Prussian railway network (Leszczycki et al. 1974; Koziarski 1993).

Like the Polish lands within the Prussian state, Galicia suffered due to its peripheral location within the new political entity in which it had found itself. The previously well-developed lands of the Cracow region were now very far from the centre of the monarchy, which radically affected their market potential and hampered their development. The improvement of life conditions, growth of efficiency in agriculture and some benefits from the (slow) economic development of the empire were practically counterbalanced by the growing birth rate. Even though most of Western Galicia escaped from the Malthusian trap at the end of the Commonwealth, due to the geographical changes which disturbed the process this did not translate into quick industrialization in the nineteenth century, but into population growth in rural areas and economic stagnation. Additionally, since the mid-nineteenth century, Galicia suffered due to the slowness of the economic development of the Austro-Hungarian Empire, which did not keep pace with the developed economies of Western Europe, including Germany; to make matters worse, Galicia was one of its least developed provinces. The Austrian Silesia was in a better situation (still worse than the neighbouring Prussian Silesia, however)—not only its industry, but also its agriculture was more modern and more efficient than those in Galicia.

Industrialization on the territory of the Congress Kingdom started relatively early when at the end of the eighteenth century Prussia industrialized the area near Siewierz (the area that was incorporated into the Kingdom of Poland after the Congress of Vienna), the state built the industrial areas in the 1820s, and industry developed in the area between Łęczyca and Kalisz and then in Łódź. However, it was not until the last decades of the nineteenth century that industry became a major branch of the economy of the Congress Kingdom, the entity with the biggest Polish population. The industrial centres created at that time (Łódź, the Kielce area, the Dabrowa basin) continued to be important development centres in Poland. However, even in these areas, industry did not have the economic significance comparable to that in Western Europe. Moreover, the industrial structure was dual, with the important sectors of traditional and backward crafts and small industry and relatively modern, large industry (Załęski 1901; Koszutski 1905, 1918; Puś 1997).

The industrialization process in the Kingdom took a different route from those in the other partitions. The failure of the state industrialization of the first half of the nineteenth century was compensated for only after the January Uprising. The disappearance of the customs border, a different model of peasant emancipation than in the rest of the Russian Empire, the development of road and railway connections with Europe, and the inflow of foreign capital (mostly German) all contributed to the dynamic development of the Kingdom. However, it should be noted that it was based mainly on the abundant supply of labour resulting from the peasant emancipation and on the branches of industry that were no longer developing technologically, for example, the textile industry; therefore, the industrialization was not accompanied by the transfer of new technologies. Additionally, it created low demand for skilled labour, which limited the market stimulus for the improvement of the education system (Misztal 1970; Pietrzak-Pawłowska 1970; Puś 2013).

The economic and political integration with Russia enforced after the January Uprising stimulated intense industrialization in the Polish lands under the Russian rule, particularly in the western provinces. Relatively modern large-scale manufacturing industry developed in and around Łódź and Warszawa and in the area near the Silesian border (Dąbrowa

Górnicza). Apart from these, there was the development of rather backward small industry, crafts and cottage industries in rural areas.

The decisive impulse for development was the change in Russian policy taking place in the late 1850s and the enforced integration of the Polish lands with the political and economic structure of Russia. The proximity of western markets and the western capital was an important factor in creating suitable conditions for economic development. At the end of the nineteenth century and at the beginning of the twentieth, the Warsaw and Piotrkow provinces achieved a level of development that was similar to or higher than that of Greater Poland, and their growth rate was higher, which manifested itself in the high level of industrialization and urbanization of these provinces.

The Warsaw area developed various branches of industry, mostly machine engineering, textile industry, metal industry, and food processing. The Lodz area developed its textile industry, predominantly cotton, on a very large scale. The area near the Silesian border developed mining and metallurgy, but also wool processing. In the area near Kielce, losing its position at the time, there were ironworks and metalworks. Chemical industry developed in Warszawa, along the Silesian border and, on a much smaller scale, in Radom near the Old-Polish Industrial Region (Misztal 1970; Pietrzak-Pawłowska 1973; Pruss 1977; Puś 1987, 1997).

The development of the Kingdom is sometimes referred to as "patchy", which is not precise. The areas of intense development, the western provinces of the Kingdom, are not exactly patches, but they are the western borderlands of Russia and the gateways to Europe. There was a sharp distinction between the faster-developing western provinces, clearly benefitting from the inflow of Russian capital and the involvement of local capital, and the eastern provinces, still at the pre-industrial stage. The western provinces developed cities and industrial towns; industrialization entailed rapid urbanization, resulting in the emergence of slums and chaotic developments.

The characteristic feature of the industrialization in the Kingdom was the emergence and development of very big enterprises using cheap labour and relatively simple technologies (labour-intensive industrialization), whose purpose was mass production for the Russian internal market and for export. Therefore, the principal industry was the textile industry, which in the mid-nineteenth century focused on cotton (and the switch from wool to cotton resulted in the radical reduction of the flocks of sheep in the region). Huge cotton mills, such as Scheibler's factory in Łódź, which employed up to 6000 workers at the end of the nineteenth century, or the linen factory in Żyrardów mentioned above, were important even on the European market, but they were competitive mainly because of the cheap labour. The biggest ironworks, Huta Bankowa in Dabrowa and Huta Hantke in Czestochowa, employed 3000–4000 workers each, and Rudzki's metalworks in Grodzisk Mazowiecki in the Warsaw area employed 9000 workers just before WWI.

Modern small- and medium-size industry developed much less dynamically, and mostly in bigger towns and cities. It was complemented by the activity of craftsmen, which was a big and rather obsolete sector with a significant representation of the Jewish minority. Thus, the dual industrial structure changed very slowly and persisted until the outbreak of WWI, even though the role of traditional manufacturing slowly declined in terms of employment (Pietrzak-Pawłowska 1967; Grochulska and Pruss 1983; Puś 1998).

Despite the emancipation reforms, agriculture evolved rather slowly in the Kingdom. Like in Galicia, the regulations allowed for the fragmentation of peasant land and the emergence of small farms. Therefore, the size and efficiency of peasant farms went down as the population grew, and there was the increase of the surplus of labour in agriculture. The situation was worse in the eastern provinces, where the agriculture was as backward as that in Galicia, while the western provinces modernized earlier due to several factors: the more developed urban labour market that could absorb more workers, better transport infrastructure, emigration, and the involvement of the more progressive part of the landed gentry. Like in the other partitions, from the early nineteenth century, the developing co-operative movement supported the modernization of agriculture. Since mid-century new industrial crops spread, such as potatoes or sugar beets, but also fruit and vegetables. This was followed by the development of the agroindustry, including sugar plants and distilleries, but its technological level was not as high as that in Greater Poland. There were also changes in the numbers and kinds of livestock. Horses replaced oxen as draught animals, and over time the production of milk, milk products, and meat grew (Pietrzak-Pawłowska 1967; Sobczak 1968; Chomać 1970; Kochanowicz 2006; Łukasiewicz 2009).

An important development barrier was the slow development of transport infrastructure. The Vistula slowly lost its importance as the principal transport route, because it was divided by customs borders between Austria and Russia, and then again, between Russia and Prussia. The road network developed, but not fast enough. Despite the efforts of the bourgeoisie of the Kingdom, the railway (state-owned or private), particularly East-West routes crossing Vistula river, developed even more slowly, as it was deliberately hampered by the Russian authorities for strategic reasons—the risk of German invasion. The first railway line, the Warsaw-Vienna Railway, was built in the 1840s, and by the end of the century, Warszawa had become relatively well connected with the bigger towns and cities of the Kingdom and with Russia and Germany; however, apart from the branch line to Kraków, there was no direct connection to Galicia (Koziarski 1993).

The development of the Kingdom, and of Warszawa in particular, stimulated the banking sector and the activity of not only industrial entrepreneurs, but also venture capitalists. Banks emerged in Warszawa, usually on the basis of the fortunes made out of banking in the previous decades, but also in Łódź, where entrepreneurs created demand for banking services. The fortune of the greatest Polish financier of the period, Leopold Kronenberg, was rooted in the banking activity of his father and was further developed on the lease of the tobacco monopoly in the Kingdom before the January Uprising. He became a venture capitalist investing in industry and the railway, and he created the biggest private bank on the Polish lands, Bank Handlowy, with numerous branches in the Kingdom and in Russia. He also owned considerable amounts of land and supported the modernization of peasant farming (Morawski 1998).

In the public service sector, a significant part was the very big military forces, maintained after the January Uprising in order to enable a quick response to the possible subsequent Polish rebellions. There was also a sizeable police force, both uniformed and undercover. Compulsory education was never fully implemented, which limited the development of the education sector. The size of public administration, while growing, also remained limited. The development of the railway and road network entailed the growth of the number of workers engaged in the transport sector and maintaining transport infrastructure, both public and private. The private service sector consisted of personal services, trade, and a relatively small modern service sector (banking, finances etc.) The personal services sector, including servants, was considerable, but it diminished as the economy modernized. The trade sector was also big, but it was scattered and mostly based on pedlars and markets and fairs; however, in big cities, it was increasingly replaced by the modern wholesale and retail trade, supported by the development of transport infrastructure (Koryś and Tymiński 2015).

The discrepancy between the provinces of the Kingdom deepened, as the western provinces (particularly the Warsaw and Piotrkow provinces) developed and the eastern ones remained backward. Their economy, based on agriculture, was burdened with the huge Russian garrisons standing in numerous towns. These areas were the sources of labour and their development was related to the demand for labour on the Polish industrial regions or in the industrial areas abroad.

The lands incorporated directly into Russia (the western provinces of Russia) developed slowly, at the rate similar to that of the eastern provinces of the Kingdom and to Austrian Galicia. Agricultural sector dominated regional economies (cf. Table 6.3). The transport network was only skeletal, and bigger cities were few and far between. An industrial area emerged around Białystok as a result of the customs border between the Kingdom and the rest of the Russian Empire; some of the industry from Łódź was moved there and some new German investments were located in that area. The development of the area lasted until the 1850s, when the customs border was lifted; subsequently, Białystok became a medium-size industrial town and a local industrial centre after the railway line between Warsaw and St. Petersburg was built. This industrial area was much smaller in size and importance than the areas of the Kingdom, and Białystok itself remained a medium-size city, with a population of over 60,000 at the turn of the century and below 100,000 just before WWI. Possibly, the emergence of the area can be related to the industrial experiences of the Grodno region, at least with respect to the human resource capital. The other bigger towns, particularly Wilno (Vilnius), did not become important industrial centres before WWI; there were some small- and medium-sized food processing, chemical (tanning), and mechanical engineering industries, while agriculture and services remained at the same development level as the eastern provinces of the Kingdom, or even lower.

While the Prussian partition industrialized along with the fast-growing Prussian economy and Galicia remained a remote and backward periphery of Habsburg's empire and its development was slow (Schulze 2007a,b; Kaps 2015), the Congress Kingdom became one of the leading regional economies of the backward and peripheral Russian Empire. In terms of development, the period after the January Uprising created favourable circumstances for benefitting from the Kingdom's western location within the empire. The most important factor quickening the pace of the development of Polish lands was the resources of cheap labour, particularly after the reforms abolishing the post-feudal restrictions on the mobility of the peasants. This enhanced the labour-intensive industrialization and eventually created the situation of sustainable development based on the transfer of labour from agriculture to industry (i.e. from the traditional sector to the modern one), resulting not from the state intervention, but from the development of the internal market and the favourable international situation.

6   Conclusions

It can be said that, during this period, the modern development and, in particular, the industrialization of the Polish lands really took off, despite the problems resulting from the fact that Poland was not a sovereign state and was divided and ruled by three different governments. However, it is doubtful that the partitions modernized Poland—one can say that their effect was similar to that of the real socialism in the twentieth century: there was modernization, but the world modernized faster. Even if the relative difference between the West and Poland remained the same as at the time of the Third Partition, the absolute difference had increased. The technological backwardness of the Polish lands relative to the Western

Europe grew, the industrial revolution started late, and the peripheral location of most of the Polish territories within the partitioning states did not encourage the transfer of modern technologies. The disparity between the economy of the British Empire, that is, the best developed economy of the nineteenth century world, and the economy (or economies) of the Polish lands was stable, with the exception of Kingdom of Poland experiencing relatively rapid development in the later part of the period.

In the brief part of the nineteenth century that is under consideration here, the Polish lands were still mostly a peripheral and backward agricultural region, and the first sector employed considerably more than half the available labour force, with a particularly high percentage in Galicia. The centres of fast industrialization were few and far between, and the industries that developed were typical of the previous technological phase, that is, they were labour-intensive rather than capital-intensive; besides, they used hardly any innovative technologies and rarely introduced technological advancements. This, in turn, is connected with the low level and slow development of the education systems in the most populated Polish regions, the Russian and Austrian partitions, and the consequent low level of human capital. The development of infrastructure was also less than satisfactory, particularly in the Kingdom of Poland and in the rest of the Russian partition, but also in Galicia. This underdeveloped infrastructure became a development barrier in the subsequent decades, in the restored sovereign state, and it determined the persistence of regional differences in the development of the Polish lands.

The prospects of the economic development based on labour-intensive industrialization were good, even though the development processes could not be enhanced by the activity of the Polish sovereign state, as a result of which the Kingdom of Poland started to slowly lose its position on the Russian market at the end of the nineteenth century. Industrialization progressed fast (except in Galicia) and was accompanied by structural social change. However, the key to development was the access to European markets and to the foreign capital to finance modernization. That is the major reason WWI caused the long-term collapse of the development process, not only in absolute measures, but also relative to other European countries.

References

Balicki, Z. (2008). *Parlamentaryzm: wybór pism*. Kraków: Ośrodek Myśli Politycznej: Księgarnia Akademicka.

Berger, J. (2010). Professor Witold Załęski (1836–1908). *Acta Universitatis Lodziensis Folia Oeconomica, 235*, 13–18.

Blobaum, R. (1984). *Feliks Dzierżyński and the SDKPiL: A study of the origins of Polish communism*. Boulder and New York: East European Monographs; Distributed by Columbia University Press.

Bończa-Tomaszewski, N. (2001). *Demokratyczna geneza nacjonalizmu: intelektualne korzenie ruchu narodowo-demokratycznego*. Warszawa: Fronda.

Brykalska, M. (1987). *Aleksander Świętochowski: biografia* (T. 1–2). Warszawa: Państwowe Instytut Wydawniczy.

Burzyński, A., & Madurowicz-Urbańska, H. (1982). *Informator statystyczny do dziejów przemysłu w Galicji: górnictwo, hutnictwo i przemysł rafineryjny (struktura zatrudnienia na tle wartości produkcji)*. Kraków: UJ.

Buszko, J. (1989). *Galicja 1859–1914: polski Piemont?* Krajowa Agencja Wydawnicza RSW "Prasa-Książka-Ruch".

Chomać, R. (1970). *Struktura agrarna Królestwa Polskiego na przełomie XIX i XX w.* Warszawa: Państwowe Wydawnictwo Naukowe.

Cieślak, E., & Biernat, C. (1988). *History of Gdańsk*. Wydawnictwo.

Cywiński, B. (1985). *Rodowody niepokornych* (Wyd. 3. rozrzesz). Paris: Editions Spotkania.

Galek, C. (2016). *Szkoła polska drugiej połowy XIX wieku w zaborze pruskim w świetle pamiętników i literatury pięknej*. Zamość: Wyższa Szkoła Zarządzania i Administracji.

Gąsowski, T. (1997). Struktura społeczno-zawodowa mieszkańców większych miast galicyjskich w okresie autonomicznym. *Zeszyty Naukowe Uniwersytetu Jagiellońskiego. Prace Historyczne, 123*, 113–135.

Główny Urząd Statystyczny. (1993). *Historia Polski w liczbach: ludność, terytorium*. Warszawa: Główny Urząd Statystyczny.

Grabski, W. (Ed.). (1916). *Rocznik Statystyczny Królestwa Polskiego =: Annuarie Statistique du Royaume de Pologne*. Piotrogród: Centralny Komitet Obywatelski Królestwa Polskiego.

Grochulska, B., & Pruss, W. (Eds.). (1983). *Z dziejów rzemiosła warszawskiego*. Warszawa: Państwowe Wydawnictwo Naukowe.

Grzybek, D. (2005). *Nauka czy ideologia: biografia intelektualna Adama Krzyżanowskiego*. Kraków: Księgarnia Akademicka.

Grzybek, D. (2012). *Polityczne konsekwencje idei ekonomicznych w myśli polskiej 1869–1939*. Kraków: Księgarnia Akademicka.

Guzicki, L., & Żurawicki, S. (1969). *Historia polskiej myśli społeczno-ekonomicznej do roku 1914*. Państwowe Wydawnictwo Ekonomiczne.

Hryniewicz, J. T. (2001). Prusy jako pośrednik w imporcie zachodnich wzorów zachowań gospodarczych i politycznych do Polski. *Przegląd Zachodni, 4,* 19–42.

Hryniewicz, J. T. (2004). *Polityczny i kulturowy kontekst rozwoju gospodarczego*. Warszawa: Scholar.

Hryniewicz, J. T. (2007). Ekonomiczne, polityczne i kulturowe czynniki różnicowania przestrzeni środkowoeuropejskiej. *Przegląd Zachodni, 2,* 21–46.

Hryniewicz, J. T. (2015). *Polska na tle historycznych podziałów przestrzeni europejskiej oraz współczesnych przemian gospodarczych, społecznych i politycznych*. Warszawa: Wydawnictwo Naukowe Scholar.

Ihnatowicz, I. (1972). *Burżuazja warszawska*. Warszawa: Państwowe Wydawnictwo Naukowe.

Jachymek, J., Sowa, K. Z., Śliwa, M., & Szaflik, J. R. (Eds.). (1996). *Chłopi, naród, kultura. T. 1: Myśl polityczna ruchu ludowego*. Rzeszów: Wydawnictwo Wyższej Szkoły Pedagogicznej.

Janczak, J. (1982). *Ludność Łodzi Przemysłowej 1820–1914. Acta Universitatis Lodziensis. Folia Historica, 11.* Łódź: Uniwersytet Łódzki. https://integro.ciniba.edu.pl/integro/192203135592/janczak-julian/ludnosc-lodzi-przemyslowej-1820-1914

Janowski, M. (2004). *Polish liberal thought before 1918*. Budapest and New York: Central European University Press.

Jaskólski, M. (2014). *Kaduceus polski: myśl polityczna konserwatystów krakowskich 1866–1934*. Kraków: Ośrodek Myśli Politycznej.

Jelonek, A. (1967). *Ludność miast i osiedli typu miejskiego na ziemiach Polski od 1810 do 1960 r.* Instytut Geografii Polskiej Akademii Nauk.

Jeż, T. T. (2009). *Rzecz o obronie czynnej i o skarbie narodowym: wybór pism*. Kraków: Ośrodek Myśli Politycznej.

Jezierski, A. (1984). *Problemy rozwoju gospodarczego ziem polskich w XIX i XX wieku*. Książka i Wiedza.

Jezierski, A., & Leszczyńska, C. (2010). *Historia gospodarcza Polski*. Wydawnictwo Key Text.

K.K. Statistischen Zentralkommision. (1916). *Berufsstatistik nach den Ergebnissen der Volkszählung vom 31. Dezember 1910 in Österreich*. Galizien und Bukowina. Bureau der K.K. Statistischen Zentralkommision, Wien.

Kaczyńska, E. (1970). *Dzieje robotników przemysłowych w Polsce pod zaborami*. Warszawa: Państwowe Wydawnictwo Naukowe.

Kaps, K. (2015). *Ungleiche Entwicklung in Zentraleuropa: Galizien zwischen überregionaler Verflechtung und imperialer Politik (1772–1914)*. Böhlau Verlag Wien.

Kawalec, A., & Wierzbieniec, W. (2011). *Galicja 1772–1918: problemy metodologiczne, stan i potrzeby badań: praca zbiorowa.* Wydawnictwo Uniwersytetu Rzeszowskiego.

Kizwalter, T. (1999). *O nowoczesności narodu: przypadek Polski.* Semper.

Kochanowicz, J. (2006). *Backwardness and modernization: Poland and Eastern Europe in the 16th–20th centuries.* Ashgate Variorum.

Kołodziejczyk, R. (1979). *Burżuazja polska w XIX i XX wieku: szkice historyczne.* Warszawa: Państwowy Instytut Wydawniczy.

Königlich Preussischen Statistischen Bureaus. (1913). *Statistisches Jahrbuch für den Preussischen Staat, 10. Jahrgang 1912.* Berlin: Verlag des Königlich Preussischen Statistischen Bureaus.

Korobowicz, A., & Witkowski, W. (2012). *Historia ustroju i prawa polskiego (1772–1918).* Warszawa: Wolters Kluwer.

Koryś, P. (2008). Romantyczny patriotyzm i pozytywistyczny nacjonalizm. Dwa style myślenia o narodzie polskim na przełomie XIX i XX wieku i ich przyszłe konsekwencje. In J. Chumiński & K. Popiński (Eds.), *Gospodarcze i społeczne skutki zaborów Polski* (Wyd. 1). Wrocław: Gajt.

Koryś, P., & Tymiński, M. (2015). *Occupational structure in the Polish territories at the turn of the 20th (1895–1900) century.* Warsaw: Faculty of Economic Sciences, University of Warsaw.

Korzon, T. (1898). *Wewnętrzne dzieje Polski za Stanisława Augusta, 1764–1794: Badania historyczne ze stanowiska ekonomicznego i administracyjnego.* L. Zwoliński.

Koszutski, S. (1905). *Rozwój ekonomiczny Królestwa Polskiego w ostatniem trzydziestoleciu: 1870–1900 r.* Księg. Warszawa: Naukowa.

Koszutski, S. (1918). *Geografja gospodarcza Polski (historycznej i etnograficznej): bogactwo i wytwórczość.* Warszawa and Lublin: M. Arct.

Koziarski, S. M. (1993). *Sieć kolejowa Polski w latach 1842–1918.* Opole: PIN-IŚ.

Król, M. (Ed.). (1982). *Stańczycy: antologia myśli społecznej i politycznej konserwatystów krakowskich.* Warszawa: Pax.

Król, M. (1985). *Konserwatyści a niepodległość: studia nad polską myślą konserwatywną XIX wieku.* Warszawa: Pax.

Król, M., & Karpiński, W. (1997). *Od Mochnackiego do Piłsudskiego: sylwetki polityczne XIX wieku.* Warszawa: Świat Książki.

Krzyżanowski, A., & Kumaniecki, K. W. (1915). *Statystyka Polski =: Handbuch der polnischen Statistik = Tableau statistique de la Pologne.* Kraków: Polskie Towarzystwo Statystyczne.

Kula, W. (Ed.). (1966). *Społeczeństwo Królestwa Polskiego: studia o uwarstwieniu i ruchliwości społecznej* (T. 2). Warszawa: Państwowe Wydawnictwo Naukowe.

Kula, W., & Leskiewiczowa, J. (Eds.). (1971). *Społeczeństwo Królestwa Polskiego: studia o uwarstwieniu i ruchliwości społecznej. T. 4: Społeczeństwo polskie XVIII i XIX wieku.* Warszawa: Państwowe Wydawnictwo Naukowe.

Kula, W., & Leskiewiczowa, J. (Eds.). (1972). *Społeczeństwo Królestwa Polskiego. T. 5: Społeczeństwo polskie XVIII i XIX wieku.* Warszawa: Państwowe Wydawnictwo Naukowe.

Kwiatek, J. (1994). *Związki Górnego Śląska z Galicją na przełomie XIX i XX wieku.* Instytut Śląski w Opolu.

Łepkowski, T. (1960). *Przemysł warszawski u progu epoki kapitalistycznej: 1815–1868.* Warszawa: Państwowe Wydawnictwo Naukowe.

Leszczycki, S., Lijewski, T., & Grzeszczak, J. (Eds.). (1974). *Geografia przemysłu Polski: praca zbiorowa* (Wyd. 2 popr). Warszawa: Państwowe Wydawnictwo Naukowe.

Łuczak, C. (1973). *Dzieje Wielkopolski: Lata 1793–1918.* Wydawnictwo Poznańskie.

Łuczewski, M. (2012). *Odwieczny naród: Polak i katolik w Żmiącej.* Toruń: Wydawnictwo Naukowe Uniwersytetu Mikołaja Kopernika.

Łukasiewicz, J. (2009). Spisy ludności w Polsce i na ziemiach polskich do 1939 r. *Wiadomości Statystyczne, 6*, 1–5.

Marzec, W. (2016). *Rebelia i reakcja: rewolucja 1905 roku i plebejskie doświadczenie polityczne.* Łódź; Kraków: Uniwersytet Łódzki; Towarzystwo Autorów i Wydawców Prac Naukowych Universitas.

Mencwel, A. (1997). *Przedwiośnie czy potop: studium postaw polskich w XX wieku.* Arch Czesława Miłosza.

Mencwel, A. (2009). *Etos lewicy: esej o narodzinach kulturalizmu polskiego* (Wyd. 1 w tej ed). Warszawa: Wydawnictwo Krytyki Politycznej.

Mielcarek, A. (2000). *Transport drogowy, wodny i kolejowy w gospodarce prowincji pomorskiej w latach 1815–1914* (Wyd. 1). Szczecin: Wydawnictwo Naukowe Uniwersytetu Szczecińskiego.

Miller, J. (2001). Strajki szkolne w Wielkopolsce w latach 1901–1907. *Przegląd Historyczno-Oświatowy, 3-4*, 73–81.

Misztal, S. (1970). *Przemiany w strukturze przestrzennej przemysłu na ziemiach polskich w latach 1860–1965.* Warszawa: Państwowe Wydawnictwo Naukowe.

Morawski, W. (1998). *Słownik historyczny bankowości polskiej do 1939 roku.* Muza SA.

Pietrzak-Pawłowska, I. (Ed.). (1967). *Zakłady przemysłowe w Polsce XIX i XX wieku: studia i materiały*. Wrocław: Zakład Narodowy im. Ossolińskich Wydawnictwo PAN.

Pietrzak-Pawłowska, I. (Ed.). (1970). *Uprzemysłowienie ziem polskich w XIX i XX wieku: studia i materiały*. Wrocław: Zakład Narodowy im. Ossolińskich Wydawnictwo PAN.

Pietrzak-Pawłowska, I. (Ed.). (1973). *Wielkomiejski rozwój Warszawy do 1918 r.* Warszawa: Książka i Wiedza.

Popławski, J. L. (2012). *Naród i polityka: wybór pism.* Kraków: Ośrodek Myśli Politycznej: Wydział Studiów Międzynarodowych i Politycznych Uniwersytetu Jagiellońskiego.

Porter, B. (2000). *When nationalism began to hate: Imagining modern politics in nineteenth-century Poland.* New York and Oxford: Oxford University Press.

Pragier, A. (1920). *Królewsko-pruska Komisja Kolonizacyjna 1886–1918.* Warszawa: s.n.

Pruss, W. (1977). *Rozwój przemysłu warszawskiego w latach 1864–1914.* Warszawa: Państwowe Wydawnictwo Naukowe.

Puś, W. (1987). *Dzieje Łodzi przemysłowej: zarys historii.* Łódź: Muzeum Historii Miasta Łodzi. Centrum Informacji Kulturalnej.

Puś, W. (1997). *Rozwój przemysłu w Królestwie Polskim 1870–1914.* Łódź: Wydawnictwo Uniwersytetu Łódzkiego.

Puś, W. (1998). *Żydzi w Łodzi w latach zaborów: 1793–1914.* Łódź: Wydawnictwo Uniwersytetu Łódzkiego.

Puś, W. (2013). *Statystyka przemysłu Królestwa Polskiego w latach 1879–1913: materiały źródłowe.* Łódź: Wydawnictwo Uniwersytetu Łódzkiego.

Romer, E., & Weinfeld, I. (1917). *Rocznik Polski: tablice statystyczne.* Kraków: Drukarnia Uniwersytetu Jagiellońskiego.

Schulze, M.-S. (2007a). *Origins of catch-up failure: Comparative productivity growth in the Hapsburg Empire, 1870–1910.* London: LSE.

Schulze, M.-S. (2007b). *Regional income dispersion and market potential in the late nineteenth century Hapsburg Empire.* London: LSE.

Ślęzak, T., & Śliwa, M. (Eds.). (2004). *Polska lewica w XX wieku: historia, ludzie, idee.* Kraków: Wydawnictwo Naukowe Akademii Pedagogicznej.

Śliwa, M. (1995). Ludwik Gumplowicz i socjalizm. *Przegląd Humanistyczny,* Warszawa, *39* 77–86.

Snyder T. (1997) Nationalism, Marxism, and modern Central Europe: A biography of Kazimierz Kelles-Krauz (1872–1905). Distributed by Harvard University Press for the Ukrainian Research Institute, Harvard University, Cambridge.

Snyder, T., Błesznowski, B., Król, M., & Puchejda, A. (Eds.). (2015). *Genealogy of contemporaneity: A history of ideas in Poland, 1815–1939*. Warszawa; Vienna: Wydawnictwa Uniwersytetu Warszawskiego; Institut für die Wissenschaften vom Menschen.

Sobczak, T. (1968). *Przełom w konsumpcji spożywczej w Królestwie Polskim w XIX wieku*. Wrocław: Zakład Narodowy im Ossolińskich. Wydawnictwo PAN.

Szczepanowski, S. (1888). *Nędza Galicyi w cyfrach i program energicznego rozwoju gospodarstwa krajowego*. Lwów: Gubrynowicz i Szmidt.

Topolski, J. (1973). *Dzieje Wielkopolski: Lata 1793–1918*. Wydawnictwo Poznańskie.

Trencsényi, B., Janowski, M., Baár, M., et al. (2016). *A history of modern political thought in East Central Europe: Negotiating modernity in the "long nineteenth century"*. Oxford: Oxford University Press.

Trzeciakowski, L. (2003). *Posłowie polscy w Berlinie 1848–1928*. Warszawa: Wydawnictwo Sejmowe: Kancelaria Sejmu.

Vnenchak, D., & Mandurowicz-Urbańska, H. (1983). *Informator statystyczny do dziejów rolnictwa w Galicji: struktura agrarna własności chłopskiej w Galicji w dobie autonomii*. Kraków: UJ.

Wapiński, R. (1980). *Narodowa Demokracja 1893–1939: ze studiów nad dziejami myśli nacjonalistycznej*. Wrocław: Zakład Narodowy im. Ossolińskich.

Wapiński, R. (1997). *Historia polskiej myśli politycznej XIX i XX wieku*. Gdańsk: Arche.

Weinfeld, I. (1922). *Rocznik Polski: tablice statystyczne*. Warszawa: Książnica Polska.

Weinfeld, I. (1925). *Tablice statystyczne Polski*. Warszawa and Bydgoszcz: Bibljoteka Polska.

Wójcik, S. (1995). *Ekonomia społeczna według koncepcji Stanisława Grabskiego*. Lublin: Wydawnictwo UMCS.

Wyczański, A. (Ed.). (2003). *Historia Polski w liczbach. T. 1: Państwo, społeczeństwo*. Warszawa: Zakład Wydawnictwo Statystycznych.

Wysokińska, A. (2016). Trwałość granic pokongresowych w krajobrazie społeczno- ekonomicznym. In: Gulczyński, A. (ed.), *Wielkie Nadzieje, wielkie rozczarowania. Ład wiedeński a europejska wspólnota*. Poznań: PTPN, 365–390.

Zagóra-Jonszta, U. (2013). Ruch spółdzielczy i działalność Franciszka Stefczyka. *Prace Naukowe Uniwersytetu Ekonomicznego we Wrocławiu. Polityka Ekonomiczna, 307*, 710–720.

Załęski, W. (1901). *Królestwo Polskie pod względem statystycznym. Cz. 2: Statystyka zajęć i przemysłu*. Warszawa: Sklad Glowny w Księgarni Jana Fiszera.

Zawadzki, W. (1963). *Polska Stanisławowska w oczach cudzoziemców.* Warszawa: PIW.

Zieliński, Z. (2011). *Kulturkampf w archidiecezji gnieźnieńskiej i poznańskiej w latach 1873–1887.* Poznań: Wydawnictwo Poznańskie.

Żor, A. (2011). *Kronenberg: dzieje fortuny.* Warszawa: Wydawnictwo Naukowe PWN.

Żor, A. (Ed.). (2015). *Jan Bloch (1836–1902): Capitalist, pacifist, philanthropist.* Warsaw: Fundacja Jana Blocha & Wyd. Trio.

7

The Window of Opportunity: Polish Lands During the Great War (1914–1921)

1 The Great War and Border Clashes 1914–1921

The outbreak of WWI interrupted the process of the social and economic integration of the Polish lands into the partitioning states. The changes of political borders and the disintegration of the empires destroyed the national markets of Russia, Austria, and Germany, but created favourable conditions for the restoration of the Polish state. However, before that happened, the Polish lands suffered considerable war damage, demographic losses resulting from migrations, and economic losses resulting from the outflow of capital. Material capital diminished because companies had been relocated, and financial capital losses resulted both from the decisions of the entrepreneurs and investors and from the collapse of the exchange rates and of the monetary systems of the states which had governed the Polish lands.

Even though according to the Polish historical tradition, WWI ended on 11 November 1918, when Polish independence was proclaimed and Germany surrendered, it seems reasonable to include the subsequent years into the war period. There was a conflict with Soviet Russia, which

© The Author(s) 2018
P. Koryś, *Poland From Partitions to EU Accession*,
https://doi.org/10.1007/978-3-319-97126-1_7

ended in October 1921 and was followed by a treaty (signed in spring 1922), which finally established the eastern border. The other borders were also drawn up in 1921, as a result of the plebiscites in Upper Silesia and part of East Prussia. The plebiscite on the Polish-Czech border was planned, but it was never conducted because of the Polish-Soviet war, and the borders were established by an international committee. In effect, it was not until the end of 1921 that the territory under the Polish administration was finally determined, and as late as in the summer of that year, the Soviet army was near Warsaw and controlled about half of that territory (Davies 1986; Roszkowski 2017).

The situation of the Polish lands changed significantly after the outbreak of WWI: as a direct armed conflict between the states that had partitioned Poland, it created an opportunity to restore the Polish state. Initially, the Russian offensive seized Eastern Galicia: in 1915, Russia captured the fortress in Przemyśl. However, in the same year, following the Gorlice-Tarnow offensive, the Austro-Hungarian and German armies regained the whole of Galicia. Through subsequent offensives between 1914 and 1915, Germany and Austro-Hungary seized part of the Russian partition, including the entire territory of the Congress Kingdom. By the end of 1914, they captured part of the western provinces of the Kingdom, including Łódź and Kalisz, which suffered serious damage during the fight. At the beginning of 1915, the Suwalki province was seized and by August the whole territory of the Kingdom followed suite—the Russian army withdrew past the rivers Niemen (Neman) and Bug. The German army subsequently captured the rest of the formerly Polish lands, including Vilnius and Grodno. Then, the situation remained unchanged despite the efforts of both sides; the only exception was the success of the Brusilov offensive in Eastern Galicia and Bukovina in 1916.

The territories newly occupied by Germans and Austrians obtained civil administration, the Government General of Warsaw (German), and the Government General of Lublin (Austro-Hungary). The Suwalki province became part of the military territory of Ober-Ost (*Oberbefehlshaber der gesamten Streitkräfte im Osten*), also comprising the formerly Commonwealth (and Lithuanian and Belorussian in the future) lands of the western provinces of Russia, the Kowno and Grodno provinces, as well as part of the Vilnius province.

In 1916, the occupying states decide to create a dependent Polish state on these territories, which was part of a plan to restructure Central Europe to serve the interests of the central powers, that is, build a system of buffer countries, dependent on Germany, on the territories seized from Russia (the idea of *Mitteleuropa*). In autumn 1916, Germany and Austro-Hungary started to create the Polish administration of the dependent Polish state, which was to be one of several countries separating Russia from Germany. At the same time, Germany supported the creation of the Kingdom of Lithuania on some of the lands of the former Grand Duchy of Lithuania (Prokš 2016; Scheer 2016).

In autumn 1917, the new authorities of the Kingdom of Poland were nominated. In 1917, independent Ukraine was created on the territories controlled by the Russian army, with the capital in Kiev (which was then seized by the Bolshevik army in 1918). The political and economic crisis in Russia, which resulted in the Russian Revolution, that is, the outbreak of two subsequent anti-Tsarist rebellions (the February and October Revolutions), and the disintegration of the imperial army contributed to the German successes in 1917, as a result of which independent Lithuania was created. The Treaty of Brest-Litovsk of 3 March 1918, between Germany and Bolshevik Russia, gave Germany control of the Polish lands, which were disjoined from Russia. The German army controlled this territory until after the war and supported the emergence of new states, including the Kingdom of Lithuania, later the Lithuanian Republic, and German protectorates, for example, the Ukrainian state.

In the spring of 1918, the Kingdom of Poland obtained formal independence from Russia. The new autonomous quasi-state had considerable internal independence, and on 7 October 1918, the Regency Council proclaimed the independence of the Kingdom of Poland from Germany, which was the first step to creating an independent state. The armistice finishing WWI guaranteed Poland's independence, but did not determine its borders. The Polish government announced its will to incorporate Greater Poland into the Polish state, and in December 1918, a Polish uprising against the German army broke out in Greater Poland. There was a risk that the former Grand Duchy of Posen would remain a part of Germany, and the Polish majority struggled for integrating Greater

Poland into Poland. After the success of the uprising, the province was governed by the Supreme People's Council, dissolved in August 1919 following the creation of the Ministry for the Former Prussian Partition. In February 1919, Greater Poland became the protectorate of the Entente, and the Treaty of Versailles of 28 June 1919 gave Greater Poland to the Polish state. Poland did not formally take over the lands of Greater Poland and Pomerania obtained under the Treaty until January 1920, but the process of the administrational integration of the lands of the former Prussian partition into the new state began six months earlier, when the customs border was abolished in June 1919 (Łuczak 1973; Davies 1986; Rezler 2016; Roszkowski 2017).

In October 1918, the government in Western Galicia was taken over by the Polish Liquidation Committee, who submitted to the government of the Kingdom of Poland and then the Republic of Poland. In Eastern Galicia, a similar function was performed by the National Council in Przemyśl, the Committee for Security and the Protection of Public Welfare in Lvov, and in Cieszyn Silesia by the National Council of the Duchy of Cieszyn. The two former bodies were dissolved at the beginning of 1919, following the creation of the Governing Commission for Galicia, Silesia, Spis, and Orava. In the Cieszyn area, the National Council was active until the territory was divided between Poland and the Czech Republic in July 1920 (Przeniosło 2010; Roszkowski 2017).

In November 1918, the Polish-Ukrainian war began in Eastern Galicia. By mid-1919, the whole province was under the control of Poland. However, between 1919 and 1923, the Entente regarded it as temporary administration, and the province itself as a disputed territory under the supervision of the Entente, which the Polish government never officially accepted. Eventually, in March 1923, Poland's sovereignty over this region was formally recognized (Klimecki 2014).

In 1918, the Bolshevik authorities rejected the Treaty of Brest-Litovsk and the German army started to cede the territories to Bolshevik Russia. In effect, the Bolshevik army occupied Minsk in December 1918 and Vilnius in January 1919. Later, as a result of an agreement signed in February 1919 between the Poles and the Germans, the Polish army started to take over the remaining positions of the German army, which led to the outbreak of the conflict between the Poles and the Bolsheviks.

The war in 1919 was successful for the Polish army. Co-operation with Ukrainians resulted in a successful offensive in Ukraine: in the spring of 1920, the Polish and Ukrainian armies captured Kiev. The Bolsheviks got the internal situation (civil war) under control, counter-attacked, and, at the end of April, after another reversal of fortunes, they reached Warszawa and took control over half of the territory of the Polish state. The Polish army won the battle of Warszawa in August 1920, which once again reversed the situation, and the Polish victory was confirmed by the successful Neman offensive. The armistice was signed in October, and the peace treaty in Riga, which established the Polish-Soviet border, in March 1921 (Davies 2003).

In 1920–1921, as a result of the Polish military success and the collapse of the Ukrainian states (including the Western Ukrainian People's Republic), the border was drawn to the east of the Curzon Line, comprising all the former Austrian Galicia and parts of the former Russian Vilnius, Grodno, Minsk, and Volhynia provinces. The planned Polish-Russian border (Curzon line) was generally outlined in the documents from the 1919, refined by the British government and put forward by Lord George Curzon, the British Secretary of State for Foreign Affairs, a year later (Eberhardt 2012). The proposed border approximately followed the eastern border of the Congress Kingdom, with former Galicia divided in the way which left Western Galicia within Poland, possibly along with Lvov and the oil-bearing Boryslav region. It is noteworthy that the Curzon Line was later used by Stalin in negotiations during WWII, and it constitutes the present-day eastern border of Poland, though with the less favourable division of Galicia, excluding Lvov from Poland.

Because of the ongoing wars, there were disturbances in the organization of the popular votes necessary to establish the northern, southern, and western borders of Poland. The plebiscite in the Duchy of Cieszyn, preceded by an armed Czech-Polish conflict in the winter of 1918–1919, did not take place. The region was divided in a way that left the Polish minority within the Czech Republic, which obtained Zaolzie (the southern bank of the river Olza) and the Karwina industrial region. The conflict and the division of this region marred the Polish-Czech relations throughout the interwar period (Knyt 2008).

The last region whose borders had yet to be established was Upper Silesia, formally under the governance of the Entente. The plebiscite, preceded by two uprisings of the Polish majority, took place in March 1921. The division of the territory after the plebiscite was carried out at variance with the decisions included in the treaty, as it was conducted on the basis of counties, not commons, mostly because of the technical difficulties with establishing the border and the considerable number of potential enclaves in both countries. Globally, Germany won the plebiscite 60% to 40%, with the greatest support in urban areas. Two shapes for the border were put forward: the French proposal was favourable for Poland, as it was to obtain the eastern counties along with the entire industrial area; and the Italian-British proposal was less favourable, as it granted Poland a relatively small south-eastern agricultural part of the region. When the proposals were made public by the Polish and the public outrage took the form of protests and strikes, the Third Silesian Uprising broke out and influenced the decision on the shape of the border. One-third of the plebiscite region was granted to Poland, along with a considerable part of the industrial area (ca three-quarters of the coal mining and half of the steel production of the region went to Poland), though it was not finally decided upon until the end of 1921, when the situation stabilized and the Inter-Allied forces took control. The final regulations were drawn up a year later, and in July, the territories granted to Poland were handed over and Polish administration was established there, which finished the process of shaping the territory and the economic structure of the new state (Szymański 1997; Towarzystwo Miłośników Ziemi Kwidzyńskiej 2000; Długoborski 2003; Lis 2015).

2   Demographic and Socio-Economic Consequences of Wars (1914–1921) in Poland

The wars inflicted heavy losses, among both soldiers (fighting in the partitioning states' armies and subsequently in the Polish army) and civilians; the estimated number of losses is 500,000 soldiers and

300,000–400,000 civilians. There are no precise data on the growth of mortality due to contagious diseases, starvation, and malnutrition, but there is no doubt that there was high level of mortality due to the epidemics of typhoid fever and cholera, the 1918 influenza pandemic, and the increase in incidences of tuberculosis. There was large-scale refugeeship—about 3.5–3.7 million people escaped or were evacuated from the Russian territories captured by Germany during the war, and later mostly incorporated into Poland, but only 2.4 million people came back to Poland, and about a million or more died (Handelsman et al. 1936; Główny Urząd Statystyczny 1993; Sula 2013).

Moreover, the birth rate decreased considerably; the data for the Prussian partition show a decline from 38 to 39 births per 1000 inhabitants in 1913–1914 to 20 births in 1917–1918 (in 1922, the number reached 34 births). In the urban areas of the Russian partition, the decline was even more significant: from 16 births in 1914 to 6 in 1918 in Warsaw, and from 24 to 5 in Lodz, respectively. The statistics from 1921 show considerable population drops: from 12.3 to 11.2 million in Congress Poland, from 5.8 to 4.1 million in the eastern provinces (the lands of the Russian partition which were not included in the Kingdom of Poland), from 8.1 to 7.6 million in the Austrian partition; it was only in the Prussian partition where the population grew from 3.8 to 3.9 million. In total, it means the drop of the population which inhabited the territory of the Second Republic of Poland from 30 to 27 million people. Some towns and cities were depopulated, for example, between 1910 to 1921 the population of Kalisz diminished from 54,000 to 45,000 people, in Łódź from 502,000 to 452,000, in Sosnowiec from 102,000 to 87,000, and in Grodno from 50,000 to 35,000 (Weinfeld 1922; Jelonek 1967). In total, population losses resulting from a decrease in the rate of natural increase (both, rise of death rate and decrease of birth rate) are estimated at 7–8 million (excluding direct victims of war and military losses). In 1921, the number of war-disabled exceeded 1% of the population (Weinfeld 1925).

War damage was considerable in the Kingdom of Poland and Galicia, resulting from the fact that Polish lands were one of the major theatres of war, the front moved on its territory several times, and many battles were fought. The data from 1921 indicate that there was damage done to about 1.7 million buildings, primarily in the

Russian and Austrian partitions, and to about 1.8 million farms (about 30% of the farms in these regions), which seriously affected agricultural output, both in crops and in livestock. There was also considerable damage to infrastructure in the Russian and Austrian partitions, where about 60% of the railway stations and bridges were damaged (Ministerstwo Robót Publicznych 1923; Weinfeld 1925) (Table 7.1).

Industry also suffered damage, which is quite well documented. In the Kingdom of Poland, the Russians evacuated part of the industry along with the employees (about 200,000 industrial and railway workers) and destroyed part of it in 1915. The Germans conducted the policy of exploitation, commandeering the resources and dismantling the machinery (including about 4250 electric engines, 900 steam and combustion engines, and 3850 machine tools). The machinery was overused and wore out significantly. In effect, by 1916, employment in the industry of the Kingdom of Poland fell by almost 80%. In the subsequent years, the employment and production levels were partially restored, but in 1918 employment in the industry of the Kingdom once again dropped to only 14% of the pre-war level, and before 1920 there were, for example, over 50% fewer spindles and 65% fewer looms than before the war. According to the estimates put forward by the Polish delegation to the Reparations Committee in Versailles, the total industrial damage on the Polish lands reached 10 billion gold francs, and the losses resulting from the German and Austrian pillage, the Russian evacuation, and direct damage during WWI were estimated at 1 billion francs (Domosławski and Bankiewicz 1936; Handelsman et al. 1936). The damage was increased in the subsequent years due to the border wars, particularly the Polish-Bolshevik War (Davies 2003; Tomaszewski and Landau 2005).

Table 7.1 Buildings destroyed during war and share of buildings rebuilt by 1925, territory of interwar Poland

	Destroyed buildings in thousands	Rebuilt until end of 1924 (%)
Poland	1818	67
Kingdom of Poland	604	71
Western provinces of Russia	648	57
Galicia	566	70

Source: Ministerstwo Robót Publicznych (1923), Weinfeld (1925)

In the aftermath of the war, the Polish sovereign state was restored. It was a fulfilment of the dreams of the Polish nation (the elite most of all), but it was also an almost inevitable consequence of the crumbling of the Eastern European empires. The war was preceded by growing ethnic tension, particularly in the Russian and German partitions, which strengthened the Poles' urge to regain independence. However, the new state was in an extremely difficult economic situation. The Polish industry had lost its connections with the internal markets of Russia, Germany, and Austria, which had been its key outlets. The new internal market was divided and disintegrated in terms of money (different currencies inherited from the partitioning countries), regulations, and institutions (different legal and institutional systems). The full integration of the state and internal market turned out to be a long-term challenge. Moreover, apart from the considerable material damage, the war caused the outflow of financial, material, and human capital as well as labour resources, which badly affected the economy. These losses are difficult to assess, but the numbers concerning the industrial damage and the population losses may give a certain idea. The cost of restoring the economy, the financial support for industry and agriculture after the war, the administration of repatriation, and the border wars contributed to the huge scale of the post-war crisis. The scale of the damage, largest in the poorest eastern provinces of the new Poland, as well as the challenge of the integration of Polish lands, impeded the implementation of social reforms which were started after the war, such as the land reform and the attempt to build the welfare state.

References

Davies, N. (1986). *God's playground: A history of Poland. Vol. 2: To the present.* Oxford: Clarendon Press.

Davies, N. (2003). *White eagle, red star: The Polish-Soviet War 1919–1920' and the miracle on the Vistula.* London: Pimlico.

Długoborski, W. (2003). *Powstania śląskie i plebiscyt w historiografii niemieckiej.* Rocz Muz W Gliwicach 367.

Domosławski, B., & Bankiewicz, J. (1936). *Zniszczenia i szkody wojenne.* Warszawa: Towarzystwo Badania Zagadnień Międzynarodowych.

Eberhardt, P. (2012). The Curzon Line as the eastern boundary of Poland: The origins and the political background. *Geographia Polonica, 1*, 5–12.

Główny Urząd Statystyczny. (1993). *Historia Polski w liczbach: ludność, terytorium.* Główny Urząd Statystyczny.

Handelsman, M., Bankiewicz, J., Gliwic, H., et al. (Eds.). (1936). *Polska w czasie wielkiej wojny (1914–1918): historja społeczna i ekonomiczna. T. 3: Historja ekonomiczna.* Warszawa: Towarzystwo Badania Zagadnień Międzynarodowych.

Jelonek, A. (1967). *Ludność miast i osiedli typu miejskiego na ziemiach Polski od 1810 do 1960 r.* Instytut Geografii Polskiej Akademii Nauk.

Klimecki, M. (2014). *Wojna polsko-ukraińska: Lwów i Galicja Wschodnia 1918–1919: pierwszy konflikt zbrojny odrodzonej Polski.* Warszawa: Bellona.

Knyt, A. (Ed.). (2008). *Zaolzie: polsko-czeski spór o Śląsk Cieszyński 1918–2008.* Warszawa: Fundacja Ośrodka Karta: Dom Spotkań z Historią.

Lis, M. (2015). *Powstania śląskie i plebiscyt ze współczesnej perpektywy.* Opole: Państwowy Instytut Naukowy – Instytut Śląski: Stowarzyszenie Instytut Śląski.

Łuczak, C. (1973). *Dzieje Wielkopolski: Lata 1793–1918.* Wydawnictwo Poznańskie.

Ministerstwo Robót Publicznych. (1923). *Zniszczenia wojenne w budowlach na ziemiach Rzeczypospolitej Polskiej: stan zniszczeń w dniu 1 stycznia.* Warszawa: Ministerstwo Robót Publicznych.

Prokš, P. (2016). "Mitteleuropa—Zwischeneuropa": niemieckie koncepcje Europy Środkowej w czasie Wielkiej Wojny w latach 1914–1918. *Stud Środ Bałkanistyczne*, 77–98.

Przeniosło, M. (2010). *Polska Komisja Likwidacyjna 1918–1919.* Kielce: Wydawnictwo Uniwersytetu Humanistyczno- Przyrodniczego Jana Kochanowskiego.

Rezler, M. (2016). *Powstanie wielkopolskie 1918–1919.* Poznań: Dom Wydawniczy Rebis.

Roszkowski, W. (2017). *Historia Polski 1914–2015* (Wyd. 12. Rozszerzone). Warszawa: Wydawnictwo Naukowe PWN.

Scheer, T. (2016). Królestwo Polskie pod okupacją Austro-Węgier w czasie I wojny światowej (1915–1918). *Doświadczenia Żołnierskie Wielkiej Wojny : Studia i Szkice z Dziejów Frontu Wschodniego I Wojny Światowej*, 27–50.

Sula, D. (2013). *Powrót ludności polskiej z byłego Imperium Rosyjskiego w latach 1918–1937.* Warszawa: Wydawnictwo Trio.

Szymański, M. (1997). Plebiscyt na Warmii, Mazurach i Powiślu w 1920 r. *Wiad Hist Czas Dla Naucz*, 193–200.

Tomaszewski, J., & Landau, Z. (2005). *Polska w Europie i świecie 1918–1939* (Wyd. nowe, rozsz). Warszawa: TRIO.

Towarzystwo Miłośników Ziemi Kwidzyńskiej (Ed.). (2000). *Plebiscyt na Powiślu—11 lipiec 1920 rok.* Kwidzyn; Sztum: Towarzystwo Miłośników Ziemi Kwidzyńskiej; Towarzystwo Miłośników Ziemi Sztumskiej.

Weinfeld, I. (1922). *Rocznik Polski: tablice statystyczne.* Warszawa: Książnica Polska.

Weinfeld, I. (1925). *Tablice statystyczne Polski.* Warszawa and Bydgoszcz: Bibljoteka Polska.

8

A Moment of Independence: Reconstruction and Economic Development of the Second Republic of Poland (1918/21–1939)

Immediately before WWI, Polish lands were mostly a backward agricultural region, and the agricultural sector of the economy employed considerably more than half the labour force (with a particularly high percentage in Galicia). Areas of intense industrialization were few and far between, and the industries which developed were typical of the previous technological stage, that is, they were labour- rather than capital-intensive. Innovative technologies were rarely used, which resulted from the low level of development of the educational systems and in particular, very low number of modern universities in the most populated Polish regions—Russian and Austrian (with the exception of Jagiellonian University in Kraków, University and Politechnic in Lwów and University and Polytechnic in Warszawa). Infrastructure was also underdeveloped, especially in the Kingdom of Poland and in the rest of the Russian partition; this turned out to be a serious detriment to development in the later decades, in the independent state.

However, the development of the Polish lands had already taken off despite the setbacks created by the lack of statehood. Unfortunately, this process was disturbed by a decade of war and destruction described in the previous chapter. The destruction in Eastern Galicia, the lands in the east (former Russian Western provinces) and in the Kingdom of Poland, wasted decades of development, and the lands that were not destroyed, like the Prussian

© The Author(s) 2018
P. Koryś, *Poland From Partitions to EU Accession*,
https://doi.org/10.1007/978-3-319-97126-1_8

partition, suffered social disintegration and the loss of the most important markets. The restored Poland was built out of three peripheral provinces of three empires; the industrial centres were elsewhere, outside Poland, and stayed there.

The integration of the Polish lands remained a challenge throughout the interwar period. In particular, as a result of Poland's unfavourable economic and geopolitical situation, the economic integration was not achieved before WWII.

1   Internal Politics

During WWI, there was a growing political conflict between the independence-oriented faction of the Polish Socialist Party and the National Democracy. It occurred in all the partitions with varying intensity, but it was particularly important in the most populous Russian partition. The results of the partial election in 1919 and the general election in 1922 showed that the middle-class National Democracy was relatively strong in Greater Poland (especially in the Posen province) and in the western provinces of the Congress Kingdom. The Polish Socialist Party had strong support in the western, more urbanized and industrialized regions of the Kingdom of Poland, and in Galicia. Another important political force in the former Kingdom and Galicia was the peasants' parties, both left-wing (*PSL Lewica*, *PSL Wyzwolenie*) and centre-right (*PSL Piast*). The communist party retained some of its influence in cities across whole country. There was also considerable support for the coalition of national minorities (Rzepecki and Rzepecki 1923; Kacperski 2007, 2013). Up to 1926, none of the political factions gained the majority of the parliament, so the political situation was unstable. The conflict was fuelled by the assassination of the first president, elected by the parliament, Gabriel Narutowicz, in 1922 (Ajnenkiel 1986; Garlicki 2012; Białokur 2013).

The first cabinet was created by the left-wing faction and its prime minister was Jędrzej Moraczewski. However, it fell as a result of the criticism of the strong right-wing faction and the lack of support from the Entente (Goclon 2009; Faryś et al. 2010). The subsequent period witnessed weak cabinets, created by coalitions (mostly centre-right) and some technocrat cabinets, the most important of which was the second cabinet created by Władysław Grabski. It was composed of specialists who were not members of parliament, and it continually sought parliamentary support. Its principal goal was curbing hyperinflation, stabilizing the budget, and conducting the currency reform. Despite constant political tension and the need to negotiate the support of the fragmented parliament, Grabski managed to continue the cabinet for almost two years (1923–1925) and implemented a number of reforms (Fronczek-Kwarta 2014).

The subsequent cabinet, headed by Aleksander Skrzyński, comprised almost the entire political spectrum (Morawski 1990). Then, in May 1926, a centre-right coalition was created of national-democratic and peasant parties (new government was headed by Wincenty Witos), but in the same month Józef Piłsudski led a successful *coup d'état*. As the former leader of the Polish Socialist Party, the former Chief of State, and the leader of the army during the Polish-Soviet war, he was still very popular with the society and had strong support in the army. He decided to take over because of his frustration caused by the fragmentation and inefficiency of the Polish parliament, the growing political instability and the economic crisis resulting in the social tension leading to protests and strikes (Ajnenkiel 1986; Garlicki 1987).

After the *coup d'état*, Pilsudski introduced semi-authoritarian government, based on the diminished power of the parliament and the strengthened power of the president (Ignacy Mościcki). In reality, Piłsudski was the actual head of state (until his death in 1935), and the government was a group of his henchmen, commonly called *Sanacja* ("Sanation"), which never turned into a political party, but was represented by political movements: the Society for the Amendment of the Commonwealth, later the Nonpartisan Bloc for Cooperation with the Government (*BBWR*, created in 1928), and since 1935, the Camp of National Unity (Wynot 1974; Chojnowski 1986; Seniów 1998).

The election of 1928 was not fully successful for *BBWR* and the parliament, with a relatively strong centre-left opposition, was dissolved in 1930. The leaders of the opposition parties, particularly of the Polish Socialist Party and of the peasant parties (*PSL Piast* and *PSL Wyzwolenie*), were accused of instigating riots and preparing a *coup d'état*, and were subsequently imprisoned. Some leaders left Poland to avoid imprisonment (this group included the peasant movement leader Wincenty Witos) (Rzepecki and Rzepecki 1928; Ajnenkiel 1989).

The next election gave the Nonpartisan Bloc for Cooperation with the Government, supported by the state structures, proper success. The position of the *Sanacja* was not even threatened by the Great Depression, which started in 1930. In 1935, the constitution was changed. In 1935, Józef Piłsudski died, which did not make *Sanacja* lose power, but led to the rise of conflicting factions within its ranks. The subsequent victory in the election (boycotted by the opposition) did not change the situation (Wynot 1974; Ajnenkiel 1989).

In the final years of the Second Polish Republic, the big opposition parties, that is, the Polish Socialist Party, National Democracy, and the peasant Polish People's Party (*PSL*), retained some influence in the local authorities, but were absolutely marginalized at the level of state politics. The popularity of the radical opposition, including nationalistic and chauvinistic groups, increased. The Polish Communist Party retained minor influence until, in 1937, Stalin invited its leaders to the USSR, arrested them, and had them killed.

The internal disintegration of the *Sanacja* political camp after Pilsudski's death created two main rival factions inside the government and the ruling elite, the military one, formed around Marshal Edward Rydz-Śmigły, and the civilian one around President Ignacy Mościcki. They arrived at a compromise and appointed General Felicjan Sławoj-Składkowski as prime minister in 1936. The political conflict within the government remained unresolved until the outbreak of WWII in September 1939 (Wynot 1971, 1974; Seidner and Wynot 1975).

The lack of political stability, the crisis of democracy, and the authoritarian government were not unique to Poland, as many European countries suffered similar problems after WWI. However, the *Sanacja* managed to create particularly effective political myths—one presenting the May 1926 *coup d'état* as a defence of democracy rather than an assault on it, another presenting the *Sanacja* period as a huge social, political, and economic success. These myths (as well as the experience of war and the post-war state socialism) blotted out the memory of the brutal methods used for solving political conflicts (such as political trials or detaining the political opponents in the Bereza Kartuska prison without formal charges or trial), the growing social unrest (resulting from the sustained class and regional economic disparities), the economic instability and inefficient economic policy, the growing political corruption, or the growing separatist tendencies posing the threat of ethnic conflicts, particularly in the south-east of the country. Finally, the greatest fault of the political elite in the late 1930s was their misguided perception of the international situation and (especially after Piłsudski's death) the erroneous assessment of the policies of the neighbouring countries and the risks connected with these policies—as a result, it occurred that Poland entered WWII without any effective military alliances (geographically remoted allies, France and Great Britain offered only minimal support for Poland in September 1939).

2   International Situation

The unstable political situation at the beginning of the new state was not conducive to building safe relations with the neighbouring countries while the state borders were being established. The creation of effective foreign policy was also hampered by the fact that the two key politicians, Józef Piłsudski and Roman Dmowski (the leader of National Democracy and the Polish representative in Versailles), held opposing views on that matter. Piłsudski favoured the idea of a union of countries (such as the Baltic republics, Ukraine, Belarus) called *Międzymorze* formed around Poland and separating it from Russia, a little like in the old Commonwealth (Wyszczelski 2015a). This plan did not succeed, Ukrainian and Belarusian states were not created, and the border conflict with Lithuania and the Polish annexation of the Wilno area marred the Polish-Lithuanian relations in the whole interwar period. The most friendly Polish neighbour was Romania and, in 1920, a treaty was signed against Russia, confirmed by the treaties of 1926 and 1931. Poland also had good relations with Latvia.

The emergence of Poland and a number of other Central European countries was Woodrow Wilson's idea for Europe, but this geopolitical change was frowned on by Russian and German politicians, because it was these two countries that contributed the territory for the newly created Poland (Gerson 1972). In the early 1920s, these two countries got closer together and signed the treaty of Rapallo in 1922. The Treaty of Locarno of 1925 and the German-Soviet Neutrality and Non-Aggression

Pact of 1926 were further steps to strengthening Germany and worsening Poland's geopolitical situation (Cienciała and Komarnicki 1984). Furthermore, the German economy was strengthened through the Young Plan. The German relations with Russia were temporarily cooled at the beginning of the 1930s and at that time the Soviet-Polish Non-Aggression Pact was signed in 1932 and the German-Polish Non-Aggression Pact in 1934. However, the Polish diplomacy was helpless when Germany's power and aggressiveness grew and Germany engineered the Anglo-German Naval Agreement in 1935, the Annexation of Austria (*Anschluss*) and Czechoslovakia (the Munich Agreement) in 1938, and the Molotov-Ribbentrop Pact (the German-Soviet Non-Aggression Pact) in 1939. The outbreak of the war in September 1939 was probably hastened by Poland's refusal to agree to reincorporate Gdańsk (Danzig) into the Reich and to allow the construction of an extraterritorial roadway along the so-called Polish Corridor, a strip of land separating East Prussia from Germany proper (Landau and Tomaszewski 1977; Davies 1986; Ajnenkiel 1999).

From the first days of its existence, Poland sought alliances with the Entente powers. France, which gave Poland military support during the Polish-Soviet War by sending the French Military Mission to Poland, was treated as the main ally. This was confirmed in 1921 by signing the Franco-Polish Military Alliance, a defensive alliance against the threats from Germany and the Soviet Union. Great Britain sought rapprochement with Germany in most of the interwar period, and the USA had resumed their isolationist policy, which made it difficult for Poland to build alliances with these countries. Eventually, in 1939, with the war ominously close, Great Britain granted Poland the guarantee of its independence, which was later turned into the Agreement of Mutual Assistance, signed a week before the war broke out.

3   Ideas

The rise of new countries in Europe and the world, the economic problems of post-war European countries, and the global crisis later, in the 1930s, resulted in the growing interest in the tools of efficient economic policy. The restoration of the pre-war world of globalization turned out unsuccessful, and numerous protectionist measures changed the economic map of Europe. Additionally, Soviet Russia established a new, non-market economic system, which for some observers seemed much more efficient than the market economy (particularly when the Soviet Russia was not hit by the Great Depression). These circumstances revived the debates on economic development, the role of state and the market, as well as of private and public property. The new economic theory of John Maynard Keynes laid the foundation for modern macroeconomics, and offered new tools for economic policy in democratic countries. Actually, it reflected the existing reality—the Great Depression forced many countries to introduce massive public investments as well as some measures of public policy to protect the unemployed, farmers, and so on. The Polish economist Michał Kalecki proposed an economic system similar to Keynes', and published his seminal book even before Keynes (López G. and Assous 2010; Toporowski 2013).

Moreover, another Polish economist, Oskar Lange, played an important role in the so-called socialist calculation debate between market socialism economists and representatives of the Austrian School of Economics. He argued that rational economic calculation was possible within his model of socialism founded on the neo-classical assumptions. He applied elements such as trial-and-error price mechanism (Walras auctions) and Pareto efficient market equilibrium to the concept of the central planning board (Boettke 2000; Kostro 2001; Temkin 2008).

Thus, during the interwar period, the relation between Polish economic debates, particularly debates on economic development, remained in much closer relations with Western European discussions than ever before. Polish economists started to apply mathematics to economic analysis relatively early—and with the growing importance of a mathematical economy, they became recognized among influential researchers in the field. Polish academics were visible even at the institutional level, for example, Władysław Zawadzki, who became a founding member of the Econometric Society (Lityńska 2004). With the growing importance of economics as a science and the growing intellectual potential of the Polish economic sciences, the problem of the development model for Poland increasingly involved professional economists. Even though some of

them were politicians representing various factions, the institutionalization of economics as a scientific discipline resulted in the discussion on
Poland's development getting professional, at least partially. The economists represented various schools of thought—from the supporters of the
Austrian school (e.g. Adam Krzyżanowski), through liberals and classical
economists (e.g. Roman Rybarski, Jerzy Zdziechowski, Edward Taylor),
and mathematical economists and the scholars involved in the general
equilibrium theory (e.g. Władysław Zawadzki, but also Oskar Lange), to
scholars conducting studies of business cycles from the statist and left-
wing point of view (e.g. Ludwik Landau and Michał Kalecki), and the
socioeconomic German school (the Grabski brothers).

They put forward diverse ideas for the solution of Poland's problems.
The liberal economists proposed the construction of the limited but very
well-organized state. They opposed the growth of bureaucracy and criticized the inefficiency of statist solutions. They regarded the market as a
self-regulating mechanism and thought that Poland should imitate the
economic leaders. The critics of classical economics, such as Michał
Kalecki, drew attention to the role of the state in alleviating the adverse
effects of business cycles. Ludwik Landau worked on the concepts of
development economics *avant la lettre*: he studied the social and wealth
disparities in Poland and in the world. He did not offer solutions, but the
research of his team in the Institute of Business Cycles and Prices helped
to identify the areas of poverty, and to analyse the economic situation of
workers or the consequences of rural unemployment. Additionally, he
and Kalecki conducted the first estimations of the Polish social income
(Kalecki and Landau 1934, 1935; Mazurek 2016).

Despite the growing involvement of economists in the discussion, the
leading role in the debate was always played by politicians. Only the basic
outlines of the main ideologies will be presented here, as it is difficult to
discuss all the details of the extremely factionalized political life of the
Second Republic of Poland.

The intellectuals connected with the Polish Socialist Party, such as
Zofia Daszyńska-Golińska and Ignacy Daszyński, thought that the modern class warfare should be conducted in the sovereign state, which had
been impossible before, when the first priority was the fight for independence. They expected the Polish state to represent the interests of the

working class and support the emancipation of the workers. Therefore, the socialists were ambivalent about private property, which they treated as a source of injustice and exploitation. At the beginning of the 1920s, Norbert Barlicki said in the Parliament, "For us socialists private property, and big private property in particular, is a privilege which is a disease of the society, a relic of the dark ages". That is why modernization should be a restructuring of the society and the economy to free the modern Polish society of exploitation, and this process should involve restructuring property. This should be done by means of democratization and delegating as much decision-making power onto the local level as possible, that is, the decentralization of the state. Similar self-governance should comprise the means of production. The socialists wanted the nationalized means of transport, tools of production and the land, to which the first step could be the land reform. The idea of co-operatives was an important component of their economic programme throughout the interwar period and, among others, it was to comprise housing and food production, which was a continuation of the tradition created during the partition period (Barlicki 1980, 36; Tomicki 1982; Śliwa 1988; Drewicz 2009).

The socialists proposed building the welfare state as the intermediate stage in the process of the modernization of the society. The funding for the implementation of their progressive ideas was to be provided by a tax system through which the wealthy would finance the modernization, and which would work as a social justice mechanism and put in practice the radical social programme formulated in the mid-nineteenth century. The main idea for the reduction of wealth disparities was the introduction of the progressive income, wealth, and inheritance taxes, and also the confiscations of estates, but on the other hand, lowering or lifting direct taxes, particularly pertaining to the basic goods.

The views of the communist parties were far more radical. Their goals did not comprise only the emancipation of the Polish working class; their aim was the emancipation of the working class in Europe and in the world. Therefore, they denied the fight for independence and the defence of independence in the Polish-Bolshevik war of 1920 as contrary to the advancement of the world. For them, the independent state was acceptable as an intermediate stage as long as it improved the economic situation of the proletariat. They wanted to abolish capitalism and build a worldwide communist republic (Czubiński 1988).

The key right-wing party was National Democracy (under various names). The nationalists promoted social solidarity, though their views on it were much less radical than those expressed on the opposite side of the political scene by socialist Norbert Barlicki. According to them, the state should represent the interests of the nation, not a class, and it should be based on the security of private property leading to entrepreneurship. In the draft of the constitution, Stanislaw Głąbiński emphasized that "the citizen's private property is inviolable. Partial or complete expropriation can be conducted only by means of the law, for reasons of the greater good and with appropriate compensation", and that "no system has been designed yet which could replace the system based on private property" (Wapiński 1980; Głąbiński 1999).

According to National Democracy, it was not only the organized and controlled state intervention, but also the individual activity and engagement that should lead to modernization. For this reason, unlike the left-wing parties, National Democracy opposed the statist policy, which they considered economically non-viable. Their criticism of statism involved the emphasis on the reduction of bureaucratic barriers, because they not only led to inefficiency, but also had adverse ethical effects due to the absence of the actual owner, and in this way they became barriers to development. Thus, the national-democratic economic journalism was focused on the criticism of statism, bureaucratic barriers, the badly designed tax system, and excessive administrational structures.

Moreover, instead of the further costly development of bureaucracy, the state should conduct the reform of the public finances aiming to lower the cost of the state, and the reform of the tax system. Unlike the socialists, the national democrats did not see taxes as an instrument of social justice, but as a tool for creating income for the state and an instrument of civic education—education towards creating honest, law-abiding citizens. Another thing that they thought Poland needed was a strong currency—the implementation of this belief was the monetary reform conducted by Władysław Grabski, a politician connected with National Democracy. Grabski and Głąbinski paid a lot of attention to the questions of public finances and the currency.

National Democracy promoted the state's activity towards the development of industry, though not statist, but focused on managing the development and creating incentives for investment and entrepreneurship. The goals of the development of Polish industry were (1) raising the incomes of the lower social classes and reducing the income disparities, (2) reducing unemployment, and (3) the absorption of the surplus rural population into the cities. The development of industry, including big industry, should eventually result in changing the status of the country from mostly agricultural into mostly industrial, and later into industrial. As the prominent politician Jan Zamorski put it, "the whole country could be covered with chimneys and factories, turn into a continuous stretch of cities and factory chimneys" (Jachymek and Paruch 2005, 160).

However, the national democrats were also convinced that the import of capital and the Polish entrepreneurship alone were not sufficient to ensure the growth of industry. For this reason, they saw the necessity to include Poland in the world economy, but in the way that would safeguard its vital interests. Poland was in need of both foreign capital and technologies; the only reservation was that the capital should be "friendly to Poland", which to some extent restricted the sources of such capital. In particular, it could not come from Germany, because that would be a threat to Poland's interests.

According to National Democrats, another key component of modernization was restructuring agriculture, particularly, solving the problem of rural overpopulation. Apart from industrialization and the development of an urban economy, the important element of the solution was the land reform conducted in a reasonable way. It was expected to create a class of small landowners rather than eliminate the big estates. The agricultural and industrial policy was to encourage the emergence of the modern social structure which Roman Dmowski wrote about at the beginning of the twentieth century, that is, based on the urban middle class. The national-democratic ideas included the anti-Semitic component, as Jews were seen as a particular threat to the process of the emergence of this modern social structure and the modern Polish middle class (Jachymek and Paruch 2005).

The conservative thinkers, including economists such as Adam Krzyżanowski, had similar views to those of the liberally oriented

National Democrats. The difference was the individualistic perspective of the former and their criticism of the idea of national solidarity and its consequences (Grzybek 2005).

During the Great Depression, the nationalist parties increasingly accepted statist solutions (similarly, moderate statism was also supported by the Christian Democrats and many Catholic thinkers). In the 1930s, the younger generation of nationalist intellectuals tried to find new economic solutions. Their considerations were influenced by the experience of the Great Depression, which resulted in their disappointment with capitalism and their fascination with the efficiency of the totalitarian states. Some more or less utopian solutions appeared, aiming to build a better world and questioning the capitalist economic model. One such idea was the one created by Adam Doboszyński, which referred to the ideas of the New Middle Ages and in fact rejected the concept of modernity. On the other hand, there were the economic ideas of the National Radical Camp (*ONR*), a radical right-wing nationalistic movement originating from National Democracy, who considered implementing totalitarian solutions. At the end of the Second Republic of Poland, the nationalistic ideas turned from loyalty to rebellious, anti-system thinking, promoting the utopia of the control of the individual exerted by institutions such as the family, the church and tradition, or the totalitarian state (Rudnicki 1985; Doboszyński 1996).

The plans of economic development and social modernization were created in the peasant parties as well. They differed in the degrees of social radicalism, but they shared some common elements. First of all, they focused on the improvement of the economic situation of the peasants. They all promoted large-scale land reform, but they did not suggest any solutions for alleviating rural overpopulation or developing other sectors of economy than agriculture (Borkowski 1987; Borkowski et al. 1995).

From 1926, the key role in the political life and the formulating of policies was played by the *Sanacja* movement. For a long time, even during the Great Depression, most of its politicians had rather liberal economic views. However, at the end of the 1920s, the left-wing statist faction of the movement emerged, which included the practitioners of economic policy, that is, state officials, such as Stefan Starzyński, who formulated one of the first proposals of state-induced development within the movement. In his *Programme for the Labour Government in Poland* (Starzyński 1926; Janus 2009), he promoted using protectionist instruments, implementing state control of manufacturing, further land reform, and administrative actions with a view to modernizing Poland. He emphasized the need for infrastructure investments, such as the construction of the seaport in Gdynia or the development of the railways. His views did not directly include statist ideas at the beginning, but later, the movement started to promote the direct involvement of the state in the economic activity when the market mechanisms and private entrepreneurship failed to create possibilities of catching up with the West any time soon. As the private resources were in short supply, statism and interventionism were to be the solutions stimulating economic development.

The fully fledged statist development programme was outlined by the *Sanacja* politician Eugeniusz Kwiatkowski. In his book *Disparities. On Poland Present and Past* (Kwiatkowski 1932), he indicated the necessity to implement a comprehensive modernization of the country, and he thought that the state should spark it off. His ideas were implemented at the end of the 1930s as the 4-year plan and the 15-year plan. They were based on the assumption that the market had failed as a mechanism of coordination, and for this reason, the state was to take over the coordination of the economic processes and simultaneously implement intense industrialization. Social change was to take a short cut—the relocation of the people to the state-owned factories and to the factory towns built at the same time was to complete the process of not only economic but also political and social modernization within 15–20 years. The statist modernization was to help reduce the development and wealth differences. It has to be noted that the programme was not only economic, but also social. This modernization was to take a different route from the one familiar to present-day reformers, and its goal was not only "the disappearance of the division into Poland A and Poland B, the advancement of the rural Poland, and the disappearance of the illiterate youth, but also the ultimate Polonization of the structure of Polish cities" (Kwiatkowski 1938). The advancement was to be paralleled by the integration of the nation, which Kwiatkowski saw in rather inclusive way.

Even though the Polish statists' views corresponded with the expectations of the society and were a natural reaction to the global economic recession, they were criticized, especially by the liberal economists from the conservative or national-democratic circles and by some business-people (though this criticism mostly stopped when Kwiatkowski included private businesses in the 4-year plan). The critics pointed out the inefficiency of the state-induced non-market coordination mechanisms, wastage, corruption, and ill-advised decisions concerning the allocation of resources. However, in the second decade of the independent state, there was a widespread belief that the statist solution was reasonable (Gołębiowski 1978; Dziewulski 1981; Lityńska et al. 2010).

Since the beginning of the Second Republic of Poland, the politicians had to face practically insolvable problems, such as the shortage of capital and of the human resources, and the unfriendly or openly hostile neighbours. Therefore, the need for modernization was strong and urgent, and taking the short cut was appealing. Additionally, the Great Depression seemed to show that the market and market capitalism were not conducive to the development process. The state, as the agent of change, determining the directions not just by means of incentives but through direct involvement during recession, seemed an appropriate solution to the people who had lost faith in capitalism, particularly considering the economic success of the Italian fascists, the German Nazis, and the Soviet communists at the time. Besides, the ideas of the Central Industrial District and the policy of the big push and the concentration of resources fascinated some economists such as Paul Rosenstein-Rodan (Rosenstein-Rodan 1943) and Michal Kalecki (López G. and Assous 2010; Ghosh 2016), who in the next decades co-created a new economic theory, the development economics.

4   Territory and Population

The Polish borders were established as a result of military conflicts between 1918 and 1921. To its west, Poland comprised most of the lands of the former Grand Duchy of Posen (the German Provinz Posen) as well as a part of the province West Preusse, including Toruń (Thorn) and Grudziądz (Graudenz), but excluding Gdańsk (Danzig) and Elbląg (Elbing). Poland obtained access to the sea, several dozen kilometres in

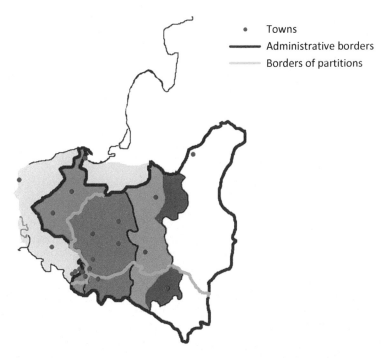

Map 8.1 Poland after WWI (1918–1939). Note: Territory of contemporary Poland shaded. Groups of voivodeships as described in Chap. 8: blue—Western; pink—Central industrial, green—Central agricultural; white—Eastern. Source: Own elaboration on the basis of various historical maps

length, from the border of Gdańsk to Lake Żarnowiec, with the Hel Peninsula (the coast line was 140 km, including the peninsula). As Gdańsk became a free city, there was not a sizeable port on the Polish coast, and the biggest coastal villages had a few thousand inhabitants each—Puck (Putzig), Gdynia (Gdingen), and Reda (Rheda), situated a little away from the shore. The access to the port in Gdańsk was guaranteed by international agreements. Puck had a small port of strategic importance, but the city authorities conducted the policy supporting German economic interests and restricted the access to the port. Therefore, it was as early as in 1920 when the decision was made to build a major seaport in Gdynia. The navy base was transferred from Puck to Gdynia and to Hel. On the southern end of the western border, as a result of the

Plebiscite and the Silesian Uprisings, most of the Upper Silesian industrial area was included into Poland (Główny Urząd Statystyczny 1993).

The northern border ran along the Gdańsk city limits and the border of the German province Ostpreusse, and then along the border with Lithuania. In 1920, the Polish army occupied the Vilnius region, inhabited mostly by Poles (about 60–70% of the population). A new dependent state, the Republic of Central Lithuania, was created in this region, and it was annexed to Poland two years later. In effect, Poland had a common border with Latvia.

The eastern border, established by the Treaty of Riga in 1921, was shared with the USSR. Poland comprised the former Grodno and Vilnius provinces, as well as western parts of the Volhynia and Minsk provinces. The entire territory of Austrian Galicia found itself within Poland, and the borders were similar to the Polish-Russian border after the Second Partition in 1793 (Roszkowski 2017).

In the south, Poland shared the border with Romanian Bukovina and with Czechoslovakia, along the Carpathian range. The disputed territory of part of Cieszyn Silesia and most of Orava and Spis found itself within Czechoslovakia, as a result of the annexation by the Czechoslovak army in 1920 and the subsequent international arbitration. In 1938, when Czechoslovakia was under pressure from Germany, the Polish government gave Czechoslovakia an ultimatum demanding the incorporation of these lands into Poland. Czechoslovakia accepted, and the territory was occupied by the Polish troops in October 1938, at the time of the German annexation of Sudetenland. The Czechs were then expelled from the region—until WWII, about 30,000 Czechs left the newly Polish land.

The territory of the restored state was 389,000 km^2 after the incorporation of Central Lithuania and in 1938 increased by 800 km^2. Most Polish lands were lowlands; the mountainous areas were in the south, mostly in the former Galicia.

The population is best presented on the basis of censuses, which were conducted every 10 years, starting from 1921 (the third census was supposed to take place in 1941) (Łukasiewicz 2009). The census of 1921 did not comprise the entire area of Poland because of the border wars and the prolonged process of taking over the plebiscite areas. Additionally, the 1921 census data are not precise because of the presence of the army in the eastern regions of the country. Between the censuses, the demographic data were supplemented on the basis of birth, death, and migration registries (Główny Urząd Statystyczny 1993).

According to the estimations of the Central Statistical Office, immediately before WWI, the territories which were later included into the restored Poland were populated with about 30 million people, mostly in the central areas, that is, in the former Kingdom of Poland, and in the aftermath of the war, the population fell to about 26 million in 1919; however, both these numbers are uncertain (the only Census in Russia took place in 1897, later data are not fully reliable). In the eastern provinces, the population fell by almost 30%, in the central areas by 13%, in the southern part by less than 10%, and in the western part by less than 5%. This was due to the higher mortality, but also (in the case of the Russian partition) to the voluntary and forcible evacuation preceding the occupation of part of the Russian territory by Germany. Further losses in the east and centre were caused by the Polish-Soviet war, and in the west, by the outflow of the German population. By 1924, the population reached almost 29 million, and in 1931, it exceeded the pre-war levels (31.7 million). In 1938, Poland had almost 35 million inhabitants. The most dynamic population growth was between 1921 and 1930, when the improvement of the economic situation was accompanied by the post-war compensatory population boom. The economic recession of the 1930s lowered the population growth rate (Główny Urząd Statystyczny 1993).

Throughout the period, there was the constant decrease of the percentage of pre-working age people (children 0–14), from 35% in 1921 to 32.5% in 1938. The percentage of post-working age people slightly grew, from 4% to 5%. The percentage of working age people grew from 60.5% in 1921 to 62.5% in 1939. The quick growth of the labour resources took place during the recession, which exacerbated the social consequences of the latter.

During the interwar period, emigration was still considerable, but by 1925, its consequences were counterbalanced by repatriation. About 580,000 people left Poland at that time, 162,000 came back from emigration and another 1,180,000 were repatriated. Between 1925 and 1930, about 960,000 left Poland and 460,000 came back. Between 1931 and 1935, as a result of the restrictions introduced in some Western countries during the recession, the outflow was down to 230,000 and similar number came back. Between 1936 and 1938, the outflow increased to almost 290,000 in 3 years, and immigration fell to 178,000 people. The main destinations were the USA (258,000 by 1930), France (over 620,000), and Germany (475,000); and—for the Jewish—Palestine (80,000 out of the 200,000 Jews who left Poland at the time). Emigrants came back mostly from Germany—about 420,000 in total. Apart from settlement emigration, there was seasonal migration, particularly to work in the German agriculture industry. According to the official statistics, between 1927 and 1938, about 410,000 people yearly went to work in Germany and almost 100,000 to Latvia.

Population growth during interwar period varied regionally. The highest growth of total population was in the former Russian partition: between 1921 and 1931, the population grew by up to 50% in the eastern provinces of Poland (formerly the western provinces of Russia) and 33% in the central provinces (former Kingdom of Poland), while just over 20% in the southern and western provinces of Poland. Moreover, population dynamics in different ethnic/religious groups were different. The Eastern Orthodox population grew more quickly than other groups, and according to the official data, the percentage of the Eastern Orthodox population grew from 10.5% to 11.8% between 1921 and 1931. In the same period, the percentage of Jewish, Greek Orthodox, and Protestant people collectively fell from 25.3% to 22.9%. According to the data from 1931, on the basis of the language used at home, the most important ethnic groups were Poles (69%), Ukrainians and Ruthenians (14%), Jews (8%), Byelorussians (3%), and Germans (2%). In terms of religious affiliation, the number of Jews was equal to 10%. Ukrainians were a majority in some south-eastern provinces, and Byelorussians in the Polesie and Nowogrod voivodeships (cf. Table 8.1). The Jewish and German populations were more scattered. The percentage of Jews was the lowest in the western provinces, that is, the former Prussian partition, and the highest in the former Russian partition, particularly in Congress Poland. The situation was reversed in the case of the German population—they lived mostly in the former Prussian partition and the industrialized cities of the former Congress Kingdom, such as Łódź, Warszawa and the Dabrowa industrial area. It should be noted, however, that the official data have been questioned by Polish historians, who indicated understating the

Table 8.1 Ethnolinguistic structure of Polish society, 1931—Share (%) of ethnolinguistic groups in total population

Voivodeship	Polish	Polish—urban pop.[a]	Ukrainian/Ruthenian	Ukrainian/Ruthenian—rural pop.[a]	Belarussian	German	Yiddish/Hebrew	Yddish/Hebrew—urban pop.[a]
Poland	68.9	68.4	13.9	18	3.1	2.3	8.6	24.3
Warszawa	70.5	70.5	0.1		0	0.2	28.5	28.5
Warszawskie	88.1	69.6	0	0	0	2.9	8.5	29.4
Łódzkie	80.1	62.7	0.1	0.1	0	5.9	13.7	29.8
Kieleckie	89.2	70.3	0	0	0	0.8	10.4	29.3
Lubelskie	85.6	61.8	3	3.6	0.1	0.6	10.5	37.5
Białostockie	71.9	56.9	0.2	0.2	12.5	0.5	11.9	38
Wileńskie	59.7	63	0.1	0.1	22.7	0.1	8.6	29
Nowogródzkie	52.4	45.4	0.1	0.1	39.1	0	7.3	40.5
Poleskie	14.1	29.7	21	b.d.	52.9	0.1	10	48.8
Wołyńskie	16.6	27.5	68.4	75.7	0.1	2.3	9.9	48.6
Poznańskie	90.5	94	0	0	0	9.2	0.2	0.3
Pomorskie	89.8	92.5	0	0	0	9.8	0.2	0.5
Śląskie	92.3	85.5	0	0	0	7	0.5	1.4
Krakowskie	91.3	79.3	2.6	3.4	0	0.4	5.6	19.3
Lwowskie	57.7	63.5	34.1	41.4	0	0.4	7.5	23.7
Stanisławowskie	22.4	40.8	66.9	78.6	0	1.1	7.4	27.4
Tarnopolskie	49.3	58.3	45.6	50.8	0	0.2	4.9	21.9

Source: Główny Urząd Statystyczny (1934) and Wyczański (2003)
[a]share of ethnolinguistic group in total urban or rural population

sizes of ethnic and religious minorities, particularly the Ukrainian minority.

Urbanization continued throughout the interwar period. WWI caused an outflow of urban population, but it started to grow already in the 1920s, and by the beginning of the Great Depression urbanization indexes attained or exceeded the pre-war levels. Then, economic hardship slowed down urbanization once again. Until the outbreak of WWII, with 20% of population living in cities larger than 10,000 inhabitants (in 1931), Poland was still mostly rural country.

5   The Society

The interwar period was the time of deep social change, influenced by a number of factors. Firstly, the intelligentsia had assumed its final shape and became the key element of the political life as a result of the accumulation of the human and social capital and of its important role in regaining independence. Both urban and rural entrepreneurs (i.e. industrialists and landed gentry) had borne the economic costs of the war, which weakened their political position. The conservative parties were also weak at the time, because they had been supported by the administration of the partitioning states, especially Austria, particularly liberal towards the Polish. Moreover, the peasants' parties never achieved the political position which would allow them to take over the government, despite the size of the peasant class in the society. Thus, the strongest political parties of the democratic period, the nationalist and socialist parties, as well as the political movements associated with the *Sanacja* later on, were created and run by the intelligentsia, and were supported by the lower classes both in urban and rural areas (Jedlicki et al. 2014).

Secondly, the emancipation of the peasants was finally concluded. The land reform conducted in 1921 gradually increased the number and size of peasant households and reduced the number of landless peasants. However, urban economy created relatively low demand for labour throughout the period, so the transformation of the peasant society into the modern industrial society was slower than before the war. Additionally, the subsequent economic recessions slowed or even reversed this process—the unemployed workers returned to the country, unable to earn a living in the city. However, the rebuilding of industry contributed to the growth of the importance of the urban working class, particularly in the western and central regions. During economic recessions, both urban and rural workers organized protests, which were particularly strong during the times of the post-war hyperinflation and the Great Depression (Borkowski et al. 1995; Mędrzecki et al. 2014).

The third factor contributing to social change was the unification of compulsory education, gradually alleviating the differences between the former partitions. However, it was a slow process due to the high cost and the limited resources. Despite that, the creation of the uniform school system at the beginning of the 1930s and its role in building the national identity can be seen as a big success of the Second Polish Republic. At the beginning of statehood, the level of literacy was extremely uneven, due to the differences between the school systems in the partitioning states. Illiteracy was practically non-existent in the post-Prussian lands, and relatively low in post-Austrian regions, particularly among the younger generations. It was the highest in the post-Russian areas, but it was unevenly distributed—the urbanized western provinces of the former Kingdom of Poland had lower illiteracy levels than the eastern ones. Illiteracy was the highest in the provinces formerly belonging to Russia (i.e. the Russian partition outside the Kingdom of Poland). Even though the general illiteracy level decreased steadily throughout the period, and thanks to compulsory education illiteracy was eradicated among the younger generations, the regional differences were visible until the outbreak of WWII. Illiteracy was higher among the Byelorussian and Ukrainian minorities than in the Polish majority, but lower among the German and Jewish groups (Stańczyk 2004; Wysocki 2005).

The success of the education system mostly concerned primary education and combating illiteracy (see Table 8.2). The higher levels, secondary and tertiary, offered high quality education, but only to few, due to the fact that the schools were not easily accessible (secondary schools were located in medium-size and big towns, universities in big cities) and could only admit a limited number of students. However, the standard of education was comparable to that offered by Western European schools (Sadowska 2001; Osiński 2007; Radziwiłł 2014).

Table 8.2 Illiteracy levels in interwar Poland

Voivodeship	1921	1931
Poland	33.1	23.1
Warszawa	15.6	10.1
Warszawskie	32.5	22.4
Łódzkie	30.3	21.4
Kieleckie	36.5	26.2
Lubelskie	35.1	24.2
Białostockie	31	23.5
Wileńskie	58.3	29.1
Nowogródzkie	54.6	34.9
Poleskie	71	48.5
Wołyńskie	68.8	47.8
Poznańskie	3.8	2.8
Pomorskie	5.2	4.3
Śląskie	2.6	1.4
Krakowskie	19.4	13.7
Lwowskie	29.2	23.1
Stanisławowskie	46	36.6
Tarnopolskie	39.2	29.8

Source: Główny Urząd Statystyczny (1934) and Wysocki (2005)

Despite the success of the education system and the state's integration/ assimilation policy, the problem of its ethnic complexity remained an issue, and the conflicts rooted in modern nationalism were never resolved. There was a high percentage of minorities whose members were unwilling to assimilate into the Polish society, such as Ukrainians, Germans or Jews, and it was a source of tension. In the south-east, especially in the areas where Ukrainians were the majority, the Polish-Ukrainian conflict sometimes turned into a guerrilla war. The Ukrainian nationalist organizations thwarted the attempts at the Polish-Ukrainian rapprochement and were determined to create their own state comprising the territories of south-eastern Poland; their activity inflicted considerable material damage and several dozen casualties, mostly in the 1920s. The Polish state responded by conducting military interventions involving civilians (1930) and by implementing the Polonization policy in the mid-1930s (Torzecki 1989; Kulińska 2009; Wyszczelski 2015b).

The Jewish minority was subject to periodic restrictions on their access to education or some professions (*numerus clausus*). There were also economic conflicts, such as boycotting Jewish shops, under the national-democratic slogan "Buy from your own kind". The conflict was particularly bitter in smaller towns due to the important role that the Jewish played as entrepreneurs, merchants, and peddlers. In the 1930s, the tension developed into violence and anti-Semitic tumults as a result of the Great Depression, and the radical ideology of some factions of the nationalist movement. The scale of these fights was much smaller than in the Polish-Ukrainian conflict, but in 1936, both sides incurred several casualties. The best known example is the Przytyk Pogrom of 1936, resulting in the death of three people and injuries of dozens (on both sides) and the demolition of the Jewish quarter (Wynot 1971; Wyszczelski 2015b).

In the mid-1930s, especially after the death of Józef Piłsudski, the Polish policy towards the minorities changed and started to involve the pressure towards their assimilation in order to create a homogeneous nation state. The attempts to implement this policy exacerbated the conflict in border areas and aggravated the mutual resentment and the friction between the Polish and the members of the minorities.

Ethnic diversity was not the only challenge for the new state. It also had to cope with the institutional differences and development disparities between the lands formerly belonging to three states: Germany, Austria, and Russia. Thus, the ethnic conflict was set against the background of huge economic differentiation: the western part of the country was relatively well developed and the eastern regions, inhabited by most of the Byelorussian and Ukrainian minorities, suffered poverty. It was as late as in the late 1930s when an effort was made to limit the economic marginalization of some regions; it involved an investment project (a 4-year plan and a 15-year plan) aiming to accelerate the development and increase the convergence of the economies of different regions of the country.

There were also considerable disparities within the sectors. Polesie, in the east, featured mostly subsistence agriculture. The lack of transport infrastructure and the difficult terrain (marshes, forests) were a barrier to creating the stimuli to modernize the sector. On the other hand, the agriculture in Greater Poland, in the west, was comparable to the commercial farming of Western Europe. In effect, the profitability varied greatly between the regions. Similar technological and organizational differences were also observed in manufacturing and services (e.g. in trade, which involved both peddling and—particularly in big cities— the development of modern wholesale and retail). In all sectors, it entailed significant income disparities at the comparable positions (Leszczyńska 2017).

Income disparities, lack of employment stability, and the recurring economic recessions made strikes and protests a common feature in Poland. They started as early as in 1920, when the railway workers went on strike in Poznań (Posen). The next year, there were hunger strikes of industrial and farm workers in Rawicz, near the German border, and the year after that, over 100,000 farm workers protested and went on strike during the harvest. All these protests in Greater Poland were the result of the rising cost of living and the falling income in the formerly Prussian region. To suppress them the police used guns, which caused casualties. About 30 casualties were also incurred in Cracow in 1923, when the Polish Socialist Party organized a general strike. In 1926, the railway workers' strike prevented the transport of the army, which contributed to the success of Pilsudski's *coup d'état*. In 1928, there was a strike in the textile industry in Łódź. The subsequent wave of protests was the result of the Great Depression, such as the ones in mining and textile industries (both in Łódź and Białystok) in 1931–1933, or the farm workers' strikes in 1933. All these protests were rooted in the economy, so the improvement of the economic situation and increasing social mobility, as well as diminishing social and ethnic tensions ameliorated the situation for a few years, though serious riots broke out in Lublin in spring 1934. In 1936, another wave of protests started. Farm workers' strikes began in the former Galicia (1936), then spread to other parts of the country, and culminated in the nationwide strike in August 1937, quelled by the police shooting several dozen people. The last wave of workers' strikes before WWII was in 1936 in Kraków, Lwów, Toruń, Gdynia, and other cities. During the Great Depression, the methods of suppressing riots became increasingly violent and, between 1931 and 1939, almost 1000 people were killed in social protests (Mędrzecki et al. 2014; Wyszczelski 2015b).

6   The Economy

Despite the development of industry, throughout the interwar period, agriculture remained the dominant sector of Poland's economy. The first years of statehood were marred by growing inflation, which later turned into hyperinflation. After 1924, all of Europe went into economic growth, and Polish industry and agriculture achieved the production levels similar to those from before WWI; however, the population had already grown. The Great Depression brought about another period of economic recession. In the mid-1930s, the state introduced elements of economic planning and state capitalism, which speeded up the post-recession reconstruction. As a result of fiscal expansion, including state investments in infrastructure and industry, the industrial potential was restored and, immediately before WWII, Poland's industrial output regained the pre-WWI levels.

For the whole period, the challenge of re-integration was only partially solved.

Throughout the interwar period one of the most pressing issues was the challenge of economic integration of Poland in terms of institutions (between former partitions), infrastructure and developmental convergence (between territories of different level of development). It occurred that economic disparities were sustained and impossible to override. From the point of view of the level of development and the structure of economy, interwar Poland could be divided into four regions[1]:

*   *The western, best developed voivodeships*: the former Prussian partition, that is, the Silesian Voivodeship (which included Cieszyn Silesia, formerly in Austria), and the Posen and Pomeranian voivodeships. They comprised about 12% of the area of Poland and 15% of the population in 1921.

---

[1] This division takes into account economic, not political and institutional, factors—i.e. historical division of Polish lands into Austrian, Prussian partition, Kingdom of Poland and former Russian western governorates. During the interwar period, economic differences slowly became more important than political and institutional ones—the unification of formal institutions were possible, economic culture, informal institutions, and geographical fate occurred to be relatively persistent.

- *The well-developed industrial central belt*: the best developed parts of the Russian partition, that is, the Kielce Voivodeship (with Czestochowa and Sosnowiec), the Lodz and Warsaw voivodeships, and the former Austrian Western Galicia, that is, the Cracow voivodeship. They constituted about 24% of the area of the country and 37% of the population.
- *The agricultural central voivodeships*: the former agricultural voivodeships of the Congress Kingdom, that is, the Lublin and Bialystok voivodeships and Lwów voivodeship. They were about 23% of the territory and 23% of the population.
- *The eastern, least developed voivodeships*: the regions formerly incorporated into Russia, that is, the Novogrod, Polesie, Volynha, Vilnius voivodeships (the latter was slightly better developed), and the former Austrian Eastern Galicia, that is, the Tarnopol and Stanislawow voivodeships. They comprised about 41% of the area of the country (and 26% of the population).

The data concerning particular voivodeships are in Table 8.3.

The regional disparities are clearly visible in the statistical data. In 1926, Polish industry used almost 29,000 engines; 9700 engines were installed in the western belt, 14,200 in the industrialized central belt, 3000 in the agricultural central belt, and 1500 in the eastern belt. The total engine power, 1.2 million horsepower, was mainly distributed in the western part, 540,000 horsepower, and the central industrialized part, 480,000 horsepower (Główny Urząd Statystyczny 1927a). Until 1938, the power of the engines installed in industry doubled, but the Central Statistical Office does not give the data for voivodeships (Główny Urząd Statystyczny 1939a, 1990).

Similarly, the total power installed in energy plants was 1700 MW; out of this number, 770 MW was in the western part, 730 MW in the industrial centre, 100 MW in the agricultural centre, and below 60 MW in the eastern part. Out of the total 4000 MWh, 40% of the energy was generated in the power plants in Upper Silesia (over 1600 MWh), the rest of the western part generated 250 MWh, the industrial central part—1750 MWh, the agricultural centre—170 MWh, and the eastern part less than 90 MWh. A unified energy system was not created until the

Table 8.3 Voivodeships: economic, and demographic data

Voivodeships	Territory	Population 1921, thousands	Population 1931, thousands	Number of engines (1926)	Cars per 10,000 inhabitants, 1938	Post offices per 100 km², 1938	Railroads (km per 100 km²), 1938	Paved roads (km per 100 km²), 1938	Industrial workers (thousands), 1938	Arable land (million of ha)	Wheat (q/ha)	Rye (q/ha)	Potato (q/ha)	Cattle (thousands)
Poznańskie	27	1968	2340		22	2.2	10.1	32.3	51.9	1.8	18.1	16	125	871
Pomorskie	16	936	1884		27	2.5	11.4	25.2	47	1.5	18.6	15.2	105	654
Śląskie	4	1125	1533		37	7	18.5	53.8	92.9	0.2	16.8	16	129	128
Western	*47*	*4029*	*5757*	*9700*					*191.8*					*1653*
Warszawskie (Warszawa included)	29	3052	3640		25	1.4	5.2	24	153	1.8	12.4	12.3	123	855
Łódzkie	19	2253	2650		16	1.2	4.8	24.7	152.1	1.2	13.8	12.6	129	633
Kieleckie	26	2536	2671		7	1.3	4.9	18.7	113.8	1.3	12.5	11.5	114	725
Krakowskie	17	1993	2300		13	3	6.5	29.8	57.4	0.9	10.7	11.6	99	807
Central-industrial	*91*	*9834*	*11,261*	*14,200*					*476.3*					*3020*
Lubelskie	31	2086	2116		5	1	4	12.3	19.1	1.4	13	12.3	139	749
Białostockie	32	1302	1263		5	0.7	4.2	11.2	20.6	1.1	9.5	10.8	105	500
Lwowskie	27	2718	3126		8	1.6	5.4	19	36.6	1.4	10	10.4	104	1071
Central-agricultural	*90*	*6106*	*6505*	*3000*					*76.3*					*2320*
Wileńskie	29	1006	1276		4	0.7	3.8	7.1	8.3	1.1	7.5	8.2	95	514
Nowogródzkie	23	801	1057		4	0.7	3.1	9.6	5.1	1.4	7.6	10.8	111	475
Poleskie	42	879	1132		3	0.4	2.9	3	6.7	1.9	9.1	10.7	107	659
Wołyńskie	30	1438	2085		3	0.7	3.4	4.2	17.7	2.2	9.4	11.4	98	915
Stanisławowskie	18	1339	1480		3	1.1	4.5	17.8	14.9	0.6	11.3	11.4	108	467
Tarnopolskie	16	1429	1600		2	1.3	5.6	21.1	7.5	1.1	11.7	11.7	113	531
Eastern	*158*	*6892*	*8630*	*1500*					*60.2*					*3561*

Source: Główny Urząd Statystyczny (1939a) and Kubiczek et al. (2006)

outbreak of the war and energy was generated and loaded regionally (Ministerstwo Przemysłu i Handlu 1933; Główny Urząd Statystyczny 1939a).

The differences between the regions are even more pronounced when studying the levels of the development of infrastructure. Dense railway networks existed in the western part, in the areas formerly belonging to Germany, and—to some extent—Austria. Roads and railways were also relatively well developed in the central parts, in the former Kingdom of Poland. Out of the 20,000 km of railways in use in 1937 (standard and narrow gauge), 5300 km were in the western part, 4800 km in the industrialized central part, 4200 km in the agricultural central part, and 5500 km in the east. Out of the 63,000 km of surfaced roads existing in Poland at the end of the 1930s, 18,000 km were in the west, 19,000 km in the industrialized central belt, less than 13,000 km in the agricultural central belt, and over 13,000 km in the east. The railway and road network density was the highest in the western part, with over 10 km of railway and 30 km of roads per 100 km^2, in the former Kingdom of Poland and Galicia it was 4–6 km of railway and 11–29 km of roads per 100 km^2, and in the east, in the formerly Russian regions, 4 km of railway and below 7 km of roads per 100 km^2 (Główny Urząd Statystyczny 1939a; Koziarski 1993).

In the interwar period, the greatest infrastructure development took place in the western and central regions, particularly in the industrialized parts. Over 1700 km of railways were constructed in that period, but only a small portion of that quantity was built in the eastern regions (the Wilno and Wołyń voivodeships). The key investments were the coal trunk line from Upper Silesia to Pomerania (over 500 km) and the lines connecting Warszawa and Radom (over 100 km) and then Kraków. The railway was also developed in Upper Silesia and Pomerania, mostly for military reasons, and in central Poland (e.g. the Warsaw junction was expanded). The road network was developed in a similar way. Between 1924 and 1938, about 20,000 km roads were built or surfaced; out of that number, 2400 km were built in the western part, over 8500 km in the central industrialized part, 4100 km in the central agricultural belt, and 5100 km in the eastern part. Therefore, most of the new railways and roads were built in the best developed regions (Główny Urząd Statystyczny 1939a; Kubiczek et al. 2006; Kamiński 2015).

Urban economy still involved a considerable role for traditional crafts. The data concerning this sector are much more scarce and were collected mostly during censuses. In 1921, out of about 1.2 million people employed in industry and mining, there were 65,000 people describing themselves as blue collar workers, 60,000 as white collar workers, and as many as 450,000 were shop owners, out of which 380,000 did not have employees. Besides, 50,000 people worked as craftsmen and cottage industry subcontractors, and another 60,000 were family members helping in the shops (Główny Urząd Statystyczny 1927b).

In 1931 (the year of the second national census), industry and mining employed about 2 million people, out of which 900,000 described themselves as industrial workers. Large-scale industrial and mining enterprises employed 450,000 people, small manufacturing enterprises, mostly workshops and cottage industry, employed 1.5 million people, out of which over 500,000 did not have employees. Despite economic development, indicated by the increase of the number of industrial workers, the traditional crafts sector and cottage industry was still significant. Additionally, at the peak of the Great Depression, as many as 500,000 people from the manufacturing sector were unemployed. The situation of many self-employed craftsmen coping with the diminished demand for their products was little better than that of unemployed industrial workers (census data 1931 from Główny Urząd Statystyczny 1939b, c)

The employment and production structure also indicated sustained considerable development disparities. A large part of the economic development took place in the areas already well developed, and infrastructure investments perpetuated the differences between the regions. This process is also visible in the statistics concerning the employment in the manufacturing industry. Out of the 440,000 people employed in 1925, 111,000 worked in the western voivodeships, 256,000 in the industrialized central voivodeships, 45,000 in the agricultural central voivodeships, and 35,000 in the eastern part (Statistical Yearbook 1925). In 1933, the respective numbers were 525,000 in total, 116,000 in the west, 325 in the industrial central belt, 49,000 in the agricultural central belt, and 35,000 in the east (Główny Urząd Statystyczny 1933). In the processing industry, 800,000 people were employed at the end of 1937, with 192,000 in the west, 467,000 in the central industrial belt, below 80,000 in the central agricultural belt, below 60,000 in the east. Apart from that, 80,000 coal miners worked in the mines of Silesia and of the areas near Łódź and near Kraków, all in the western and industrialized central regions. Between 1925 and 1937, the regional distribution of industrial employment was stable: 24–25% in the western voivodeships, 58% in the industrialized central voivodeships, 10% in the agricultural central voivodeships, 6–7% in the eastern voivodeships (Główny Urząd Statystyczny 1939a).

In the agricultural central voivodeships, employment in industry, even in 1931, was low, though modern branches played a certain role. In the Bialystok voivodeship, 30% of the workers were employed in the textile industry, in the Lublin voivodeship 18% worked in the metal industry, in the Lvov voivodeship 11% were employed in chemical industry and 18% in mining. In the eastern voivodeships, employment in industry was very low, and the industries were labour-intensive and obsolete. The dominating industries were the wood industry (employing 70% of the workers in the Polesie voivodeship, almost 50% in the Stanislawow voivodeship, and 20–30% in the other voivodeships, with the exception of the Tarnopol voivodeship, where the number was 14%), food processing (over 60% in the Tarnopol voivodeship and between 10% and 23% in the other voivodeships), and mineral processing (48% in the Volhynia voivodeship, mostly in cement works). In the Vilnius voivodeship, paper industry employed 15% of the workers, and in the Novogrod voivodeship chemical and mineral processing industries—respectively, 15% and 20%. The excavation of oil in the Stanislawow voivodeship gave employment to 20% of the workers in this voivodeship (Główny Urząd Statystyczny 1927b, 1938, 1939b, c).

In 1937, mining constituted 11% of the total employment in industry and mining. Eighty-eight per cent of that number worked in the Silesian, Kielce and Cracow voivodeships, mainly in coal mining. In the same year the modern branches of manufacturing industry, metal industry, electrical engineering, chemical, and textile industries employed 46% of all industrial and mining workers. Twenty-one per cent of these workers were employed in the western part, 73% in the central industrial part. In

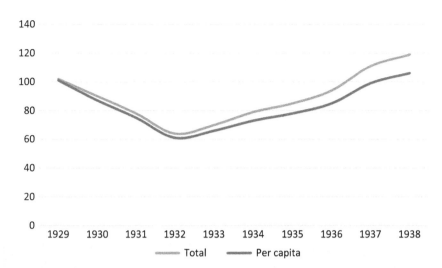

Graph 8.1 Value of industrial output (total and per capita), constant prices of 1928 (1928 = 100). Source: Kubiczek et al. (2006)

the Silesian voivodeship, 38% of workers were employed in mining and almost 30% in the metal industry and electrical engineering. In the Lodz voivodeship 72% workers were employed in the textile industry; in Kielce and Warsaw voivodeships, over 30% were employed in metal industry and in electrical engineering (Główny Urząd Statystyczny 1939a).

Until 1931, industrial output increased and there was a change in the structure of the value added in industry. There was a gradual growth in the role of the modern sectors, even though the traditional manufacturing sector retained its significant percentage in employment. During the Great Depression, the industrial output rapidly decreased, and then stabilized at a significantly lower level (Graph 8.1). The policy of fiscal expansion and state capitalism implemented in 1936 led not only to restoring the industrial base, but to restructuring the production. State investments in heavy industry and metallurgy, chemical industry, mechanical engineering, arms, aviation, and auto industry caused the increase of the percentage of these branches in the global output. The growing demand for electrical power in industry stimulated the development of energy production, particularly the investments in power plants based on coal and hydroelectricity in the central areas.

Before WWI, the key industrial investments were private, but during the interwar period, with the shortage of internal capital and difficulties in obtaining external financing, the key role in developing large-scale industry (particularly outside Upper Silesia) was played by the state, while the private entrepreneurs invested in restoring the production capacity after the war and maintaining the production during the Great Depression (Kofman 1986). Even though the political debate concerning the role of the state in the economy continued throughout the interwar period, in 1935, the policy of active state involvement was implemented by Eugeniusz Kwiatkowski, the deputy prime minister and Minister of the Treasury. The 4-year plan developed for that purpose involved the state-financed re-industrialization of Poland. The investment focused on one region selected for development, the area comprising parts of the Kielce, Lublin, Cracow, and Lvov voivodeships. It was centrally located, densely populated, and sparsely industrialized, with high hidden unemployment in the country and a low standard of living. The industrial and infrastructural investments aimed to restructure employment, stimulate internal demand, and make the region, called the Central Industrial Area (*COP*), a springboard for further development, like the other industrial areas in Poland. The industries that were developed in the area were designed to become the basis for the modernization of the army, and therefore, the focus was on heavy industry, arms industry and chemical industry (Samecki 1998; Gołębiowski 2000; Koryś 2015).

During the interwar period, the implementation of Poland's industrial policy involved the state's functioning both as the grassroots investor and as the capital investor. Immediately after the war, the state took over some of the enterprises commandeered during the war and managed by the authorities of the partitioning states. One of the most important enterprises like this was the modern nitrogenous fertilizer production plant in Chorzów, claimed by both Poland and Germany, and the dispute had to be resolved by the Court of International Justice attached to the League of Nations (Popkiewicz and Ryszka 1959). While the fiscal expansion was relatively limited, the state played an important role as an owner (e.g. railways were state owned, as well as a part of strategically important industry) (Łapa 2002; Musiał 2013). The state functioned as a leading capital investor later, during the Great Depression, for example, partially or completely taking over many large-scale enterprises such as the Żyrardow linen factory, the Scheibler & Grohman textile factory in Łódź, or mines and industrial enterprises in Silesia. The state also conducted direct investments, such as the construction of a nitrogenous fertilizer production plant in Mościce (1927–1930), which employed about 3200 workers and was expected to make Poland independent of the import of fertilizers. The second half of the 1930s was the time of intense state investments in the new industrial area, *COP*. Some of the investments were conducted by state-owned joint-stock companies (Landau and Tomaszewski 1977, 1978, 1983; Samecki 1998).

In the mid-1930s, the state-owned banking conglomerate managed by the Bank of State Economy (*BGK*) (Landau 1998) also became the owner of the biggest industrial group in Poland. The bank was practically the sole provider of loans for the state and private industrial investments. In this way, state institutions became the main co-ordinator of the economic processes in the manufacturing sector, as the owner, investor, and creditor. Private investors, dependent on the state-controlled credit, adjusted their investment decisions to the state industrial policy. This can be exemplified by the construction of a machine tools factory in Rzeszów by the Cegielski enterprise (encouraged to take part in COP development and invest in Rzeszów instead of Poznań), which became part of the 4-year plan and the development of the Central Industrial Area (*COP*) (Samecki 1998; Gołębiowski 2000).

The investment aims of the Central Industrial Area, where the state was the owner, investor, and credit provider, were mostly achieved ahead of schedule, and the project itself became a symbol of the efficiency of the government of the restored Poland. However, this propaganda image, created in part by some eminent writers (e.g. Melchior Wańkowicz), who wrote articles and book about the Central Industrial Area (Wańkowicz 1939), was not completely true. The state's fiscal expansion, the control of the distribution of credit, and the support for state-owned enterprises led to the marginalization of private enterprises, which was particularly visible in the period of the restoration of the economy after the Great Depression. Developing one region of the country (according to the model of "big push" *avant la lettre*, which later inspired the creators of development economics, such as Paul Rosenstein-Rodan) limited the development potential of other areas and impeded the process of economic convergence. Moreover, most probably many of the investments were not cost-effective, which was officially justified by the urgency to satisfy the army's demand for modern armaments; however, in reality, the Central Industrial Area was not able to meet it on time. The divergence of the civilian and military aims of the project resulted in the inefficient allocation of investment resources and later of the means of production. The project itself was conducted very fast and involved incurring huge costs in a small area (in less than 4 years, the investments in the *COP* constituted almost 30% of all the state investments in the interwar period), which entailed the increasing economic problems of the state, including inflation and the need to raise taxes. Additionally, even though some enterprises achieved their production aims, most of the developmental goals of the project were not fulfilled. Just like the state investments conducted in the same area between 1820 and 1840, state-funded industrialization failed to change the economic and social situation of the region—this time, possibly, because of the outbreak of the war and another disruption of the continuity of economic development (Landau and Tomaszewski 1989; Kofman 1992; Landau and Roszkowski 1995; Landau 2011; Szlajfer 2012; Musiał 2013; Leszczyński 2017).

The modernization of the other two sectors, agriculture and services, was significantly slower than in the manufacturing industry. In agriculture, the stimulus for change was the land reform introduced by the regulations from 1920 and 1925, whose implementation lasted throughout the interwar period; by 1939, the aims of the reform were achieved in 60%. The land that was parcelled out was state-owned or purchased from landowners. The process was gradual, based on the voluntary decisions of the landowners selling land to the state at market prices and of farmers taking out state-guaranteed 40-year loans for the purchase of land.

Agriculture remained the sector with the biggest employment. It was also the key factor in mitigating the effects of the successive recessions caused by the war (1918–1920), hyperinflation (1923–1925), and the Great Depression. Some people who lost employment in industry and services in cities would return to their villages, where unemployment was hidden, that is, the increased number of labourers did not contribute to the increase of agricultural output. Additionally, agriculture was badly affected by war damage, and later, after 1929, it was hit by the price slump and rapid decline of demand during the Great Depression. In effect, throughout the interwar period, the growth of agricultural output was slow, mostly because of the limited investment potential of the peasant farms and landed gentry estates. There were persistent efficiency disparities between the former partitions, especially between the relatively modern agriculture in the western parts and the mostly subsistent agriculture of some of the eastern regions (Mieszczankowski 1983; Roszkowski 1991; Mędrzecki et al. 2014).

The services sector was also dominated by traditional low-productive services, such as small trade, peddling, small-scale services (e.g. informal financial services), personal services (e.g. domestic service). This sector, particularly crafts and trade, was important in the employment of the Jewish minority. Modern services were represented by public services as well as by the modern services sector developing particularly in big cities (Tomaszewski and Landau 2005; Mędrzecki et al. 2014).

The Second Polish Republic was determined to take part in international relations, including international trade. These ambitions were difficult to achieve because of the collapse of the economic order in Central Europe after WWI and because of the difficult economic situation of the country: throughout the interwar period, Poland's economy was at the level below that from 1913. Directly after the restoration of the state, Poland had a negative trade balance (the data are incomplete, however), and the staple exports were food and raw materials, particularly coal. The new state used protectionist mechanisms to secure its economic independence and support its industry. Protectionism was particularly strong during the Great Depression and the implementation of the anti-crisis policy adopted by Kwiatkowski. The instruments used to stimulate export were, for example, export bonuses and undercutting the prices of exports, and import was limited by tariffs, restrictions on currency transfers abroad, licences for the import of goods, and the compulsory exchange of foreign currencies (Landau and Tomaszewski 1989; Tomaszewski and Landau 2005; Landau 2011).

Nevertheless, throughout the period, Polish foreign trade was relatively low. Export reached its peak at the end of the 1920s, at 2.8 billion zlotys and about 10% of the GDP (1929). Import was at a similar level at the time, 3.4 billion zlotys in 1928. During the Great Depression, between 1932 and 1935, trade collapsed and the Polish export dropped to 0.9–1.1 billion zlotys and import to 0.8–0.9 billion. Then, there was a slow increase of trade, but by 1938 it did not achieve even half the levels from before the Great Depression (in nominal prices). In 1929, Polish trade constituted about 1% of the global trade, and in 1938 it returned to this level after the decrease caused by the recession. Since the construction of the seaport in Gdynia, much of the Polish foreign trade was conducted by sea—between 1930 and 1938, the percentage of the value of trade in Gdańsk and Gdynia grew from 28% to 63%, and the trade in Gdynia alone grew from 5% to 48% (Główny Urząd Statystyczny 1939a, 1990).

In 1922, Poland gained much of the Upper Silesian coal mining area and became one of the leading coal producers and exporters in Europe. Poland's main trade partner and importer of coal was Germany, which influenced the investment policy of the state, particularly during the growing economic and political tensions between Poland and the Weimar Republic (the so-called customs war between Poland and Germany, which lasted between 1925 and the 1930s). It resulted in the decline of Polish industrial production by up to 20%, particularly in Upper Silesia, and in the intensified state investment in infrastructure, particularly in the port in Gdynia and in the coal trunk line from Upper Silesia to Gdynia (Popkiewicz and Ryszka 1959; Kotlarz et al. 2017).

In the 1930s, Poland's main trade partners were Germany, Great Britain, the Netherlands, France, Czechoslovakia, and the Scandinavian countries. In 1928, almost two-thirds of Polish export was to Germany, Great Britain, and Czechoslovakia, and 55% of Polish import was from Germany, the USA, and Great Britain. This structure slowly changed, and in 1938 Sweden became the third most important importer of Polish goods, mostly coal: half of the Polish export was directed to Great Britain, Germany, and Sweden, and almost half of Polish import was from Germany, the USA, and Great Britain. Germany remained the crucial economic partner of Poland for the whole period, despite permanent political tensions.

In terms of value, Poland's primary exports were coal, zinc, timber, and wood, but also raw and processed agricultural products. The most important manufactured goods were textile products and iron and steel. The main imports were machinery, chemical products, and means of transport, but also cotton and wool for the Polish textile industry. Data show that the only internationally competitive branch was the textile industry (developed in the former Kingdom of Poland). Thanks to low labour costs, there was also demand for the coal mined in Upper Silesia and the adjacent mining areas. At first, the sole buyer was Germany, but thanks to the development of port infrastructure and the construction of the coal trunk line to Gdynia, the market gradually diversified (Gazeł 1939; Główny Urząd Statystyczny 1939a).

The *sine qua non* of participating in international trade was a stable and reliable currency. Thus, the persistent challenge for the government was to achieve and then ensure the stability and exchangeability of the currency, in order to enter the gold standard currency system and to remain in it. Later, in the 1930s, this "adherence to gold" deepened and prolonged Polish economic depression (Knakiewicz 1967; Wolf 2007). The beginning of statehood was marked with unstable public finances and the hyperinflation of the currency, the Polish mark. The cabinet of 1924–1925, led by Władysław Grabski, stabilized the budget, and their currency reform, which introduced the Polish zloty, stabilized the prices. Polish Loan Bank (*Polska Krajowa Kasa Pożyczkowa*), a national bank created by the German administration during WWI, was replaced by a modern central bank, the Bank of Poland, plc (*Bank Polski SA*). The stabilization of rates of exchange was based on loans from the USA. After the reform, the Polish zloty became an exchangeable currency and the Polish authorities regarded it as a symbol of the stability and credibility of the Polish state, which resulted in their effort to introduce the zloty into the gold system, but also in their reluctance to devalue it during the Great Depression (Morawski 1998; Leszczyńska 2006, 2010, 2013).

Poland's public finances were periodically in a bad shape, despite the efforts to the contrary. After the restoration of the state, the budget was not stable until 1924; also, during the Great Depression, the budget was challenged by tax arrears and budget deficits. Public spending was the highest just before the Great Depression—even during the period of Kwiatkowski's fiscal expansion the level of expenditure was 15% lower than at the end of the economic boom of the 1920s (Morawski 2008). For the whole period, state incomes were relatively low (due to the poverty of the society); thus, the natural consequence of a politics of a relatively stable budget (after hyperinflation) was relatively low level of public spending (Koryś 2015).

The tax system was inefficient and heterogenous—based on the tax systems of the former partitioning empires (full uniformity of tax law throughout Poland was only achieved in the mid-1930s). The huge income disparities resulted in a sizeable population not paying direct taxes, but also—in the regions of subsistent agriculture—sometimes, not even subject to indirect taxes. Income tax was payable on incomes over 1500 zlotys per household, which both in 1929 and in 1938 applied to only 1.1–1.2 million people (civil servants excluded) (Landau 1969; Jezierski and Leszczyńska 2010; Leszczyńska 2016).

The data and information presented above suggest rather sluggish economic growth of Poland during the interwar period. Unfortunately, the available estimates of the Polish GDP allowing to approximate the dynamics of economic growth in the interwar period are divergent and comprise only part of the period (usually after 1929). Poland was one of the main theatres of WWI, as it was described in the previous chapter, and 1920 was the time of border wars and a humanitarian disaster resulting from the epidemics of the typhoid fever and the Spanish flu; thus, the war surely had a prominent negative effect on the Polish GDP per capita. The data concerning agricultural and industrial output show that the post-war recession (during hyperinflation period) gained momentum in 1924. Production declines in some branches took place until 1925, and then there was a decline in international trade because of the Polish-German customs war (Skibiński 1933; Gazeł 1939; Klimiuk 2011). It was as late as after 1925, when the real restoration took place, after the macroeconomic stabilization achieved by Władysław Grabski and the subsequent adjustments drawn up mostly by Jerzy Zdziechowski. Throughout the subsequent year, the recession firstly in agricultural sector continued due to poor harvest (while the industry was being reconstructed), and later, in industry and agriculture, due to the decline of the trade with Germany. Thus, the period of cyclical economic expansion started as late as in 1926 and was significantly shorter in Poland than in Western Europe, even though the Polish economic cycle seems similar to that of Germany. Economic recession occurred slightly later in Poland than in other European countries—growth of industrial output could be observed until almost the end of 1929. The period after 1929 has been studied more closely by Polish economists and historians, and there are more estimates. All of them indicate a deep plunge of the GDP per capita in the years 1930–1935 and then the return to the levels from before the recession.

Most estimates place the moment of regaining the pre-recession levels at 1937 or 1938. The industrial output data show the pre-recession levels in 1937. Thus, in terms of economic development, the interwar period was either partial failure or very limited success. The industrial potential was to a large extent rebuilt, the process of urbanization and the growing role of modern sector in the national economy were restored, and sluggish but continuous changes in agriculture were observed until the Great Depression. On the other side, endogenous and exogenous demand shocks undermined long-term growth regularly. All in all, before WWII, the GDP per capita was close to that from 1929 and from 1913 (Kalecki and Landau 1934, 1935; Łaski 1956; Knakiewicz 1967; Landau 1976).

7   Conclusion

In the interwar period, Poland did not manage to achieve developmental success. Regaining independence alone did not turn out to be a sufficient window of opportunity. The unfavourable international environment, the shortage of local capital resources, the war damage, the relatively low percentage of industry in the global product of Polish economy, and internal social tensions hampered economic development.

The long-term consequences of partitions turned out to be comparably costly. Partitions resulted not only in the divergence of economic growth in Polish regions, but also in different institutional, legal, education, and monetary systems. To some extent, the challenge of integration exceeded the capacity of the restored country. It turned out to be successful in some spheres (the unification of law, administration, monetary system, education), while in others the dynamics of change was sluggish, and even the processes of regional de-convergence occurred (particularly the eastern provinces stayed behind the relatively well-industrialized western and central provinces) (Trenkler and Wolf 2005; Wolf 2005).

Moreover, throughout the interwar period, Poland was troubled by social and ethnic conflicts resulting from the persistent economic disparities. Social integrity was low due to social, ethnic and political tensions, and there were strong regional and social divisions, for example, between urban and rural societies. Economic reforms were not fully successful, and the recurring economic recessions worsened the situation of the lower classes. All this shows that the social problems resulting from the poverty of a nation, the wars, and partitions were not resolved. The crisis of the parliamentary system after 1926 limited the representation of the interests of some social groups in the authorities, which diminished the chances to find effective solutions to the problems.

Besides, there were some errors in the economic policy, such as overvaluing the zloty during the currency reform or the delay in implementing fiscal expansion during the Great Depression. The anti-crisis policy itself, based on not only fiscal expansion and interventionism, but also on nationalization, in the long term, could have become a barrier to development.

References

Ajnenkiel, A. (1986). *Od rządów ludowych do przewrotu majowego: zarys dziejów politycznych Polski 1918–1926* (Wyd. 5). Warszawa: Wiedza Powszechna.

Ajnenkiel, A. (Ed.). (1989). *Historia sejmu polskiego. T. 2 cz. 2: II [Druga] Rzeczpospolita*. Warszawa: Państwowe Wydawnictwo Naukowe.

Ajnenkiel, A. (Ed.). (1999). *Rok 1918: odrodzona Polska w nowej Europie*. Warszawa: "Neriton" & Instytut Historii PAN.

Barlicki, N. (1980). *Muszą zamilknąć spory na lewicy: wybór pism*. Warszawa: Książka i Wiedza.

Białokur, M. (2013). *Prezydent Gabriel Narutowicz i polityczny gorący grudzień 1922 roku: zbiór studiów*. Bielsko-Biała; Opole; Warszawa: Wydawnictwo Cum Laude.

Boettke, P. J. (Ed.). (2000). *Socialism and the market: The socialist calculation debate revisited*. London and New York: Routledge.

Borkowski, J. (1987). *Ludowcy w II Rzeczypospolitej* (Cz. 1–2). Warszawa: Ludowa Spółdzielnia Wydawnicza.

Borkowski, J., Inglot, S., & Wydawnictwo Uniwersytetu Wrocławskiego. (Eds.). (1995). *Historia chłopów polskich* (Wyd. 2). Wrocław: Wydawnictwo Uniwersytetu Wrocławskiego.

Chojnowski, A. (1986). *Piłsudczycy u władzy: dzieje Bezpartyjnego Bloku Współpracy z Rządem*. Wrocław: Zakład Narodowy im. Ossolińskich.

Cienciała, A. M., & Komarnicki, T. (1984). *From Versailles to Locarno: Keys to Polish foreign policy, 1919–1925*. Lawrence: University Press of Kansas.

Czubiński, A. (1988). *Komunistyczna Partia Polski: (1918–1938): zarys historii*. Warszawa: Wydawnictwa Szkolne i Pedagogiczne.

Davies, N. (1986). *God's playground: A history of Poland. Vol. 2: To the present*. Oxford: Clarendon Press.

Doboszyński, A. (1996). *O ustroju Polski*. Warszawa: Wydawnictwo Sejmowe.

Drewicz, M. (2009). *Głęboka przemiana rewolucyjna: sejmowa debata nad reformą rolną w Polsce w 1919 roku: w 90 rocznicę*. Lublin: Wydawnictwo Werset.

Dziewulski, K. (1981). *Spór o etatyzm: dyskusja wokół sektora państwowego w Polsce międzywojennej 1919–1939*. Warszawa: Państwowe Wydawnictwo Naukowe.

Faryś, J., Wątor, A., & Walczak, H. (Eds.). (2010). *Od Moraczewskiego do Składkowskiego: gabinety Polski odrodzonej 1918–1939*. Szczecin: Wydawnictwo Naukowe Uniwersytetu Szczecińskiego.

Fronczek-Kwarta, A. (2014). *Polityka finansowa i gospodarcza rządu Władysława Grabskiego w okresie reformy walutowo-skarbowej (1923–1925)*. Poznań: Wydawnictwo Nauka i Innowacje.

Garlicki, A. (1987). *Przewrót majowy*. Warszawa: Czytelnik.

Garlicki, A. (2012). W szóstym dniu urzędowania. *Polityka Warszawa, 2887*, 65–67.

Gazeł, A. (1939). *Handel zagraniczny Polski z uwzględnieniem ruchu przez porty*. Gdynia: Instytut Bałtycki.

Gerson, L. L. (1972). *Woodrow Wilson and the rebirth of Poland 1914–1920: A study in the influence an American policy of minority groups of foreign origin*. Hamden: Archon Books.

Ghosh, J. (2016). Michal Kalecki. In *Handbook of alternative theories of economic development* (pp. 475–484). Edward Elgar Publishing.

Głąbiński, S. (1999). *Stanisław Głąbiński o ustroju państwa polskiego i parlamentaryzmie*. Warszawa: Wydawnictwo Sejmowe: Kancelaria Sejmu.

Główny Urząd Statystyczny. (1927a). *Rocznik statystyki Rzeczypospolitej Polskiej. R. 4, 1925/1926*, Warszawa: Główny Urząd Statystyczny.

248   P. Koryś

Główny Urząd Statystyczny. (1927b). *Pierwszy powszechny spis Rzeczypospolitej Polskiej z dnia 30 września 1921 roku: Mieszkania. Warszawa: Ludność. Stosunki zawodowe: Tablice państwowe.* Warszawa: Główny Urząd Statystyczny.

Główny Urząd Statystyczny. (1933). *Statystyka przemysłowa 1931.* Warszawa: Główny Urząd Statystyczny.

Główny Urząd Statystyczny. (1934). *Drugi Powszechny Spis Ludności z dnia 9 grudnia 1931 r: wyniki ostateczne opracowania spisu ludności z dn. 9.XII.1931 r. w postaci skróconej dla wszystkich województw, powiatów i miast powyżej 20 000 mieszkańców Rzeczypospolitej Polskiej.* Warszawa: Główny Urząd Statystyczny.

Główny Urząd Statystyczny. (1938). *Drugi powszechny spis ludności z dn. 9. XII.1931 r: Polska: Stosunki zawodowe – ludność w rolnictwie.* Z. 94 b, Warszawa: Główny Urząd Statystyczny.

Główny Urząd Statystyczny. (1939a). *Mały rocznik statystyczny 1939.* Warszawa: Główny Urząd Statystyczny.

Główny Urząd Statystyczny. (1939b). *Drugi powszechny spis ludności z dn. 9. XII.1931 r: Polska: Stosunki zawodowe – ludność poza rolnictwem (część 1).* Z. 94 c, Warszawa: Główny Urząd Statystyczny.

Główny Urząd Statystyczny. (1939c). *Drugi powszechny spis ludności z dn. 9. XII.1931 r: Polska: Stosunki zawodowe – ludność poza rolnictwem (część 2).* Z. 94 d, Warszawa: Główny Urząd Statystyczny.

Główny Urząd Statystyczny. (1990). *Mały rocznik statystyczny Polski: wrzesień 1939 – czerwiec 1941.* Warszawa: Zakład Wydawnictw Statystycznych GUS.

Główny Urząd Statystyczny. (1993). *Historia Polski w liczbach: ludność, terytorium.* Główny Urząd Statystyczny.

Goclon, J. A. (2009). Rząd Jędrzeja Moraczewskiego 17 XI 1918 – 16 I 1919 r. (struktura, funkcjonowanie, dekrety). *Przegląd Nauk Historycznych, 2,* 99–138.

Gołębiowski, J. (1978). *Spór o etatyzm wewnątrz obozu sanacyjnego w latach 1926–1939.* Kraków: Wydawnictwo Naukowe WSP.

Gołębiowski, J. (2000). *COP: dzieje industrializacji w rejonie bezpieczeństwa 1922–1939.* Kraków: Wydawnictwo Naukowe AP.

Grzybek, D. (2005). *Nauka czy ideologia: biografia intelektualna Adama Krzyżanowskiego.* Kraków: Księgarnia Akademicka.

Jachymek, J. & Paruch, W. (Eds.). (2005). *Więcej niż niepodległość: polska myśl polityczna 1918–1939* (Wyd. 2). Lublin: Wydawnictwo Uniwersytetu Marii Curie- Skłodowskiej.

Janus, P. (2009). *W nurcie polskiego etatyzmu: Stefan Starzyński i Pierwsza Brygada Gospodarcza 1926–1932.* Kraków: Wydawnictwo Avalon.

Jedlicki, J., Janowski, M., Micińska, M., & Korecki, T. (2014). *A history of the Polish intelligentsia.* Peter Lang Edition.

Jezierski, A., & Leszczyńska, C. (2010). *Historia gospodarcza Polski.* Warszawa: Key Text.

Kacperski, K. (2007). *System wyborczy do Sejmu i Senatu u progu Drugiej Rzeczypospolitej.* Warszawa: Wydawnictwo Sejmowe.

Kacperski, K. (2013). *System wyborczy do parlamentu drugiej Rzeczypospolitej w pracach Sejmu i Senatu pierwszej kadencji (1922–1927).* Warszawa: Wydawnictwo Sejmowe.

Kalecki, M., & Landau, L. (1934). *Szacunek dochodu społecznego w r. 1929.* Warszawa: Instytut Badania Koniunktur Gospodarczych i Cen.

Kalecki, M., & Landau, L. (1935). *Dochód społeczny w r. 1933 i podstawy badań perjodycznych nad zmianami dochodu.* Warszawa: Instytut Badania Koniunktur Gospodarczych i Cen.

Kamiński, P. (2015). *Mapa dróg w Polsce zbudowanych w latach 1918–1939: skala ok. 1:1 750 000.* Warszawa: GDDKiA & PTR Kartografia.

Klimiuk, Z. (2011). *Stosunki handlowe Polski i Niemiec w okresie międzywojennym (1918–1939): problemy handlu zagranicznego obu krajów na tle międzynarodowych stosunków gospodarczych i politycznych.* Lublin: Wydawnictwo Polihymnia.

Knakiewicz, Z. (1967). *Deflacja polska 1930–1935.* Warszawa: Państwowe Wydawnictwo Ekonomiczne.

Kofman, J. (1986). *Lewiatan a podstawowe zagadnienia ekonomiczno-społeczne Drugiej Rzeczypospolitej: z dziejów ideologii kół wielkokapitalistycznych w Polsce.* Warszawa: Państwowe Wydawnictwo Naukowe.

Kofman, J. (1992). *Nacjonalizm gospodarczy – szansa czy bariera rozwoju: przypadek Europy Środkowo-Wschodniej w okresie międzywojennym.* Warszawa: Wydawnictwo Naukowe PWN.

Koryś, P. (2015). The state as an enterpreneur: Reorientation of the economic policy of the Republic of Poland in late 1930s and the development of state capitalism. *Ekonomia, 42,* 109–132.

Kostro, K. (2001). *Hayek kontra socjalizm: debata socjalistyczna a rozwój teorii społeczno-ekonomicznych Friedricha von Hayeka.* Warszawa: DiG.

Kotlarz, G., Dąbrowski, H., Wieczorek, E. (2017). *Magistrala węglowa: najciekawsze linie kolejowe Polski.* Rybnik: Eurosprinter.

Koziarski, S. (1993). *Sieć kolejowa Polski w latach 1918–1992.* Opole: Państwowy Instytut Naukowy.

Kubiczek, F. & Wyczański, A. (Eds.). (2006). *Historia Polski w liczbach. T. 2: Gospodarka.* Warszawa: Zakład Wydawnictw Statystycznych.

Kulińska, L. (2009). *Działalność terrorystyczna i sabotażowa nacjonalistycznych organizacji ukraińskich w Polsce w latach 1922–1939*. Kraków: Księgarnia Akademicka: Fundacja Centrum Dokumentacji Czynu Niepodległościowego.

Kwiatkowski, E. (1932). *Dysproporcje: rzecz o Polsce przeszłej i obecnej*. Kraków: Nakładem Towarzystwa Szkoły Ludowej.

Kwiatkowski, E. (1938). *O wielkość Rzeczypospolitej: przemówienie wygłoszone w Sejmie w dn. 2 grudnia 1938 r*. Warszawa: Nakładem tygodnika "Polska Gospodarcza".

Landau, Z. (1969). Płace w Polsce w okresie kryzysu gospodarczego lat 1930–1935. *Roczniki Dziejów Społecznych Gospodarczych Poznan, 30,* 94–121.

Landau, Z. (1976). National income in historical research. *Acta Poloniae Historica, 33,* 93–119.

Landau, Z. (1998). *Bank Gospodarstwa Krajowego*. Warszawa: Oficyna Wydawnicza Szkoły Głównej Handlowej.

Landau, Z. (2011). Kwiatkowskiego wizja gospodarki Polski. *Zeszyty Naukowe Uczelni Warszawskiej, 33,* 95–116.

Landau, Z., & Roszkowski, W. (1995). *Polityka gospodarcza II RP i PRL*. Warszawa: Wydawnictwo Naukowe PWN.

Landau, Z., & Tomaszewski, J. (1977). *Druga Rzeczpospolita: gospodarka – społeczeństwo – miejsce w świecie: (sporne problemy badań)*. Warszawa: Książka i Wiedza.

Landau, Z., & Tomaszewski, J. (1978). *Trudna niepodległość: rozważania o gospodarce Polski 1918–1939*. Warszawa: Książka i Wiedza.

Landau, Z., & Tomaszewski, J. (1983). *Sprawa żyrardowska: przyczynek do dziejów kapitałów obcych w Polsce międzywojennej*. Warszawa: Książka i Wiedza.

Landau, Z., & Tomaszewski, J. (1989). *Lata interwencjonalizmu państwowego 1936–1939*. Warszawa: Książka i Wiedza.

Łapa, M. (2002). *Modernizacja państwa: polska polityka gospodarcza 1926–1929*. Łódź: Ibidem.

Łaski, K. (1956). *Akumulacja i spożycie w procesie uprzemysłowienia Polski Ludowej*. Warszawa: Książka i Wiedza.

Leszczyńska, C. (2006). Polska bankowość centralna 1828–1989: Bank Polski, Polska Krajowa Kasa Pożyczkowa, Bank Polski SA, Narodowy Bank Polski. *Bank i Kredyt, 2,* 43.

Leszczyńska, C. (2010). *Zarys historii polskiej bankowości centralnej*. Warszawa: Narodowy Bank Polski.

Leszczyńska, C. (2013). *Polska polityka pieniężna i walutowa w latach 1924–1936 w systemie Gold Exchange Standard*. Warszawa: Wydawnictwa Uniwersytetu Warszawskiego.

Leszczyńska, C. (2016). Level of living of Polish citizens in the interwar period, and its diversification. *Roczniki Dziejów Społecznych Gospodarczych, 4*, 93–120.

Leszczyńska, C. (2017). Przemysłowe peryferia. Polska Północno-Wschodnia w latach 1870–1939. *Optimum Studia Ekonomiczne, 2*, 93–118. https://doi.org/10.15290/ose.2017.02.86.07

Leszczyński, A. (2017). *Leap into modernity: Political economy of growth on the periphery, 1943–1980*. Frankfurt am Main: Peter Lang Edition.

Lityńska, A. (2004). Władysław Zawadzki – życie i twórczość. *Zeszyty Naukowe Akademii Ekonomicznej w Krakowie, 632*, 105–111.

Lityńska, A., Giza, W., & Skrzyński, T. (2010). *Spór o etatyzm w polskiej myśli ekonomicznej w okresie dwudziestolecia międzywojennego*. Kraków: Wydawnictwo Uniwersytetu Ekonomicznego.

López, G. J., & Assous, M. (2010). *Michał Kalecki*. Basingstoke and New York: Palgrave Macmillan.

Łukasiewicz, J. (2009). Spisy ludności w Polsce i na ziemiach polskich do 1939 r. *Wiadomości Statystyczne, 6* , 1–5.

Mazurek, M. (2016). "Bezdroża kapitalizmu": Ludwik Landau i jego statystyczna wizja globalnych nierówności. *Stan Rzeczy Teoria Społeczna*, 127–143.

Mędrzecki, W., Leszczyńska, C., & Instytut Historii im. Tadeusza Manteuffla (Polska Akademia Nauk) (Eds.). (2014). *Praca i społeczeństwo Drugiej Rzeczypospolitej: zbiór studiów*. Warszawa: Instyut Historii PAN.

Mieszczankowski, M. (1983). *Rolnictwo II Rzeczypospolitej*. Warszawa: Książka i Wiedza.

Ministerstwo Przemysłu i Handlu (Ed.). (1933). *Statystyka zakładów elektrycznych w Polsce 1930, 1931, 1932 =: Statistique de la production et de la distribution de l'énergie électrique en Pologne 1930, 1931, 1932*. Warszawa: Stowarzyszenie Elektryków Polskich.

Morawski, W. (1990). *Polityka gospodarcza rządu Aleksandra Skrzyńskiego*. Warszawa: Państwowe Wydawnictwo Naukowe.

Morawski, W. (1998). *Słownik historyczny bankowości polskiej do 1939 roku*. Warszawa: Muza SA.

Morawski, W. (2008). *Od marki do złotego: historia finansów Drugiej Rzeczypospolitej*. Warszawa: Wydawnictwo Naukowe PWN.

Musiał, W. (2013). *Modernizacja Polski: polityki rządowe w latach 1918–2004*. Toruń: Wydawnictwo Naukowe Uniwersytetu Mikołaja Kopernika.

Osiński, Z. (2007). *Janusz Jędrzejewicz – piłsudczyk i reformator edukacji (1885–1951).* Lublin: Wydawnictwo Uniwersytetu Marii Curie- Skłodowskiej.

Popkiewicz, J., & Ryszka, F. (1959). *Przemysł ciężki Górnego Śląska w gospodarce Polski międzywojennej: 1922–1939: studium historyczno- gospodarcze.* Opole; Wrocław: Instytut Śląski & Ossolineum.

Radziwiłł, A. (2014) Ideologia wychowawcza sanacji i jej odbicie w polityce szkolnej w latach 1926–1939. *Kwart Pedagog,* 227–306.

Rosenstein-Rodan, P. N. (1943). Problems of Industrialisation of Eastern and South-Eastern Europe. *Economic Journal, 53,* 202–211. https://doi.org/10.2307/2226317

Roszkowski, W. (1991). *Landowners in Poland 1918–1939. East European Monographs.* Distributed by Columbia University Press, Boulder and New York.

Roszkowski, W. (2017). *Historia Polski 1914–2015* (Wyd. 12. rozszerzone). Warszawa: Wydawnictwo Naukowe PWN.

Rudnicki, S. (1985). *Obóz Narodowo Radykalny: geneza i działalność.* Warszawa: Czytelnik.

Rzepecki, T., & Rzepecki, K. (1928). *Sejm i Senat 1928–1933: podręcznik zawierający wyniki wyborów w województwach, okręgach i powiatach, podobizny posłów sejmowych i senatorów, statystyki i mapy poglądowe.* Poznań: Wielkopolska Księgarnia Nakładem Karola Rzepeckiego.

Rzepecki, T., & Rzepecki, W. (1923). *Sejm i Senat 1922–1927: podręcznik dla wyborców zawierający wyniki wyborów w powiatach, okręgach, województwach.* Poznań: Wielkopolska Księgarnia Nakładem Karola Rzepeckiego.

Sadowska, J. (2001). *Ku szkole na miarę Drugiej Rzeczypospolitej: geneza, założenia i realizacja reformy Jędrzejewiczowskiej.* Białystok: Wydawnictwo Uniwersytetu w Białymstoku.

Samecki, W. (1998). *Centralny Okręg Przemysłowy 1936–1939. Wstępna faza programu uprzemysłowienia Polski.* Series: *Acta Universitatis Wratislaviensis: Ekonomia, 3.* Wrocław: ydawnictwo Uniwersytetu Wrocławskiego.

Seidner, S. S., & Wynot, E. D. (1975). The camp of national unity: An experiment in domestic consolidation. *Polish Review, 20,* 231–236.

Seniów, J. (1998). *W kręgu piłsudczyków: poglądy ideowo-polityczne "Gazety Polskiej": (1929–1939).* Kraków: Wydawnictwo Uniwersytetu Jagiellońskiego.

Skibiński, S. (1933). *Zagraniczny handel towarowy Polski i Anglji.* Warszawa: s.n.

Śliwa, M. (1988). *Polska myśl socjalistyczna: 1918–1948.* Wrocław [etc.]: Zakład Narodowy im. Ossolińskich.

Stańczyk, E. (2004). Analfabetyzm w Polsce w okresie dwudziestolecia międzywojennego. *Acta Universitatis Wratislaviensis. Przegląd Prawa i Administracji, LXIII,* 197–212.

Starzyński, S. (1926). *Program rządu pracy w Polsce.* Warszawa: Droga.

Szlajfer, H. (2012). *Economic nationalism and globalization: Lessons from Latin America and Central Europe.* Leiden and Boston: Brill.

Temkin, G. (2008). *Dyskusje o gospodarce socjalistycznej: Marks, Lange, Mises, Hayek.* Warszawa: Wydawnictwo Polskiego Towarzystwa Ekonomicznego.

Tomaszewski, J., & Landau, Z. (2005). *Polska w Europie i świecie 1918–1939.* Warszawa: Wyd. TRIO.

Tomicki, J. (1982). *Lewica socjalistyczna w Polsce 1918–1939.* Warszawa: Książka i Wiedza.

Toporowski, J. (2013). *Michal Kalecki: An intellectual biography. Volume I: Rendezvous in Cambridge, 1899–1939.* New York: Palgrave Macmillan.

Torzecki, R. (1989). *Kwestia ukraińska w Polsce w latach 1923–1929.* Kraków: Wydawnictwo Literackie.

Trenkler, C., & Wolf, N. (2005). Economic integration across borders: The Polish interwar economy 1921–1937. *European Review of Economic History, 9,* 199–231.

Wańkowicz, M. (1939). *Sztafeta: książka o polskim pochodzie gospodarczym.* Warszawa: Biblioteka Polska.

Wapiński, R. (1980). *Narodowa Demokracja 1893–1939: ze studiów nad dziejami myśli nacjonalistycznej.* Wrocław: Zakład Narodowy im. Ossolińskich.

Wolf, N. (2005). Path dependent border effects: The case of Poland's reunification (1918–1939). *Explorations in Economic History, 42,* 414–438.

Wolf, N. (2007). Should I stay or should I go? Understanding Poland's Adherence to Gold, 1928–1936. *Historical Social Research, 32,* 351–368.

Wyczański, A. (Ed.). (2003). *Historia Polski w liczbach. T. 1: Państwo, społeczeństwo.* Warszawa: Zakład Wydawnictw Statystycznych.

Wynot, E. D. (1971). "A necessary cruelty": The emergence of official Anti-Semitism in Poland, 1936–1939. *The American Historical Review, 76,* 1035. https://doi.org/10.2307/1849240

Wynot, E. D. (1974). *Polish politics in transition: The Camp of National Unity and the struggle for power: 1935–1939.* Arch Czesława Miłosza.

Wysocki, T. (2005). Umiejętność czytania i pisania w grupach wyznaniowych zamieszkujących Polskę w świetle wyników Spisu Powszechnego z 1931 roku. *Rozprawy z Dziejów Oświaty, 44,* 105–135.

Wyszczelski, L. (2015a). *Polska mocarstwowa: wizje i koncepcje obozów politycznych II Rzeczypospolitej: międzymorze, federalizm, prometeizm, kolonie i inne drogi do wielkości.* Warszawa: Bellona.

Wyszczelski, L. (2015b). *Konflikty narodowe i wewnętrzne II Rzeczypospolitej: mroczne obszary dziejów II RP: konflikty z sąsiadami, opór mniejszości narodowych, strajki chłopskie i robotnicze.* Warszawa: Bellona.

9

Under the Nazi and Soviet Rule: Polish Lands During World War II (1939–1945)

For more than a century, the partitions, displacements of territory, and resettlements of the population remained an important barrier for institutional enhancements and economic development. In 1939, the two decades of efforts to reintegrate the Polish state after regaining sovereignty were ended by the outbreak of the war, which began another, ultimate, wave of partitions, displacements of territory, as well as extermination and resettlements of the population in Poland.

WWII started with the attack of the German army on Poland on 1 September 1939, and on 17 September, the USSR attacked Poland from the east. By the end of September, the whole territory of Poland was occupied—the last Polish troops surrendered in the first week of October. The Polish territory was divided between Germany and the USSR, as stated by the Molotov-Ribbentrop Pact. Additionally, the Wilno region was occupied by Lithuania, and parts of southern Poland by Slovakia. In June 1941, after the German attack on the USSR, the entire Polish territory found itself under German occupation. In 1944 the Soviet army entered the territory of the former Commonwealth, and in spring the war moved to the present-day territory of Poland. At the same time, the Polish underground army made an attempt to liberate some of the Polish

© The Author(s) 2018
P. Koryś, *Poland From Partitions to EU Accession*,
https://doi.org/10.1007/978-3-319-97126-1_9

territory before the Soviets (Operation Tempest) and organized the Warsaw Uprising in August 1944; both these actions were unsuccessful, and the German army did not withdraw until the Soviet offensive. The fights on the territory of present-day Poland lasted until May 1945, which made Poland the country where the military warfare lasted the longest, from September 1939 to May 1945 (Davies 1986).

When the Soviet army invaded Poland on 17 September 1939, many members of the cabinet and the military high command left Poland and went to Romania, where they were interned. The Polish Government-in-Exile was formed, first in France, then—after the fall of France to Germany in June 1940—in London. The office of prime minister was held by Władysław Sikorski from 1939 until his death in an aeroplane crash in 1943, then by Stanisław Mikołajczyk, then Tomasz Arciszewski. This government was internationally recognized; however, the USSR suspended its relations with the Polish Government-in-Exile in 1943 and in 1944 recognized the Polish Committee of National Liberation (*PKWN*) as the Polish government. It was dominated by communists and created with the support of the USSR; later, it proclaimed itself the Provisional Government of the Republic of Poland and became one of the main agents in introducing the socialist system in Poland, alongside the quasi-parliamentary State National Council (*KRN*), created by Stalin in Moscow in December 1943 (Davies 1986; Roszkowski 2017). Then, the Polish state was reconstructed according to the plan designed by Stalin. Both the Polish Committee of National Liberation and the Provisional Government of the Republic of Poland comprised mainly communists, but also members of other parties, the Polish Socialist Party, the agrarian party SL, and SD, representing small business. The presence of other parties was supposed to make these governments appear multi-partisan, but by that time Poland had already been officially included into the Soviet sphere of influence and given new borders. This decision was made outside Poland and without any Polish participation or will by the leaders of the anti-German coalition during conferences in Teheran (1943), Moscow (1944), and Yalta (1945). During these meetings, Winston Churchill, prime minister of the United Kingdom, Joseph Stalin, first secretary of the Communist Party of the Soviet Union, and Franklin D. Roosevelt, President of the USA, carved out the shape of the post-war world including the division into spheres of influence, Soviet and Anglo-American (Western).

Despite the absence of the Polish government on the Polish territory occupied by the German army, the Polish underground government and military structures (the Polish Underground State, the Home Army) were created on a scale far larger than anywhere in Europe. Their allegiance was to the Polish Government-in-Exile in London. Some guerrilla activity was conducted (urban guerrilla, partisan warfare, terrorist attacks), but it was limited due to the savage German reprisals. The main activity was the sabotage of German arms production and transport infrastructure. Importantly, The Home Army provided the western powers with intelligence concerning German concentration camps, the Holocaust, German military facilities and technologies, and so on. Apart from the Home Army, the Polish resistance movement included other military organizations, such as the communist People's Guard (since 1942, known as People's Army); the Peasants' Battalions, created in 1940 and in 1943 partly incorporated into the Home Army; the National Armed Forces; and others, connected with various political movements. At the peak of their activity, the Polish underground military forces totalled well over 500,000 soldiers (1944), most of them unarmed or poorly armed, however.

The territory occupied by Germany was divided into the part incorporated into Germany (the former Prussian partition and some of the lands of central Poland) and the General Governorate (*Generalgouvernement für die besetzten polnischen Gebiete*), which was later meant to become a separate quasi-state. The lands incorporated to the German state, 92,000 km² with 10.6 million inhabitants, comprised Greater Poland and the Łódź region (these lands were named *Warthegau*), Pomerania, Upper Silesia along with the industrial area near Dąbrowa, northern Masovia, and the Suwalki region. The General Governorate, comprising the rest of the former Kingdom of Poland and Western Galicia, comprised 95,000 km² and 11.5 million inhabitants. The areas occupied by the USSR, 201,000 km² with 13 million inhabitants, were incorporated into the respective republics, the Byelorussian and Ukrainian SSRs. After the German invasion of the Soviet Union, Eastern Galicia and Lwów were incorporated into the General Governorate, the Bialystok region was incorporated into Germany, and the other regions were under military administration (Madajczyk 1987; Łuczak 1996).

In the regions incorporated into Germany, the state quickly restored and developed the industry and introduced the policy of extreme ethnic discrimination and cleansing, for example, expropriations and deportations of the Polish population and the concentration and extermination of Jews. The policy aimed at eliminating the Polish intellectual and economic elites and creating the German majority (in short time over 500,000 Germans were settled, mostly in Warthegau: in Greater Poland and in the area around Łódź). The policy also included moving Polish children to Germany for adoption and Germanization (40,000–120,000 people), as well as racial evaluation and segregation according to the assessment of the person's "capability of re-Germanization". By the end of 1940, approximately 1.5 million Polish nationals were expelled from homes, and almost 500,000 were deported to the General Governorate (the expulsions were conducted in Warthegau, Silesia, and Pomerania). German settlement started in Warthegau and the Ciechanow area. In short time over 500,000 Germans were settled in these areas, mostly in Warthegau: in Greater Poland and in the area around Łódź. Polish Jews from Warthegau were deported to Łódź and settled in the ghetto. By 1942, much Polish-owned property had been confiscated, such as trade and industrial enterprises as well as 900,000 farms. These territories were included into the German legal system, and the Polish were deprived of civil rights, including access to education. They were treated as slave labour resources (Madajczyk 1973; Łuczak 1979).

The General Governorate was treated as a German colony, made dependent on Germany by means of confiscating and eliminating industry, lowering the standard of living of the local population, and treating it as a forced labour reserve. Germany conducted a slash-and-burn economic policy, aimed at the maximum exploitation of the labour force and of the existing production capacity without the intention of sustaining it. Initially, part of the industry was relocated to Germany, which resulted in a rapid decrease of industrial production and the growth of unemployment. Later, the industry was partially restored because of the Soviet-German war, as the General Governorate was a good supply base due to its proximity to the theatre of war. In 1943, Germans started to relocate some industrial activity to the General Governorate, due to the frequent Allied bombings of the

German territory. While withdrawing from Poland during the Soviet offensive, Germans destroyed most of the industrial facilities. In the General Governorate, the big and Jewish-owned properties were confiscated, but small properties owned by ethnic Poles, including peasant farms, were not. Jews were deprived of civil rights, were subject to forced labour, and were required to wear special armbands. Municipalities designed districts where the Jewish population was to live, and between 1940 and 1941 the biggest ones (the ghettoes in Kraków and Warszawa) were closed. There were also special districts designed for the German population employed in the public and economic administration, the military, and the police. The Polish population retained the basic civil rights, including access to primary and vocational education in Polish. The secondary and tertiary education as well as research institutions were abolished. The new areas for German settlement were designed and the deportation of the Polish citizens from these regions was organized (in the first stage, the mass deportations comprised the area around Zamość, from where several hundred thousand people were deported to make room for Germans) (Madajczyk 1973; Winstone 2014).

In the Soviet occupation zone, the authorities conducted the policy of mass deportations of the Polish population into the remote areas of Russia, which comprised 370,000 people in the years 1940–1941. Other forms of ethnic discrimination concerned mostly the Polish elites, and a particularly vivid example is the fate of several thousand officers of the Polish army, interned as prisoners of war and subsequently executed (the Katyn massacre). Several hundred thousand men were conscripted to the Red Army. The Polish property was confiscated: all industrial and trade enterprises, craftsmen's workshops, and big agricultural estates. In 1940, the land collectivization policy was introduced. The standard of living of the Polish population lowered rapidly due to lowering the wages, increasing the work time, confiscation of property, and currency exchange. However, due to the shorter period of the Soviet occupation, the lack of planned extermination policy, and considerable percentages of Byelorussian and Ukrainian populations, the scale of the Soviet atrocities on the Polish territories annexed by the USSR was much smaller than that committed under the German occupation.

In 1940, the Germans started to build concentration camps on the Polish territory. At first, they were forced labour camps with very high mortality due to hard labour, bad hygiene, harsh conditions, and insufficient nutrition, but later, they turned into death camps conducting well-organized extermination. The biggest of these facilities was Auschwitz-Birkenau, whose prisoners worked in the nearby IG Farben chemical plant. Mass extermination comprised Polish and European Jews, Romani and—to a lesser extent—Slavic people. Most concentration camps were situated in Poland, whose central European location, and a huge Polish-Jewish population, facilitated the logistics of one of the most sinister elements of the German policy, planned genocide called the "Final Solution to the Jewish Question" (*Endlösung der Judenfrage*) (Łuczak 1979; Madajczyk 1987; Snyder 2010; Winstone 2014).

The organized extermination of Jews, Poles, and Gypsies was conducted in death camps, ghettoes, and forced labour camps, but there were also other means, such as the so-called pacifications of villages (i.e. executing some or all the villagers and torching the whole village), public executions, roundups and kidnapping people in the street to force them into slave labour in Germany or concentration camps, or taking away children with a view to Germanization, slave labour, or death. Additionally, the German authorities fuelled ethnic resentments and inspired anti-Jewish violence, called pogroms, among the local Polish, Lithuanian, Byelorussian, and Ukrainian populations (one of the biggest pogroms where the Polish population was involved in inflicting the violence was the one in Jedwabne in 1941). Moreover, the harsh conditions in German factories, both in the General Governorate and on the territories annexed to Germany, resulted in high mortality among the Polish workers. Besides, the Polish population suffered huge losses in the ineffective Polish anti-German military action in 1944, Operation Tempest, particularly in the Warsaw Uprising; the German reprisals involved the death of several hundred thousand people, including many civilians.

The population losses of the Polish Republic were mostly the result of the German policy of exterminating the non-German population (cf. Table 9.1). The losses reached about 20% of the pre-war population, and the Jewish and Gypsy populations were affected much more than other groups. The catastrophic human losses entailed the depopulation of urban areas and the loss of human capital on a scale which cannot be compared with any other country severely affected by the war, including

Table 9.1 Population balance of Poland 1939–1950

	Total	Poles	Jews	Germans	Other minorities
Population 1939	35,000,000	24,300,000	3,200,000	800,000	6,700,000
Natural increase 1939–1945	1,300,000	1,000,000	–	–	300,000
Total human losses	–6,000,000	-3,100,000	–2,800,000	–	–100,000
War emigration	–1,500,000	–500,000	–200,000	–600,000	–200,000
Border changes USSR	–6,700,000	–700,000	–	–	–6,000,000
Population gain on recovered territories	1,100,000	1,100,000	–	–	–
Re-immigration 1946–1950	200,000	200,000	–	–	–
Deportations to USSR 1944–1947	–500,000		–	–	–500,000
Natural increase 1946–1950	2,100,000	2,100,000	–	–	–
Population 1950	25,000,000	24,400,000	200,000	200,000	200,000

Source: Piesowicz (1987)

Germany and the USSR. Moreover, the Polish suffered a moral crisis on an unprecedented scale, resulting from the policy of the systematic elimination of the elites, mass extermination, and turning the whole Polish nation into slaves, along with extremely harsh anti-Jewish measures introduced by the German authorities (among the countries occupied by Germany, Poland was the only place where providing help to Jews was punishable by death). The phenomena which appeared within the Polish population included looting, the persecution of Jews, collaboration with the Germans in giving away the Jews hiding in Polish homes, blackmail (giving shelter to Jews for money), and even taking part in anti-Jewish violence. The scale of these phenomena was relatively small, but still they contributed to numerous casualties among Jews and in the future in the lowering of the moral standards, which later facilitated the implementation of the communist rule, based on the similar terror as the Nazi regime.

Material losses, resulting from the slash-and-burn exploitation of the material capital, depreciation, war damage, and planned destruction conducted by the withdrawing German army, were enormous. Warszawa was

Table 9.2 Distribution of direct material losses by area and sector of economy (in comparison to September 1939)[a]

Voivodeship	Losses as a share of pre-war assets, geographical distribution (%)	Sector of economy	Losses as a share of pre-war assets (%)
Total losses	100	Total assets	38
Białostockie	4	Agriculture	35
Gdańskie	5	Forestry, hunting, fishing	28
Kieleckie	8	Industry, mining, crafts and energy sector	32
Krakowskie	5	Trade	65
Lubelskie	3	Transport and communication	50
Łódzkie	9	Post and telegraph	62
Pomorskie	5	Public administration, banks and insurance	60
Poznańskie	9	Cultural and historical heritage	43
Rzeszowskie	4	Schools and academic institutions	60
Śląsko-Dąbrowskie	6	Health service	55
Warszawskie	7	Military equipment	100
Warszawa	35	Buildings	30

Source: Biuro Odszkodowań Wojennych (1947)
[a]Data covers the territory of post-WWII Poland, with the exclusion of Western and Northern Territories

practically annihilated—all the industry and most of the infrastructure and residential buildings were destroyed (as shown in table 9.2, destruction of Warszawa was responsible for 35% of Polish war losses). Other Polish cities were also considerably damaged, for example, Łódź and Poznań. There was also a substantial level of destruction or damage to the transport infrastructure—bridges, railways, and roads (cf. Table 9.2).

The war resulted in huge human and material losses for Poland, and the GDP per capita again fell well under that in 1913. The scale of the damage on the territories, which were part of Poland before 1939 and stayed within its borders after 1945, was significantly bigger in WWII than in WWI. The difference was enormous, especially in terms of population losses, particularly if we consider the number of children not born because of the war. The actual population loss was increased by the emigration (the majority of the soldiers of the Polish Western Army and the workers of the London administration, as well as part of the war emigrants, decided against returning to Poland and stayed in the West) and by border changes and relocations on the territories included into the USSR in 1945 (not all Polish population of these areas managed to be repatriated). The war losses entailed the change of the employment structure—non-agricultural and highly qualified workforce was affected much more than other groups, as the extermination targeted Jews and the intelligentsia (Zaremba 2012; Leder 2014).

Additional material losses were the territories incorporated into the USSR in 1945, partially compensated for by the acquisition of the eastern parts of Germany granted to Poland the Yalta Treaty. These territories, although their infrastructure and industry were well developed in comparison to the other regions of Poland, had suffered war damage and the slash-and-burn Soviet policy immediately after the war. In the aftermath of the war, Poland became part of the Soviet sphere of influence, which in the long term became a serious development barrier.

War crimes, huge human losses, collapse of formal and informal institution, and mass displacements of population resulted in the corrosion of the moral standards of the Polish society and the disintegration of the values system (Wyka 1984). This resulted in the emergence of immoral practices, such as looting, blackmail, and corruption. The attitudes of "amoral familism" were enhanced by general insecurity, living under the constant fear for life and awaiting economic disaster (Zaremba 2012). The moral crisis contributed to the increase of violence in social relations, including the emergence of anti-Jewish behaviours, often inspired by the German or (later) communist authorities.

Moreover, the war resulted in another period of institutional discontinuity, displacement of territory, and unprecedented population loses and moves. In this way, the world war hampered the economic development of Poland once again. The direct effect of the war was strengthened by the inclusion of Poland into the Soviet zone. Thus, the struggle of the Polish interwar governments to make Poland a part of Europe (or the Western world) was unsuccessful.

As a result of the war, the newly established state faced not only the challenge of the post-war reconstruction, quite common across Europe, but also the challenge of the integration of new lands into its territory and institutional arrangement. The population was decimated by war and emigration, and the loss of human capital was even higher than crude demographic losses. Moreover, the Polish society had to rebuild the institutions and social relations, after the war experience which damaged its structure, size, and moral fabric. And all this happened in a new institutional arrangement, the Soviet one, which was inefficient in economic terms and hostile to private property, market, entrepreneurship, pre-war elites, and pre-war traditions.

References

Biuro Odszkodowań Wojennych. (1947). *Sprawozdanie w przedmiocie strat i szkód wojennych Polski w latach 1939–1945.* Warszawa: Biuro Odszkodowań Wojennych przy Prezydium Rady Ministrów.

Davies, N. (1986). *God's playground: A history of Poland. Vol. 2: To the present.* Oxford: Clarendon Press.

Leder, A. (2014). *Prześniona rewolucja: ćwiczenie z logiki historycznej* (Wyd. pierwsze). Warszawa: Wydawnictwo Krytyki Politycznej.

Łuczak, C. (1979). *Polityka ludnościowa i ekonomiczna hitlerowskich Niemiec w okupowanej Polsce.* Poznań: Wydawnictwo Poznańskie.

Łuczak, C. (1996). *Pod niemieckim jarzmem: kraj Warty 1939–1945.* Poznań: PSO [Pracownia Serwisu Oprogramowania].

Madajczyk, C. (1973). Założenia generalne i charakter przesiedleń hitlerowskich. *Studia Historiae Oeconomicae, 8,* 4–34.

Madajczyk, C. (1987). *Die Okkupationspolitik Nazideutschlands in Polen 1939–1945.* Berlin: Akademie.

Piesowicz, K. (1987). *Demograficzne skutki II wojny swiatowej.* Studia Demograficzne.

Roszkowski, W. (2017). *Historia Polski 1914–2015* (Wyd. 12. rozszerzone). Warszawa: Wydawnictwo Naukowe PWN.

Snyder, T. (2010). *Bloodlands: Europe between Hitler and Stalin.* New York: Basic Books.

Winstone, M. (2014). *The dark heart of Hitler's Europe: Nazi rule in Poland under the general government.* I. B. Tauris.

Wyka, K. (1984). *Życie na niby: Pamiętnik po klęsce.* Warszawa: Wydawnictwo Literackie.

Zaremba, M. (2012). *Wielka trwoga: Polska 1944–1947: ludowa reakcja na kryzys.* Kraków: Znak.

10

Communist Modernization? Economic Development of Poland Under State Socialism (1945–1989)

The process of regaining sovereignty and subsequently establishing the communist regime in Poland started in summer 1944, but parts of the territory of the arising "new" Poland remained under German control until the end of WWII. Then, Poland faced serious development challenges, which resulted from the loses of population and territory, inclusion of new lands, the resettlement of the German population of these new lands to Germany, from the destruction of industry, towns and infrastructure, but also from internal conflicts. Large part of Polish lands were devastated by war. Poland's capital, Warszawa, was totally destroyed. The new lands of Poland, called the Recovered Territories or Western and Northern Lands, relatively well developed, after the expulsion of Germans, were entirely depopulated. As a consequence, the post-war development began from a very low level. Actually, once again, Poland was de-industrialized—not only due to infrastructural damage, but also due to the loss of human capital: industrial workers, engineers, and managers.

Anyway, in the first years after WWII, Poland experienced rapid growth, which resulted from the reconstruction process. Unfortunately, at the same time, the new, communist economic policy resulted in the

© The Author(s) 2018
P. Koryś, *Poland From Partitions to EU Accession*,
https://doi.org/10.1007/978-3-319-97126-1_10

growing inefficiency in economy. Since the 1950s, the gap between Poland and Western Europe—experiencing the golden years of post-war reconstruction—and also other neighbouring communist countries, rapidly expanded, and this process (with short break in early 1970s) lasted until the collapse of the People's Republic of Poland. Once again, institutional discontinuity, displacements of the territory, and resettlement of the population cast a shadow on the economic development of Poland and the prosperity of the Poles. As a result, just before the system transformation, the gap between Poland and the global technological leader, the USA, in both relative and absolute values, was among the widest in modern history.

However, unconsciously, the foundation for the economic success of the Third Republic of Poland was laid: Poland became an industrialized country, and mass education resulted in the eradication of illiteracy. Urbanization reduced the share of the rural/peasant population, and the post-war baby boom and echo-boom resulted in a significant increase of the population and of the labour force. After the dramatic post-war resettlements, the population of Poland within the new borders became nearly homogeneous, ethnically, which almost eliminated ethnic conflicts. Finally, after decades of efforts, the Western and Northern Lands became an integral part of Poland's territory and Germany confirmed the shape of the Polish-German border.

1   Internal Politics of Communist Poland

Even though the decisions concerning Poland were taken in Yalta in January 1945, until 1947, it was not clear in what form the communist party would govern Poland. As decided in Yalta, the parliamentary function was performed by the State National Council, in which the biggest parties were the communist Polish Workers' Party (*PPR*) and the Polish Socialist Party (*PPS*), the latter already dominated by the proponents of the rapprochement with the communists; these two parties created the so-called Democratic Bloc along with the peasant party People's Party (*SL*) and the Democratic Party (*SD*), acting in Poland. The main opposition party was PSL, the Polish People's Party, connected with the Polish emigration and headed by the ex-prime minister of the Polish

Government-in-Exile, Stanisław Mikołajczyk. The president of the State National Council was Bolesław Bierut from the Polish Workers' Party, and the vice presidents were the pre-war politicians, Wincenty Witos and Stanisław Grabski. The new Polish cabinet, the Provisional Government of National Unity, headed by Edward Osóbka-Morawski (formally from the socialist party, but close to the communists), was mostly composed of communists, but it also included members of the other democratic parties. Mikołajczyk became deputy prime minister and his party got the ministries of education and public administration. The new cabinet was soon recognized by other countries, including the USA and Great Britain, which completely marginalized the Polish Government-in-Exile. The Polish government's policy was strongly influenced by the USSR, through the communist ministers and through the Soviet officers and advisors in the military and security forces (Karpiński 2001; Roszkowski 2011).

In the spring of 1946, the people's referendum was held with a view to the legitimization of the communist rule. The three questions were about abolishing the senate, consolidating the system based on the land reform and nationalization, and confirming the western borders on the Oder and the Lusatian Neisse rivers. The results were less favourable than expected, particularly concerning the abolishment of the senate (PSL did not recommend the affirmative response); therefore, the results were falsified with the help of officers of the Soviet security forces. In January 1947, the first Polish legislative election was held, and its results were also falsified: the official results showed 80% support for the Democratic Bloc, while the scarce records of the authentic results indicate a clear-cut victory for PSL, the opposition party. The coalition of the Polish Workers' Party and the Polish Socialist Party assumed power, and the falsification of the results did not bring about significant protests. In 1948, the two coalition parties united as the Polish United Workers' Party (PUWP, Polish abbreviation: *PZPR*), where the socialist faction was eventually marginalized. The new party ruled Poland until 1989, and the actual power centre was in its Central Committee. The cabinet and the prime minister were marginalized, and the subsequent elections, held every four years with falling turnouts, only confirmed the enforced dominance of the PUWP and proved the lack of any real choice, despite the presence of the two other parties—Democratic Party and United People's Party (*ZSL*) (a rump people's party created from the peasant *SL* and the remnants of *PSL*)—whose members obtained selected positions in the cabinet. The office of president was abolished (Karpiński 2005).

In the years 1944–1949, three internal conflicts were still going on in Poland. The first one, sometimes called an anti-communist resistance in Poland, was the activity of military groups from the Home Army and National Armed Forces that opposed the new political system. Most of these groups were defeated by 1947, though some lasted longer. The second one was the increasing conflict with the partisans from the Ukrainian Insurgent Army, active in south-eastern Poland and in the former East Galicia incorporated into the USSR. In order to defeat it, the authorities conducted the deportation of Ukrainians from Poland to the Soviet Union (1944–1946) and Operation Vistula (1947–1950), involving the forced resettlement of the Ukrainian minority within Poland. The third conflict was in the western part of post-war Poland, on the so-called Recovered Territories, that is, on the formerly German lands incorporated into Poland as compensation for the Polish lands incorporated into the USSR. It was connected with the activity of the underground German resistance, *Werwolf*, who were particularly active in Upper Silesia and near Szczecin (Stettin) and Gdańsk (Danzig). The mass expulsion of Germans and the activity of the security forces eliminated the German underground by the end of the 1940s (Jankowiak 2004; Motyka 2011; Markowska 2013; Pisuliński 2017).

The new system was finally consolidated at the end of the 1940s, when the internal conflicts were brought under control, the power was seized by the communist/socialist coalition. The communist leader Bolesław Bierut was appointed president and the two ruling parties united to create the PUWP. The authorities intended to conduct the full nationalization of the economy (including agriculture) and its militarization by means of the 6-year plan. They implemented the process of "Stalinization", which lasted until Stalin's death. It involved restructuring the state, the society, and the economy through terror and direct violence, to create a system that imitated the Soviet model. Another element of this process was the growing Soviet influence on the Polish political life, and the event which epitomized this trend was appointing Marshal of the Soviet Union Konstantin Rokossovsky as Marshal of Poland and Poland's Defence

Minister. Stalin's death in 1953 triggered the process of dismantling this system, which gained momentum in 1956. In March, Bolesław Bierut died in Moscow; in June, there were the first mass protests (including the general strike) against the communist rule, and in October, there was a change of policy—Rokossovsky and other Soviet officers were removed from office. The leader of the USSR, Nikita Khrushchev, after a visit in Warsaw, given the international tension and the Soviet intervention in Hungary, decided to accept the changes (Karpiński 2001; Roszkowski 2011).

After a brief period of liberalization (1956–1957) the policy of the party (now under the leadership of Władysław Gomułka) became stricter, and some of the institutions and solutions implemented during the de-Stalinization were revoked. The situation stabilized but, in the 1960s, opposition movements started to emerge, both revisionist (aiming to liberalize the system) and, gradually, anti-system. The criticism from intellectuals grew, to which the authorities responded by launching a propaganda campaign, initially directed against the intelligentsia, and then fiercely anti-Semitic, leading to ethnic purges in public institutions, including universities and the army. It resulted from the competition of interest groups within the communist party, but also from the increasing conflict between the "right wing" of the party and the liberal intelligentsia, partly of Jewish origin. Its culmination was the March 1968 political crisis (student protests in Warsaw and other academic centres were suppressed by the police force and communist militia; the protesters were later persecuted). The purges resulted in the emigration of several thousand Polish citizens of Jewish origin, usually well-educated and highly qualified, including such intellectuals as Leszek Kołakowski and Zygmunt Bauman. The crisis contributed to the consolidation of the democratic opposition and the emergence of its leaders, such as Jacek Kuroń and Adam Michnik. The emigrants of that time, such as Aleksander Smolar, as well as some members of the Polish diaspora, for example, Jerzy Giedroyć, got involved in the Polish cultural and political enterprises abroad and worked to connect them with the opposition movement in Poland (Eisler 1991; Stola 2000; Karpiński 2001).

The team at the helm came unscathed from the anti-Zionist campaign and the political crisis of March 1968 and was not moved until the workers' protests against the price rises in Gdańsk in December 1970, when the suppression of the strike involved tens of fatalities. The new leader was Edward Gierek, who made another attempt to liberalize the system, this time economically, not politically. He wanted to strengthen the position of the communist party by means of improving the economic situation of the dissatisfied majority, raising the wages, increasing investment in consumption and housing, and instigating the rapprochement with the West. The next crisis, the first symptom of which were the workers' protests in Radom and Ursus in 1976 and which increased over the years, led to a wave of strikes and the emergence of the *Solidarność* (Solidarity) trade union in August 1980. *Solidarność* became a mass social movement and the meeting ground for political forces as different as the intellectual opposition, independent workers' unions, and organizations connected with the Catholic Church. Thus, it was an attempt to connect the tradition of the fight for independence, Christian values, and left-wing ideas. The president of the union was Lech Wałęsa, and the leadership included activists from the opposition groups of the 1970s (such as Jacek Kuroń, Adam Michnik, Antoni Macierewicz), from independent trade unions (such as Lech Wałęsa), and from Catholic organizations (such as Tadeusz Mazowiecki) (Holzer 1990; Karpiński 2005; Kamiński and Waligóra 2010).

Edward Gierek fell from power, which—after a brief transition period—was assumed by the former Minister of Defence, Wojciech Jaruzelski, who yielded to the Soviet pressure and introduced martial law (Dudek 2003). This *Solidarność* was delegalized and its key leaders imprisoned. The USSR, involved in the war in Afghanistan, relinquished the intervention in Poland, yet again. Ever since Gierek, the communist ideology became more of a veneer, while the system became increasingly authoritarian, and the social peace was achieved through terror as well as financial transfers. The departure from the communist ideas is even more visible during the incumbency of Jaruzelski, especially since the mid-1980s, when his team made attempts to deregulate the economy, while some of the party officials enfranchised themselves using its assets and access to permits sanctioning economic activity (Grala 2005).

However, this did not solve the economic problems, and the next wave of social resentment came in the late 1980s (1988–1989). It led to the negotiations with the opposition (the Polish Round Table and the confer-ence in Magdalenka) and the negotiated controlled handover of power. This was made possible by the growing economic and political problems of the USSR, who was unable to prevent the disintegration of the com-munist bloc (Dudek 2014).

2   International Situation

After the war Poland was included into the Soviet sphere of influence, in the "outer" Soviet empire, behind the Iron Curtain; this determined the nature of its international relations. Initially, Poland was included in the process of creating the new global order—it became a founder member of the UNO (even though a Polish representative could not attend the UNCIO, as the USSR no longer recognized the Polish Government-in-Exile), the International Monetary Fund, and the World Bank. However, over the 1940s, the Polish relations with the West gradually worsened, and in 1947 they came to a halt, when the Polish communist authorities rejected the offer of the participation in the European Recovery Plan (the so-called Marshall Plan). In 1950, Poland withdrew from the IMF and the World Bank (Davies 1986; Marer and Siwiński 1988). In the same year, it lost the status of the "most favoured nation" in the trade with the USA (restored in 1960). Poland became a closed country—international mobility was heavily restricted (except for the repatriation of the Polish and the expulsion of the Germans) (Stola 2012), foreign trade with the West was very limited. In the Stalinist era, the political isolation of Poland, mostly towards the West, was the greatest of the whole post-war period.

Simultaneously, the integration of the eastern bloc was promoted and new international institutions were created to support it, that is, the Council for Mutual Economic Assistance (Comecon) and the Warsaw Pact. They were supposed to be the equivalent of the Western institutions of economic and military integration, such as ECSC, EC, and NATO. The co-operation within the Warsaw Pact, enforced by the USSR, was effec-tive, but the integration model of the Comecon was not successful. The socialist countries had little incentive to undertake international co-operation; additionally, the co-operation within the Comecon was expected to be based on bilateral relations between enterprises, not on market exchange and free movement of factors of production, and it involved extensive bureaucratic control, which made the co-operation even less appealing. Consequently, the economic relations within the Comecon were mostly comprised of bilateral relations of particular countries with the USSR, and Poland was no exception (Berend 1998).

The relations with the USSR were close but one-sided—the Soviet empire kept control of the situation in Poland. This control was exercised both directly, through keeping a sizeable garrison of the Soviet army, primarily near the western border of Poland (in 1945, there were about 300,000 Soviet soldiers on the Polish territory; according to the agreement of 1957 between Poland and the USSR, the Red Army could station up to 66,000 soldiers in Poland, in 1989 there were about 60,000), and indirectly, through the control and the actual authority of the Communist Party of the USSR over the Polish United Workers' Party. Moreover, the Red Army had their secret warehouses of nuclear heads on the Polish territory. In the years 1945–1947, the Red Army and People's Commissariat for Internal Affairs (NKWD) took part in suppressing the post-war Polish and Ukrainian partisan activity. Later, the Soviet military forces stationed in Poland were never used to bring the situation in Poland under control—though in October 1956 they were put on red alert. After October 1956, the Soviet influence on Polish politics and economy gradually decreased, what may be described as change of Polish status from informal Soviet colony to a dominion (Pearson 2002).

The political and economic relations with the USSR became weaker in the subsequent periods of liberalization, particularly in 1956 and in 1980–1981. In turn, in 1981, the USSR, engaged in the conflict in Afghanistan, refused to support General Jaruzelski and conduct a direct intervention aiming to abolish *Solidarność*. However, the USSR really relinquished the control over Poland only as a result of its internal crisis, which began in the mid-1980s (Dudek 2003, 2014; Paczkowski 2003, 2015).

The dominance of the bilateral relations with the USSR discouraged building intense relations with the other countries of the region. In effect, the horizontal relations with eastern bloc countries were adequate, though neither particularly strong nor warm, and there was not a country with which they were stronger than with others. Additionally, very much unlike in the unstable Poland, in the other countries, the regimes were fossilized for decades: in Czechoslovakia, Gustav Husak was in power from 1969, in Hungary, Janos Kadar from 1956, Erich Honecker in East Germany from 1971, Nicolae Ceausescu in Romania from 1967, Todor Zhivkov in Bulgaria from 1954—and they all kept their offices in the parties and the states until the end of the 1980s. The Polish instability and the successive political crises were perceived as a token of the weakness of the Polish communist party, and the rebellious Polish society was considered a dangerous example. The social support from Poland for the Hungarian revolution in 1956 made Poland less than credible for the communist regime of Hungary; on the other hand, the Polish army took part in suppressing the Prague Spring in 1968, and this made Poland unpopular with the people in Czechoslovakia, which was enhanced by the old resentment resulting from the border conflict of 1918–1939.

In the 1960s a certain attempt to bring Poland closer to other socialist countries involved allowing tourism without the visa, and, in the case of the local border traffic (e.g. with Czechoslovakia), even without the passport, only with a pass. Even though this did not create conditions for workers' mobility, only for recreational travel, it was a substitute for integration processes. The scale of this traffic was considerable, and it largely had a commercial character, contributing to reducing some consumer goods distribution problems in the centrally planned economies. Over the 1960s, the number of Polish people who travelled to other socialist countries grew from 200,000 per year to over 800,000 in the mid-decade. The peak was reached in the next decade, when the number of tourist trips exceeded 10 million. The scale of arrivals was similar (Kochanowski 2015).

After 1956, particularly in the 1960s, Poland tried to take an active part in supporting the development of Third World countries. Polish scientists conducted research on that topic, and economists, for example, Michal Kalecki, advised governments on how to reform the economy. Big construction projects (infrastructural and industrial) were carried out by Polish companies in many Third World countries. The peak of these relations was in the 1960s, then, due to political changes in the Third World and growing internal economic problems, the Polish activity in this area diminished.

Finally, after the liberalization of 1956, there was some improvement in the relations with the West. An important factor determining the international position of Poland was the fact that the Polish territory was moved to the west at the expense of Germany. The change was decided on during the Potsdam Conference, but Poland was not certain how stable the situation was, and this marred the relations between Poland and West Germany. East Germany officially recognized the Polish western border in 1950, but West Germany did so as late as in 1970, as a consequence of a certain improvement in the relations resulting from the conciliatory activity of the Polish Catholic Church (the letter of the Polish bishops from 1965) and the rapprochement between the USSR and West Germany (a similar treaty was signed by West Germany and the USSR six months earlier and was ratified by Germany at the same time as the one between Poland and Germany). The improvement in relations facilitated the relocation of the *Spätaussiedler*, "late emigrants", to Germany, in the family reunification process. This resulted in considerable emigration to West Germany in the 1970s.

Poland gradually opened up and this resulted in more intense diplomatic relations, the transfer of technologies (e.g. through buying patents), the increase of foreign exchange, and the growing number of short-term and long-term travels to the West. One of the first effects was the support of France and Great Britain for the Polish western border at the end of the 1950s. The events of 1968 and 1970 slowed down this process, but in the 1970s Poland took an active part in implementing the socialist bloc's policy of the rapprochement with the capitalist world. It participated in the organization of the Conference on Security and Co-operation in Europe, developed diplomatic relations with many western countries, including the USA, and received visits from western politicians. Poland's economic growth was financed from western loans. In 1978, the Polish cardinal Karol Wojtyła became Pope John Paul II and started to play an important role as an informal ambassador of the Polish nation. His visits to Poland in 1979, 1983, and 1987 were very significant in consolidating the democratic opposition in Poland.

The relations with the West deteriorated after the suppression of workers' protests in 1976 and stalled after introducing martial law in 1981. The USA introduced economic sanctions against Poland, such as suspending state indemnity, suspending the "most favoured nation" trade status, restricting the access to new technologies, banning fishing on the American territorial waters, banning Polish airplanes from entering the American airspace, among others. These sanctions, along with the decrease in the prices of coal and the growing economic recession in Poland, in 1981, led to a situation where Poland was unable to repay its debts in full and lost its creditworthiness.

The relations were resumed in the mid-1980s as a result of the liberalization of the internal policy by General Jaruzelski's regime and the improvement in the relations between the USSR and the USA. In 1981, Poland applied for reinstatement as an IMF member (which was recommended by the economic experts of *Solidarność*) and was accepted in 1986. In 1988 the authorities started to liberalize the economy in response to the growing inflation and political tensions. The reformatory process involved negotiations with the opposition and an agreement, endorsed by the Western countries. Simultaneously, there was the process of the disintegration of the relations within the Council for Mutual Economic Assistance and of the system of co-operation of the socialist states, which existed on paper until 1991, but the eastern bloc countries had already started to prefer to co-operate with the West. In Poland, it meant a certain improvement in the relations between Jaruzelski's regime and the West after suspending and then lifting martial law in 1983 (Berend 1998, 2009; Ther 2016).

3   Ideas

The discussions on the shape of post-war Poland started during the war. The programmes of the reconstruction of the state were created by the Polish groups working abroad, both in London and in Moscow. Their ideas concerned the territory of the future state (they raised the question of better access to the Baltic, moving the western border to the west and including East Prussia into Poland) and the future economic system.

Generally, all the groups, both in London and in Moscow, aimed at enlarging the social and workers' rights, conducting the land reform and creating a mixed system, involving elements of both market and controlled economy. The substantial differences among the London groups concerned the scope of the land reform, the ways of taking over the property and the scope of the state's involvement in the economy. The national-democratic SN (the Nationalist Party) was closest to reconstructing the capitalist system, while the post-*Sanacja*, socialist and peasant groups saw the need for bigger involvement of the state and limiting the role of market mechanisms in co-ordinating the economic processes. The programme of the communists from Moscow was principally similar to that of the London socialists—during the war, they did not reveal the intention to introduce the full nationalization and Stalinization of the economy.

Many London politicians, writers working in Poland, and communists from Moscow agreed that given the lack of local capital and dramatic war damage the best strategy for the post-war reconstruction would be using the potential of government and public institutions as a springboard for development. The pre-war experience of the construction of the Central Industrial District indicated that it was feasible and potentially effective. The concept appearing most often was the idea of a multi-sector economy, with the dominating public sector and the private and co-operative sectors existing simultaneously. There was also a consensus concerning retaining elements of market mechanisms, particularly in agriculture, services, and small manufacturing. The land reform of 1944 was conducted within this framework—the rural modernization was expected to eliminate the old ownership rights of landowners (landed gentry), spread ownership among the lower classes, and finally eliminate the great property, according to the plans of the communists and some of the left-wing and peasant political groups (Przybysz 1992; Wapiński 1997).

After the war, the London Government-in Exile and other political groups of emigrants lost their importance, and the programme for the post-war reconstruction and development of socialist Poland was first created within the Provisional Government of National Unity, and then it became more radical and followed the programme of the communist party. The development was to be based on controlled economy. The first plan, the 3-year plan, was created in the Central Planning Committee by Czesław Bobrowski and his team (Kowalik 1992, 2006). It was the plan to reconstruct the Polish economy and to make it encompass the economy of the post-German lands. At that time, the architects of the change, for example, Hilary Minc, were preparing the final justification for eliminating the market mechanism and private property, which were seen as the relics of the old system and barriers to further social and economic development. The ultimate restructuring of the economy and its mechanisms was included in the 6-year plan (for the years 1950–1955), implementing the full-scale centralization and control of the economy along with enforced industrialization and the militarization of industry like in the USSR (Kaliński 1971; Landau and Tomaszewski 1985). The theoretical background for the new structure of the economy was provided by Oskar Lange, a widely recognized representative of econometrics, and a group of young economists educated in the USSR, such as Włodzimierz Brus. In the 1950s, socialist (Marxist) economics was being institutionalized as a science and it replaced all the remainders of "bourgeois economics". At the same time, this new form of economics became the most important among Marxist social sciences (Connelly 1996, 2000; Czarny 2016; Zysiak 2016).

In the Stalinist model agriculture, nationalized and communalized like the Soviet kolkhozes and sovkhozes, was to maintain the food supply for the dynamically developing industry. The elimination of private property (i.e. peasant farming), was supposed not only to lead to that end, but also to eliminate the relics of the past. Thus, from the perspective of the Marxist theory, it was the next logical step towards social change—after the widely supported land reform eliminating big property and its social base for the benefit of the masses, the collectivization was expected to finalize the social change in the country by means of eliminating all private property (Dobieszewski 1993; Kaliński 2014).

Similarly, trade was only to serve the development of industry and of cities. The main goal of economic development was the development of industry, in close connection with the industry of the leader of the world economy, the USSR. Industrialization was not only meant as an economic process (seen as the only way to catch up with the West) aimed at eliminating the backward, obsolete sector of the economy, but it was also a means to changing the social structure. An important category in the considerations on development was accumulation (understood as the accumulation of resources for industrial investment), which was expected to be the instrument of industrialization and the springboard for social change. According to economists such as Kazimierz Łaski (1956), maximizing the rate of accumulation justified postponing higher individual consumption until later periods, and in reality it justified lowering the standard of living and investing in capital-intensive industries. From this perspective the collectivization and elimination of private property in agriculture and the self-dependence of individual farming was meant to facilitate the process of accumulation and the transfer of resources from the traditional sector (agriculture) to the modern one. The Stalinist modernization model was an example of Manichean thinking about modernity organized around the fight against the enemies of the people (such as wealthier farmers, private shopkeepers and entrepreneurs, or western spies) who were responsible for blocking the path of reason and progress. Within economy, at least two enemies were easy to identify: private trade and non-collectivized agriculture. Hilary Minc's "battle for trade" was extremely successful, but the collectivization of agriculture, despite some advancements, was never fully implemented (Kowalik 1992; Wagener 1998; Czarny 2016).

After Stalin's death, the idea of socialism changed, particularly in terms of the economic system. Intellectuals and professional economists, including Brus and Lange (who in the 1950s turned into the internal critics of the party policy), questioned the idea of centralization and tried to find ways to reform the socialist economy, aiming to restore its potential to achieve the main goals of socialism. One of the creators of the reform programme was the greatest Polish economist of the time, Michał Kalecki. The aims were the decentralization, democratization, and communalization of the economy (i.e. reversing the Stalinist centralization), by delegating the decision-making power onto the lower levels of the economic hierarchy, sometimes to the level of the autonomous enterprise, the management of which would be influenced by the workers' self-government. This was expected to improve the efficiency of the enterprises, the distribution of the national income with a view to satisfying the citizens' consumption needs, and conceptually, it was an attempt to implement the democratic management of the economy. Planning was also partially decentralized. The authorities briefly considered implementing these reforms under the pressure of social unrest, some laws were passed but not fully implemented (e.g. on introducing the workers' self-government into enterprises), and the decentralization was abandoned at the end of the 1950s (Łukawer 1996, 2004; Koryś 2007; López and Assous 2010; Ghosh 2016; Koryś and Tymiński 2016a).

From the beginning of the 1960s, there was the growing criticism of the economic development process and of Poland's policy. The critics were economists, such as Brus and Stefan Kurowski, but also opposition leaders, such as Jacek Kuroń and Karol Modzelewski, who proposed the full democratization of the system in order to bring back the importance of the working class instead of the party nomenclature. The economists indicated the inability of the socialist system to compete with capitalism (Kurowski), and advocated increasing the autonomy of the enterprises and the decentralization of economic decision-making (Brus). The idea of maximum accumulation was increasingly replaced with maximizing the wages and consumption. The plan of communist modernization was radically criticized by the emerging anti-system opposition. At the end of the 1960s, the organization *Ruch* ("Movement") published a manifesto "Years go by", where they indicated the insurmountable development barriers caused by the mono-party system. The leaders of *Ruch* were soon arrested and the organization disappeared (Eisler 1991; Karpiński 2001; Friszke 2010).

Further attempts at reforms, after the discussions concerning the inefficiency of the socialist economy, were formulated in the mid-1960s. The set of reforms of Bolesław Jaszczuk was based on "selective development" and "material incentives". The former, inspired by the development economics worked on by such Polish economists as Kalecki, Lange and Ignacy Sachs (Mazurek 2016), involved increasing the competitiveness of the economy by the selection of branches of industry for state-supported development and by the elimination of other branches. The particular focus was on export potential. The selection was to be made by a team of bureaucratic experts (which resembled the solutions used in the developing capitalist countries, such as the "Asian tigers"), but this idea did not take into account the high level of corruption and nepotism in the Polish economy and the low competences of the communist bureaucrats. "Material incentives" mostly concerned the rationalization of wages. The introduction of the piecework system was expected to increase efficiency; however, other reasons for low efficiency were not explored, such as low innovativeness, ineffective management, and the bad organization of the enterprises (Kaliński 1995; Łukawer 1996; Rybiński 2011).

After the period of social tension of 1968–1970, another development model was created by the entourage of Edward Gierek, where the leading economists were Paweł Bożyk and Andrzej Karpiński. The reconstruction and return to the centralization of the economy (this time sectorial) was to help to make use of the "untapped reserves" of development potential. The new idea was the creation of the Great Economic Organizations (WOGs), modelled on big corporations, managed by specialists educated in the newly created business management university departments. The creation of big industrial conglomerates was expected to strengthen the autonomy of the central economic administration within the state-party structures, and the form of planning was changed. The partial opening to the world was to facilitate the access to the external, Western investment loans. This model was criticized by several groups, that is, by the democratic opposition (Waldemar Kuczyński, Jadwiga Staniszkis, Maria Hirszowicz), by the emigration circles and within the party. The consequence of its implementation was a recession, and the last attempts at designing the reforms of the system were its direct result (Brus and Łaski 1989; Koryś 2007).

On the one hand, they were the reforms postulated by the opposition, particularly during the period of the legal activity of *Solidarność* (1980–1981); the scope of the reforms formulated by Solidarity's experts and advisors was considerable, but they were primarily a response to the current recession. In the long term, the solutions comprised some deregulation of economy, and then its partial commercialization and orientation on the market. The advisors of the time were, for example, Leszek Balcerowicz and Ryszard Bugaj, but also Kurowski, Kuczyński, and Staniszkis. A philosopher from Kraków, Mirosław Dzielski, formulated an interesting idea, where the nomenclature would be partially enfranchised in exchange for allowing a system transformation. At the end of the 1980s, Janusz Lewandowski and Jan Szomburg created the idea of mass privatization. On the other hand, the government was looking for solutions for alleviating recession, initially through limiting the grey economy and corruption, and later through the liberalization of economy—in effect, the last reforms implemented by the cabinet of Mieczysław Rakowski mostly anticipated the institutional changes of the system transformation (Grala 2005; Luszniewicz 2008, 2009; Koryś and Tymiński 2016a).

The prevailing conviction of the communist period was that the agent of change was the state and its institutions. All the successive ideas of reforms and attempts at accelerating the development up to the end of the 1980s were based on this assumption. The opposition of the time of the Solidarity Movement did not offer an alternative development paradigm.

4   Territory and Population

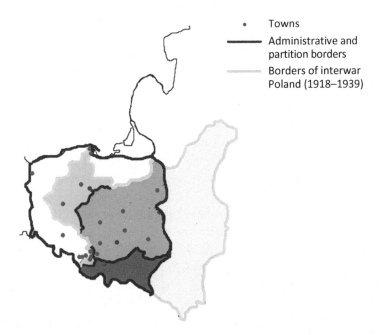

Map 10.1 Poland after 1945. Note: Territories of historical partitions: green—Prussian, pink—Russian and grey—Austrian. Western and Northern territories in white. In yellow—eastern territories of interwar Poland, incorporated by USSR, currently constitute the territories of Lithuania, Belarus, and Ukraine. Cities located in these territories (incl. Lvov and Vilnius) not marked. Source: Own elaboration on the basis of various historical maps

The Polish borders were established during the Potsdam Conference; later, they were only very slightly changed. The eastern border was moved to the west, to the Curzon line; all the eastern provinces of the Second Polish Republic, along with two important cities, Lvov and Vilnius, found themselves outside Poland. Most of these regions were inhabited by the Polish minority. As compensation for its eastern territories lost to the USSR, the post-war Poland obtained the eastern provinces of Germany ("the Recovered Territories" or Western and Northern Lands): the whole (or almost whole) Upper and Lower Silesia, Pomerania, West Prussia, part of East Prussia (divided between Poland and the USSR) and part of Brandenburg. These territories were either strongly urbanized and industrialized (e.g. Silesia), or were Germany's agricultural supply base (e.g. Pomerania, East Prussia). On the coast, in addition to Gdynia, which was a Polish port built after 1918, Poland took over two important port cities, Gdańsk (Danzig) and Szczecin (Stettin) (cf. Map 10.1).

The biggest change to the eastern border was made in 1951, when Poland relinquished part of the Lublin Voivodeship near Sokal (now in Ukraine), with a railway line and coal deposits, in exchange for a mountainous area in the east of the present-day Podkarpackie Voivodeship. Further changes were planned, but they were given up after Stalin's death. The border, which is the present-day border between Poland and Russia, Lithuania, Byelorussia, and Ukraine, started in the north on the Vistula Spit, followed an artificial, mostly straight line until it reached the Bug River, which it followed for about 200 km, as far as the border between the Byelorussian and Ukrainian Soviet Republics in the USSR. The next fragment was an artificial straight line as far as the San River, which it followed to the source. Then it followed the Bieszczady ridge southwards as far as the border with Czechoslovakia.

The border with Czechoslovakia was drawn up along the pre-war Polish-Czech border, and in the newly acquired Polish territories, it mostly followed the pre-war Czech-German border along the ridges of the Sudetes and several northern ranges within the Carpathian Mountains. In 1945, there was a brief border conflict, which did not bring about any changes. The Polish established their administration for the disputed territory of part of Cieszyn Silesia and most of Orava and Spis, but later, the Soviet military administration was established for this area and finally, it was granted to Czechoslovakia. In 1947 Poland and Czechoslovakia signed a treaty of friendship, and in 1958 an agreement finishing the border dispute. Very slight changes to the border were made in 1958 and in 1976.

The border with East Germany, like the one with Czechoslovakia, was mostly natural, along the Lusitian Neisse and the Oder rivers, then along the western edge of the Oder Valley, up to the Stettin Lagoon, which it cut in two. The islands Wolin and part of Usedom found themselves within Poland. This border was confirmed by the treaty of Zgorzelec in 1950. It was slightly changed between 1949 and 1951. The northern border was a sea border, one of the longest sea borders in the history of Poland—400 km, which is over 700 km along the coastline.

Directly after the war, Poland had a population of about 24 million people in 1946 and about 25 million in 1950. The data from this period are not fully reliable because of the huge scale of migration: the expulsions of the Germans, the repatriation of Polish nationals from the territories incorporated into the USSR, the returns of the Poles from the West and from Siberia, from labour camps, or from slave labour and concentration camps in Germany. The expulsions of the Germans comprised 3.5 million people, who were forced to leave the Polish Recovered Territories and move to Germany (mostly West Germany). Simultaneously, over a million people were relocated from the former eastern regions into Poland, with another 600,000 who had run away from Ukraine, afflicted by ethnic conflict and the front. The next wave of relocations took place in 1955–1959 and comprised about 220,000 people. On the other hand, the expulsions of Ukrainians from Poland to the USSR comprised about half a million people. The year 1950 marks the beginning of the quick growth of the population of Poland, the post-war baby boom. In 1960, the population reached 30 million (29.8 million, according to the census data), in 1970 it exceeded 32.5 million, in 1978—35 million, and in 1988—37.9 million. Population growth was recorded despite the growing international migration, because of the increasing life expectancy and the echo baby boom in the late 1970s and early 1980s. Total Fertility Rate decreased gradually from 3.5 to 2.0 (Wyczański 2003; Gawryszewski 2005).

The structure of the population considerably changed throughout the period due to the increasing life expectancy and decreasing fertility. The share of pre-production-age population slowly decreased. Between 1950 and 1960, the percentage of pre-production-age people (0–14) grew from 29% to 33% because of the baby boom, but it fell to 26% in 1970 and 25% in 1988. The percentage of the post-production-age people grew steadily from 8% in 1950 to 13% in 1970 and 15% in 1988. The percentage of working-age population grew from 1960 (57%) to 1980 (62.5%), and then decreased slightly to 60% in 1988 due to the society's ageing process with a certain counterbalancing effect of the echo baby boom. Some part of the economic growth observable in the first half of the 1970s can be explained by the favourable situation on the labour market and the increase of the share of the working-age population (demographic dividend), which caused production growth even with low increase of efficiency.

Population growth was paralleled by rapid urbanization. Warszawa remained the biggest city, except in the year 1946, when the number of inhabitants was only 480,000, as a result of the destruction of the city during and after the Warsaw Uprising and the expulsion of the population by the Germans. In 1946, Łódź had about 500,000 inhabitants, Kraków—300,000, Poznań—270,000. Seven other cities, including Gdańsk and Wrocław, had the population of above 100,000 people. By 1950, the population of Warszawa had grown to 800,000, in 1970 it exceeded 1.3 million, and in 1988—1.6 million people. In 1988, Łódź had the population of over 800,000 people, Kraków—700,000, Wrocław—600,000, Poznań—almost 600,000, Gadńsk—over 450,000, and Szczecin—400,000. The biggest metropolitan areas, Greater Warsaw and the Upper Silesian conurbation, had over 2.5 million inhabitants each. There were over 40 cities with above 100,000 inhabitants (Jelonek 1967; Wyczański 2003; Kuklo et al. 2014).

In 1946, 6.4 million people lived in cities and towns bigger than 5000 inhabitants (about 27%). In 1950, it was 8.5 million people (34%). Next, the percentage of the urban population climbed to 43% in 1960, 50% in 1970, and almost 60% in 1988. In 1950, the rural population started to stabilize at the level of over 15 million people; between 1960 and 1970, it fell to below 15 million and stabilized at this level until the end of the 1980s. Simultaneously, some formally rural areas became parts of the growing metropolitan areas and, in the 1960s, a new phenomenon emerged, "the peasant-workers"—that is, the owners of small farms who had workers' jobs in factories, and their commute was often organized by the factory (Gołębiowski et al. 1974). In the early 1970s, at the peak of this phenomenon, the number of such workers exceeded 1.2 million people. It was a feature of under-urbanization, characteristic of the socialist countries, which stemmed from the insufficient investment in housing and the consequent shortage of permanent accommodation in cities, but also from the policy of avoiding the full agglomeration of the workforce in order to avert the risk of protests. It slowed down social change and the development of cities, and incurred high maintenance costs of infrastructure (roads, temporary accommodation), but also allowed enterprises to pay very low wages, as the farms were the livelihoods and the wages were an additional income allowing "the peasant-workers" to buy quasi-luxury goods, both perishable, such as alcohol or cigarettes, and durable, such as TV sets or furniture. In the 1990s, this form of employment was unsustainable, but the farms and the return to the country to some extent cushioned the effects of the growth of unemployment in peripheral regions at the beginning of the transformation period.

Throughout the period, the population grew primarily in industrial regions, and the growth was enhanced by the increasing demand for labour, causing substantial internal migrations. There was increase in the population of both big cities and bigger industrial areas. The population of the Katowice Voivodeship in Upper Silesia (in its shape up to the administrative reform of 1975) grew by almost 40%, from 2.7 million to 3.7 million, that of the Szczecin Voivodeship grew by 40%, that of the Gdańsk Voivodeship even more rapidly, by 60%, that of Warszawa by over 60%, Kraków and Wrocław by over 40% each, Poznań—almost 40%. In the same period the populations of the Kraków and Poznań voivodeships outside the cities remained stable, and the populations of the eastern voivodeships and the less-developed central and western voivodeships grew more slowly than the whole of Poland or, at most, at the same rate. Even Łódź and the Lodz voivodeship developed relatively slowly in this respect. In 1975, an administrative reform was conducted and the new division turned 16 voivodeships into 49, so the units became much smaller and there appeared big economic disparities between the different units, for example, the rural and industrial ones. In the new administrative division, the population growth took place in several urban voivodeships. Population kept growing in Warszawa and Greater Warsaw (the population in the latter grew from 2.2 million to 2.4 million), in the Katowice region (from 3.5 to 4 million), in the Poznań, Wrocław, Gdańsk, and Szczecin voivodeships (growth by about 100,000 people each), and a few other voivodeships where industry developed (respective growth by over 100,000 people or more). The dominant direction for the migrations was towards the centre, but some local industrial centres also became significant destinations, such as Rzeszów, the Legnica-Głogów area, or Wałbrzych (Wyczański 2003; Gawryszewski 2005; Kuklo et al. 2014).

From the late 1960s, emigration became an important phenomenon, not only the expulsions immediately after the war, but also the voluntary emigration to the West. The official data state that over 20,000 people a year emigrated between the years 1960 and 1990, but these data are undervalued, and the scale of emigration was much bigger. Over a million people left Poland in the 1970s and the 1980s as the so-called late emigrants, *Spätaussiedler*. In the 1980s, over a million people emigrated because of political repressions and for economic reasons (some of them as the "late emigrants"). Another socially significant wave of emigration was the emigration of Polish Jews, particularly intense in 1956 and in the late 1960s (Stola 2012).

As a result of the changes of the territory and the internal migrations, throughout the period (except the first decade, when the relocations and expulsions were still under way) Poland was almost homogeneous ethnically and in terms of religion. In 1946, over 10% of the population of the Polish territory were German; a year later, the percentage became very small. After the relocations, a small and scattered minority were Ukrainians. The dominant faith was Roman Catholicism (the percentage of the baptized was 93–95%). The Russian Orthodox Church constituted about 1% in 1980, and there was a marginal percentage of Protestants. The number of Jews fell from 56,000 in 1950 to 1,500 in 1980.

After the movement of the borders in 1945, the Polish territory remained stable throughout the period. However, inside Poland, there were deep changes of the demographic structure. They resulted from political decisions (expulsion of the Germans, repatriation, relocations) as well as spontaneous processes (birth rate, increasing life expectancy, internal migrations). The socialist state tried to moderate some of these processes (c.g. by creating the "peasant-workers" class, restrictions on the migration to the biggest cities, or the housing investment strategy).

During state socialism, Poland became an urbanized country. Since the 1960s, the development of cities relatively slowed down due to the significance of the "peasant-workers" as the industrial workforce, which hampered the outflow of the rural population to urban areas, and in the subsequent decades due to economic recession. The rapid urbanization until the late 1960s was a sign of a structural change in the economy, and particularly of the growth of the importance of the modern industrial sector, which was another stimulus for development. The subsequent slowdown of urbanization resulted from political decisions as well as the structural problems of the socialist economy. The crisis of the state in the final 15 years of its existence influenced demographic processes; in particular, the urbanization process was not completed, and some labour resources were irrecoverably lost through emigration.

5   The Society

The Polish society created in the aftermath of the war was dramatically different from that of the inter-war period. The social groups disproportionally affected by the war were the Polish Jews, the Polish bourgeoisie and petit bourgeoisie, and the Polish political, economic, and cultural elite, including the intelligentsia. During the war, about 3 million Polish Jews lost their lives and only about half a million survived (about 100,000 on the territories occupied by Germany). This affected the post-war population structure, because before the war the Jewish population was over-represented among townspeople and the intelligentsia, that is, in urban economy in general (trade, services, and industry); consequently, the population loss among the urban population and among highly qualified workers was disproportionately higher than in the rest of the society. Similar consequences ensued from the German- and Soviet-planned elimination of the Polish elite. Poland's population loss is estimated at 22% (the highest of all the countries participating in the war), but it lost

40% of its medical doctors, a third of its teachers, scientists, and scholars, and 26% of its lawyers. These losses were aggravated by the war and post-war emigration (including that of the Polish Jews, which was the highest in 1956) as well as the communist state's policy of repression and expropriation towards most of the pre-war elite (Biuro Odszkodowań Wojennych 1947; Wyczański 2003).

The losses did not only impede the post-war reconstruction and modernization of the country through the shortage of qualified human resources, but also led to profound social changes. Intense urbanization meant the migration of the rural population into cities, but also entailed massive social advancement onto the social positions previously held by the victims of the war. With the state policy of intense industrialization, this process quickly resulted in creating the socialist industrial society. Cities often assumed a distinctive half-rural character, where the inhabitants of the public housing estates had an urban career and a quasi-rural lifestyle.

The significance of the working class grew rapidly as a result of industrial investments, and the demand was for both qualified and unqualified workers, and last, but not least, communist ideology. The end of the 1960s was the first time in the Polish history when more than half the population lived in urban areas, and the most numerous social group were the industrial workers and miners. In the 1970s, the manufacturing sector employed almost 40% of the workforce, while the agricultural and service sectors employed about 30% each. Poland had transformed from an agrarian economy into an industrial one, and consequently, the two major migration directions were from the countryside to the city and from the less industrialized regions to the more industrialized ones (Fallenbuchl 1974).

Apart from upward mobility and internal migration from the rural to urban areas, an important factor stimulating social change in the initial period of post-WWII Poland was the colonization of the depopulated Recovered Territories, that is, the formerly German lands obtained by Poland after the war, from which the German population had been evacuated or expelled. The new settlers arrived as a result of spontaneous migration from the centre of Poland and the repatriation of the Polish population from the eastern territories incorporated into the USSR. This created a motley community of pioneers, uprooted by the war or relocation and thrown into a new place, many of whom dreamed of returning home or feared the return of the Germans. The economic policy concerning the Recovered Territories (Western and Northern lands) involved the prevalence of state ownership of land, resulting in the emergence of social structures which differed from those in the other regions—the new society was less religious and less influenced by the traditional intelligentsia, and it was structured in a more modern way, with a higher percentage of urban population and the higher percentage of industrial and agricultural landless workers. The relocations usually significantly improved the newcomers' standard of living, as the quality and density of infrastructure was much higher on the formerly German lands than elsewhere in Poland, even considering the war damage and the savage looting of these regions by the Red Army at the end of the war and immediately afterwards (Kociszewski 1999).

The historic conditions which allowed the upward mobility of almost the whole society and the policy of the elimination of the private sector in the economy and big private property were the environment that created the most egalitarian society in the entire Polish history. Social disparities disappeared mostly as a result of the elimination of the elite or depriving them of their property during and after the war, but also due to the enrichment connected with the post-war upward mobility, even if much slower than in the capitalist countries. The standard of living was improved as a consequence of the mobility from rural to urban areas, but also of the improvement of the quality of life both in cities and in the country, including the rural electrification and the development of the public services infrastructure—such as gas supply and sewage systems in towns, the railways, public transport, schools, and hospitals. The quality of public services also improved, particularly at the time when rapid industrialization ceased to be the first priority. Education developed intensely, because upward mobility was connected with the demand for increased qualifications, and the access to medical services improved. A national social security system was built, though it did not comprise farmers until the 1970s, when they became eligible for old-age pension in return for transferring the ownership of their farm to the state. The lower social strata appreciated the equality, the upward social mobility, and the unprecedented access to public services, and in 1980s it expected all these achievements to remain unchanged during the system transformation (Leder 2014; Piatkowski 2018).

The success of the policy of developing education was proven by the disappearance of illiteracy, the rapid growth of the level of education in subsequent generations (as measured, e.g. by the average number of years spent in education), and the growing access to tertiary education. In the 1950s, universities developed rapidly (particularly the Warsaw University, the Jagiellonian University in Kraków, and the technical universities in Warszawa, Gliwice, and Kraków), but it came to a halt after 1968. Between 1945 and 1989, many new tertiary education institutions were created, from strictly academic, through technical, to ones focusing on a particular field, for example, teacher training or agriculture.

The development of industry entailed many unfavourable consequences, such as the degraded natural environment in industrial regions, increasing air and water pollution, the degradation of urban and natural landscape similar but on a scale much larger than that in the capitalist countries of Europe, but also the emergence of social degradation areas both in industrial cities and state-owned agriculture, with pathologies such as alcoholism, domestic violence, and—later—drug abuse.

Up to Stalin's death, the Polish communist state was totalitarian, and then it turned into authoritarian. In this system, there was no other way to express discontent or to conduct political struggle than strikes and demonstrations. The first strikes connected with the workers' low wages took place in the 1940s (such as the dockers' strike in Gdańsk in 1946 or the strikes in Łódź in 1945–1946), but the protests did not become political until the mid-1950s. Starting from the 1956 revolution, the characteristic feature of the communist system in Poland was the political-economic cycle. The periods of contraction in the economic cycle entailed a significant lowering of the standard of living, sometimes including the shortage of some food products and irregular food supply in cities, and this led to protests, which then became political and usually resulted in the change of the leadership of the communist party. Such waves of protests took place in 1956 (Władysław Gomułka became the new leader), in 1970 (Gomułka was replaced by Edward Gierek), in 1980 (Gierek was replaced by Stanisław Kania and then by Wojciech Jaruzelski), and in 1988 (the result was the Round Table negotiations with the opposition, the free elections, and the transformation of the system). The protests of the intelligentsia in March 1968 were not supported by the workers, and the great workers' protests of December 1970 were not supported by the fledgling democratic opposition, decimated after 1968. The subsequent protests of 1976 were quickly pacified, but they were an opportunity for the opposition and the independent workers' movement to start to co-operate, which during the protests in 1980 led to the emergence of *Solidarność* as a nationwide mass social movement (Karpiński 2001, 2005; Bałtowski 2009).

The growing threat of workers' protests as well as the emergence of the democratic opposition in the late 1960s proved that the ideology of the workers' state bore little relation to reality. It turned out that the process of the emancipation of the working class and the establishment of a society of socially and economically equal citizens, promised by the communist regime, had failed. The result of the disillusionment of workers were the subsequent waves of protests—the signs of the struggle for real social and political emancipation of workers. The scale and scope of the protests were larger in each successive wave: in 1956, the protests took place in Poznań and then Warszawa, in 1970, in all the main cities on the coast (Gdańsk, Gdynia, Szczecin, Elbląg) and a few cities in other regions, in 1980—all over Poland (Tarkowski 1994; Karpiński 2001).

The other social class on which the communist system was to be based were the peasants (slowly transforming into farmers). The starting point was the land reform of 1944, in which all estates over 50 hectares were parcelled out. It was conducted much more brutally than the one before the war, and the former owners did not only have to relinquish their land without compensation, but were not even allowed to live near their former properties. When the German ownership of land was abolished on the Recovered Territories, part of the land was given to farmers. In total, about 1.5 million hectares were used for setting up state-owned agricultural enterprises, whereas 6 million hectares were parcelled out to create over 700,000 new peasant farms, which eliminated the problem of landless peasants. However, the authorities did not get the peasants' allegiance, which they had expected, particularly after the attempt at enforced collectivization of the late 1940s and the early 1950s. The attempt failed, and in 1956, the authorities gave up the plan to abolish private ownership in agriculture, due to the vast size of the rural population, the power of the Catholic Church, and the low efficiency of state and collective agriculture, which, from the mid-1950s, made the industrialized cities vulnerable to food shortages. In effect, the agricultural sector in Poland remained private, which was unique in the Soviet bloc. However, the party policy did not support private agriculture, and most of the resources for the development of agriculture were directed to the big state-owned farms. In this way, the under-invested private sector produced the huge majority of agricultural output, both for the internal market and for export. This situation fossilized the economic relations in the country— the modernization of agricultural production was slow, and the outflow of the population into the other sectors was relatively poor, particularly in comparison with the Western European countries at a similar level of development, such as Spain or Portugal. At the end of the 1980s, the scope of the social change was much smaller in the country than in the city, and the Polish countryside was overpopulated, very traditional in terms of its culture and values and sustaining a backward peasant economy (Borkowski and Inglot 1995).

The third important social class, which played a vital role first in the formation, then in the critique, and finally, in the transforming of state socialism, was the intelligentsia. This group, whose resources of cultural and social capital were much greater than those of material capital, was specific both to the region of Central-Eastern Europe and to the socialist society. It played the key role both in creating the socialist system (as a vehicle for social emancipation and modernization) and in dismantling it, by organizing the democratic opposition, creating the *Solidarność* programme, and later taking part in the process of the transformation of the system. The intelligentsia had an inclusive character, which made it a very influential group throughout the period, particularly because the system created very poor conditions for forming the political and economic elite (Jedlicki et al. 2014). The entry into intelligentsia was regulated by the members of intelligentsia recognizing an individual as one of them. Whereas one had to be born into or buy one's way into the landed gentry, one could become a member of the intelligentsia on the basis of academic merit or artistic achievement and the acquisition of proper manners.

The fourth separate social class was the communist *nomenklatura*, a group of party and state officials who constituted the political elite of the communist party (it consisted of members of other social groups, including *intelligentsia* and workers). Its importance was based on the system of appointing the party and state leaders at all levels on the basis of semi-formal, exclusive list of the people who were eligible for these positions. The role of this group was crucial in the functioning of the communist economy (and in the early stages of the system transformation), because its members held the key positions in the state and economic administration, which additionally gave them access both to the network of political and economic relations, informal knowledge and to the opportunities for personal enrichment. (Tarkowski 1994; Szelényi et al. 1995; Tymiński 2001, 2011).

A social group that emerged in the late 1960s and was increasingly tolerated by the authorities (even though most of the names given to them by the public were derogatory) was the group of private entrepreneurs, such as agricultural producers in the vicinity of big cities, lease-holders of shops and small state-owned manufacturing plants, and later, private entrepreneurs and businessmen involved in joint ventures with foreign partners, usually Polish emigrants. The role of private entrepreneurship gradually grew over the years. Even though it was on the fringes of the system primarily based on state ownership and central planning, it vastly contributed to easing the shortages on the consumer market. This role was particularly visible in the 1980s (Knyt and Wancerz-Gluza 2004).

The element that played an important part in the functioning of the socialist state and society was the apparatus of control and repression, that is, the police force and the security service, closely connected with the judicial system and with the *nomenklatura*. It was based on police surveillance, infiltration, and collecting information about the citizens, but also on different forms of persecution, such as arrests, assaults, or even assassinations. During martial law, an additional means of oppression was the internment of opposition members, and during the periods of workers' or students' protests (1956, 1968, 1970, 1980–1981) direct interventions were conducted by the riot police and the army (e.g. in 1956 in Poznań, in 1970 in Gdańsk, in 1981 during the implementation of martial law). In 1968, the students' demonstrations were suppressed by means of the police and communist militia, that is, armed groups of party activists from Warszawa factories.

The socialist economic system involved the nationalization of all enterprises, long-term central planning, and the state control of all economic

activity; however, the lack of market mechanisms resulted in the suboptimal allocation of resources and permanent disequilibrium of the economy. Inefficient planning and management created the permanent
shortage of products and services, and the state control rendered many
operations illegal, such as the exchange of foreign currencies. The result
was the emergence of many illicit or informal practices, such as the black
market, the grey economy, corruption, bribery, collusion, and nepotism—often unavoidable both for citizens and for industry. Some of these
practices were even formalized, for example, the "internal export" system,
where people could buy goods (even cars and flats) for foreign currencies
even though it was illegal to exchange the currency (it was legal to possess
foreign currencies, though, e.g. received as a gift from the family abroad).
Corruption and clientelism helped to obtain administrative decisions or
simply raw materials for industrial production, and in the 1980s the
functioning of private companies involved informal networking with the
party and local officials and bribing bureaucrats. Such mechanisms undermined the moral fabric of the society, which became particularly visible
during the late communist and early post-communist period.

The grey economy and corruption were the mechanisms making it
possible to survive in the planned economy, as they reduced the inefficiency generated by the planners' decisions and introduced the element
of the market. Similarly "black market" became a kind of underpinning
of official market of consumer goods (which was in the state of persistent
disequilibrium). Therefore, even though these practices were indictable,
the authorities tolerated them, and even partly controlled them by means
of the secret intelligence service (Sikora 2013; Kochanowski 2015; Koryś
and Tymiński 2016b).

In the period between 1945 and 1989, the Polish society underwent
profound social and economic changes, as a result of which it turned into
an industrial society. Simultaneously, some modernization processes were
hampered by the totalitarian or (later) authoritarian political control, the
extensive *nomenklatura*, and the centrally planned economy. Therefore, the
urbanization process was not completed, and much of the population
remained in the poorly urbanized regions. In many areas of life, the social
and economic relations were fossilized, for example, in the Polish rural communities. The social processes in the newly inhabited areas (i.e. in the

Recovered Territories, the formerly German lands) were different from those in other regions, where mobility (including social mobility) was lower.

The attempts of the creation of a new socialist society, equal and without hierarchies, seemed to be a costly illusion. Thus, in later stages of communism, more and more elements of property, market, and hierarchies were introduced. New hierarchies, rooted in economic and political structures of state socialism arose (as *nomenclatura*), but simultaneously, traditional hierarchies of social prestige and economic wealth persisted.

6   Economy

While analysing the post-war economic development of Poland, one should consider the huge scale of war damage, the characteristic features of state socialism as a political and economic system, and the results of the dramatic changes of borders and migrations of the population. Because of the war damage, immediately after the war, the first priority was the reconstruction and restoration of at least the basic production capacity of agriculture and industry. Another priority, aiming to ensure sustainable growth, was the integration of the formerly German lands into the Polish economy, that is, populating the cities, restoring the industry, and re-establishing long-distance internal trade and linkages between various industries and vertical supply chains. As far as the communist ideology is concerned, at least at the beginning, it was perceived as the road to successful modernization, as there was a widespread belief in the effectiveness of the communist "development economics", both in Poland and in other countries on the Soviet side of the Iron Curtain. In Poland, there seemed to be a certain continuation of the economic policy, from the state capitalism of the late 1930s, through the nationalization and expropriation policy of the German occupation during the war, to the communist economic policy. In fact, to a great extent, the process of the nationalization of big and medium-size industry took place before the People's Republic of Poland was even created, during war (Jezierski and Petz 1988; Jezierski and Leszczyńska 2010).

The economic policy of the socialist Poland was formed between 1945 and 1960. The starting point was the strategic planning implemented in the early stages of the reconstruction and the colonization of the post-German lands and in the land reform of 1944, which in fact abolished the old ownership rights and eliminated most of the market-oriented farms. In effect, the system that emerged in agriculture, based on small farms, turned out to be extremely resilient to collectivization and nationalization. Strategic planning was the basis for the 3-year plan for 1947–1949, created by the Central Planning Commission. Some pre-war politicians and economists were involved in the initial stages of the reconstruction, for example, Eugeniusz Kwiatkowski (Kowalik 2006; Koryś 2007).

However, strategic planning was soon replaced by the Stalinist ideas of total nationalization. At the end of the 1940s, the authorities started the collectivization of agriculture, nationalized the co-operative movement, and started to control the prices, eliminating both the market mechanism and private entrepreneurship. The "battle for trade", conducted between 1947 and 1949 by Hilary Minc, the main architect of the economic policy of the Stalinist period, obliterated the vestiges of market economy through the nationalization of larger enterprises and economic and political repression against owners of smaller establishments. The full expression of the utopian idea of the non-market economy was the 6-year plan for the years 1950–1955, the main aim of which was the forced industrialization and militarization of economy, imitating the model adopted in the USSR. Simultaneously, agriculture underwent fast-paced (but short-term) collectivization, resulting in a rapid decrease in food production, which was unexpected for the authorities and led to workers' protests in 1956 and the downfall of Hilary Minc (Kaliński 1971, 1995).

The Stalinist-era economy attained a high rate of economic growth, as a result of the brutal accumulation of capital (through the collectivization of agriculture and taking over the surplus agricultural production, as well as taking over trade enterprises along with the capital and income potential) and the financial and technological transfers from the USSR. The point of reference was low, however, as the Polish economy was still working to reach the pre-war production levels. Statistically, it approached them in around 1950, but only due to the incorporation of the post-German territories, which were at a much higher level of industrialization and infrastructure development than the former Polish eastern regions.

The pre-war Polish regions took much longer to return to the development level of the late 1930s, for example, the port in Gdynia did not reach the pre-war transhipments level until 1965. The focus was on heavy industry, and coal mining was one of the best-invested branches of the economy; its pre-war levels of production were attained at the end of the 1940s (the post-German areas included), but the levels from 1944 to 1945 were not achieved until the mid-1950s. The first big investment in steel production was the construction of the Nowa Huta gigantic steelworks near Kraków, opened in 1954; before that, the formerly German ironworks and steelworks were repaired and made operative. The dynamic growth of the 1950s, aimed to catch up with Western Europe, and comparable to that of the peripheral capitalist European countries (Spain, Portugal), was not to be maintained or repeated in the Polish economy. In the subsequent decades, despite sustained industrialization efforts, the distance to the West persisted or grew.

The symbol of that period of industrialization was Nowa Huta. The construction of gigantic steelwork lasted from 1949 to 1971, and the plant reached its maximum production capacity in the late 1970s, when it produced over 6 million tons of steel, employing almost 40,000 workers. The decision to locate the investment near Kraków was made for various reasons: technological (access to the Vistula river), economic (labour resources from Kraków, high population density in the surrounding rural region, the vicinity of Upper Silesia with its qualified human resources, and the coal and iron ore deposits), but also political. Kraków was a stronghold of opposition, which was proved by the unfavourable for communists results of the referendum (1946) and the general election (1947). The steelworks and the adjoining workers' housing estate were expected to change the social structure of Kraków and turn it into a modern, socialist industrial city, dominated by the working class. The design of the steelworks and the technology, particularly the solutions used in the initial stage of the enterprise, came from the USSR (Golonka-Czajkowska 2013; Pozniak 2014).

It is worth noting that even though Polish research and development produced numerous designs and new technological solutions, it did not always meet all the needs and in many branches of industry it had to be supported by foreign licences. Until the 1960s, these licenses came mostly from the USSR and the socialist countries—the great oil refinery in Płock, one of the flagship investments of the 1960s, was built on the basis of Polish and Soviet technologies. Gradually, though, there was the process of opening up to Western European technologies, international relations and trade, and the importance of the import of Western technologies steadily grew. As a consequence, many new investments relied on Western European or Japanese technologies (such as the nitrogen fertilizer production plant in Puławy, the car production plants in Warszawa under FIAT licence, or production of electric locomotives in Wrocław and Poznań under the British licence) (Jezierski and Leszczyńska 2010).

The development in the 1950s can be regarded as the unsustained economic model of the People's Republic of Poland. The accumulation enabled a leap forward, but due to central planning, the resources were usually allocated to the wrong (suboptimal) goals, which led to overinvestment and the decrease of the capacity to absorb the subsequent investments. The symptoms were the growing shortages of materials for production and the falling quality of the manufactured goods. The focus on investment in heavy industry led to very little increase in the standard of living, even with the very low starting point. Whatever improvement there was in this respect was connected with urbanization and migration from the country to the city, rather than with the development of the consumer goods and services sectors.

The Stalinist economic model collapsed in the mid-1950s and the economic reforms introduced by the new party leadership (Władysław Gomułka) aimed at reversing the Stalinist system, that is, decentralizing the economy and increasing the influence of the workers (through workers' councils in factories). It was an attempt at the democratic management of the plants and, to some extent, economy. In terms of the macro-economy, de-Stalinization meant a decrease the level of accumulation and investment, particularly in capital-intensive sectors, and directing a bigger portion of the domestic production to individual consumption. Agricultural sector also profited from de-Stalinization. The forced collectivization in agriculture was stopped and reversed, and the higher productivity of private farms contributed to alleviating the problems with food supply. In effect, the system of co-operatives created by force was disintegrated, and a large part of agriculture remained private for the whole communist period.

After 1958, the ideas of decentralization and democratization of the economy were suddenly dropped and there came the decade of stability, with lower investment rates and attempts to increase the people's standard of living. The economy was undergoing dynamic structural changes, that is, the movement of the labour force from the first to primarily the second sector and increasing urbanization. All this translated into economic growth, not resulting from the Solow residual (Total Factor Productivity), but from the productivity increase caused by the structural change in national economy, that was reflected by the change of the structure of the employment in the sectors (decline in the share of those employed in traditional sectors and an increase in the share of those employed in modern sectors of the economy). The beneficial effect of the structural change started to decline in the 1960s, when Poland had become a primarily industrial country and the supply of workers in less productive employment (e.g. agricultural) to be moved into more productive employment declined. From 1956, the growing share of the global production output, however still small in comparison with the western economies, was consumer goods (Landau 1969; Jezierski and Petz 1988; Orłowski 2010; Vonyó 2017).

From the moment when the structural transformation of economy was achieved, economic growth could be maintained mostly by means of the growth in the productivity of the factors of production, first of all by the growth of labour productivity. However, it was very difficult for the centrally planned economy to control labour productivity—the allocation of human capital proved to be extremely inefficient or even irrational (with many poorly educated party officials who held important managerial posts and many well-educated members of the intelligentsia on "inner emigration"). Additionally, the demographic pressure grew, as the baby boomers started to enter the labour market in the late 1960s. Another important element that could have stimulated growth was innovations, but the 1960s showed the decreasing capacity of socialist economies, including that of Poland, for innovativeness. In effect, abandoning the reforms in the late 1950s, the lack of success in increasing the efficiency at the level of the economy as well as that of the enterprise, and inflation at the end of the 1960s, led to another wave of economic recession. Like in the previous decade, as soon as the contraction phase of the investment cycle started to affect the people, they started to protest. Particularly, the workers' protests in December 1970 shook the political scene (Landau and Roszkowski 1995; Roszkowski 2008; Bałtowski 2009).

The new development policy aimed at restoring economic balance took shape in the reforms of 1968, created by Boleslaw Jaszczuk, based on the ideas of "selective development" and "material incentives". The concept of selective development, probably inspired by development economics, was based on choosing the branches of industry whose development would be supported by the state, thus increasing the competitiveness of the economy, and stopping the other branches. The selection was made by a group of experts, as there was no market mechanism, and the main criterion was the export potential. The "material incentives" concerned the payments. Piecework wages were introduced to enhance efficiency; however, this goal was not achieved. Another reform that Jaszczuk tried to implement was making the prices similar to those in the West, with relatively more expensive food and cheaper manufactured goods (Fallenbuchl 1980; Landau and Roszkowski 1995).

The change of economic policy introduced by Jaszczuk was not successful, and the attempt to change the structure of the prices without the compensatory growth of wages led to a perceptible decrease of real incomes. The workers' response was the 1970 protests, which led to the downfall of Władysław Gomułka. Edward Gierek, the new party leader, put forward economic reforms that were supposed to revive the Polish economy. Interestingly, they were a mixture of new solutions and the reiterated Stalinist centralization tendencies. At the beginning of the 1970s, the Polish economy did gain momentum, due to the import of capital and technologies, financed by foreign loans, and the export of coal with extremely advantageous terms of trade. Several institutional and administrative reforms were conducted, such as the new territorial division, or creating the WOGs (Large Economic Organizations), which were large conglomerates of state enterprises. They took over the enterprises' legal authority and were expected to implement modern management models in order to achieve greater competitiveness on the global markets. However, modern management was incompatible with central planning, and the corruption affected structure of investment policy, so the WOGs were not successful.

The investment expansion was effective until the mid-decade, then the symptoms of overinvestment started to show again: the capital was dispersed, the investment projects were not properly co-ordinated and there were shortages of materials and labour resources, and all these phenomena translated into the decline of the national economy. The problems were aggravated by the stabilization (and then, decline) of oil prices and world markets in general, which led to stabilizing (and, later, decline of) the price of coal (which had risen rapidly in the first half of the decade), and the deterioration of the terms of trade (Kuczyński 1979)—in late 1970s coal remained major export product of Polish economy.

Like in the preceding decade, in the 1970s, the development of industry was based on foreign licences, but mostly Western, not Soviet. Car industry was developed in co-operation with FIAT, the tractor factory Ursus replaced the Polish designs with the Massey-Ferguson licence, the technology for the huge oil refinery in Gdańsk was Italian. The construction of the greatest investment of that period and one of the biggest in the whole socialist era in Poland, the Huta Katowice steelworks (about 50,000 people were involved in its construction), also involved the Western (but also partially Soviet) technology (Fallenbuchl 1983).

The early symptoms of the crisis were the workers' protests and unrests in 1976. After these protests, Gierek changed the economic policy and decided to increase the expenditure on consumption, in order to prevent further social protest; however, it was not effective, as the costs of ill-advised investment projects were growing, the foreign demand for coal was falling, the Polish economy did not have much export potential and the internal tensions were building up. The incongruities of the socialist economy were even strengthened by Gierek's new policy. The growing crisis of the second half of the 1970s was increasingly pointed out by economists, both from the socialist side and the ones connected with the opposition. The event which revealed the depth of the crisis was the particularly snowy and frosty winter of 1979/1980, which revealed the hidden tensions within the national economy, resulting in inflation, shortages, and the energy crisis, which hampered production and affected the people. The recession started in 1978 and culminated in 1980, triggering the Solidarność movement (Karpiński 2001; Bałtowski 2009).

It seems that at some point, controlled economies experienced development barriers, and that the development success based on structural transformation was unsustainable. The movement of the labour force from the traditional sector to the modern one created extensive growth, but it ceased to occur in Poland in the 1970s, as most of the labour force had already left the traditional sector and—voluntarily or forcibly—had moved mostly to the industrial sector. Gierek made an attempt to redirect the economy from extensive into the intensive development path inside the institutional framework of state socialism by means of the import of technologies and aggressive fiscal expansion. This attempt failed, which resulted in a structural economic crisis and prolonged recession (Berend 1998, 2009; Turnock 2003; Orłowski 2010; Vonyó 2017).

An important reason for that failure was the fact that the reforms were financed from foreign loans with high debt service costs, taken out by the Polish government, both from governments and from private banks. By the end of the 1960s, Poland had little debt, as industrialization and infrastructure development were still financed mostly from Poland's own resources, but the debt quickly grew over the 1970s. In 1970, the total debt was 1 billion dollars in current prices (i.e. about 6.5 billion dollars in 2011 prices), in 1976 it was 12 billion, and in 1980—25 billion in current prices (66.3 billion in 2011 prices). Simultaneously, in the second half of the decade, the ratio of short-term debts to export incomes approached 0.5. In effect in 1981 maturing debt payments (including the current account deficit) in dollars and other currencies was 11 billion dollars, whereas the export income (after the decrease of the coal prices) was lower than 8.5 billion dollars (Olszański 2002; Morawski 2011).

As a result, at the beginning of 1982, the Polish government lost credit worthiness, which became the next stage of economic destabilization. Without the inflow of foreign currency and affected by the American economic sanctions, the country went into stagnation, which lasted until the system transformation in 1989. The authorities made continual attempts at reforms and the deregulation of the economy practically until the end of the socialist state. In the first half of the 1980s, the reforms aimed to give the enterprises greater autonomy and self-governance, but also to limit the grey economy and corruption. In the second half of the 1980s, some elements of market economy were introduced; it seems that the Polish party leaders tried to transform the economy but retain the political control (not unlike the Chinese model). Despite these attempts at reforms, the stagnation continued. Poland was partly an autarky and had limited access to foreign markets, and the economy was riddled with shortages of goods, growing inflation, and the lack of investment capacity of the state, which was proved by the unfinished big construction projects all over the country. At the end of the 1980s, inflation got out of control and turned into hyperinflation (Marer and Siwiński 1988; Slay 1994; Simatupang 2003; Bałtowski 2009).

Throughout the post-war period, the regional industrial development structure was relatively stable. Even though the industrialization policy was to comprise the whole country, the existing industrial facilities were concentrated in certain areas and, even if some convergence took place, it was slow. The key industrial areas, both in terms of industrial output and the level of industrial employment, were Upper Silesia and the adjacent Dabrowa basin. The industrial areas around Warszawa and Łódź also retained their importance. The reconstructed industry of Lower Silesia and the shipping industry of Szczecin and Gdańsk (and also Gdynia) were vital points on the industrial map of the Recovered Territories. There were also new industrial areas developing around big cities. In particular, after the construction of the Nowa Huta steelworks Kraków gained importance as an industrial city, and in the 1960s and 1970s other new centres emerged, connected with the development of, for example, oil refinement (Płock), mining and processing of minerals, mechanical industry, or light industry. The pre-war industrial centres in south-east Poland (built as the state-initiated industrialization projects) partially retained their importance (Misztal 1970; Pietrzak-Pawłowska 1970; Leszczycki et al. 1974; Lijewski 1978; Dwilewicz and Morawski 2015).

Over time, two important industrial areas, Upper Silesia and the Łódz area, started to lose their position in the economy. The share of the Katowice voivodeship (in its shape before the 1975 division) in the manufacturing output fell from 36% in 1950 to 18% in 1975. It was caused by the development of other regions, but also by the lack of investment in machinery and new technologies, as well as the wear and tear on the machinery (what was common in socialist block, e.g. in the 1980s the machinery in East Germany was on average 2–3 times older than that in the West Germany). The situation was similar in the textile industry in Łódź. The factories, nationalized after the war, still used the de-capitalized, obsolete machinery (Andrzej Wajda shot his film about the nineteenth-century industrial Łódź, *The Promised Land*, on location in the original factory buildings, with the period machinery still in use). The resources saved by minimizing the maintenance and modernization of the existing industrial facilities were directed to the less developed regions, but the investments were not sufficient to transform them and make them lose their agricultural, peripheral character. In effect, despite the investment effort and considerable debt, and despite the obvious industrialization, in relation to the West, the Polish economy was as underdeveloped in the 1980s as it was in the 1950s, when the pre-war German factories were being taken over and repaired.

The growth rate of industrial output and industrial employment was high. Between 1946 and 1980, industrial employment grew from 1.4 million to 5.2 million people. According to the official sources, in the same period, the value of global industrial output grew 15 times and the growth of the value added is estimated at 11 times; the actual growth was probably lower, though industrial output must have grown considerably due to the growth of industrial employment and certain growth of efficiency. In the 1980s, workers' efficiency ceased to grow, the industrial employment had also reached its peak at the turn of the 1970s, and the global industrial output stabilized (production grew in the private sector, but it was too small to affect the global output) (Kubiczek et al. 2006).

The whole socialist period in Poland was also the time of industrial and infrastructure development. In particular, the development of industrial infrastructure involved the dynamic development of the electrical grid, including the transmission and distribution networks (up to the 1980s). By the end of the 1960s, the electrification of the country was completed. Initially, only the pre-war power plants were modernized, but from the 1960s big, modern power plants were constructed in the areas of coal and lignite deposits; in the 1960s, they were the coal-fired plants in Upper Silesia and the lignite-based ones in Greater Poland (Konin) and Lower Silesia (Bogatynia); in the 1970s, the system was developed and more coal-fired power plants were built, including the ones in Kozienice and Połaniec on the Vistula, and near Szczecin on the Oder. Big lignite deposits were discovered near Bełchatów in central Poland, and the power station constructed there was the biggest in Poland. The most costly element of the power system was to be a nuclear power station in Żarnowiec, built under Soviet licence: started in 1982, slowed down after the Chernobyl disaster in 1986, was not completed before 1989, and was finally dropped after the transformation.

Also, the network of oil and gas pipelines, including large transmission oil and gas pipelines crossing the country in an East–West direction and the dense and growing network of gas distribution pipelines covered the country. Natural gas, prevailing part of which was imported from USSR, became important source of energy for industry and households.

Development of transport infrastructure was rapid, but nonetheless slower than that in the capitalist countries. Generally, immediately after the war, the infrastructure was greatly damaged. In total, there were about 90,000 km of surfaced roads in Poland. Road density differed significantly between the regions, with 16 km per 100 km^2 in the east of Poland and 57 km per 100 km^2 in Lower Silesia. By 1954, the total length of surfaced roads approached 100,000 km and by 1980 the average road density grew to 47 km per km^2. Until the beginning of the 1970s, only local and regional roads were constructed, but Gierek's investment policy also included the construction of trunk roads. In 1989, the total length of roads was over 200,000 km. The development of railways was less dynamic, and mostly comprised local and regional lines. There was intense electrification of trunk and regional lines, and by 1989, 10,000 km had been electrified. In the 1970s, two big investment projects were constructed, the coal trunk line from Upper Silesia (and Kraków) to Warszawa (it was built between 1971 and 1977, and was designed to reach Gdańsk, but the construction was dropped because of the recession) and a broad-gauge line from Upper Silesia to the USSR (built 1976–1979; it was used for transporting iron ore from the Ukraine in the USSR to the Huta Katowice steelworks and for exporting coal and sulphur to the USSR). There was also the development of transport infrastructure in cities, such as tramways and the Warsaw underground railway, started in the 1980s (Koziarski 1993; Kaliński 2011).

The development of agriculture in the socialist economy followed two parallel tracks: private and state-owned. Apart from the brief period of collectivization, the sector was dominated by private ownership; however, due to legal constraints, the slowness of the outflow of the rural population to the cities (resulting from the limited demand for labour in the urban economy) and the fear of nationalization, the process of farm consolidation was very slow. For this reason, before 1989 and later much of the country's agriculture was conducted on small fields, inconveniently scattered among the other owners' properties. Private agriculture was underinvested, and the state support for its development was very limited. In effect, peasant subsistence farming prevailed, particularly in central and eastern Poland, with traditional technology, multiple produce, and low marketable output. From the late 1950s, there existed also private market-oriented farms, mostly near the big cities, where the produce (fresh flowers, fruit and vegetables) was sold (Gorzelak 1987, 2010; Jezierski and Leszczyńska 2010).

According to the communist ideology, the foundations of agricultural production were to be State Agricultural Farms (*PGR*) and co-operatives, which were equivalents of Soviet sovkhozes and kolkhozes respectively. The failed attempt at collectivization resulted in the disappearance of co-operatives, but the state farms became an important part of the sector, due to the huge areas they cultivated, the vast numbers of workers they employed, and the huge financial resources they obtained. In 1950, state farms cultivated about 10% of arable land, and by 1980, the area had grown to almost 20%. In 1989, they employed half a million workers and obtained at least 50% of the public funding allocated to agriculture. According to some scholars, the state farm was a reincarnation of the old-time agricultural estate, with its exploitation of the workers, dependence of workers on the flats, infrastructure, and livelihood it provided, or limited workers' mobility; the difference was that this time the estate was owned by the state.

Between 1950 and 1980, the global agricultural output grew by 82%, which is a very small growth rate given the steady level of employment, new investments, and a considerable increase of the area of cultivated land. It became the growing economic and social problem, due to the population growth and increase of incomes in urban economy, which resulted in the growing demand for agricultural products. This indicates significant underinvestment or ineffective allocation of resources, but also development barriers for small private farms. The result of increasing inefficiency of agricultural sector was a growing disparity between the standard of living in the city and in the country. The process of incomplete urbanization, which was discussed above, slowed down the structural change of the rural areas. As food remained relatively attractive for export, the slowness of the growth of agricultural production, large-scale export and growing internal demand posed a threat of food shortages on the internal market, particularly in the periods of poor harvest (e.g. at the turn of the 1970s).

Like in agriculture, the era of state socialism hampered modernization in the service sector, particularly in trade and banking. As a result of the "battle for trade" of the late 1940s, most trade was nationalized. Internal trade was neglected throughout the socialist period, and the availability of consumer goods was limited not only by the actual shortages, but also by inefficient, centrally planned distribution. Until 1989, trade was mostly state-owned or co-operative, which was in fact state-owned as well. Private lease holders played a marginal role as regards the turnover, but they were of key importance in delivering the end products to the marketplace, thus alleviating the shortages. The permanent shortages in state-owned retail outlets made it possible for private entrepreneurs to make a good profit, though they ran the risk of being accused of profiteering, and the regulations, tax system, and social security were unclear and involved many instruments that interfered with doing business and discouraged people from getting involved in it; for instance, the punitive measures, both in the form of fines and imprisonment (or even death penalties for fraud in the state trade system) could bear no relation to the crime, even if there was a crime. Wholesale trade was supposed to be replaced by planned distribution, but in reality the system was complemented by informal co-ordination mechanisms (e.g. corruption, nepotist networks, planning negotiation).

Because of the autarkic development model, foreign trade played an insignificant role in the socialist economy of Poland. There was little trade either with the capitalist countries or the socialist bloc, and the negative trade balance was a permanent feature. The main imports were fuels and energy, which grew from 7.5% of the global import value in 1960 to 18% in 1980, and in 1980 constituted 23% of imports from the Comecon countries (it was primarily the import of oil and natural gas from the USSR). The staple export was coal, which in 1975 constituted 20% of export value and 30% of export to the capitalist countries. The main export of manufactured goods was electrical machinery. After a temporary decline, agricultural produce and food played an increasing role in the import, and in 1980 it constituted 15% of import. Over time, trade with countries outside the Comecon increased; in 1956, the export to Comecon countries was 60% of the global export, with over 10% to capitalist,[1] Western countries; in 1960, the Comecon export was 53% and the export to capitalist countries—38%; in 1980, it was 54% and 44%, respectively; and in 1988, the export to capitalist countries slightly exceeded that of the Comecon countries. In 1956, import from the socialist countries was 66% of the global import, and that from the capitalist countries was over 10%; in 1960, it was 60% and 30%; in 1980—53% and 45%; and in 1988—40% and 53%, respectively. Economic integration with other socialist countries within Comecon, mostly enforced by the USSR, was the strongest between 1950 and 1970. Later, the falling importance of the trade within the Comecon and the growing trade outside it seems to indicate the failure of the project, or at least of Poland's participation in it, which was due to decreasing Moscow's pressure and weak bilateral contacts between countries.

The banking sector restored after the war was mostly co-operative or state-owned, but it was still nationalized (1946) and restructured following the Soviet model (1948–1950). There were state banks providing services for each sector and retail banking, and the National Bank of Poland (*NBP*) as a central and loan bank; there were also two state-owned joint-stock companies (*Polska Kasa Opieki SA* and *PKO Bank Polski SA*) providing services for trade with the West. In the mid-1950s, as much as 91% of loans were provided by the NBP. After 1956, some co-operative banking for farmers was restored, co-ordinated by the Bank of Agriculture (*Bank Rolny*). The subsequent reforms did little to change the extremely centralized state banking system, strictly connected with the specific features of the Polish currency, used only as a medium of exchange within the country, but not as a store of value (as the authorities could always conduct a currency reform in which the savings would be lost) or a measure of value (as the prices were arbitrary) (Jezierski and Petz 1988; Leszczyńska 2010; Morawski 2011).

In the socialist Poland an important element of development, or lack thereof, was international exchange. The Polish currency, *złoty* was not exchangeable, either with the capitalist world or within the Comecon, where the substitute of exchangeable currency was the so-called transfer-

---

[1] Export to Third World countries constituted the remaining part.

able rouble. The western currencies had two rates of exchange—official and black market. The former was statistical in nature, and the state used it in foreign trade, whenever possible. The latter was illegal, as currency exchange was banned in Poland until the end of the 1980s. Neither rate really corresponded to the purchasing power parity. In the late 1980s, the average salary in Poland expressed in dollars at the black market rate was as low as 20–30 dollars a month.

The money played limited role in socialist economy. Such approach to money allowed for using it as a means to expropriate some of the citizens in the initial stages of the socialist state; the currency reforms of that time involved exchanging money for only partial compensation. The prices were centrally regulated; the periods of social protests, caused by the growth of prices (due to shortages), brought about increases of wages and inflation (in 1953–1954, 1974–1980, 1982), but it was usually quickly curbed. However, in the late 1980s, the economic recession, the growing supply of money, and the liberalization of the economy led to hyperinflation—in 1989, the price growth rate exceeded 250% a year (Jezierski and Leszczyńska 2010).

Throughout the socialist period, the quality of public services in Poland gradually increased. From the mid-1950s, public housing intensified and standardized technologies were increasingly used, for example, the large-panel system building. An increasing percentage of the population had access to plumbing and sewer systems, although until the end of the socialist system, it mostly comprised the urban population. Education also developed, and it entailed enhancing the quality of human capital; however, this did not affect productivity much, due to the obsolete structure of the economy and the wrong kinds of incentives within it (the controlled system rewarded complicity rather than creativity and initiative). The comparison with the capitalist countries of the southern peripheries of Europe shows that the enhancement of human capital did not translate into economic growth to the extent it probably could have. Free compulsory education, medical care, social security, public housing, and modern labour law contributed to improving the standard of living and security of the people and were all elements of what Winicjusz Narojek called "the socialist welfare state" (Narojek 1991), which from the 1970s, or even earlier, was the price the state offered to pay for maintaining social peace. The recession of the late 1970s showed that this model was unsustainable in state socialism. The fall in the standard of living of the Polish people was one of the main factors determining the scale of the protest in 1980 (though later it turned into a political protest against the communist system in general) (Fallenbuchl 1980, 1985; Jezierski and Leszczyńska 2010; Orłowski 2010).

The question remains how the Polish economy developed in the communist era, and how it compared to other countries. Even though data collection methods differed and there is not a simple straightforward way to compare the socialist and capitalist countries, some relatively credible extrapolations can be made, due to Poland's formal and geographical (but also, to some extent, political and legal) continuity over the last 70 years. Moreover, since the 1980s, the estimations of GDP have been conducted according to the western methodology, and the studies of the domestic product were also carried out before that time. Additionally, there exist estimates of the Polish GDP/national income made for 1970–1980, for the World Bank (Fallenbuchl 1985). However, it is difficult to determine the levels for 1945–1950, as there are no reliable data on the actual state of the post-German lands in comparison with their pre-war condition. It is very difficult to evaluate the effect of moving the Polish border to the west, that is, relinquishing the poorly developed eastern regions and gaining the well-developed Silesia and the modern agricultural provinces of Pomerania and Masuria.

The development rate at the time of reconstruction is likely to have been very high, but we cannot present precise estimates for that period. In the period of 1946–1950, there seem to be three tracks of the restoration of the economy in Europe: it was very dynamic in Austria and Germany (with the average growth rate up to 16%), slower in the countries in the Soviet sphere of influence (average growth rate up to 10%), and relatively low in Western European countries (average growth rate over 7%). In Poland, the rate might have been similar to that in Germany, both because the military activity was conducted on the Polish territory practically until the very end of the war and because the new Polish territory comprised important German industrial areas. On the other hand, however, the growth rate might have been lower because of the demographic factors (in economic terms, the extermination of the Polish citizens meant the loss of human capital), the slash-and-burn policy of the

Red Army, and the enforced economic system. Thus, the growth rate was probably between 10% and 15% a year between 1946 and 1950, and the GDP per capita in 1946 was probably about 55–70% of that in 1950, that is, 1350–1700 G-K dollars. In this case, the pre-war level (according to Maddison Project database) was achieved in 1948 or 1949. However, it has to be noted that it concerned a different territory and a different population from those in 1939.

After a period of quick growth, it slowed down in the mid-1950s, which entailed the rise of social protests. The stabilization of the early 1960s brought another wave of economic growth, and then, after the slowdown at the turn of the 1960s, there was a "leap forward" of the first half of the Gierek decade. After 1975, there was a decline, which lasted until the early 1990s. That was the time when industrial output decreased.

After four decades of state socialism, the economy collapsed, with almost no signs of recovery. It is worth noting, however, that Poland was not unique in that respect, as most of the socialist countries experienced an economic collapse, or at least a major growth reduction in the 1970s, and it turned out to be irreversible. That was the moment when the development of the peripheral (socialist) East and the (capitalist) Western centre diverged once again, scissors-fashion.

The 1980s was the time of the collapse of state-owned industry, agriculture, and services, but it was also the time of the rapid development of the private sector. It was no longer restricted to private agricultural producers and lease-holders of shops who contributed to reducing the shortages and partial restoration of economic equilibrium; there was a rising number of small and medium-size entrepreneurs active in the growing number of branches of industry, including manufacturing (e.g. car parts, clothes, furniture) and food processing, which played an important role in meeting the food demand in big cities. Many successful businesspeople of the 1990s actually started their economic activity in the 1980s. The high demand resulting from the shortages created opportunities for a runaway financial success, and the development of the enterprise was not limited by the competition (as the size of market, in comparison with the size of the private sector, was almost unlimited), but by legal constraints, which led the entrepreneurs to co-operate (or even collude) with members of the party or repression apparatus. Unfortunately, the impact of the sector on the condition of the whole economy remained limited until the transformation.

Due to the industrial investment, in the year 1989, Poland was a country with extensive yet obsolete and badly kept industrial and transport infra-structure, and numerous highly qualified yet demoralized labour force. The post-Stalinist period was the time of the emergence of microeconomic development barriers within the system, connected with the transition of a totalitarian system into a bureaucratic autocracy. Managing a backward economy by means of terror and violence was effective in the short term, but with the growing complexity and the political changes, new management tools were required, and there were not any. Central planning had serious flaws, which were compensated for by the growing importance of informal connections, such as nepotism or clientelism. Promotion and managerial success did not depend on competences and management skills, but on the person's contacts, which in effect often led to a paralysis in decision-making, as the managers avoided taking any risks. Additionally, with no market mechanisms, there were no effective incentives for either enterprises or peo-ple. At the macroeconomic level, the growing problems were the falling efficiency of industry, the constantly low efficiency of agriculture, and the ineffective allocation of investment resources. An important factor was the increasing financial problems, hampering the economic relations with for-eign partners and limiting the investment potential. All this translated into the growing disparity between the Soviet bloc countries and the West in terms of technology, efficiency, standard of living, and the condition of infrastructure; in the long run, it became the reason why the Soviet bloc countries lost the ability to sustain the socialist system.

How can we sum up the development in this period? Undoubtedly, Poland became an industrial country. According to the census in 1950, industry employed 23% of the labour force, and at the end of the socialist period, it was almost 40%. In Europe, it was a very high proportion, but the industry had low efficiency and was based on obsolete technologies; in reality, the Polish industrialization once again reached only the level of the second industrial revolution (if we consider the branch structure and the level of technological advancement).

7   Conclusions

It cannot be questioned that the socialist period was the time of the dynamic economic growth, and from certain moment also improvement of the standard of living, even though it was much slower than in the West.

The statistics and analyses conducted in the socialist countries indicated that in the 1960s they were gaining ground on the West, which seemed credible within the accepted development model and rapid industrialization. The scale of industrial output of the socialist countries started to resemble that of the capitalist world. However, what the statistics did not show was that it resulted from the different allocation of capital and human resources, or that there was a huge disparity between the Western and socialist economy in terms of complexity, the quality of products, and their innovativeness. One of the biggest cognitive errors of the Marxist economic doctrine was the focus on material production. This idea of economic development did not include the production towards fulfilling the needs of individual consumption or developing public services aiming to improve the citizens' quality of life, because these were perceived as a non-productive sphere of economy and reduced to the minimum. This was the thinking which determined the public investment, which, in the controlled economy, meant all the investment. And this was at the time when the Western economies were undergoing a profound transformation, as a result of which the service sector became more important than manufacturing. For a long time, the error in the perception of the services was not noted, as there were no comparable measures of development. The different ways to calculate the domestic product and the lack of realistic exchange rates led to erroneous conclusions on both sides of the Iron Curtain, though it was as early as in the late 1960s that the West started to notice the symptoms indicating that the socialist states developed less quickly than previously expected. However, it was not until the 1970s that the first Polish GDP estimations using Simon Kuznets methodology were conducted for the World Bank.

The socialist theoreticians had dreamed of building national, state-owned industries, which would pass through the infant stage and become competitive on the global markets. In Poland, this dream did not come true, and after 40 years of intense industrialization the process had to be started over again.

References

Bałtowski, M. (2009). *Gospodarka socjalistyczna w Polsce: geneza – rozwój – upadek.* Warszawa: Wydawnictwo Naukowe PWN.

Berend, T. I. (1998). *Central and Eastern Europe, 1944–1993: Detour from the periphery to the periphery.* Cambridge: Cambridge University Press.

Berend, T. I. (2009). *From the Soviet bloc to the European Union: The economic and social transformation of Central and Eastern Europe since 1973.* Cambridge, UK and New York: Cambridge University Press.

Biuro Odszkodowań Wojennych. (1947). *Sprawozdanie w przedmiocie strat i szkód wojennych Polski w latach 1939–1945.* Warszawa: Biuro Odszkodowań Wojennych przy Prezydium Rady Ministrów.

Borkowski, J., Inglot, S. (Eds.). (1995). *Historia chłopów polskich* Wrocław: Wydawnictwo Uniwersytetu Wrocławskiego.

Brus, W., & Łaski, K. (1989). *From Marx to the market: Socialism in search of an economic system.* Oxford: Clarendon Press.

Connelly, J. (1996). Internal bolshevisation? Elite social science training in Stalinist Poland. *Minerva, 34,* 323–346. https://doi.org/10.1007/BF00127070

Connelly, J. (2000). *Captive university: The Sovietization of East German, Czech and Polish higher education, 1945–1956.* Chapel Hill: University of North Carolina Press.

Czarny, B. (2016). *Szkice o ekonomii w Polsce w latach 1949–1989: ekonomia w państwie totalitarnym.* Warszawa: Oficyna Wydawnicza Szkoła Główna Handlowa.

Davies, N. (1986). *God's playground: A history of Poland. Vol. 2: To the present.* Oxford: Clarendon Press.

Dobieszewski, A. (1993). *Kolektywizacja wsi polskiej: 1948–1956.* Warszawa: Fundacja im. Kazimierza Kelles-Krauza.

Dudek, A. (Ed.). (2003). *Stan wojenny w Polsce 1981–1983.* Rzeszów: IPN & Komisja Ścigania Zbrodni Przeciw Narodowi Poleskiemu.

Dudek, A. (2014). *Reglamentowana rewolucja: rozkład dyktatury komunistycznej w Polsce 1988–1990.* Kraków: Społeczny Instytut Wydawniczy Znak.

Dwilewicz, Ł., Morawski, W. (Eds.). (2015). *Historia polskich okręgów i regionów przemysłowych* (T. 1). Warszawa and Zalesie Górne: Pracownia Wydawnicza & Akant.

Eisler, J. (1991). *Marzec 1968: geneza, przebieg, konsekwencje*. Warszawa: Państwowe Wydawnictwo Naukowe.

Fallenbuchl, Z. (1985). *National income statistics for Poland, 1970–1980*. The World Bank.

Fallenbuchl, Z. M. (1974). *The impact of the development strategy on urbanization: Poland 1950–1970*. Windsor: Department of Economics University of Windsor.

Fallenbuchl, Z. M. (1980). *Polityka gospodarcza PRL*. London: Odnowa.

Fallenbuchl, Z. M. (1983). *Transfert de technologie entre l'Est et l'Ouest: le cas de la Pologne 1971–1980*. Paris: Organisation de Coopération et de Développement Économiques.

Friszke, A. (2010). *Anatomia buntu: Kuroń, Modzelewski i komandosi*. Kraków: Znak.

Gawryszewski, A. (2005). *Ludność Polski w XX wieku*. Warszawa: Instytut Geografii i Przestrzennego Zagospodarowania im. Stanisława Leszczyckiego PAN.

Ghosh, J. (2016). Michal Kalecki. In *Handbook of alternative theories of economic development* (pp. 475–484). Edward Elgar Publishing.

Gołębiowski, B., Gałaj, D., & Spółdzielnia Wydawniczo-Handlowa "Książka i Wiedza" (Eds.). (1974). *Chłoporobotnicy o sobie: studium autobiografii*. Warszawa: Książka i Wiedza.

Golonka-Czajkowska, M. (2013). *Nowe miasto nowych ludzi: mitologie nowohuckie*. Kraków: Wydawnictwo Uniwersytetu Jagiellońskiego.

Gorzelak, E. (1987). *Polityka agrarna PRL*. Warszawa: Państwowe Wydawnictwo Naukowe.

Gorzelak, E. (2010). *Polskie rolnictwo w XX wieku: produkcja i ludność*. Warszawa: Szkoła Główna Handlowa.

Grala, D. (2005). *Reformy gospodarcze w PRL (1982–1989): próba uratowania socjalizmu*. Warszawa: Wydawnictwo Trio.

Holzer, J. (1990). *Solidarność 1980–1981: geneza i historia* (Wyd. 1). Warszawa: krajowe. Omnipress.

Jankowiak, S. (2004). Wysiedlenia Niemców z Polski po II wojnie światowej. Pamięć Sprawiedl Biul Gł Kom Badania Zbrod Przeciwko Nar. *Pol Inst Pamięci Nar*, 139–160.

Jedlicki, J., Janowski, M., Micińska, M., & Korecki, T. (2014). *A history of the Polish intelligentsia*. Peter Lang Edition.

Jelonek, A. (1967). *Ludność miast i osiedli typu miejskiego na ziemiach Polski od 1810 do 1960 r*. Instytut Geografii Polskiej Akademii Nauk.

Jezierski, A., & Leszczyńska, C. (2010). *Historia gospodarcza Polski*. Warszawa: Key Text.

Jezierski, A., & Petz, B. (1988). *Historia gospodarcza Polski Ludowej 1944–1985* (Wyd. 3 zm). Warszawa: Państwowe Wydawnictwo Naukowe.

Kaliński, J. (1971). *Bitwa o handel: 1947–1948*. Warszawa: Książka i Wiedza.

Kaliński, J. (1995). *Gospodarka Polski w latach 1944–1989: przemiany strukturalne*. Warszawa: Państwowe Wydawnictwo Ekonomiczne.

Kaliński, J. (2011). *Autostrady w Polsce czyli Drogi przez mękę*. Warszawa and Łódź: Księży Młyn.

Kaliński, J. (2014). *Economy in communist Poland: The road astray*. Warsaw: Institute of National Rememberance. Commission of the Prosecution of Crimes against Polish Nation.

Kamiński, Ł., & Waligóra, G. (Eds.). (2010). *NSZZ "Solidarność" 1980–1989. T. 2: Ruch społeczny*. Warszawa: Instytut Pamięci Narodowej – Komisja Ścigania Zbrodni przeciwko Narodowi Polskiemu.

Karpiński, J. (2001). *Wykres gorączki: Polska pod rządami komunistycznymi*. Lublin: Wydawnictwo Uniwersytetu Marii Curie-Skłodowskiej.

Karpiński, J. (2005). *Ustrój komunistyczny w Polsce*. Warszawa: Wydawnictwo Wyższej Szkoły Przedsiębiorczości i Zarządzania im. Leona Koźmińskiego.

Knyt, A., & Wancerz-Gluza, A. (Eds.). (2004). *Prywaciarze 1945–1989*. Warszawa: Karta.

Kochanowski, J. (2015). *Tylnymi drzwiami: "Czarny rynek" w Polsce 1944–1989* (Wyd. 2, przejrz. i popr). Warszawa: Wydawnictwo W.A.B. – Grupa Wydawnicza Foksal.

Kociszewski, J. (1999). *Proces integracji gospodarczej ziem zachodnich i północnych z Polską*. Wrocław: Wydawnictwo. AE.

Koryś, P. (2007). Idea nowoczesności w działaniach i planach partii komunistycznej w Polsce 1945–1980. Przegląd problematyki. In E. Kościk & T. Głowiński (Eds.), *Gospodarka i społeczeństwo w czasach PRL-u (1944–1989): Wrocławskie Spotkania z Historią Gospodarczą, spotkanie 2* (pp. 440–455). Wrocław: Gajt.

Koryś, P., & Tymiński, M. (2016a). Od socjalizmu do socjalizmu. Koncepcje reform gospodarczych w PRL po wybuchach społecznych w 1956 i 1980 r. *Dzieje Najnow, 48*, 125–140. https://doi.org/10.12775/DN.2016.4.06

Koryś, P., & Tymiński, M. (2016b). The unwanted legacy. In search of historical roots of corruption in Poland. *Sociologija, 58*, 203–219.

Kowalik, T. (1992). *Historia ekonomii w Polsce 1864–1950*. Wrocław and Warszawa: Zakład Narodowy im. Ossolińskich.

Kowalik, T. (2006). *Spory o ustrój społeczno-gospodarczy w Polsce: lata 1944–1948*. Warszawa: Wydawnictwo Key Text: Instytut Nauk Ekonomicznych PAN.

Koziarski, S. (1993). *Sieć kolejowa Polski w latach 1918–1992.* Opole: Państwowy Instytut Naukowy.

Kubiczek, F., Wyczański, A., & Zakład Wydawnictw Statystycznych (Eds.). (2006). *Historia Polski w liczbach. T. 2: Gospodarka.* Warszawa: Zakład Wydawnictw Statystycznych.

Kuczyński, W. (1979). *Po wielkim skoku.* Warszawa: Niezależna Oficyna Wydawnicza.

Kuklo, C., Łukasiewicz, J., & Leszczyńska, C. (2014). *Poland in Europe.* Warszawa: Zakład Wydawnictw Statystycznych.

Landau, Z. (1969). Tempo wzrostu gospodarki Polski Ludowej. *Kwart Hist, 76,* 300–318.

Landau, Z., & Roszkowski, W. (1995). *Polityka gospodarcza II RP i PRL.* Warszawa: Wydawnictwo Naukowe PWN.

Landau, Z., & Tomaszewski, J. (1985). *The Polish economy in the twentieth century.* London and Sydney: Croom Helm.

Łaski, K. (1956). *Akumulacja i spożycie w procesie uprzemysłowienia Polski Ludowej.* Warszawa: Książka i Wiedza.

Leder, A. (2014). *Prześniona rewolucja: ćwiczenie z logiki historycznej.* Warszawa: Wydawnictwo Krytyki Politycznej.

Leszczycki, S., Lijewski, T., & Grzeszczak, J. (Eds.). (1974). *Geografia przemysłu Polski: praca zbiorowa.* Warszawa: Państwowe Wydawnictwo Naukowe.

Leszczyńska, C. (2010). *Zarys historii polskiej bankowości centralnej.* Warszawa: Narodowy Bank Polski.

Lijewski, T. (1978). *Uprzemysłowienie Polski 1945–1975: przemiany strukturalne i przestrzenne.* Warszawa: Państwowe Wydawnictwo Naukowe.

López, G. J., & Assous, M. (2010). *Michal Kalecki.* Basingstoke and New York: Palgrave Macmillan.

Łukawer, E. (1996). *Z historii polskiej myśli ekonomicznej: 1945–1995.* Warszawa: Olympus.

Łukawer, E. (2004). *Miejsce koncepcji Oskara Langego w poglądach na model funkcjonowania gospodarki socjalistycznej.* Kraków: Wydawnictwo Akademii Ekonomicznej.

Luszniewicz, J. (2008) *Solidarność, samorząd pracowniczy, transformacja systemu: o programie gospodarczym Sieci Organizacji Zakładowych NSZZ "Solidarność" wiodących zakładów pracy (rok 1981).* Warszawa: Szkoła Główna Handlowa.

Luszniewicz, J. (2009). Wizje reformy gospodarczej w koncepcjach pierwszej Solidarności 1980–1981. In E. Kościk & T. Głowiński (Eds.), *Między zacofaniem a modernizacją: społeczno-gospodarcze problemy ziem polskich na przestrzeni wieków: Wrocławskie Spotkania z Historią Gospodarczą, spotkanie IV.* Wrocław: Gajt.

Marer, P., & Siwiński, W. (1988). *Creditworthiness and reform in Poland: Western and Polish perspectives*. Indiana University Press.

Markowska, M. (Ed.). (2013). *Wyklęci: podziemie zbrojne 1944–1963*. Warszawa: Ośrodek Karta.

Mazurek, M. (2016). "Bezdroża kapitalizmu": Ludwik Landau i jego statystyczna wizja globalnych nierówności. *Stan Rzeczy Teoria Społeczna*, 127–143.

Misztal, S. (1970). *Przemiany w strukturze przestrzennej przemysłu na ziemiach polskich w latach 1860–1965*. Warszawa: Państwowe Wydawnictwo Naukowe.

Morawski, W. (2011). *Dzieje gospodarcze Polski* (Wyd. 2). Warszawa: Difin.

Motyka, G. (2011). *Od rzezi wołyńskiej do Akcji "Wisła": konflikt polsko-ukraiński 1943–1947*. Kraków: Wydawnictwo Literackie.

Narojek, W. (1991). *Socjalistyczne "welfare state": studium z psychologii społecznej Polski Ludowej*. Warszawa: Wydawnictwo Naukowe PWN.

Olszański, P. (2002). *Historia polskiego zadłużenia międzynarodowego na tle wydarzeń społecznych i politycznych*. Warszawa: Szkoła Główna Handlowa.

Orłowski, W. M. (2010). *W pogoni za straconym czasem: wzrost gospodarczy w Europie Środkowo-Wschodniej 1950–2030*. Warszawa: Polskie Wydawnictwo Ekonomiczne.

Paczkowski, A. (2003). *The spring will be ours: Poland and the Poles from occupation to freedom*. University Park, PA: The Pennsylvania State University Press.

Paczkowski, A. (2015). *Revolution and counterrevolution in Poland, 1980–1989: Solidarity, martial law, and the end of communism in Europe*. Rochester and Warsaw: University of Rochester Press; Institute of Political Studies of the Polish Academy of Sciences.

Pearson, R. (2002). *The rise and fall of the Soviet Empire* (2nd ed.). New York: Palgrave.

Piatkowski, M. (2018). *Europe's growth champion*. New York: Oxford University Press.

Pietrzak-Pawłowska, I. (Ed.). (1970). *Uprzemysłowienie ziem polskich w XIX i XX wieku: studia i materiały*. Wrocław: Ossolineum.

Pisuliński, J. (2017). *Akcja specjalna "Wisła"*. Rzeszów: Libra PL.

Pozniak, K. (2014). *Nowa Huta: Generations of change in a model socialist town*. Pittsburgh, PA: University of Pittsburgh Press.

Przybysz, K. (Ed.). (1992). *Wizje Polski: programy polityczne lat wojny i okupacji 1939–1944*. Warszawa: Elipsa.

Roszkowski, W. (2008). *Gospodarka: wzrost i upadek systemu nakazowo – rozdzielczego*. Warszawa: Wydawnictwo Naukowe PWN.

Roszkowski, W. (2011). *Najnowsza historia Polski: 1945–1956*. Warszawa: Świat Książki.

Rybiński, K. (Ed.). (2011). *Dekada Gierka: wnioski dla obecnego okresu modernizacji Polski*. Warszawa: Wyższa Szkoła Ekonomiczno-Informatyczna.

Sikora, M. (2013). Koncesjonowany kapitalizm: Służba Bezpieczeństwa MSW a "spółki polonijne" w PRL (1976–1989). *Dzieje Najnow, 45*, 125–146.

Simatupang, B. (2003). *The Polish economic crisis: Background, circumstances and causes*. Taylor & Francis.

Slay, B. (1994). *The Polish economy: Crisis, reform, and transformation*. Princeton, NJ: Princeton University Press.

Stola, D. (2000). *Kampania antysyjonistyczna w Polsce 1967–1968*. Warszawa: Instytut Studiów Politycznych Polskiej Akademii Nauk.

Stola, D. (2012). *Kraj bez wyjścia? migracje z Polski 1949–1989*. Warszawa: IPN & Komisja Ścigania Zbrodni przeciwko Narodowi Polskiemu.

Szelényi, I., Treiman, D., & Wnuk-Lipiński, E. (Eds.). (1995). *Elity w Polsce, w Rosji i na Węgrzech: wymiana czy reprodukcja?* Warszawa: ISP PAN.

Tarkowski, J. (1994). *Władza i społeczeństwo w systemie autorytarnym*. Warszawa: ISP PAN.

Ther, P. (2016). *Europe since 1989: A history*. Princeton: Princeton UP.

Turnock, D. (2003). *The East European economy in context: Communism and transition*. Routledge.

Tymiński, M. (2001). *PZPR i przedsiębiorstwo: nadzór partyjny nad zakładami przemysłowymi 1956–1970*. Warszawa: Wyd. Trio.

Tymiński, M. (2011). *Partyjni agenci: analiza instytucjonalna działalności lokalnych instancji PZPR w przemyśle (1949–1955)*. Warszawa: Wydawnictwa Uniwersytetu Warszawskiego.

Vonyó, T. (2017). War and socialism: Why Eastern Europe fell behind between 1950 and 1989: Why Eastern Europe fell behind. *The Economic History Review, 70*, 248–274. https://doi.org/10.1111/ehr.12336

Wagener, H.-J. (1998). *Economic thought in communist and post-communist Europe* (H.-J. Wagener, Ed.). London: Routledge.

Wapiński, R. (1997). *Historia polskiej myśli politycznej XIX i XX wieku*. Gdańsk: Arche.

Wyczański, A. (Ed.). (2003). *Historia Polski w liczbach. T. 1: Państwo, społeczeństwo*. Warszawa: Zakład Wydawnictw Statystycznych.

Zysiak, A. (2016). *Punkty za pochodzenie: powojenna modernizacja i uniwersytet w robotniczym mieście* (Wyd. I). Kraków: Nomos.

11

In Pursuit of the Western World: Poland Between the Transition and the EU Accession (1989–2004)

In 1989, a political and economic crisis in the USSR and its satellite states caused the collapse of the geopolitical order established in Yalta, determining the situation of Eastern European countries. The Iron Curtain separating the region from the rest of Europe disappeared, the communist regimes in the satellite states and then in the USSR fell, the Soviet sphere of influence dissolved, and its countries underwent a system transformation, which turned them back into market economies. After an initial slump, in 1991, a lasting period of stable development began, quite exceptional in the region in the last two centuries.

1 Internal and International Political Situation

The political transformation of Poland and the whole region took place at the turn of the 1980s. In Poland, the high point was the general election of 4 June 1989, preceded by the negotiations between the party leaders and the opposition (the so-called Polish Round Table, as a result of which, e.g. the Senate and the Office of President were re-established).

© The Author(s) 2018
P. Koryś, *Poland From Partitions to EU Accession*,
https://doi.org/10.1007/978-3-319-97126-1_11

The transformation itself was a longer process, which began in the mid-1980s, when General Jaruzelski's regime softened its policy and martial law was lifted. In the second half of the 1980s, there were attempts to liberalize the economic system and create favourable conditions for the development of the private sector within the one-party system. The deregulation of the economy begun at that time paved the way for the system transformation in the early 1990s (Roszkowski 2015; Ther 2016).

The initial stage of the transformation was connected with a high level of unpredictability concerning both the internal and international situation. It was uncertain how strong the communist party was and how determined it was to use the force at its disposal to protect its status. However, it quickly turned out that almost the whole party elite decided to take part in the transformation and there was no risk of a political coup similar to that organized by Yanayev in the USSR. Another unpredictable point was how stable the democratic parliamentary institutions were, but it turned out that the change was firm, and even the post-communist party's electoral victory in 1993 did not stop or avert it.

The international situation was also difficult to predict. On the one hand, the Red Army troops stationed in Poland in considerable numbers until 1992, which initially brought about fears of an intervention, or at least of attempts to interfere with Poland's internal affairs, but these fears soon subsided. The status of Poland's western border further complicated Poland's international position. At the time of transformation, West Germany had not formally recognized Poland's western border, and the USSR was its de facto guarantor. On the other hand, it was uncertain what the West would do—in retrospect, the integration was expectable, but it was not at all obvious at the beginning of the transformation. The situation of the other eastern bloc countries was also precarious (Dudek 2004, 2014).

The geopolitical changes entailed the disintegration of the previous alliances. The Warsaw Pact and the Comecon ceased to exist in 1991. From 1989, the new priority of the Polish foreign policy was the rapprochement with the West and creating alliances ensuring that Poland would not return to the Soviet sphere of influence. Earlier, after WWI, pursuing the same priorities made Poland party to several political and military treaties as well as bilateral economic agreements in the 1920s and

1930s; also, an important element of that policy was creating a gold-based Polish currency proving Poland's credibility. Now, in the 1990s, the rapprochement with the West had to involve working towards the re-establishment of a market economy and the participation in the NATO and the European Union.

In 1989, Poland signed the treaty with the EEC. In 1991, the association agreement was signed (Europe Agreement) and it came into force in 1994; in 1992, the Free Trade Agreement came into force. In 1994, Poland applied for the EU membership, and the accession negotiations lasted from 1998 to 2002. In 2003, the Treaty of Accession was signed and Poland organized a referendum on membership, as a result of which Poland became a member of the European Union on 1 May 2004. Simultaneously, the process of military integration with the West took place, as Poland was invited to be a part of NATO in 1997, and became a member in 1999 (Trzeciak 2012).

Both of the main priorities of the Polish foreign policy were endorsed by practically all the important political forces of the period 1989–2004, including the post-communists. The political divisions were determined by the internal conflicts between the post-communists and the traditional anti-communists, and not by actual differences in the ideas concerning economic, social, or foreign policy.

Symbolically, the day of the election of 4 June 1989 is the end of the socialist rule in Poland. The election was only partially free, as 65% of the seats in the Parliament were reserved for the communist party (PUWP) and its coalition parties, ZSL and SD, and 35% for non-PUWP members, but all the seats allowed for non-PUWP members were taken by the candidates connected with Lech Wałęsa's Citizens' Committee. In the aftermath, a new cabinet, headed by Tadeusz Mazowiecki, was formed by the coalition of the Citizens' Committee and ZSL and SD. The election to the Senate was entirely free and 99 out 100 seats were won by the candidates of the Citizens' Committee. The National Assembly elected Wojciech Jaruzelski as president (by the votes of the PUWP and some coalition members), but his term in office was shortened and in 1990 a direct presidential election was held. Lech Wałęsa won in the run-off, beating the populist candidate, Stanislaw Tymiński. In 1991, Mazowiecki was replaced by Jan Krzysztof Bielecki from the Liberal-Democratic

Congress. The deputy prime minister and minister of finance in both cabinets was Leszek Balcerowicz, the main architect of the economic system transformation (Paszkiewicz 2000; Dudek 2004, 2013).

The first entirely free election was held in 1991, later than in some other countries of the eastern bloc. The parliament elected at the time was composed of several political parties; the factionalized post-Solidarity Movement (of which the strongest party was the Democratic Union, with 13% of the seats) and the post-communist parties; the descendant of the PUWP called SLD, which got 13%; and the peasant party PSL, which got 10%. The fragmentation of the parliament hindered the creation of a lasting coalition. The cabinet did not have the majority; its prime minister was Jan Olszewski from PC, a post-Solidarity party led by Jarosław Kaczyński. The cabinet was dismissed in June 1992, after passing an act requiring the vetting of all the higher state officials (concerning the information whether they had collaborated with the security apparatus before 1990). The two successive cabinets did not have the majority and in 1992 the president dissolved the parliament, but before that, an act was passed making amendments to the constitution.

The election of 1993 brought the defeat of the post-Solidarity Movement, many factions of which did not even get into the parliament because of the 5% entry threshold, though collectively they got 25% of the votes. The party created by President Wałęsa achieved a very poor result, about 5%. The strongest parties were the post-communist SLD (37% of the seats) and the peasant PSL (29%); they created a stable majority in the Sejm (the lower parliamentary house) and they had 73% of the Senate seats as well. The coalition created the cabinet headed by the leader of PSL, Waldemar Pawlak. He resigned in 1995 because of internal conflicts, and the same coalition created a new cabinet headed by Józef Oleksy from the other coalition party, SLD. In the same year, the presidential election was won by the young leader of the post-communist SLD, Aleksander Kwaśniewski (in the run-off election, he defeated Wałęsa 52% to 48%). In 1996, a new cabinet was formed by Włodzimierz Cimoszewicz from SLD. In 1997, a new Polish constitution was adopted after long discussions and a referendum.

The post-Solidarity Movement that took part in the election in 1997 got divided into two blocs, the liberal Freedom Union (UW, 13% of the seats) and the right-wing AWS (44%). The SLD improved its result, which, however, did not translate into more seats (36%), and PSL only got 6% of the seats. In the Senate, AWS got 51% of the seats, SLD 28%, and UW 8%. In effect, the cabinet was formed by the AWS-UW coalition, the prime minster was Jerzy Buzek, and the cabinet lasted until the next election.

At the end of the decade, further institutional changes were required, and four big socio-economic reforms were conducted, concerning medical aid, education, old-age pensions, and territorial division. They were expected to decentralize the state and modernize the social security system, thus modernizing the welfare state institutions in Poland.

In 2000, the next presidential election verified the level of the support for the post-Solidarity Movement. The incumbent Aleksander Kwasniewski got 54% and won, defeating Andrzej Olechowski (supported by the leader of the UW, though not its official candidate), who got the result of 17%, Marian Krzaklewski (from the ruling AWS), who got only 16%, and Wałęsa himself. The cut in support for the post-Solidarity Movement was also visible in the subsequent parliamentary election.

Before the election of 2001, the post-Solidarity Movement underwent profound changes. In 2000, in the UW party election, Bronisław Geremek defeated Donald Tusk, who subsequently left the party and created a new one, the Civic Platform (PO), along with some UW members and the groups which had campaigned for Olechowski in the presidential election. AWS also split, as a new group called Law and Justice (PiS) was formed around Lech Kaczyński, the minister for justice in the AWS-UW cabinet, and his twin brother, Jarosław. The left-wing SLD won (along with a small party called the Labour Union, or UP; they got 47% of the seats), PO got 14%, PiS 10%, and PSL 9%, while neither AWS nor UW reached 5% entry threshold. Another two parties in the Sejm were the populist *Samoobrona* ("Self-defence"), which got almost 12% of the seats, and the nationalistic League of Polish Families (*Liga Polskich Rodzin*, LPR) (8%). SLD obtained 78% of the seats in the Senate. The coalition SLD-UP-PSL was formed, and its cabinet was headed by Leszek Miller, the leader of SLD. Several corruption allegations and investigations concerning the highest officials led to a split within the coalition, but Miller's cabinet continued as a minority cabinet of SLD-UP. On the 1 May 2004, Poland became a member of the European Union; Leszek Miller resigned on the next day, and was succeeded by Marek Belka, who was prime minister until the election in 2005.

Throughout the period, there were no major instances of questioning the results of the elections or their validity. The succession, continuity, and participation of post-communist parties in the new political system as well as the absence of objections as to the way elections were conducted were a proof that Poland had consolidated democracy. In turn, the successes of populist movements (the presidential candidacy of Tymiński, *Samoobrona* and far-right movements, such as the League of Polish Families headed by Roman Giertych) and the persistent popularity of post-communist parties indicated that transformation resulted not only in huge economic success, but also in unsolved social problems, including the relative deprivation of a part of the society (due to the collapse of state-owned agriculture, large-scale long-term unemployment in the urban economy, etc.) and its division into the winners and losers of the system transformation.

2   Ideas

The possibility of a system transformation emerged as a topic of discussion among the Polish intellectuals in the 1980s. The Polish People's Republic was originally founded on the communist elite's belief in the agency of the state, but from the mid-1980s there was growing criticism of the state-controlled planned economy. During the Solidarity period, the discussions concerned the new social order based on communitarian values. Its important element was the decentralization of the economy, but not necessarily its privatization. Later, as the debates on the future of Poland started to involve the younger generations of intellectuals, both on the side of the government and the opposition, the belief that the economy had to be liberalized and—at least partially—privatized started to dominate. Many of the proponents of the transformation (including Leszek Balcerowicz) had studied at American universities, and that is where they were first introduced to the free market ideas (Luszniewicz 2009; Brzechczyszyn 2010; Koryś 2011; Koryś and Tymiński 2016a).

In 1989, an attempt was made to adapt the relatively modern institutional solutions, stemming both from the economic reforms implemented in the Western economies (the liberalization of the economy of Great Britain, the USA, and Germany) and from the system transformations in peripheral, poorly developed countries. What the West recommended to the countries suffering prolonged economic crisis, including high government debt, was the solution provided by the International Monetary Fund, based on the experiences of the economic policy based on the monetarist theory of Milton Friedman. These measures brought positive results in Latin America, and a similar solution for Poland was put forward. The actual shape of the idea of transformation was vastly influenced by American advisors, such as Jeffrey Sachs, and Polish economists working abroad, such as Jan Vincent Rostowski and Stanisław Gomułka (Portes et al. 1993; Sachs 1993; Gomułka et al. 2011; Gomułka 2013).

They formulated the proposal of shock transformation, based on the Washington Consensus, and it was treated as the optimum solution throughout the transformation period (Balcerowicz 1997; Balcerowicz et al. 2009). Most political groups accepted the trajectory of change which it involved, though the social democrats and post-communists suggested a social adjustment. Some reservations concerning the way privatization was conducted (though not concerning the privatization itself) were expressed by right-wing groups as well as some social critics, who indicated the clientelist character of some political connections and the involvement of the communist secret service in the process (Łoś and Zybertowicz 2000). Anyway, the transformation model was not criticized by any of the mainstream political groups, including the post-communists; criticism was expressed by the populists, the radical left wing, and some of the nationalistic right-wing extremists. The part of the society (loosers of transformation process, usually politically inactive) welcomed the left-ist' and populists' ideas of enfranchising the workers of enterprises as opposed to the "thieving" privatization, but also the renationalization of the key sectors of the economy, abandoning the liberal shock transformation and adopting the social market economy model—"the third path", or gradual transformation.

Transformation was also criticized by left-wing economists, such as Ryszard Bugaj or Grzegorz Kołodko, as well as more radical leftist thinkers like Tadeusz Kowalik, who used to be advisor of *Solidarność* or Kazimierz Poznański, working in the USA (Poznański 1996, 2001; Kołodko 2000; Bugaj and Kulpińska-Cała 2004; Kowalik 2009; Bugaj 2015). They indicated the development costs of the excessively rapid structural changes and the discrepancy between the programme prepared by Western experts and the local needs. They also emphasized the fact that the social costs of privatization were very high and unequally distributed, as they involved mass bankruptcies of the main employers, that is, the state-owned industrial and agricultural enterprises. More radical critics pointed out the under-pricing of the enterprises sold to the foreign capital (the sell-off of the national capital) and adopting the peripheral development model. They indicated the much too high social costs of the transformation, the emergence of crony capitalism, and choosing the Latin American model instead of the Western European one; that is, abandoning the idea of creating the welfare state and allowing the rapid growth of income disparities. A non-left-wing economist and management theorist Witold Kieżun presented an even more radical view, that the transformation resulted in the loss of Poland's economic potential, the sell-off of the national capital, and the impoverishment of the population (Kieżun 2011). Even though this criticism contained some truth, the authors tended to confuse global processes and local phenomena. In retrospect, many (if not most) of their points seem unfair or exaggerated.

In the 1990s, the political consensus concerning modernization was built around the rapprochement with the West by means of the integration with Western political, economic, and military structures, particularly the EU and NATO. This integration and the ensuing introduction of the western institutional and legal standards were expected to facilitate modernization and promote the convergence with Western Europe. The Polish intellectual consensus concerning the model of modernization was parallel to the early Western debates on the transition period, perceived as a step towards building a modern society. In this perspective, the EU accession and the prompt implementation of EU regulations and institutions was perceived as the next, ultimate step towards the Europeanization of Poland.

Simultaneously, the new wave of Western (but also Polish) research on the transition period focused on the problems emerging in the post-socialist states and societies. In this view, the process of modernization was slowed down by the unpredicted impact of the institutions and regulations originating from the communist *ancient regime*, as well as by the persisting social habits created in that period. They resulted in the slow-down of economic growth and delaying the catching-up process. Some researchers and intellectuals indicated the persistent distinctive features of post-communist societies, such as large-scale corruption and nepotism. In comparison with the optimistic view of the theoreticians of modernization, this new wave of interpretations was much more pessimistic.

Still, it is worth noting that until the EU accession, the path of transformation was almost unanimously seen as proper and successful (with some complaints concerning the persistent corruption). Critique was marginal and practically invisible, even though some critics indicated the growing social and economic problems, which turned out to be important for the Polish politics in the coming years.

3   Territory and Population

The initial period of transformation was riddled with changes of the international situation, as between 1989 and 1993 all the neighbouring states ceased to exist. East Germany united with West Germany in 1990, Lithuania announced its independence in the same year, and the Soviet empire disintegrated a year later. In 1991, the treaty of Białowieża stated that the sovereign states of Russia, Byelorussia, and Ukraine were created (their borders with Poland were along the old borders with the USSR). On 1 January 1993, Czechoslovakia split into the Czech Republic and Slovakia. Thus, since 1993 Poland has had borders with Russia, Lithuania, Byelorussia, Ukraine, Slovakia, the Czech Republic, and Germany; however, the three neighbouring countries turned into seven without any changes to the Polish border.

In turn, a major change in the internal administrative division of Poland happened in 1997, when the administrative reform brought back the three-level administration (voivodeships divided into counties, divided into communes) and the bigger voivodeships (16 instead of 49) to enable their capitals to develop into regional administrative and economic centres.

During the transformation period, the population size stabilized and urbanization practically stalled. However, throughout the period, the birth rate decreased, from the peak number of births, over 700,000 in 1982 to about 350,000 at the turn of the century. The total fertility rate also declined, quickly falling below 1.3 (Wyczański 2003; Okólski 2004; Główny Urząd Statystyczny (GUS) 2014).

As a result, the share of working-age people in the population grew quickly, particularly from the end of the 1990s, when the echo baby boom started to enter the labour market. The demographic dividend was not fully incorporated into the Polish economy (as it also happened during the interwar period and in the 1970s). It resulted in the persisting high level of unemployment throughout the 1990s and, in effect, in the persisting low wages. This made Poland attractive for foreign direct investments (FDI), but also contributed to the emigration of the Polish people, as a result of which in 2004 about 1 million Polish citizens lived outside Poland (and another million emigrated in the years following the EU accession) (Jaźwińska-Motylska et al. 2001; Grabowska-Lusińska and Okólski 2009).

The transformation of the economy led not only to emigration, but also to internal migration. The population of some industrial and peripheral regions started to fall (e.g. the population of Upper Silesia and of Łódź), and the peripheral agricultural and rural areas underwent rapid population ageing and depopulation. There was also the new phenomenon of urban sprawl—metropolitan areas spread onto the increasingly distant suburbs. Population growth was observed in some cities, which became the regional administrative, academic, or international services centres (Warszawa, Kraków, Wrocław, Poznań); this growth was not fully recorded in the official statistics due to inefficient registration procedures, but in fact in the second decade of the twenty-first century, Kraków overtook Łódź in terms of population and became the second biggest city of Poland, and the Warsaw metropolitan area had grown almost as big as the Upper Silesian conurbation.

While at first sight Poland remained impressively stable in terms of population and territory during the transformation, actually, some major changes happened. To begin with, the geopolitical changes resulted in the fact that Poland's three neighbours turned into seven. Furthermore, the demographic processes (decrease of fertility, increase of life expectancy) resulted in the demographic dividend as well as the process of the ageing of the Polish society. Moreover, internal migration reflected the changing structure of the economy, with the growing role of some economic centres and the decline (also populational) of others. Finally, once again in the Polish history, emigration resulted in the rapid outflow of the population and human capital, but similarly to late nineteenth century labour emigration, it was forced by purely economic, not political, reasons.

4   The Society

The transformation resulted not only in a successful transition to market economy, but also in a deep social change. The twentieth century brought the economic emancipation of peasants and workers, and the system transformation created the modern industrial and market society, with its characteristic social structure as well as its internal conflicts. The period 1989–2004 was the time of tensions typical of the process of creating such a modern society and the upward mobility of various groups, involving the overhaul of the class relations in comparison with the society of the late state socialism.

Socialism fossilized some social structures in Poland. For instance, peasant economy persisted in communist Poland due to the lack of incentives for the modernization of small private farms throughout the communist period and due to the absence of large-scale market mechanisms. The social and economic framework typical of traditional peasant households (focus on subsistence, not development) remained almost unchanged until the 1980s. Moreover, the social processes fundamental for the modernization of the society, such as urbanization and rural-urban migration, were limited (which resulted in so-called under-urbanization, that is, relatively low level of urbanization induced by political decisions). Additionally, the communist social policy prevented the creation of the modern bourgeoisie and middle class. Thus, the transformation involved many social changes taking place rapidly and simultaneously, and resulted in the replacement of peasants by the class of modern farmers, the rise of the modern bourgeoisie, and the replacement of the intelligentsia by the capitalist middle class, including specialists and professionals. Moreover, the transformation was the time of rebuilding the civic society and social trust, greatly weakened by the decades of the communist rule. Consequently, the structure of the Polish society started to resemble the structure of Western European societies (Giza-Poleszczuk et al. 2000; Piatkowski 2018).

The industrial working class declined during the first years of the transformation, as the deregulation, privatization, and macroeconomic reforms resulted in the crisis of the industrial sector, and in the quick growth of efficiency in the medium term. Therefore, the demand for industrial workers fell because of the wave of bankruptcies of big enterprises and because of the redundancies in the ones which survived; moreover, the newly created enterprises employed relatively few people. Similarly, the transformation completed the prolonged and difficult process of creating market-oriented agriculture, which ultimately led to the disappearance of the peasant class. As late as during the transformation and the EU accession, the Western press showed photographs from Poland featuring horse-drawn carts or tilling with a horse-drawn plough, but these were rare instances at the time, as agriculture was modernized very rapidly. In this way, peasants and workers, the two classes whose emancipation had fuelled social change in Poland during the nineteenth and twentieth centuries and who had played a crucial role in the egalitarian socialist society, disappeared as a result of the transformation, and were replaced by modern social classes (Giza-Poleszczuk et al. 2000; Domański 2004, 2015).

A new upper class started to form from the beginning of the transformation. Initially, fortunes were made because of the transfer of state property to some politicians and entrepreneurs closely connected with the communist party, though some of the party members "enfranchised" in this way were not successful in the free market economy. Later, the new upper class started to emerge due to the financial success of the most talented or skilful professionals, entrepreneurs, and managers of foreign companies investing in Poland (Gardawski 2001; Jasiecki 2002; Jarosz and Kozak 2015).

Another result of the transformation was, as mentioned above, the emergence of the numerous modern urban middle class. A big part of this class was the former urban intelligentsia, which now ceased to suffer the discrepancy of the factors of social status (income, level of education and position in society), and with efficient use of social capital it developed into the class of professionals and intellectuals. The other big group which slowly evolved into middle class was that of the owners of small- and medium-size manufacturing, services, or agricultural enterprises (some of them established their businesses in 1980s and others in the market economy after 1989). The middle class grew quickly and achieved considerable social and political importance; therefore, the parties representing its views, either liberal or conservative, obtained substantial support, which increased towards the end of the period. The rise of the middle class, both in size and in wealth (even though it remained considerably less affluent than its Western counterpart), contributed to the stability of the transformation and to Poland's commitment to European integration.

Apart from the benefits for large social groups, the transformation had an adverse effect on other groups of people, mostly from the lower class. Some of its members benefitted from the upward mobility opportunities, but others were among those badly affected. The decline of big state-owned industry and agriculture resulted in the emergence of unemployment, urban and rural poverty, and the increasing income gap. Peasant farms were able to absorb part of the surplus labour force at the expense of lowering the standard of living, but the greatest social crisis appeared in the declining industrial areas and in the areas of predominant state agriculture; the inhabitants of the latter, mostly on the post-German territories, suffered poverty and lack of prospects. The successive governments made attempts to alleviate the problem, but with limited success. These adverse processes, however, had little bearing on the transformation process, because the social and economic marginalization was paralleled by the lack of strong enough political representation. Such people, if they voted at all, frequently supported post-communist left-wing or populist parties. They contributed to the success of the populist politician

Stanisław Tymiński, who appeared out of nowhere and got into the presidential run-off election, and to the success of the populist political movement *Samoobrona* ("Self-defence"), which emerged from the farmers' protests against the import of food. Also, some far-right parties (such as the League of Polish Families) and conservative Catholic movements (such as the *Radio Maryja* Family) tried to attract the voters who perceived themselves as victims of the transformation (Jarosz 2008; Jarosz and Kozak 2015).

Actually, the growing disparities and the relative deprivation of a part of the society went mostly unnoticed by the more successful part of the society. The less successful did not exactly "lose" in the process, as the improvement of the standard of living and the growth of income comprised practically everyone, but the changes were much slower in the lower social strata and—as the new studies indicate—the income disparity gradually increased (even though up to 2004 it was lower than in most Western societies).

The income gap was growing between well-paid, white-collar workers in Warszawa and other big cities and manual workers from the declining industrial districts and from peripheral regions, as well as public sector workers. In particular, underpayment in the public sector contributed to the persistence of some adverse social phenomena, for instance, corruption. Even though it was different from that in state socialism, throughout the 1990s, corruption, both street-level and large-scale, was not only very common, but socially accepted. The change in this respect did not occur until the beginning of the twenty-first century, when the big corruption scandals of the SLD-PSL government brought about the defeat of the ruling parties in the 2003 election (Koryś and Tymiński 2016b).

An important factor fuelling the social change at the time was education. Primary and secondary education substantially improved, particularly in the poorer and less developed regions, and it was at least partly adjusted to the needs of the modern economy. This contributed to the growth of the participation in tertiary education, made possible by the increased admission to state universities and by the dynamic development of private tertiary education institutions. The success was measured not only by the rise of the number of graduates (up to 50% in each successive cohort in the late 1990s), but also by the enhancement of the quality of teaching resulting from reforms, novel approaches, and new technologies.

Even though the social and political changes after 1989 were exceptionally dynamic, they were conducted peacefully. The period 1989–2004 was the time of the formation of modern social structures, which was done much later than in the other countries due to the adverse, fossilizing effect of state socialism. Apart from the political change, the social change was the greatest success of the transformation (even though it resulted in the growing disparities in the society). The simple measure of this success is the Human Development Index. In 1990, it equalled 0.712; between 1990 and 2000 it grew by 0.97% a year (one of the fastest rates among well-developed countries) and reached 0.8 in 2003.

5   The Economy

The final decades of the economy of state socialism were the time of impending economic disaster, analysed in the previous chapter. In the mid-1970s, Poland's GDP per capita again reached about a third of the GDP per capita of the economic leader, the USA, and almost 50% of that of Germany (so did Hungary's and Bulgaria's, and in Czechoslovakia the GDP per capita was higher than in Poland by about 25%). That was the peak of the development capacity of the region. In 1989 Poland's GDP per capita was 10% lower than a decade before (so the scale of the slump and the persistency of the recession were comparable to that in Greece in 2010s, but with the lower affluence level to begin with). The other socialist countries also had the economic growth rates of about 0, but still Poland's GDP per capita in 1989 was only 90% of Bulgaria's, 80% of Hungary's, and 65% of Czechoslovakia's. Additionally, at the time, the well-developed countries started to develop much faster than the backward socialist states. Any positive Gerschenkron effect of backwardness disappeared.

In 1989, the communist authorities tried to shirk the responsibility for the recession, which they did not know how to overcome, and in a probably unpredicted result, the system transformation took place. The economic policy of the transformation was created by Leszek Balcerowicz, who was minister of finance in the years 1989–1991 and 1997–2001.

The transformation itself started under the communist rule, and its first stage (or the stage of the transformation *avant la lettre*) was the set of reforms liberalizing the activity of enterprises (including the private ones) implemented by the minister of industry in the last socialist cabinet, Mieczysław Wilczek, an experienced entrepreneur from the socialist era. But the crucial, second stage of transformation was the set of reforms of 1989, prepared by Leszek Balcerowicz along with American advisors, one of whom was Jeffery Sachs. It was called shock therapy because of the huge pace of the deregulation of the controlled economy. The rapidity of the changes was meant to avert the risk of social resentment during the brief economic slump caused by the transformation (Holmes and Roszkowski 1997; Kofman and Roszkowski 1999; Bałtowski 2009; Berend 2009; Dudek 2014).

The changes comprised a structural adjustment to the framework determined by the Washington Consensus. In particular, they consisted of measures aimed at curbing inflation, reducing the budget deficit, balancing the internal market through the price mechanism, overcoming the shortages, making the activity of state enterprises economically viable (by their commercialization, but also by the elimination of the inefficient ones), and their subsequent privatization. The Polish currency became fully convertible. The economic balance was regained by around 1992. Further reforms entailed changes to the tax system, the currency (the redenomination of 1995), the retirement system, and the social security system. The last wave of the four system reforms took place in 1999.

The further reforms comprised the tax system, the currency (the redenomination of 1995), the retirement system, and the social security system. The last wave of the four system reforms took place eight years after the transformation, in 1999 (Balcerowicz 1997; Balcerowicz et al. 2009).

As a result of the reforms, a relatively modern institutional system was established. However, it had a mixed, "patchwork" character, as some of the institutions and regulations were formed in state socialism and were only adjusted and partly changed in the new system. Thus, the institutional transformation was partly evolutionary, which helped the people survive the difficult time, but preserved some of the flaws of the previous system and created problems caused by the imperfection of the adjustments and modifications.

The structural change in economy in the aftermath of the transformation comprised all the sectors, manufacturing, agriculture, and services. In the initial phase, the industrial sector collapsed as a result of the change of regulations and a radical change in the economic environment. In state socialism, the economy was practically autarkic, and opening it to the market, enfranchising the state enterprises and creating the possibility of bankruptcy clearly showed the low competitiveness of much of state-owned industry. Many state enterprises went bankrupt at the beginning of the transformation, and in consequence, industry went through a profound structural change, fuelled by privatization and foreign investment. In 1989, the industrial employment rate was 36%, in 2000 it fell to 31%, and in 2004, to 29%. The demand for labour was limited, and thus, this structural change in economy resulted not only in the relative growth of employment in the service sector, but also in the emergence of a high rate of unemployment, which was higher than in the developed capitalist economies and than in state socialism, and was usually higher than 15% (periodically up to 20%). It persisted until 2004, and even longer; in absolute numbers, the peak of unemployment, over 3 million people, was reached in 2003, and from that moment, both the rate of unemployment and the number of the unemployed declined. This phenomenon was accompanied by the low participation rate, resulting in a large share of working-age population outside the labour market (Kubiczek et al. 2006).

The restructuring of industry entailed the change of its geographical distribution and the structure of production. Some of the principal industrial regions, with traditional branches of industry and strong trade unions, lost their dominant position, as they were located too far from the western border to be attractive for foreign investors. For that reason, western urban centres gained importance and developed industrial production, especially Poznań and the urban areas of Lower Silesia. Even though Upper Silesia remained the biggest industrial area of the country, its economic significance considerably lowered.

As to the branch structure of industry, the modern branches developed: car industry (a large-scale geographical relocation took place in this industry, and the production was gradually moved to the west and south of Poland: unlike in the communist period, a large part of production was and still is exported, and thus, the factories were located closer to Western Europe), household appliances and high tech. The branches which were developed in state socialism lost importance, particularly heavy industry and mining.

While the industrial sector developed and was modernized very quickly, transport and electrical infrastructure developed relatively slowly. The railway network shrank due to the liquidation of unprofitable local lines, mostly in post-German regions, where the infrastructure density was still considerably higher than in the rest of Poland. Railway transport of people and cargo declined in relation to the more flexible road transport, and the state did not generate incentives to avert that trend. The road network developed steadily; the length of surface roads grew from 216,000 km to 254,000 km, and by 2000 the construction or modernization of a few lengths of motorways and expressways (in many cases the construction begun in the 1980s) was completed. More were constructed in 2000–2004, but the development of the trunk road network did not gain momentum until later (Kaliński 2011).

The power grid also developed slowly. The Polish and Western European systems became connected and synchronized in the 1990s, which enabled the exchange across borders. New blocs were added in the coal-fired power stations, but generally, the Polish power plants were getting obsolete. The gas and oil distribution infrastructure were developed, while the modernization of transmission infrastructure was rather slow. At the beginning of the twenty-first century, wind power production started to develop. On the other hand, the telecommunication sector underwent huge changes, due to the privatization and the development of cellular technology. Telephone lines, which were previously a rationed good, with waiting lists for services amounting to years between request and installation, disappeared overnight, with privatization and entrance of mobile telephony providers.

Similarly, agriculture underwent profound changes. State-owned agriculture, particularly the state farms, was liquidated in the first years of the transformation. In 1990, State Agricultural Farms employed about 400,000 workers; in the subsequent year, the employment was halved. The State Agricultural Farms which operated in the market conditions were gradually liquidated and sold out. Some of the land was returned to the pre-war owners, some was sold, the rest remained state property. The process of dissolving State Agricultural Farms was completed in 1995, a few continued to exist as state-owned companies (Łapińska-Tyszka et al. 1997).

Private agriculture was also restructured. The privatization of State Agricultural Farms and the process of land concentration led to the emergence of big agricultural estates and farms. The traditional peasant economy finally declined (as another mark of successful post-transformational modernization), which was indicated by the growing average area of the farm and the decrease in employment in agriculture. The agricultural output declined and its structure changed. Rye production halved between 1989 and 2005, potato production fell by 75%, and cattle production almost halved. The farms became better equipped with machinery. At the end of the period, the global output was lower, but the quality of the produce was much higher. Agricultural export and import had a considerable share in the Polish foreign trade, but this share was declining. The employment in agriculture was falling much faster than the rural population. In 1989, it was still 29% of all employment; in 1997, it fell below 20%, and in 2004, it was only 17%. These levels were still higher that in Western Europe, but many of these were ageing farmers owning small farms, which often were not passed on to successors (for this reason, the decline of agricultural employment has not ended yet). In consequence, employment fell, and labour efficiency in agriculture grew despite some decline in production (Szuman 1999).

The service sector was privatized and modernized; as a result, the employment in services grew both in numbers and in proportion to the employment in the other two sectors. In 1989, the employment level in services was the same as in industry (36%); in 1999, it exceeded 50%; and in 2004, it was almost 54%. The restructuring of the service sector was connected with the privatization of trade and banking. After the privatization both sectors were fragmented, and their concentration was based on foreign capital, which was invested in the most profitable segments of the sectors and modernized them very quickly. Modern banking and financial and insurance services started to develop. New solutions were introduced and some stages of the development were skipped due to the involvement of foreign investment; however, it resulted in the high share of foreign capital in this sector, particularly in commercial banking. On the other hand, the employment in public service sector was very high, but employees (particularly the highly qualified ones) remained underpaid (compared to the private sector), and it resulted in the loss of human capital.

At the beginning of the transformation, the Warsaw Stock Exchange was established and became the foundation of the capital market in Poland and one of the channels of privatization. In 1995, a mass privatization programme was conducted, where the citizens obtained bonds of National Investment Funds, incorporating and managing the assets of 500 enterprises, constituting 2–5% of the national assets. The economic and social goals of the programme were achieved only in part—it had limited educational value and it did not contribute to transforming the Poles into the society of owners. The economic benefits for the enterprises were scarce, and the cost of the programme, particularly the fees for the investment funds, turned out to be high.

Foreign trade gained importance in the new market environment. The share of export in the GDP grew from 25% in 1990 to 29% in 2005, and the respective numbers for import are 16% and 33%. The value of trade increased (between 1990 and 2004 export grew four times and import eight times), and the balance of trade was negative throughout the period. In 2004, Poland's export constituted about 0.8% of the world export. In 1989, Poland's main trade partner was the USSR (about 20% of export in current prices went to this country and 18% of import came from this country); the other important partners were West Germany (respectively, 14% and 16%, together with East Germany: 18% and 20%), Great Britain and Czechoslovakia in export (7% and 6%, respectively), and Austria, Czechoslovakia, and Switzerland in import (6%, 6%, and 5%). The change of the branch structure of industry and the change of international economic relations resulted in the change of the geographical structure of the Polish foreign trade. In 2004 Poland's main trade partner was Germany (28% of export and 25% of import). The important recipients of the Polish export were France and Italy (6% each), and the Polish import came from Russia (9%, mostly natural gas and oil) and Italy (7%). In 2004 as much as 80% of Polish export went to the EU countries (including the new members) and 68% came from the EU. The branch structure of foreign trade also changed. Both in export and in import the share of energy resources declined between 1990 and 2005 (in export, from 11% to 5% in current prices, in import from 22% to 12%), and the share of manufactured goods considerably increased in import (from 11% to 21%), and of machines, appliances, and transport machinery in export (from 26% to 39%) (Czarny and Śledziewska 2009; Główny Urząd Statystyczny 2017).

To sum up, the most important effect of the transformation was a prolonged period of economic growth after a relatively short recession at the beginning, resulting from the dynamic changes, the collapse of the controlled economy, and curbing inflation. In 1991, when stable economic growth began, the Polish GDP per capita was not even a quarter of that of the USA. Poland no longer tried to catch up with the West by means of industrialization inspired and financed by the state, but this time, it made an effort to imitate the West, building the market and reforming the institutions, using the institutional and financial support of Western Europe and the USA, and it began a period of extraordinary growth. Until 2004, Poland's GDP per capita grew each year; between 1990 and 2004, it grew threefold, and then grew each year up to 2017, reaching almost 50% of the GDP per capita of the USA.

6   Conclusions

The Polish transformation was a remarkable success; it was extraordinary in the Polish history and also in the region, in comparison with the other countries that also underwent a system transformation at the time (Piatkowski 2013, 2018; Branko Milanovic 2014). It resulted in profound social changes, which modernized the Polish society in terms of social structure, education, and urbanization.

The post-communist period was also the period of successful imitation as well as cultural and institutional diffusion. The transformation model, many institutional adjustments and regulatory reforms, the modernization of industry, and the service sector were the result of the inflow of ideas, knowledge, and capital from the West. Also, the state institutions underwent the process of rapid Europeanization—it was modernized through the implementation of institutional and legal solutions elaborated in the process of European integration.

Moreover, the transition to modern market economy proved to be extremely successful in terms of economic development. It resulted in a very long period of economic growth, which was also the time of catching-up with the leaders of global economy. The Polish economic transformation was among the most successful ones in Central-Eastern Europe. At the time of the accession to the European Union, the Polish economy was already relatively modern, open, and globalized. Like the economies of many other countries in the region, it was becoming the manufacturing department of "the European factory" (as a result of direct investment, some European manufacturing was relocated here, for the mutual benefit). The subsequent years showed that the changes of the period between 1989 and 2004 prepared Poland well for the accession to the European Union.

References

Balcerowicz, L. (1997). *Socjalizm, kapitalizm, transformacja: szkice z przełomu epok*. Warszawa: Wydawnictwo Naukowe PWN.

Balcerowicz, L., Baczyński, J., & Koźmiński, J. (2009). *800 dni: krótka historia wielkiej zmiany 1989–1991*. Warszawa: Polityka.

Bałtowski, M. (2009). *Gospodarka socjalistyczna w Polsce: geneza – rozwój – upadek*. Warszawa: Wydawnictwo Naukowe PWN.

Berend, T. I. (2009). *From the Soviet bloc to the European Union: The economic and social transformation of Central and Eastern Europe since 1973*. Cambridge, UK and New York: Cambridge University Press.

Branko Milanovic. (2014). For whom the wall fell? A balance sheet of the transition to capitalism. *The Globalist*. Retrieved June 10, 2018, from https://www.theglobalist.com/for-whom-the-wall-fell-a-balance-sheet-of-the-transition-to-capitalism/

Brzechczyszyn, K. (2010). Program i myśl polityczna NSZZ Solidarność. In Ł. Kamiński & G. Waligóra (Eds.), *NSZZ "Solidarność" 1980–1989. T. 2: Ruch społeczny*. Warszawa: IPN – Komisja Ścigania Zbrodni przeciwko Narodowi Polskiemu.

Bugaj, R. (2015). *Plusy dodatnie i ujemne czyli Polski kapitalizm bez solidarności*. Warszawa: Wydawnictwo Poltext.

Bugaj, R., & Kulpińska-Cała, K. (Eds.). (2004). *Polska transformacja ustrojowa: próba dyskursu – zarys perspektyw.* Warszawa: Fundacja Innowacja: Wyższa Szkoła Społeczno- Ekonomiczna.

Czarny, E., & Śledziewska, K. (2009). *Polska w handlu światowym.* Warszawa: Polskie Wydawnictwo Ekonomiczne.

Domański, H. (2004). *O ruchliwości społecznej w Polsce.* Warszawa: Instytut Filozofii i Socjologii Polskiej Akademii Nauk.

Domański, H. (2015). *The Polish middle class.* Frankfurt am Main and New York: Peter Lang.

Dudek, A. (2004). *Pierwsze lata III Rzeczypospolitej: 1989–2001.* Kraków: Wydawnictwo Arcana.

Dudek, A. (2013). *Historia polityczna Polski: 1989–2012.* Kraków: Społeczny Instytut Wydawniczy Znak.

Dudek, A. (2014). *Reglamentowana rewolucja: rozkład dyktatury komunistycznej w Polsce 1988–1990.* Kraków: Społeczny Instytut Wydawniczy Znak.

Gardawski, J. (2001). *Powracająca klasa: sektor prywatny w III Rzeczypospolitej.* Warszawa: Wydawnictwo IFiS PAN – Instytutu Filozofii i Socjologii Polskiej Akademii Nauk.

Giza-Poleszczuk, A., Marody, M., & Rychard, A. (2000). *Strategie i system: Polacy w obliczu zmiany społecznej.* Warszawa: Wydawnictwo IFiS PAN – Instytutu Filozofii i Socjologii Polskiej Akademii Nauk.

Główny Urząd Statystyczny. (2014). *Polska 1989–2014.* Warszawa: Główny Urząd Statystyczny.

Główny Urząd Statystyczny. (2017). *Rocznik Statystyczny Handlu Zagranicznego 2017.* Warszawa: Główny Urząd Statystyczny.

Gomułka, S. & Kowalik, T. (Eds.). (2011). *Transformacja polska: dokumenty i analizy 1990.* Warszawa: Wydawnictwo Naukowe Scholar.

Gomułka, S. (Eds.). (2013). *Transformacja polska: dokumenty i analizy 1991–1993.* Warszawa: Wydawnictwo Naukowe Scholar.

Grabowska-Lusińska, I., & Okólski, M. (2009). *Emigracja ostatnia?* Warszawa: Wydawnictwo Naukowe Scholar.

Holmes, L. T., & Roszkowski, W. (Eds.). (1997). *Changing rules: Polish political and economic transformation in comparative perspective.* Warsaw: ISP PAN.

Jarosz, M. (Ed.). (2008). *Wykluczeni: wymiar społeczny, materialny i etniczny.* Warszawa: Instytut Studiów Politycznych PAN.

Jarosz, M., & Kozak, M. W. (2015). *Eksplozja nierówności?* Warszawa: Instytut Studiów Politycznych PAN: Oficyna Naukowa.

Jasiecki, K. (2002). *Elita biznesu w Polsce: drugie narodziny kapitalizmu.* Warszawa: Wydawnictwo IFiS PAN – Instytutu Filozofii i Socjologii [Polskiej Akademii Nauk].

344   P. Koryś

Jaźwińska-Motylska, E. & Okólski, M. (Eds.). (2001). *Ludzie na huśtawce: migracje między peryferiami Polski i Zachodu.* Warszawa: Scholar.

Kaliński, J. (2011). *Autostrady w Polsce czyli Drogi przez mękę.* Łódź: Księży Młyn.

Kieżun, W. (2011). *Drogi i bezdroża polskich przemian.* Warszawa: Ekotv.

Kofman, J., & Roszkowski, W. (1999). *Transformacja i postkomunizm.* Warszawa: ISP PAN.

Kołodko, G. W. (2000). *From shock to therapy: The political economy of postsocialist transformation.* Oxford: Oxford University Press.

Koryś, P. (2011). To jest Polska i chcemy mieć rozwiązania polskie. NSZZ Solidarność jako ruch modernizacyjny. In *Polska Solidarności. Kontrowersje, oblicza, interpretacje.* Kraków: Ośrodek Myśli Politycznej.

Koryś, P., & Tymiński, M. (2016a). Od socjalizmu do socjalizmu. Koncepcje reform gospodarczych w PRL po wybuchach społecznych w 1956 i 1980 r. *Dzieje Najnowsze, 48,* 125. https://doi.org/10.12775/DN.2016.4.06

Koryś, P., & Tymiński, M. (2016b). The unwanted legacy. In search of historical roots of corruption in Poland. *Sociologija, 58,* 203–219.

Kowalik, T. (2009). Retrieved from www.polskatransformacja.pl. Warszawa: Warszawskie Wydawnictwo Literackie Muza.

Kubiczek, F., Wyczański, A., & Zakład Wydawnictw Statystycznych (Eds.). (2006). *Historia Polski w liczbach. T. 2: Gospodarka.* Warszawa: Zakład Wydawnictw Statystycznych.

Łapińska-Tyszka, K., Fedyszak-Radziejowska, B., & Perepeczko, B. (1997). *Nowi gospodarze dawnych PGR: przekształcenia państwowego rolnictwa.* Warszawa: PAN. IRWIR.

Łoś, M., & Zybertowicz, A. (2000). *Privatizing the police-state: The case of Poland.* Houndmills, Basingstoke and New York: Macmillan Press and St. Martin's Press.

Luszniewicz, J. (2009). Wizje reformy gospodarczej w koncepcjach pierwszej Solidarności 1980–1981. In E. Kościk & T. Głowiński (Eds.), *Między zaniechaniem a modernizacją: społeczno-gospodarcze problemy ziem polskich na przestrzeni wieków: Wrocławskie Spotkania z Historią Gospodarczą, spotkanie IV.* Wrocław: Gajt.

Okólski, M. (2004). *Demografia zmiany społecznej.* Warszawa: Scholar.

Paszkiewicz, K. A. (Ed.). (2000). *Partie i koalicje polityczne III Rzeczypospolitej.* Wrocław: Wydawnictwo Uniwersytetu Wrocławskiego.

Piatkowski, M. (2018). *Europe's growth champion.* New York: Oxford University Press.

Piatkowski, M. M. (2013). *Poland's new golden age: Shifting from Europe's periphery to its center.* The World Bank.

Portes, R., Gomułka, S., & Rosati, D. (Eds.). (1993). *Economic transformation in Central Europe: A progress report.* London and Luxembourg: Centre for Economic Policy Research; Office for Official Publications of the European Communities.

Poznański, K. (1996). *Poland's protracted transition: institutional change and economic growth 1970–1994.* Cambridge [etc.]: Cambridge University Press.

Poznański, K. (2001). *Obłęd reform: wyprzedaż Polski.* Warszawa: Ludowa Spółdzielnia Wydawnicza.

Roszkowski, W. (2015). *East Central Europe: A concise history.* Warszawa: Instytut Studiów Politycznych Polskiej Akademii Nauk: Instytut Jagielloński.

Sachs, J. (1993). *Poland's Jump to the market economy.* Cambridge, MA and London: MIT Press.

Szuman, A. (1999). Przeobrażenia struktury społeczno-zawodowej ludności Polski w XX wieku. *Ruch Prawniczy, Ekonomiczny i Socjologiczny, LXI,* 187–202.

Ther, P. (2016). *Europe since 1989: A history.* Princeton: Princeton UP.

Trzeciak, S. (2012). *Poland's EU accession.* London and New York: Routledge.

Wyczański, A. (Ed.). (2003). *Historia Polski w liczbach. T. 1: Państwo, społeczeństwo.* Warszawa: Zakład Wydawnictw Statystycznych.

12

Conclusion: Two Centuries of Catching-up to the West

The modern Polish economic history is extremely difficult to describe. Poland did not exist as a sovereign state and party to international relations for more than half of the 250 years covered in this book: in the period of partitions between 1795 and 1918, and during the German and Soviet occupation between 1939 and 1945 (Soviet until 1941). The years between 1772, the beginning of the period of history described here, and 1795, the Third Partition, are the time of the disintegration of the state, when the scope of real sovereignty was limited by the policy of the neighbouring states, particularly Russia's. For almost three decades of the first half of the nineteenth century there were autonomous quasi-states on the Polish lands, embodying the Enlightenment ideas in their political and socio-economic goals (the Duchy of Warsaw, which was the protectorate of France, the Kingdom of Poland, which was the protectorate of Russia, the Free City of Cracow and—to a much lesser extent—the Grand Duchy of Posen in Prussia). With a few exceptions in some periods (the Duchy of Warsaw, the Kingdom of Poland up to 1830, the Free City of Cracow), the real autonomy of these political entities was limited, even concerning their internal affairs. In the second half of the twentieth century, there was a sovereign Polish state, but it was within the Soviet sphere

© The Author(s) 2018
P. Koryś, *Poland From Partitions to EU Accession*,
https://doi.org/10.1007/978-3-319-97126-1_12

of influence and in reality its sovereignty in terms of international relations and the choice of its constitution and internal policy was significantly limited by the political objectives of the USSR.

The political impermanence of Poland on the international arena
affected its internal policy. When Poland was independent, it was often
a part of the political *avant-garde* of the region, or even Europe, like
when the very modern Constitution of 1791 was created, or when Poland
gave social rights and suffrage to women at the beginning of its existence
in 1918, or during the "self-limiting" revolution of the *Solidarność*
Movement, or on 4 June 1989, when the half-free election sparked off "the
autumn of nations". However, the political discontinuity hampered the
development of modern political movements and the elaboration of modern ideas. In the nineteenth century, the lack of independence entailed the
lack of internal policy creating a modern nation (and a modern nation
state). The fragmented state did not conduct an independent modernization policy for 100 years, and the elite focused on regaining or preserving
independence rather than on stimulating the process of modernization. It
was only after 1989 that the situation became conducive to change and
development.

The political discontinuity was reflected in the political ideas. In the
modern period, the Polish ideas of development were derivative rather
than original, and their authors struggled with the question of how to
create or re-create the modern state, while the problem of how to catch
up with the developed Western economies was of secondary importance.
As early as in the mid-eighteenth century, Polish thinkers started discussing the problem of the need to modernize the economy, that is, to adjust
its development to the changes happening in Western Europe, and these
ideas grew even stronger during the reign of the last king of the
Commonwealth, Stanisław August Poniatowski. The imitation of the
model of the modernization organized by the enlightened state was a
popular idea at the time of the Duchy of Warsaw and in the Kingdom of
Poland until 1830. That is the time when the main division line emerged
between the proponents of the different ways to modernize Poland, the
line which has been periodically revived in various forms ever since.

From the decline of the Commonwealth at the end of the eighteenth
century forth the criticism of modernization following the Western model
was scarce—even though it existed, and obtained limited support during

periods of economic crises or recessions (as Great Depression) and in early communist period (when the part of intelligentsia believed in communism as a modernizing solution). Practically all the important political factions in the last 200 years supported Westernization (at least verbally), with the exception of the communist party ruling in Poland from 1945 to 1989. The division line was about the way to conduct the modernization, its dynamics, and points of reference, rather than its goals.

The differences between the proposals of modernization concerned first of all the scope of the social and institutional reforms. It was visible with regard to the enfranchisement of the peasants (which was finally conducted by the partitioning states). The conflict was about how fast the reform should be conducted, and what its scope should be, as even though the freedom for the peasants was undisputed, the scope of ownership was debatable. Secondly, the model of modernization was problematic. On the one hand, there were the (usually liberal) proponents of the institutional reform; on the other hand, there were the (usually etatist or interventionist) believers in the fiscal and investment expansion of the state. Their positions were obviously more nuanced, but very crudely this conflict can be presented as the contrast between the bottom-up modernization: from the modern institutional arrangement to the modern society and the spontaneously emerging modern economy, and the modernization from above, from the state- or private-funded factories (as a metaphor of the modern organization of the society) to the modern society.

The former, more liberal view, shared by entrepreneurs, some economists, and rather few politicians was—and is—based on the belief that the direct intervention of the state may do more harm than good to the economy. This belief is not always true, but it seems that when the institutions are relatively weak, like in Poland, the state as the modernizing factor is not very effective. It is my opinion that the experience of the failed, make-believe modernization of the socialist state ensured the prevalence of this view during the transformative reforms and brought about enormously successful modernization.

The other view, dominating in almost the whole period discussed here, was based on the belief that in the situation of backwardness the state is the only entity capable of initiating and implementing economic and social modernization. In other words, it was the conviction that in the case of the shortage of private capital and the lack of human capital, infrastructure and technology, state intervention can stimulate the economy in the long term and make it attain the same level as, or even—as the communists believed—surpass the West (by means of creating infrastructure or industrialization). This belief underpinned the investments conducted by Staszic, and then by Drucki-Lubecki in the eighteenth and early nineteenth centuries; it also underlay the 4-year plan designed by Eugeniusz Kwiatkowski and its 15-year continuation, which were supposed to reduce the social and regional disparities in the Second Republic of Poland and make it catch up with the West. The goal was to build the foundation for further capitalist development by means of etatist tools, and the fundamental conviction was that the state, embodied by state officials and bureaucrats, had all the expertise concerning the organization of this process. Admittedly, these ideas were adopted in the West, as the cameralist policy of the Kingdom of Prussia or the American New Deal. However, these solutions were either abandoned as ineffective (like in Prussia, after the humiliating defeat in the Napoleonic war), or essentially different (like the New Deal, where the dominant role was still played by the private sector, even if supported by the state policy). It is worth noting that sometimes Polish economic liberals, who did not believe in the state as an engine of modernization, shared with etatists the mechanistic view of societal modernization (from—in this case private, not public one—factory to modern society).

Poland's discontinuous political status was paralleled by territorial dislocations. Throughout the period, there was the gradual loss of territory in the east, taken over by Russia. Poland's eastern border moved towards the west in each successive incarnation of the state. Additionally, Poland's western border was moved in the same direction after WWII. In effect, the overlap of the territories of all the successive Polish states is very small. The present-day Polish territory comprises less than 40% of the Commonwealth in its shape after the First Partition in 1772, and only slightly more than 50% of the territory of the Second Republic of Poland. Additionally, after 1945, about 30% of Poland's territory found itself within its borders for the first time in the historic period covered by this book, though some of this area had been a part of Poland before it (i.e. before 1772).

The territorial changes entailed significant relocations of the Polish population. In the nineteenth century, the relocations were the result of establishing the borders of the partitioning states. Later, in the aftermath of the subsequent uprisings (1830–1831 and 1863–1864), there were considerable international migrations, which meant an outflow of part of the elite and—in economic terms—can be seen as a serious, permanent loss of human capital. The ethnic structure of the central and eastern regions of the former Commonwealth was affected by the Russian regulations concerning the settlement of Jews (establishing the Pale of Settlement), which resulted in the rapid growth of the Jewish population in the western provinces of the Russian Empire, particularly in towns, and in the migration of Russian Jews to the Kingdom of Poland, because the territory of Jewish settlement in Russia was diminished, Jews were expelled from Moscow and St. Petersburg and there were numerous pogroms and anti-Jewish tumults in Russian cities at the turn of the nineteenth century.

In the twentieth century, the relocations of the population were the result of war and border changes. Large-scale migrations occurred during and after WWI, such as the voluntary and forced relocations of the population of the Congress Kingdom into Russia and back, or the emigration of the German population from the territories incorporated into the newly established Second Republic of Poland. The next demographic shock took place on the Polish lands during WWII. As a result of German and Soviet policy, about 6 million Polish citizens lost their lives, including up to 3 million citizens of Jewish origin (as a result of the German policy of *Endlösung*), which practically annihilated the Jewish minority in Poland. The post-war period was a time of enormous forced relocations of the population, resulting from the border changes and from the communist party's policy towards ethnic minorities. The Germans still living in the post-German regions were expelled within the subsequent decade, the Ukrainian and Lemko minorities were relocated within Poland and to the USSR; some of the Polish population from the formerly Polish regions incorporated into the USSR were repatriated, and considerable numbers of people migrated from the central and eastern areas to the western post-German lands.

From the last decades of the nineteenth century onwards, the Polish lands were the scene of mass labour migrations. Even though they stopped during wars or periods of closing the borders, the successive waves of migration—before WWI, in the interwar period, the family-reunification emigration to Germany of the 1970s, the post-Solidarity emigration of the 1980s, and the post-EU-accession emigration (not described here)— attained a considerable scale, both in numbers and in proportion to the size of local labour force. These migrations were a response to the low nominal and real wage levels and to the inability of sufficiently rapid structural change in the economy to keep up with the demographic change and demand for gainful employment. The size of local urban labour market was limited, and international migration substituted the migration to the cities, like in many other peripheral regions.

The two centuries of modern history were the time of Poland's political, territorial, and, to a certain extent, demographic discontinuity. Border changes, political temporariness, and migrations strongly affected the transformation of the institutions and the social structure, as well as their present form. The process of social modernization started at the end of the eighteenth century, but it was derailed and delayed by wars and recessions. The unsuccessful attempt at state-induced industrialization at the beginning of the nineteenth century, halted after the November Uprising, failed to create an urban industrial society in the Kingdom of Poland. This failure and the defeat of the uprising held this process back for several decades, while it was taking place in the Prussian partition and was practically non-existent in the Austrian Galicia. The enfranchisement reforms emancipated the peasants, but in most of the Polish lands failed to bring about the emergence of modern agriculture and sustained small-scale subsistence farming instead. That model slowed rural-urban migration, which was not stimulated anyway because of the low demand for labour from the modern sectors, particularly in Galicia and the western provinces of the Russian Empire, and in the Congress Kingdom up to the 1870s.

The industrialization of the Polish lands at the turn of the nineteenth century started to change the social and occupational structure of the society. Yet, the economic structure it created in large parts of Poland was dual in nature, with a limited number of modern industrial centres and endless agricultural, rural and backward peripheries. The change, however quick and seemingly permanent, with hopes of a successful transformation of the peripheries in the near future, was abruptly stopped by WWI. As a result, the social structure of the Second Republic of Poland was obsolete, with subsistence peasant agriculture, traditional manufacturing based on crafts and hand production (once more, the dual industrial structure was recreated), and archaic, dispersed trade. The attempt at top-down modernization conducted in the second half of the 1930s, when the state-led industrialization was expected to lead to the social change, brought little success, due to the limited resources of the state, the smallness of the territory impacted by the intervention, and the outbreak of WWII.

In the aftermath of the war, the social structure of Poland was disrupted again, and the demographic loss involved the disappearance of a substantial portion of the upper and middle classes. Additionally, the annihilation of the Polish Jews, constituting much of the lower middle class and playing a vital role in trade and the SME manufacturing sector, particularly in eastern and central parts of the country, left gaping holes in the social and professional structure of Poland. In effect, after the war and post-war displacement of territory and resettlements the Polish society became a mono-ethnic (like it had never been in history), mostly peasant. The post-war relocations and reconstruction brought large-scale upward social mobility, which was made possible by the huge number of vacant positions in the social and professional structure, and by the colonization of the post-German lands, which were better urbanized and industrialized than the other Polish regions, particularly the areas from which the settlers originally came.

As a result, in the first decades of the socialist Poland an socialist industrial society was formed, with the growing proportion of the urban working class. The crisis of industrialization model, resembling the Second Industrial Revolution in technology, organization of production, and enterprise structure, soon stopped the upward mobility opportunities, and the standard of living of the newly formed working and middle class in the successive decades became increasingly unfavourable compared with their aspirations. Further social change and modernization turned out impossible in the totalitarian, and then authoritarian communist regime and centrally planned economy. Unintended by communists fossilization of the social structure was enhanced by the growing tensions within the system, as the ruling party made every effort to retain the power and the control of the economy and the society, which was increasingly less productive and increasingly more distressed by the over-whelming corruption, clientelism, and nepotism of the socialist bureau-cracy. This resulted in the successive waves of social unrest, in which the economic demands were increasingly supported with political ones. The success of the *Solidarność* Movement of 1980–1981, and then in 1989 the capitulation of the socialist government, returning to the negotia-tions with the opposition and agreeing to the system transformation, can be regarded as the success of the workers' emancipation effort made throughout the state socialism period. Even though the results of the transformation turned out different from the workers' expectations, as the urban working class gradually disappeared, many of its members and their children gained unprecedented opportunities to fulfil their goals and ambitions.

The transformation itself resulted in the rapid adjustment of the social structure to the model characteristic of the modern industrial and post-industrial societies. In particular, for the first time in the history of Poland, the strong and relatively affluent middle class was formed on the basis of the emerging structures of a modern market economy. It strongly influenced the transformation process itself, and the three key elements of the Polish long-term economic success were the talent and diligence of Polish entrepreneurs, who quickly acquired the rules of the market econ-omy, the flexibility of the intelligentsia, who turned into a class of profes-sionals and specialists, and the growing numbers of qualified workers. Admittedly, however, the transformation brought the growth of social disparities and the sense of relative deprivation among the lower classes.

In view of the particularly adverse political and social processes within the period discussed in this book, how can Poland's economic develop-ment be interpreted? The territorial fragmentation and changes as well as the mass relocations of the population rendered the conditions for devel-opment far more difficult than those in many other regions of Europe. The division of the territory up to WWI destroyed the uniform internal market and economically connected the particular regions of Poland with external metropoles during the Industrial Revolution and the first globalization. In effect, all the macroeconomic aggregates presented in this book describing Poland's development at that time are artificial, because the Polish lands were integral parts of three Central- and East-European empires.

In the twentieth century, Poland was restored twice, each time on a different territory, and both times, particularly after WWII, the population underwent mass relocations and big structural changes in the aftermath of the war. Even though a uniform economic organism was rebuilt, these experiences hampered its development. After WWI, the period of stability had to be preceded by the reintegration of the internal market and the creation of a homogeneous institutional structure. It was a long process, impeded by the successive economic difficulties, such as hyperinflation, the customs war with Germany or the Great Depression, and by the disadvantageous international situation; therefore, it was not finished before the outbreak of WWII.

The fragmentation of the political space of Eastern and Central Europe during the interwar period allowed for the creation of nation states in this region, but it also resulted in the disintegration of the existing market structures and the free trade zones (Austrian, German, and Russian), which adversely affected economic development, particularly that of the Second Republic of Poland. The Russian market, which had been one of the key markets for the Polish economy, was completely lost due to the autarkic policy of the USSR, and the access to the other key market, German, was also considerably limited.

Thus, after the economically unsuccessful interwar period, it was after WWII when appropriate conditions were finally created for the reconstruction of a uniform internal market, despite the war damage, war losses, and another mass relocations. Unfortunately, Poland could not take advantage of the favourable conditions which were the springboard for development, for example, the southern European countries equally damaged by the war, because the political and economic system imposed by the USSR was a permanent, insurmountable barrier to dynamic development, due to the inherent inefficiency of central planning, the ineffective management model of the economy and of enterprises, and the anti-development political and social institutions created and sustained by the communist regime.

As a result, between 1914 and 1989, Poland (or the Polish lands in the periods when the Polish state did not exist) developed slowly because of both endo- and exogenous barriers to development. However, it was not a time without success; after WWI, the involvement of a part of the

Polish political elite and the favourable circumstances put Poland back on the map, and the communist rule rebuilt the homogeneous structure of the state and promoted industrialization and the development of transport, power, and communications infrastructure. Admittedly, these changes were costly both economically and socially, and in 1989, a good deal of the infrastructure and industrial facilities were obsolete or worn; however, the capital accumulated in this way and the relatively high labour and human capital resources turned out to be important factors determining the high rate of Poland's development during the transformation. Besides, the relatively successful adaptation of the Western models in the initial stage of the structural reforms created the institutional framework for the rapid development after 1989.

However, it has to be noted that the development during the transformation was mostly extensive—it was based on the proper, effective management of the existing material capital, the cheap and easily available labour and the human capital. Furthermore, the inflow of foreign investment and capital alleviated the problem with which generations of Polish reformers had been grappling for 200 years, the shortage of local capital. Additionally, the demographic situation at the time created exceptionally favourable conditions for development, particularly the demographic dividend—a rapid growth of the resources due to the echo baby boom of the 1980s entering the job market and a simultaneous rapid fall of total fertility rate (TFR), which temporarily lowered the demographic dependency ratio. The development in that period had features of dependent development—it was based on three factors, the low wage level (in relation to Western Europe) and converging productivity, particularly in the modern sectors of the economy; the availability of the labour force and high unemployment; and the inflow of direct investment into labour-intensive rather than capital-intensive sectors. The Polish companies were mostly in the midstream of global value chains, with relatively low value added.

The accession to the European Union brought further advantages, gradually increasing Poland's credibility as a country suitable for foreign investment, as it effectively adopted better institutional solutions and improved the efficiency of its public institutions. The influx of European funding started already in the mid-1990s and gradually increased, helping to improve the quality of transport infrastructure and public services, but also supporting the development of the private sector, which was particularly important for small- and medium-size enterprises.

Let us try to analyse the scale of the present and past success and failure in a broader perspective. However, in the case of Poland, such analysis presents considerable difficulties because of its particular history. Over the last 200 years, Poland has suffered not only the discontinuity as a political entity, but also repeated changes of its territory and population. At the beginning of the period under discussion, Poland had a territory of over 730,000 km². Then it was partitioned and ceased to exist, and when it was restored by Napoleon (the Duchy of Warsaw) and Alexander I (the Kingdom of Poland), it was only on a far smaller area. Both these political entities were relatively small and constituted about 50% and 40% of the present-day territory of Poland, respectively. This area was included into the Polish states restored after WWI (in its entirety) and WWII (except a small area in the north-east). The Second Republic of Poland had an area of almost 390,000 km²; its western border was almost identical to the one before the First Partition, but in the east, the territory was significantly reduced. The present-day territory of Poland, shaped after WWII, only partly covers the area of the Commonwealth from before the partitions (the common area is about 200,000 km², less than 30% of the territory of the Commonwealth) or of the Second Republic (the overlap constitutes about half of the territory of the Second Republic and about two-thirds of present-day Poland). The territorial changes were followed by mass migrations, primarily in the aftermath of wars, particularly WWI and WWII.

In effect it is hardly possible to measure the economic development of the Polish lands in comparison to other countries. The study of the present-day territory, tempting as it seems, is necessarily biased because of the territorial and population changes. For instance, up to 1945, the western part of present-day Poland was inhabited by Germans, and its economic development in the nineteenth century took place within Germany; however, during and after WWII, the area was destroyed by war activity and the slash-and-burn policy of the Soviet occupation, and its German population was almost entirely expelled and replaced with Poles, so the history of its economic development can be seen as having started anew. The border change, the population exchange, and the destruction of infrastructure render all comparisons between the pre- and post-WWII periods questionable. This is probably the most compelling example, but similar difficulties appear while comparing, for example, the territories of the Second Republic of Poland or the Commonwealth.

In light of these challenges, I will focus on the development of the area which was part of all the Polish sovereign and autonomous political entities, that is, the Commonwealth after the First Partition, the Duchy of Warsaw, the Second Republic of Poland, the Polish People's Republic and the present Polish Republic. This common area corresponds to the territory of the Congress Kingdom (except the aforementioned north-east sliver). Its population was relatively immobile (in the Polish context), though its size and structure were affected by, for example, the relocations of Jews from Russia at the end of the nineteenth century, the Holocaust, or the internal migrations connected with the development of Warsaw as an administrative and academic centre.

Table A.5 in Annex presents the GDP per capita of the area in question in light of the estimates and data concerning the GDP per capita of Poland. It can be seen that particularly in the periods of political stability this area had a higher growth rate than that of the rest of Poland. In the periods of political discontinuity (such as the time after 1830), the area of the Kingdom of Poland developed similarly to the other Polish lands. This may indicate the significance of political and territorial discontinuity in hindering development. If the development of the area of the former Congress Kingdom is compared with that of the neighbouring countries with experiences of political discontinuity but much smaller territorial and population dislocations, that is, Czechoslovakia and Hungary, the effect of these phenomena is even more pronounced. The gap between these two countries and the area of the Congress Kingdom (comparable in terms of the area and population sizes) grew steadily from WWI onwards.

In this context, it is important to compare Poland to other countries in the region which were similar in some respects but had a different institutional path dependency. Both the bourgeois Czechoslovakia (here, always compared as one entity) and Hungary developed at a similar rate throughout the period. The gap between Poland and these countries

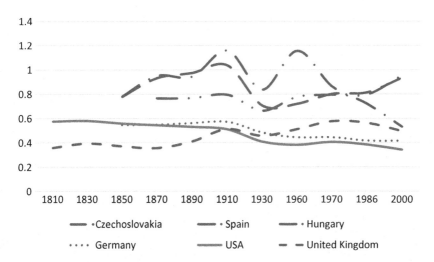

1.4
1.2
1
0.8
0.6
0.4
0.2
0
1810 1830 1850 1870 1890 1910 1930 1960 1970 1986 2000

- •Czechoslovakia   — • Spain   — • Hungary
•••• Germany   — USA   — — United Kingdom

Graph 12.1 GDP per capita of the territory of the Kingdom of Poland (Russian partition) in comparison to neighbouring countries and leaders of growth. Source: As in Table A.5 in Annex

started to grow after WWI, but it does not seem to be connected with the existence of the divergent economic models in history, but rather with challenges of political reintegration of Polish lands in sovereign state and war losses and destruction (see Graph 12.1).

In state socialism, regions of central and eastern Poland developed relatively quickly (the GDP per capita of the Congress Kingdom between 1960 and 1986 grew from about 110% to 115% of the Polish average, mostly because of the relatively slower development of the urbanized regions of south-western Poland). Anyway, the area's catching up with the neighbouring socialist countries and with the West was limited. Between 1960 and 1986, the gap between this area and Hungary remained stable, and in the case of Czechoslovakia it slightly narrowed (respectively, the GDP per capita of this area was 78% and 80% of the GDP per capita of Hungary, and 72% and 81% of Czechoslovakia). The changes after 1989, particularly the shock therapy, the reconstruction of the market system and restoring Warszawa as the main political and economic centre of Poland created favourable conditions for dynamic economic development and catching up with the other countries. In 2000 the GDP per capita of the area of the former Congress Kingdom was about

93% of the GDP per capita of the Czech Republic and Slovakia and 95% of that of Hungary.

It is possible that, apart from the successful shock therapy, the institutional factor which determined the economic success of the period was the unique structure of agriculture. Unlike Hungary or Czechoslovakia, Poland retained individual private ownership and basic market mechanisms, which might have facilitated the emergence of the institutions of the capitalist economy after 1989.

Poland's situation in relation to the leaders of growth, both the neighbouring Germany and the global leaders, that is, Great Britain in the nineteenth century and the USA in the twentieth century, was even worse, as it is shown on Graph 12.1. Over the subsequent decades of the nineteenth century gap remained stable, but successive decades of war, recurring costs of re-integrations of the state, and introduction of the socialist economy resulted in stabilization of aforementioned relation (or even further decline, as in case of Germany) on very low levels and further deep decline in early period of transformation in 1990s. The catching-up period started once again in late 1990s and is continuing until 2018. Thus, without experience of permanent displacements of territory and populations and extremely destructive wars, the history of Polish development in modern Europe would be similar to the histories of Polish neighbours, CEE countries. They are still much less developed than Western Europe, but better than poor countries in Eastern Europe, Central Asia, and many other regions.

To sum up, the periods of relative decline of Polish economic development in relation to the global leaders can be observed primarily during the early industrialization (in Great Britain) and then between WWI and the fall of communism. This may lead to some conclusions concerning the economic history of Poland, as described here.

Firstly, the imperfect Polish social, economic and political institutions did not have a significant influence on development in the nineteenth century. In relation to the countries of the economic centre, the gap started to grow as a result of the differences in the timing of industrialization as well as institutional discontinuity (the beginning of the growth of the gap is marked by the final loss of autonomy in 1830 and the inability to conduct the self-dependent economic policy). Then in the twentieth century the key factors were the disintegration of internal markets as a result of the outbreak of WWI and the cost of the reintegration of the state (the recurrent changes of the territory of the independent state), but also war damage and the post-WWII introduction of the communist system and dismantling the market.

Secondly, in the case of Poland, a planned modernization effort brought hardly any effect. The results were far from expected in the case of state-induced industrialization conducted by Staszic (1820–1830), or Kwiatkowski's industrial policy, or the attempts of communist modernization in the versions devised by Stalin or Gierek. Instead of helping to narrow the gap, they resulted in widening it (though in the case of Kwiatkowski's reforms, there are not enough data to determine their success, or lack thereof, and the project itself was interrupted by the outbreak of the war, probably on the verge of the emergence of fiscal problems). Possibly the reason was not only the inefficiency of the state investment policy (and, more broadly, of the allocation of resources), which is an obvious explanation, but not sufficient in the context of the development experience of the South-East Asian countries. An important factor might be the fact that the state's investment decisions were hasty attempts to solve development problems, rather than strategic decisions aimed at sustaining development. In this sense, the decisions concerning fiscal expansion may have actually been overdue. The situation changed after Poland's accession to the EU, when the inflow of European development funds helped to sustain economic growth for next decades.

Thirdly, the context of Poland's development was extremely unfavourable, and that is where we can find many reasons for the backwardness and delayed convergence, postponed until the system transformation. In 1989 practically all exogenous barriers to development ceased to exist—the transformation was the last period of political discontinuity, but this time, it brought about the positive results of the restoration of liberal democracy and market economy, and the inclusion of Poland into the global flow of income. The favourable conditions were enhanced by the policy of the USA and European countries, and later, the European funds and the EU's integration process, which positively affected the quality of Polish regulations and institutions. Fifty years after the war, the new territory was fully integrated in terms of economy and social structure, and the negative effects of territorial changes and migrations were no longer perceived. In the new market environment, the communist investment in infrastructure and education finally started to bring profit, and the adaptation of the population to the market rules was quick and relatively smooth. These were probably the key factors which laid the foundation for the extraordinary economic success of the last decades.

*   *   *

The two centuries of the economic history of Poland discussed here were the time of development and attempts to catch up with the West. Most of the time, these attempts brought limited success at best, as throughout the industrial period Poland remained significantly less advanced than the global technological leader. Throughout the twentieth century, Poland's growth rate was even lower than that of other similar, neighbouring countries. It seems that the existing human, labour, and capital resources were not managed efficiently enough, which was often determined by external factors; however, some of these external factors were in fact the long-term results of the ill-advised decisions of Poland's political leaders. Additionally, not all the ideas and designs for development were prudent—apart from the persistent belief in state-induced modernization ensuring the leap forward, there was the constant mistake of ignoring the local conditions, which were rarely considered either as barriers, potentially hampering the implementation of the grand designs, or as possible factors accelerating the development. Poland was a backward, peripheral country imitating the solutions applied in the top economies of the time, and, unsurprisingly, this strategy long failed to bring positive results; it was only after 1989, when the extremely favourable international situation made the reception of external models, properly adjusted to the local conditions, enable the long-awaited development success.

Economic development has been high in Poland for an exceptionally long time, almost three decades (1991–2018), without periods of recession. It confirms the great success of the transformation reforms and the correctness of the strategies adopted by the reformers. The first decade of the twenty-first century, particularly after 2004, that is, in the post-EU accession period, not discussed in this book, brought the further, increasing inflow of European funding, stimulating the economy and supporting the convergence. The European funds helped to accelerate the modernization of the infrastructure and increase the attractiveness of the country for foreign investment; they advanced the improvement of public services and supported private entrepreneurship. However, at the time, the demographic dividend started to diminish, which potentially threatens the long-term sustainability of the current development model.

In forthcoming decades, the scale of the contemporary success will be measured by the ability of Poland's economy to remain among the best developed and most advanced economies of the world. I sincerely hope that this time it will be the Polish people who decide, and not external factors.

Annex

Table A.1 Population of Poland (contemporary borders), thousands of people

	1810	1825	1843	1857	1868	1890	1910
Prussian part	5091	6451	8083	9353	10,350	12,345	14,158
Russian part	3267	3494	4628	5168	5856	8258	12,205
Austrian part	1158	1416	1646	1853	1968	2300	2690
				1931	1960	1970	1986	2000

	1931	1960	1970	1986	2000
Prussian part	5757 (14,567)	12,790	14,442	17,029	17,612
Russian part	11,706	12,567	13,498	15,722	15,286
Austrian part	3766	4170	4627	5324	5358
Northern and Western territories (1939)	8810				
Eastern territories of interwar Poland (incorporated by USSR after 1945)	12,800				

Source: Own calculations (Główny Urząd Statystyczny 1993; Wyczański 2003; Gawryszewski 2005)
Note: For year 1931, population of Prussian part in borders of Second Republic of Poland (in brackets in contemporary borders, including Northern and Western Territories), population of Northern and Western territories and population of Eastern territories (Kresy) incorporated by USSR after WWII

© The Author(s) 2018
P. Koryś, *Poland From Partitions to EU Accession*,
https://doi.org/10.1007/978-3-319-97126-1

Table A.2 Urbanization rates (populations of towns 5000+ as a share of total population)

	1810 (%)	1825 (%)	1843 (%)	1857 (%)	1868 (%)	1890 (%)	1910 (%)
Austrian part	4	4	5	6	8	13	19
Russian part	3	5	5	7	12	18	29
Prussian part	6	8	10	12	15	20	29
Poland, contemporary territory	5	6	7	9	13	18	27

	1921 (%)	1931 (%)	1950 (%)	1970 (%)	1988 (%)	2010 (%)
Poland, contemporary territory	21	24	34	49	60	58

Source: Own calculations (Karpineć 1932; Jelonek 1967) and various statistical yearbooks of the Republic of Poland

Note: For years 1921 and 1931, only the territory of the Second Republic of Poland

Table A.3 Population of the largest cities and towns of Polish lands, 1810–1990. Thousands of people

1810	1868	1910	1931	1960	1990
78 Warszawa	255 Warszawa	895 Warszawa	1178 Warszawa	1171 Warszawa	1655 Warszawa
68 Wrocław	**208 Wrocław**	**512 Wrocław**	**625 Wrocław**	723 Łódź	852 Łódź
56 Wilno	**89 Gdańsk**	424 Łódź	605 Łódź	490 Kraków	748 Kraków
44 Lwów	*87 Lwów*	**236 Szczecin**	*316 Lwów*	**443 Wrocław**	**642 Wrocław**
37 Gdańsk	**76 Szczecin**	*210 Lwów*	**269 Szczecin**	418 Poznań	589 Poznań
24 Kraków	*60 Wilno*	*205 Wilno*	247 Poznań	**297 Gdańsk**	**465 Gdańsk**
21 Szczecin	56 Poznań	**170 Gdańsk**	**229 Gdańsk**	**279 Szczecin**	**412 Szczecin**
17 Elbląg	50 Kraków	157 Poznań	221 Kraków	275 Katowice	380 Bydgoszcz
16 Poznań	36 Łódź	143 Kraków	*196 Wilno*	240 Bydgoszcz	367 Katowice
10 Brzeg	**31 Elbląg**	99 Sosnowiec	**130 Zabrze**	**194 Zabrze**	350 Lublin
10 Świdnica	28 Bydgoszcz	80 Białystok	127 Katowice	188 Lublin	268 Białystok
9 Legnica	**23 Legnica**	75 Częstochowa	118 Bydgoszcz	**186 Bytom**	259 Sosnowiec
8 Głogów	22 Płock	73 Chorzów	118 Częstochowa	168 Częstochowa	257 Częstochowa
8 Grudziądz	22 Tarnów	**68 Bytom**	113 Lublin	153 Gdynia	251 Gdynia
8 Zielona Góra	**21 Gorzów Wlkp.**	**67 Gliwice**	**111 Gliwice**	150 Chorzów	**230 Bytom**
8 Stargard Szczeciński	21 Lublin	**67 Legnica**	109 Sosnowiec	**139 Gliwice**	226 Radom
8 Nysa	20 Chorzów	65 Lublin	**99 Bytom**	135 Radom	**222 Gliwice**
7 Przemyśl	**19 Nysa**	**63 Zabrze**	91 Białystok	135 Ruda Śląska	213 Kielce
7 Kalisz	**18 Głogów**	**59 Elbląg**	81 Chorzów	134 Sosnowiec	**203 Zabrze**
7 Rawicz	**17 Stargard Szczeciński**	58 Bydgoszcz	78 Radom	126 Białystok	200 Toruń

Source: Own estimations (Karpineć 1932; Jelonek 1967) and various statistical yearbooks.
Note: In bold towns located in Western and Northern Territories (and Gdańsk). In italicized towns from the eastern territories of the Second Republic of Poland (Kresy). In this table, only contemporary Polish names are used

Table A.4 Regional shares of GDP (contemporary borders)

GDP	1790	1810	1830	1850	1870	1890	1910	1930	1960	1970	1986	2000
Prussian partition	58.2	61.7	65.0	65.4	64.0	59.8	53.6	49.0	40.4	39.2	40.8	43.6
– Of which Western and Nortern territories								35.0	23.4	23.3	24.9	25.5
Austrian partition	12.5	10.5	10.0	8.8	8.2	7.4	6.5	8.0	12.5	14.1	11.7	12.2
Russian partition	29.2	27.9	25.0	25.9	27.8	32.7	39.9	41.0	46.9	46.7	47.5	44.2

Source: Own calculations (Zieliński 1974; Główny Urząd Statystyczny 1989; Bukowski et al. 2018)
Note: Calculations for the communist period based on corrected estimations of National Income (Material Product System). Methods of correction, like in Fallenbuchl (1985), Główny Urząd Statystyczny (1989)

Table A.5 Regional GDP per capita in Poland (contemporary borders, G-K dollars 2011)

GDP	1790	1810	1830	1850	1870	1890	1910	1930	1960	1970	1986	2000
Prussian partition	1625	1727	1931	2237	2644	3358	4479		5832	7621	10,286	13,384
Austrian partition	1359	1289	1358	1492	1787	2234	2882		5534	8547	9434	12,310
Russian partition (Kingdom of Poland)	1217	1217	1370	1574	2033	2746	3868		6891	9705	12,970	15,633
Poland	1431	1491	1687	1954	2348	3006	4065	3879	6253	8613	11,275	14,132

Source: Own calculations (Zieliński 1974; Główny Urząd Statystyczny 1989; Bukowski et al. 2018; Inklaar et al. 2018)
Note: See comments for Table A.4. For years 1790–1910 GDP per capita estimations from Bukowski et al. (2018), since 1921 from Inklaar et al. (2018)

Table A.6 Occupational structure

Russian part	1810 (%)	1830 (%)	1860 (%)	1897 (%)	1921 (%)	1936 (%)
I	78	73	74	68	74	52
II	9	9	13	12	17	25
III	13	18	13	20	9	23

Prussian Part	1810 (%)		1867 (%)	1895 (%)	1921 (%)	1936 (%)
I	70	X	66	55	68	38
II	13	X	16	26	14	32
III	17	X	18	19	18	29

Austrian part	1810 (%)		1880 (%)	1900 (%)	1921 (%)	1936 (%)
I	81	X	80	82	82	64
II	9	X	6	6	7	15
III	10	X	14	12	10	20

Western and Northern Territories	1936 (%)	1950 (%)	1988 (%)
I	28	50	23
II	32	25	36
III	40	25	41

Poland	1810 (%)	1859/1867/ 1869 (%)	1895/1897/ 1900 (%)	1921 (%)	1931 (%)	1950 (%)	1970 (%)	1988 (%)	1995 (%)
I	76	71	64	76	70	57	38	27	28
II	10	13	18	10	13	23	35	36	30
III	14	16	18	14	17	20	27	37	42

Source: Sobieszczański (1860), Załęski (1876, 1901), Grossmann (1925), Tipton (1976), Kociszewski (1999), Szuman (1999) and Koryś and Tymiński (2015) and various statistical yearbooks of Russia, Prussia, Germany, and Austria in the nineteenth century and the Republic of Poland in the twentieth century
Note: Year 1810—data for Duchy of Warsaw (Russian, Prussian and Austrian parts). Year 1921 and 1931, see note for Table A.1 in Annex. Territories of partitions included only in the contemporary territory of Poland, cf. Map 11.1

Bibliography

Bukowski, M., Koryś, P., Leszczyńska, C., et al. (2018). Urban population and economic development: Urbanization and approximation of GDP per capita in history—The case of the Polish lands in the 19th century. *Mimeo.*

Fallenbuchl, Z. M. (1985). *National income statistics for Poland, 1970–1980.* Washington, DC: World Bank.

Gawryszewski, A. (2005). *Ludność Polski w XX wieku.* Warszawa: Instytut Geografii i Przestrzennego Zagospodarowania im. Stanisława Leszczyckiego PAN.

Główny Urząd Statystyczny. (1989). *Dochód narodowy Polski według województw w 1986 r.* Warszawa: Zakład Badań Statystyczno-Ekonomicznych Głównego Urzędu Statystycznego i Polskiej Akademii Nauk.

Główny Urząd Statystyczny. (1993). *Historia Polski w liczbach: ludność, terytorium.* Główny Urząd Statystyczny.

Grossmann, H. (1925). *Struktura społeczna i gospodarcza Księstwa Warszawskiego na podstawie spisów ludności 1808–1810.* Warszawa: Główny Urząd Statystyczny.

Inklaar, R., de Jong, H., Bolt, J., & van Zanden, J. (2018). *Rebasing "Maddison": New income comparisons and the shape of long-run economic development.* Groningen Growth and Development Centre, University of Groningen.

Jelonek, A. (1967). *Ludność miast i osiedli typu miejskiego na ziemiach Polski od 1810 do 1960 r.* Warszawa: Instytut Geografii Polskiej Akademii Nauk.

© The Author(s) 2018
P. Koryś, *Poland From Partitions to EU Accession,*
https://doi.org/10.1007/978-3-319-97126-1

Karpineć, Ì. (1932). *Ilość osad miejskich byłej Galicji i podział ich na miasta i miasteczka*. Lwów: asa im. J. Mianowskiego, Instytut Popierania Polskiej Twórczości Naukowej.

Kociszewski, J. (1999). *Proces integracji gospodarczej ziem zachodnich i północnych z Polską*. Wrocław: Wydawnictwo Akademii Ekonomicznej.

Koryś, P., & Tymiński, M. (2015). *Occupational structure in the Polish territories at the turn of the 20th (1895–1900) century*. Faculty of Economic Sciences, University of Warsaw.

Sobieszczański, F. M. (1860). *Kalendarz wydawany przez Obserwatoryum Astronomiczne Warszawskie na rok zwyczajny 1861*. Warszawa: Obserwatoryum Astronomiczne Warszawskie.

Szuman, A. (1999). Przeobrażenia struktury społeczno-zawodowej ludności Polski w XX wieku. *Ruch Prawniczy, Ekonomiczny i Socjologiczny, LXI*, 187–202.

Tipton, F. B. (1976). *Regional variations in the economic development of Germany during the nineteenth century*. Wesleyan University Press.

Various Statistical Yearbooks of Austria, Prussia, Germany, Russia (until 1918) and Republic of Poland (after 1918).

Wyczański, A. (Ed.). (2003). *Historia Polski w liczbach. T. 1: Państwo, społeczeństwo*. Warszawa: Zakład Wydawnictw Statystycznych.

Załęski, W. (1876). *Statystyka porównawcza Królestwa Polskiego: ludność i stosunki ekonomiczne*. Warszawa: Gebethner i Wolff.

Załęski, W. (1901). *Królestwo Polskie pod względem statystycznym. Cz. 2: Statystyka zajęć i przemysłu*. Warszawa: Skład Glowny w Ksiegarni Jana Fiszera.

Zieliński, M. (1974). Próba określenia rozmiarów dysproporcji międzyregionalnych w stopie życiowej ludności i sposobów ich zmniejszenia. *Annales Universitatis Mariae Curie-Skłodowska, 8*, 123–134.

Index

A

Abramovitz, Moses, 9
Accumulation, 298
Acemoglu, Daron, 3, 13
Agrarian reform, 24, 95, 107, 116,
    123, 132, 140, 143, 156, 168,
    177
Agricultural output, 306
Agriculture, 138, 140, 240, 241,
    292, 305
Agroindustry, 137, 140, 141
Akamatsu, Kanamu, 11, 13
Aldcroft, Derek, 2, 4
Alexander I Romanov, 82, 357
Alexander II Romanov, 130
Amoral familism, 263
Amsden, Alice, 9, 13
Anglo-Polish Agreement of Mutual
    Assistance (1939), 212

Annexation of Austria (*Anschluss*),
    212
Annexation of Czechoslovakia, 212
Anti-communist resistance in
    Poland, 268
Anti-Jewish measures, 261
Anti-Jewish violence, 261, 263
Anti-Semitism, 162
Apparatus of control and repression,
    293
Arciszewski, Tomasz, 256
Army, 36, 44, 46, 47, 50, 52, 63, 64,
    68, 78, 80–82, 84, 85, 94, 98,
    101, 107, 196–200, 209, 222,
    230, 238, 240, 255, 257, 259,
    261, 262, 268, 269, 272, 273,
    289, 293, 311, 322
Assembly, 120
Augustus II Wettin, 43

Augustus III Wettin, 43, 47
Austria, 47, 79, 195
Austrian partition, 116, 119
    backwardness, 106
    education, 135
    Josephine reform, 93, 97
Austrian School of Economics, 213
Autumn of nations, 348
Autonomy of Galicia, 120
AWS, 325

B

Backwardness, 7–15, 17, 21, 40,
    186, 335, 349, 361
    in Poland, recognition, 49
    social reforms, 49
Badeni, Kazimierz, 120, 151
Balcerowicz, Leszek, 280, 324, 326,
    327, 335, 336
Balicki, Zygmunt, 160
Banking, 307
Banking crisis of 1793, 69, 96
Bank of Agriculture, 308
    May 1926 *coup d'état*, 210
Bank of Poland, 102, 136, 243
Bank of State Economy, 239
Bar Confederation, 44, 45, 48
Barlicki, Norbert, 215
Battle for trade, 278, 296, 307
Bauman, Zygmunt, 269
Bazar, 132, 137
Bełchatów, 304
Belka, Marek, 326
Berend, Ivan, 3
Bereza Kartuska, 210
Biała, 141
Białowieża, 329

Białystok, 140, 141, 230, 257
Bielecki, Jan Krzysztof, 324
Bierut, Bolesław, 267–269
Bieszczady Mountains, 282
Biskupski, James, 4
Black market, 294, 309
Bobrowski, Czesław, 277
Bobrza, 103
Bobrzyński, Michał, 16, 151, 157
Bochnia, 54, 141
Bogatynia, 304
Border conflicts (1918–1921), 273
Boryslav-Drohobycz area, 178
Borysław, 178
Bourgeoisie, 94, 137, 287
Bożyk, Paweł, 280
Brandenburg, 282
Braudel, Fernand, 7, 15
Bródno, 166
Brus, Włodzimierz, 277–279, 324
Brzeg, 92
Budget, 64, 69, 98, 101, 209, 243,
    336
Bugaj, Ryszard, 280, 328
Bujak, Franciszek, 5
Bulgaria, 273
Burke, Edmund, 62
Buzek, Jerzy, 325
Bydgoszcz, 56
Byelorussia, 329
Byelorussian minority, 229

C

Cameralist model, 88
Camp of National Unity, 209
Carpathian Mountains, 222, 282
Cash rent, 140

Catching-up, 2, 11, 18, 26, 329, 342, 347–363
Catholic Church, 291
Ceausescu, Nicolae, 273
Cegielski, Hipolit, 137, 173
Cegielski enterprise, 239
Census, 90
    of 1790–1791, 57
    of 1921, 222
    of 1931, 222, 235
    Duchy of Warsaw (1808, 1810), 57, 99
    Poland of 1789, 46
    Post-WWII censuses (1950, 1988), 6, 358, 361
    Prussian census, 79, 99
    Rodecki table (1828), 106
    Russian census of 1897, 161, 175
Central bank, 308
Central Industrial Area, 238–240
Central Industrial District, 220, 276
Central Lithuania, 222
Central Planning Commission, 296
Central Planning Committee, 277
Central-Eastern Europe (CEE), 20, 36, 342, 360
Centrally planned economy, 299
Chemical industry, 239
Chernobyl disaster, 304
Chinese model, 302
Chłapowski, Dezydery, 132
Chorzów, 238
Christian Democrats, 218
Chrzanów, 141
Churchill, Winston, 256
Ciechanow, 258
Cieszkowski, August, 121
    Commission of National Education, 45

Cieszyn, 282
Cimoszewicz, Włodzimierz, 324
Cities, 284
    Commonwealth of Poland and Lithuania, 55
Citizen's Committee, 323
Civic Platform (PO), 325
Coal mining, 136, 141, 242, 275
Code of Civil Law (Napoleon), 81
Collectivization, 306
    of agriculture, 259, 278
Colonization of the post-German lands, 296
Comecon, 308
Commission of National Education, 45
Committee for Security and the Protection of Public Welfare, 198
Commonwealth, 15, 16, 35–40, 43, 45, 46, 48, 52, 54–61, 63, 68–70, 77, 79, 82–86, 88, 90–93, 96, 97, 106, 108, 120, 126, 143, 157, 176, 180, 196, 209, 211, 255, 348, 350, 351, 357, 358
Commonwealth of Poland and Lithuania, 211
    banking system, 68
    cities, 37
    Dutch loans, 68
    economic development, 60
    ethnic and religious minorities, 57
    First Partition, 54
    GDP per capita, 61
    Golden Age, 35
    Jews, 58
    manufacturing sector, 65
    model of development, 63

Commonwealth of Poland and
    Lithuania (*cont.*)
  Second Partition, 54
  Sejm in Grodno, 47
  state incomes, 63
  taxation, 63
  urban economy, 66
Communes of Polish People, 121,
    123
Communist Party of the Soviet
    Union, 272
Conference in Magdalenka, 271
Conference in Moscow (1944), 256
Conference in Teheran (1943), 256
Conference in Yalta (1945), 256
Constitutions of Poland, 210, 216,
    324
  Duchy of Warsaw, 87
  Free City of Cracow, 84
  Kingdom of Poland, 94
  of Poland 3rd May, 46
Corruption, 60, 69, 136, 263, 294,
    307
Corvée, 38, 95, 119
Council for Mutual Economic
    Assistance (COMECON),
    271, 275
Cracow Uprising, 120, 134, 162
Creditworthiness, 302
Crimean War, 117, 130
Crony capitalism, 328
Crude oil production, 141
Curzon, George, 199
Curzon line, 282
Customs border, 140
Czartoryski, Adam, 84, 124
Czartoryski family, 121
Czechoslovakia, 222, 282

Czech-Polish conflict, 199
Czech Republic, 198, 199, 329, 360

D

Dąbrowa baisin, 129, 139, 257
Dąbrowa Górnicza, 105, 138, 166
Dąbrowski, Jan Henryk, 84
Daszyńska-Golińska, Zofia, 214
Daszyński, Ignacy, 156, 214
Davies, Norman, 3, 35, 36, 196,
    198, 199, 202
Davout, Marchal
  decline of, 43
Debates on emancipation, 117
December 1970, 270, 291, 293, 300
Decree abolishing serfdom, 119
Dembowski, Stanisław, 123
Demographic dividend, 284, 330,
    331, 356, 363
Democratic Bloc, 266
Democratic Party, 267
de Sismondi, Jean, 122
De-Stalinization, 298
Development economics, 220
Development gap, 122
Dincecco, Mark, 14
Discontinuity, 109
Dmowski, Roman, 156, 159, 160,
    169, 211, 217
Doboszyński, Adam, 218
Drucki-Lubecki, Xawery, 89, 101,
    350
Drzymała, Wojciech, 165
Duchy of Cieszyn, 222
Duchy of Łowicz, 85, 98
Duchy of Siewierz, 78, 85, 98, 105
Duchy of Warsaw, 80, 97, 101

army, 98
cities, 91
fiscal revenue, 98
Jews, 92
population, 92
tax system, 97
Dutch loans, 68
Dutch Republic, 15, 47, 49
Działyński, Tytus, 121
Dzielski, Mirosław, 280

E

Early industrialization, 8, 12, 360
Eastern Galicia, 257
East Galicia, 268
East Germany, 273, 274, 283, 303
East Prussia, 129, 282
Econometric Society, 213
Economic destabilization, 302
Economic development, 1–3, 7, 10,
    12, 14, 17–20, 22, 26, 60, 62,
    86, 88, 89, 105, 121, 123,
    127, 156–158, 160, 171, 172,
    180, 182, 187, 207–246, 255,
    263, 265–314, 342, 354, 355,
    357, 359, 360, 362
Economic growth, 244
Economic policy, 1, 10, 12, 18, 25,
    160, 327, 335, 360
  big push, 220
  building the industrial
    bourgeoisie, 105
  cameralism, 96, 97, 105
  cameralist model, 88
  centrally planned economy, 294,
    299
  mercantilism, 106

state-led industrialization, 24, 103
state socialism, 265, 295
Economic recession of 1980s, 275,
    309
Economy of Second Republic of
    Poland
  customs war with Germany, 355
  15-year plan, 219
  4-year plan (1936–1940), 219
  Grabski macroeconomic
    stabilization policy, 244
  hyperinflation of 1923–1924, 355
ECSC, 271
Education, 227, 290
Elbląg, 56, 92, 220, 291
Emancipation of the working class,
    291
Emigration, 224, 280
  World War II, 262
Employment, 236
Employment structure, 263
Endlösung der Judenfrage, 260
Energy crisis, 301
Enforced collectivization, 291
Enfranchisement, 83, 87, 116–118,
    123, 124, 132, 134, 166, 169,
    172, 349, 352
Enfranchising of the workers, 327
Enlightenment, 45
Enlightenment in Poland, 49
Entrepreneurs, 311
Epstein, Stephan R., 14, 131
Estate, 306
Ethnic and religious minorities, 226
Ethnic structure, 286
Europe Agreement, 323
European Union, 19, 323
Evans Brothers' factory, 139

Evans, Lilpop and Rau, 139
Export-oriented industrialization,
     10, 11, 19
Extermination, 25, 255, 258–261,
     263, 310
Extractive institutions, 3, 13, 17

F

Familia, Czartoryski family, 48, 51
Familia, Czartoryski house, 44
Far-right movements, 326
Feldman, Wilhelm, 6
Fertility, 283
FIAT, 298
Fiedler's factory, 139
15-year plan, 219
First Partition, 45, 53, 54, 63, 64,
     79, 350, 357, 358
Fiscal capacity, 14
Fiscal revenues, 98
Folwark, 62
Forced resettlement of the German
     population, 265, 268, 271
Foreign licences, 297, 301
Foreign loans, 302
Foreign trade, 307
4-year plan (1936–1940), 219
France, 47, 98, 274
Franco-Polish Military Alliance, 212
Free City of Kraków, 82, 84, 97,
     116, 128
Freedom Union (UW), 324, 325
French Revolution, 51
Friedman, Milton, 327

G

Galicia, 5, 83, 92, 106, 119
Galician Slaughter, 120, 134

Garczyński, Stefan, 50
Gawryszewski, Andrzej, 6
Gdańsk, 54–56, 81, 92, 96, 212,
     220, 242, 268, 270, 282, 286,
     290, 291, 293, 303
Gdańsk Voivodeship, 285
Gdynia, 221, 230, 242, 291, 297,
     303
General Governorate, 257, 258, 260
German concentration camps, 257
German historical school of
     economics, 127
Germanization, 133
German-Polish Non-Aggression Pact
     (1934), 212
German-Soviet Neutrality and
     Non-Aggression Pact of 1926,
     211–212
Germany, 195, 261
Gerschenkron, Alexander, 8, 9, 13,
     18, 335
Geyer, Ludwik, 119, 131, 139
Giedroyć, Jerzy, 269
Gierek, Edward, 270, 280, 290,
     300–302, 305, 361
Giertych, Roman, 326
Głąbinski, Stanisław, 216
Gołębiowski, Jerzy, 18
Gołuchowski, Agenor, 120, 151
Gomułka, Stanisław, 216, 327
Gomułka, Władysław, 269, 290,
     298, 300
Gorlice, 178
Governing Commission for Galicia,
     Silesia, Spis and Orava, 198
Government General of Lublin, 196
Government General of Warsaw, 196
Government-in Exile, 276
Grabski, Stanisław, 122, 156, 214,
     267

Grabski, Władysław, 19, 122, 156, 162, 209, 214, 216, 244
Grand Great Duchy of Posen, 82, 83, 220
Great Britain, 15, 47, 49, 274
Great Depression, 218, 230, 231, 235, 242
Great Emigration, 123, 135
Greater Poland, 5, 56, 97, 108, 129, 133, 136, 137, 208, 229, 257
cities of, 91
Great Northern War, 48
Grodek, Andrzej, 5
Grodno, 67, 201
Growth rate, 310
Grudziądz, 220
Grzybek, Dariusz, 6, 156–158
Guzicki, Leszek, 6, 156
Gypsies, 260

H

Habsburg, Joseph II, 24, 186
Habsburgs, 48
Hayek, Friedrich, 8
Heavy industry, 136
Hel, 221
Hirszowicz, Maria, 280
Hohenzollerns, 48
Holocaust, 17, 257
Home Army, 257, 268
Honecker, Erich, 273
Hotel Lambert, 121, 124
Hryniewicz, Janusz, 16, 177
Human capital, 299
Human Development Index, 335
Hungarian revolution of 1956, 269
Husak, Gustav, 273
Huta Bankowa, 138

Huta Katowice, 301, 305
Hyperinflation, 231, 309

I

Ideas
agrarism, 218
anti-Semitism, 217
backwardness, 88
battle for trade, 278
cameralism, 49, 88, 89
communism, 216
concepts of anti-communist opposition, 280
concepts of post-WWII Polish economy, 276
conservatism, 218
de-Stalinization after 1956, 279
development economics, 214
economic schools in interwar Poland, 214
enlightened absolutism, 49
French Enlightenment, 49
Great Depression, 218
Great Emigration, 123, 124
import substitution, 89
January Uprising, 124
Kaleckians' economics, 213
Keynesism, 213
liberalism, 87
loyalist policy, 126
mass privatization, 280
mathematical economics, 213
modernization, 87
nationalism, 216, 217
organic work, 127
Polish Jacobin ideas, 52
positivism, 127
post-war reconstruction, 276

Ideas (*cont.*)
reception of French Revolution, 70
Romanticism, 122
Scottish Enlightenment, 49
socialism, 215
social reform, 127
Stalin model, 277
statism, 219
Utopia of the non-market economy, 296
IG Farben, 260
Ihnatowicz, Ireneusz, 6
Illiteracy, 227, 290
IMF, 271, 275, 327
Immigrants, 138
Immoral practices, 263
Import substitution, 9–11, 13, 18
Inclusion to the nation, 263
Inclusive institutions, 3, 13, 14, 17
Industrialization, 137, 139, 234, 303
Industrialization, first wave of, 9
Industrial output, 304
Industrious revolution, 12, 13
Industry, 202
Infant industry, 9
Inflation, 301
Informal co-ordination mechanisms, 307
Institute of Business Cycles and Prices, 214
Institutionalization of Marxist economics, 277
Intelligentsia, 127, 226, 287, 290, 292, 299
extermination, 263
Internal migrations, 285–288

International Monetary Fund (IMF), 271, 275, 327
International trade, 242, 243
Investment mania of the late 1780s, 69
Iron Curtain, 271, 321

J

Jagiellonian University, 135, 290
Janos, Andrew, 4
Janowski, Maciej, 4, 158
January Uprising, 118, 162
decree abolishing serfdom, 119
Japan, 9
Jaruzelski, Wojciech, 270, 272, 275, 290, 322, 323
Jaszczuk, Bolesław, 279, 300
Jedlicki, Jerzy, 4, 6, 18
Jelonek, Andrzej, 6, 161, 201
Jewish ghettoes, 259
Jews, 57, 228, 241, 258–260, 269, 286, 287, 351
Commonwealth of Poland and Lithuania, 57, 58
Jezierski, Andrzej, 5, 38, 174
Jezierski, Franciszek Salezy, 51
Joseph II Habsburg, 49
Josephine reforms, 79, 97
June 1956, 269, 293
June 1976, 270

K

Kaczyński, Jarosław, 324
Kadar, Janos, 273
Kalecki, Michał, 213, 214, 220, 273, 278, 279

Kalinka, Walerian, 125, 157
Kaliński, Janusz, 5, 338
Kalisz, 89, 92, 106, 108, 136, 139, 201
Kamienna, 103
Kania, Stanisław, 290
Kaps, Klemens, 5, 178, 186
Karpiński, Andrzej, 159, 280
Karwina, 199
Katowice, 285, 303
Katyn massacre, 259
Kawalec, Agnieszka, 5, 179
Keynes, John Maynard, 213
Khrushchev, Nikita, 269
Kielce, 67, 103, 129, 136, 139, 236
Kiev, 163, 170, 197, 199
Kieżun, Witold, 328
Kingdom of Galicia and Lodomeria, 120
    assembly, 120
Kingdom of Lithuania, 197
Kingdom of Poland, 82, 83, 116, 118, 128, 138, 202, 208, 257
    budget, 101
    education, 132
    fiscal revenues, 102
Kizwalter, Tomasz, 6, 158
Kochanowicz, Jacek, 3, 16, 35, 166, 184
Kołakowski, Leszek, 269
Kollontaj, Hugo, 51
Kołodko, Grzegorz, 328
Konarski, Stanislaw, 51
Konin, 304
Korzon, Tadeusz, 57, 157, 177
Kościuszko, Tadeusz, 47
Kostrowicka, Irena, 5
Kowalik, Tadeusz, 6, 328

Kozienice, 304
Kraków, 54, 56, 92, 94, 97, 130, 134, 170, 230, 234, 305
Kronenberg, Leopold, 119, 131, 184
Krosno, 141
Krysiński, Dominik, 86
Krzaklewski, Marian, 325
Krzyżanowski, Adam, 156, 162, 176, 214
Kuczyński, Waldemar, 280
Kujawski, Aleksandrow, 140
Kula, Witold, 16, 35, 39, 61, 166
Kuroń, Jacek, 269, 279
Kuznets, Simon, 313
Kwaśniewski, Aleksander, 324, 325
Kwiatkowski, Eugeniusz, 219, 296, 350, 361

L

Labour emigration, 135, 286
Labour-intensive industrialization, 7–15, 18, 140, 182, 186, 187
Labour market, 299
Labour migration, 129
Labour rent, 52
Labour Union, UP, 325
Lake Żarnowiec, 221
Landau, Ludwik, 214
Landau, Zbigniew, 3, 5, 202
Land Credit Society, 102
Landless peasants, 57, 58, 95, 107, 226, 291
Land reform of 1944, 276, 296
Lange, Oskar, 8, 213, 278, 279
Lannes, Marchal, 98
Late industrialization, 8, 9, 11, 12, 24, 151–187

Latvia, 211
League of Nations, 238
League of Polish Families (LPR),
    325, 326, 334
Leap forward, 298
Łęczyca, 106, 108
Leder, Andrzej, 17
Legnica, 92
Legnica-Głogów area, 286
Łepkowski, Tomasz, 6, 158
Leszczyńska, Cecylia, 5, 174
Leszczyński, Stanisław, 47, 49
Leszek, Miller, 165, 325, 326
Lewandowski, Janusz, 280
Lignite, 304
Lin, Justin, 12, 13
List, Friedrich, 121
Lithuanian Republic, 197
Little Divergence, 17
Livezeanu, Irina, 4
Łódź, 108, 129, 131, 138, 166, 201,
    230, 239, 257, 258, 262, 290,
    303
Longue durée, 7
Lower Silesia, 91
Łowicz, 65
LPR, 325
Łubieński family, 136
Lublin, 56
Łuczak, Czesław, 5
Ludwikowski, Rett, 6
Łukawer, Edward, 6
Lwów, 54, 56, 92, 130, 134, 170,
    230, 257

M

Macierewicz, Antoni, 270
Maddison Project, 311
Małowist, Marian, 15

Manufacturing sector, 137, 139
March 1968, 269, 290, 293
Marshall Plan, 271
Martial law in 1981, 275, 293
Marx, Karl, 122
Masovia, 109, 257
Mass deportations in Soviet zone,
    259
Massey-Ferguson, 301
Material incentives, 279, 300
Material losses, 262
Mazowiecki, Tadeusz, 183, 270, 323
Mechanical engineering industry,
    136
Michnik, Adam, 269
Middle class, 94
Międzymorze, 211
Mikołajczyk, Stanisław, 256, 267
Milanovic, Branko, 21, 341
Miłkowski, Zygmunt, 159
Military territory Ober-Ost, 196
Mill, John Stuart, 122
Minc, Hilary, 277, 296
Ministry for the Former Prussian
    Partition, 198
Minsk, 163, 198, 199, 222
Mint, 102
Mitteleuropa, 197
Modernization, 1, 50
Modzelewski, Karol, 279
Molotov-Ribbentrop Pact, 212, 255
Moraczewski, Jędrzej, 208
Morawski, Wojciech, 5, 38, 184
Morewood, Steven, 4
Mościce, 239
Mościcki, Ignacy, 210
Moscow, 269
Munich Agreement (1938), 212
Musiał, Wojciech, 6
Myrdal, Gunnar, 14

N

Napoleon's Civil Code, 119
Narojek, Winicjusz, 309
Narutowicz, Gabriel, 208
National Armed Forces, 257, 268
National Bank of Poland, 308
National Council in Przemyśl, 198
National Council of the Duchy of
    Cieszyn, 198
National Democracy, 208, 210, 216
Nationalization of the economy, 268
National Radical Camp, 218
NATO, 323, 328
Nazi German settlements, 220, 259
Neisse, Lusatian, 267
Nepotism, 22, 136, 329, 354
New Silesia, 96
Nicholas II Romanov, 130
Nieśwież, 65
1976 Strikes, 291, 301
1988 Polish strikes, 270
Nitrogen fertilizer production plant
    in Puławy, 298
Niwka, 105
Nobility, 16, 17, 36–39, 93, 126,
    167, 169, 172, 174
    obligatory verification, 130
    social structure, 59
Nomenklatura, 292, 294
Nonpartisan Bloc for Cooperation
    with the Government, 209,
    210
North, Douglass C., 13, 14, 20
November Uprising (1830–1831), 4,
    82, 94, 108, 122, 130, 162
Nowa Huta, 297, 303
Nuclear power, 304
Numerus clausus, 228

O

Obligatory verification, 130
O'Brien, Patrick, 14
Occupational structure, 235, 288
October 1956, 269, 272, 274
Oder, 267
Oil and gas pipelines, 305
Oil refinery in Gdańsk, 301
Oil refinery in Płock, 298
Old Polish Industrial Area, 103
Olechowski, Andrzej, 325
Oleksy, Józef, 324
Oligarchy, 60
Olza, 199
Opatówek, 139
Operation Tempest, 256, 260
Operation Vistula (1947–1950), 268
Orava, 222, 282
Organized extermination, 260
O'Rourke, Kevin, 15
Oskar Lange, 8

P

Pale of Settlement, 162
Panki, 105
Partitions of Commonwealth of
    Poland and Lithuania
    Austrian Partition, 1, 79
    First partition, 45
    Partition treaty, 93
    Prussian Partition, 79
    Russian Partition, 80
    Second Partition, 46, 47
    territorial division, 90
    Third Partition, 47
PC, 324
Peasants, 17, 36–39, 95, 151, 152,
    155, 156, 158, 163–170, 172,

174, 177, 179, 181, 183, 184, 186, 291, 324, 331–333, 339, 349, 352, 353
cash rent, 140
corvée, 93
cottagers, 58
debates on emancipation, 117
emancipation of, 50
enfranchisement, 134
inclusion to the nation, 127
January Uprising, 119
labour rent, 140
landless peasants, 95
land reform, 226
parties, 208
the peasant-workers, 285
private farms under communism, 305
second serfdom, 36
serfdom, 50
serfdom abolishment—Josephine reforms, 79
social structure, eighteenth century, 57
subsistence farm, 107
Peasants' Battalions, 257
People's Army, 257
People's Guard, 257
Piątkowski, Marcin, 3, 13, 16, 17, 21, 22, 35, 332, 341
Piłsudski, Józef, 156, 159, 169, 209–211, 229
Piotrków, 106
PKO Bank Polski SA, 308
Plebiscite in Upper Silesia (1921), 196, 200
Płock, 298, 303
Podymne, 63

Pogrom in Jedwabne, 260
Poland, Lesser, 56, 103, 136
Połaniec, 304
Polesie, 229
Polish-Bolshevik War (1919–1921), 215
Polish Committee of National Liberation, 256
Polish-Czechoslovak border, 282
Polish Democratic Society, 121, 123
Polish-German border, 274, 283
Polish-German customs war, 244
Polish Government-in-Exile, 256, 271
Polish Liquidation Committee, 198
Polish-Lithuanian Commonwealth, 43, 52
Polish Loan Bank, 243
Polish minority in Czech Republic, 199
Polish People's Party, 210, 267
Polish Round Table, 271
Polish Socialist Party, 208–210, 214, 230, 266
Polish-Soviet War (1919–1921), 212
Polish-Ukrainian conflict, 228
Polish-Ukrainian war, 198
Polish Underground State, 257
Polish United Workers' Party, 267, 272
Polish Workers' Party, 266
Polish zloty, 243
Political myths, 210
Polska Kasa Opieki SA, 308
Pomerania, 5, 129, 133, 137, 234, 282
Poniatowski, Michał, 65, 348

Poniatowski, Stanisław August, 43, 44, 48
Pope John Paul II, 274
   Potsdam Conference, 274
Population, 283
Population loss, 260, 287
Portugal, 292
Post-communism, 26, 322–324, 326, 327, 329, 333, 341
Post-war reconstruction, 288
Potato blithe, 138
Potsdam Conference, 282
Poznań, 56, 91, 92, 132, 137, 230, 262, 284–286, 291, 293
Poznański, Izrael, 131
Poznański, Kazimierz, 328
Prague Spring 1968, 273
Prebisch-Singer hypothesis, 10
Private entrepreneurs in socialism, 293
Private sector, 311
Proclamation of Połaniec, 52
The Promised Land, 303
Propination monopolies, 120, 141
Protestants, 286
Provisional Government of National Unity, 276
Provisional Government of the Republic of Poland, 256
Prussia, 46, 48, 78
Prussian partition, 116, 121, 136
   agrarian reform, 107
   cities, 92
   education, 133
   ethnic structure, 132
Przemyśl, 56, 130
Przytyk Pogrom, 229
PSL, 324, 325

PSL Lewica, 208
PSL Piast, 208, 209
PSL Wyzwolenie, 208, 209
Public housing, 309
Puck, 221
Pula, James, 4
Puławy, 298
PZPR/PUWP, 267

R

Radom, 234, 270
Radziwill family, 65, 66
Railroads, 234
Rakowski, Mieczysław, 281
Ránki, Gyorgy, 3
Rawicz, 230
Recession, 301
Reconstruction process, 265
Recovered Territories, 265, 283, 288, 291, 303
Reda, 221
Red Army, 322
Reds' faction, 124
Refugees, 201
Regency Council, 197
Rębieliński, Rajmund, 18, 103, 105
Repatriation of Ukrainians from Poland to the Soviet Union, 268
Reparations Committee in Versailles, 202
Repphan Brothers' factory, 139
Resettlement of the Ukrainian minority, 268
Restoration (1918), 156
Reymont, Władysław, 158

Ricardo, David, 86
Riga, 199
Robinson, James, 3, 13
Rodecki, Franciszek, 106
Rokossovsky, Konstantin, 268
Roman Catholicism, 286
Romania, 211, 222
Roosvelt, Franklin D., 256
Rosenstein-Rodan, Paul, 220, 239
Rostowski, Jan V., 327
Roszkowski, Wojciech, 4
Round Table, 290
Ruch Underground Movement, 279
Ruhr, 137
Rural proletariat, 95, 133
Rural-urban migration, 331
Rusiński, Władysław, 5
Russia, 44, 48, 117, 130, 195
Russian Orthodox Church, 286
Russian partition, 116, 118, 129
Russian Revolution, 197
Rutkowski, Jan, 5
Rybarski, Roman, 214
Rydz-Śmigły, Edward, 210
Rzeszów, 239, 286
Rzewuski, Henryk, 125

S

Sachs, Ignacy, 279
Sachs, Jeffrey, 327, 336
Samoobrona, 325, 326, 334
Sanacja, 209, 210, 218, 226
Sandomierz, 56
Saxon House, 43
Saxony, 48
Say, Jean-Baptiste, 86
Scheibler, Karol, 138

Scheibler & Grohman textile factory,
    239
Scottish Enlightenment, 86
Second industrial revolution, 312
Sejm
    of 1780, 45
    Great Sejm, 46, 52
    in Grodno, 1793, 46
    Partition Sejm, 48
    Silent Sejm of 1717, 48
Selective development, 300
Self-governance, 302
Serfdom, 16, 36, 50, 52, 79, 87, 88,
    95, 116–119, 135, 140, 142
Services, 241
Service sector, 307
7-Years' War (1756–1763), 48
Sienkiewicz, Henryk, 158
Silesia, 136, 236, 282
Silesian Plebiscite, 222
Silesian Uprisings, 222
Sikorski, Władysław, 256
6-year plan (1950–1955), 268, 277,
    296
Skarbek, Fryderyk, 86
Skodlarski, Janusz, 5
Skrzyński, Aleksander, 209
Sławoj-Składkowski, Felicjan, 210
SLD, 324–326, 334
Small Emigration, 135
Smith, Adam, 62, 86
Smoczyński, Rafał, 17
Socialist calculation debate, 213
Socialist economy, 294, 360
    accumulation, 298
    Bank of Agriculture, 308
    Bank of State Economy, 239
    battle for trade, 278, 296, 307

black market, 294
collectivization, 298
collectivization of agriculture,
    278, 296
creditworthiness, 302
de-Stalinization after 1956, 269
economic destabilization, 302
economic recession of 1980s, 275,
    309
enforced collectivization, 291
foreign debt, 293
foreign licences, 297, 301
foreign loans, 302
hyperinflation of 1980s, 303
institutionalization of Marxist
    economics, 277
nationalization of the economy,
    268
private entrepreneurs in socialism,
    293
public housing, 309
6-year plan (1950–1955), 277
socialist welfare state, 309
Stalinist-era economy, 296
state-owned agriculture, 311
state socialism, 295
3-year plan (1947–1949), 276
winter of 1979/1980, 301
Socialist welfare state, 309
Social mobility, 288, 289
Social reforms, 23, 43, 45, 49,
    115–143, 203
Social structure, 6, 7, 21, 36, 38,
    170, 331, 335, 341, 352–354,
    361
Sokal, 282
Solidarność Movement, 270, 272,
    280, 291, 301

Solow residual, 299
Sosnowiec, 161, 166, 201, 232
South America, 9
South-East Asia, 11
Soviet-German war, 258
Soviet military forces in Poland, 272
Soviet-Polish Non-Aggression Pact
    (1932), 212
Soviet Russia, 213
Soviet Union, 257, 261, 272
Sowa, Jan, 16, 35
Spain, 292
Spätaussiedler, 274, 286
Spis, 222, 282
Spring of Nations, 116, 120, 121,
    130, 162
Stalin, Joseph, 199, 256, 361
Stalinist-era economy, 296
Stalinization, 268
Stańczyk party, 125
Standard of living, 289, 310
Staniszkis, Jadwiga, 280
Starzyński, Stefan, 218
Staszic, Stanislaw, 51, 89, 103, 161,
    350, 361
State Agricultural Farms, 306, 339
State capacity, 14, 16
    Commonwealth, 43
State income, 63, 243
State National Council, 256, 266
State-induced development, 9, 11
State-led accelerated
    industrialization, 89
State-led industrialization, 89, 240
State-owned agriculture, 311
State-owned industry, 311
Statism, 239
Stefano, Biancini, 4

Stefczyk, Franciszek, 180
Steinkeller, Piotr, 131
Stettin, 92
Strikes, 166, 230, 290
    1883 strike in Żyrardów, 166
    1892 strike in Łódź, 167
    1905 strike, 155, 167
    1920 strike in Poznań, 230
    1920 strike in Rawicz, 230
    1923 strike in Cracow, 230
    1926 strike of railway workers,
        230
    1931 strike in Białystok, 230
    1931 strike in Łódź, 230
    1933 farm workers strike, 230
    1936 farm workers strike, 230
    1945–1946 strikes, 290
    1956 June strike, 269
    1956 October strike, 272
    1970 December strike, 300
    1976 June strike, 269
    1980 protests, 286
    school strikes, 165, 170
    strike in Września, 165
Structural change, 299
Subsistence farm, 306, 352
Sudetenland, 222
Sums of Bayonne, 81, 98
Supiński, Józef, 126, 157, 158
Supreme People's Council, 198
Surowiecki, Wawrzyniec, 87–89
Suwalki, 257
Sweden, 48
Świdnica, 92
Świętokrzyskie Mountains, 103
Systemic transformation, 3, 321,
        322, 324, 326, 327, 335, 341,
        354, 361
Szczecin, 268, 282, 285, 286, 291,
        303, 304

Szlajfer, Henryk, 4
Szomburg, Jan, 280

T

Targowica Confederation, 44, 46, 53
Tax system, 244
Taylor, Edward, 214
Tepper, Piotr, 68
    The Enlightenment reform, 44
Textile industry, 107, 140, 141, 239
Third Republic of Poland, 266
Third World countries, 273
Thomas, Robert P., 13
3-year plan (1947–1949), 277, 296
Tilly, Charles, 14
Tomaszewski, Jan, 3, 6
Topolski, Jerzy, 5, 61
Toruń, 54, 56, 140, 220, 230
Tourism, 273
Trade, 307
Trade partners, 242
Transferable ruble, 309
Transport infrastructure, 137, 140,
        141, 234, 305
Treaty of Brest-Litovsk, 197, 198
Treaty of Locarno, 211
Treaty of Rapallo, 211
Treaty of Riga, 222
Treaty of Versailles, 198
Turkey, 49
Turnock, David, 4
Tymiński, Stanisław, 323, 334
Tyzenhaus, Antoni, 53, 59, 67

U

Ukraine, 197, 199, 281, 329
Ukrainian Insurgent Army, 268
Ukrainian minority, 229

UNCIO, 271
Under-urbanization, 331
United People's Party, 267
UNO, 271
Upper Silesia, 78, 91, 129, 140, 200,
222, 234, 257, 268, 285, 303,
305
Urban economy, 235
Urbanization, 91, 284
Ursus, 270, 301
USSR, 255

V

Vagabonds, 95, 105
Versailles, 211
Vistula Country, 160
Vistula River, 54
Volhynia, 222
Voltaire, 62
von Klimo, Arpad, 4
von Reden, Friedrich Wilhelm, 78

W

Wajda, Andrzej, 303
Wałbrzych, 286
Wałęsa, Lech, 270, 323–325
Wańkowicz, Melchior, 239
Wapiński, Roman, 6, 152, 160
War damages, 38, 39, 63, 80, 195,
201, 241, 245, 261, 263, 276,
289, 295, 355, 361
Walras auctions, 213
War of the Polish Succession, 47
Warsaw
mint, 102
Warsaw Pact, 271, 322
Warsaw Uprising, 256, 260

Warszawa, 55, 56, 65, 67, 91, 129,
131, 136, 138, 139, 166, 234,
291, 303, 305
Warthegau, 257, 258
Washington Consensus, 327, 336
Wawelbergs family, 119, 131
Weber, Max, 12
Weingast, Barry R., 14
Werwolf, 268
Western and Northern Lands, 265,
282
Western Europe, 1, 8, 9, 13, 20,
36–39, 155, 169, 172, 174,
180, 181, 328, 332, 338, 339,
341, 348, 356
Western Galicia, 79, 257
Western Ukrainian People's
Republic, 199
West Germany, 274
West Prussia, 129, 282
White collar workers, 334
Whites' faction, 131
Wieliczka, 54, 97, 141
Wielopolski, Aleksander, 18, 118,
125, 131
Williamson, Jeffrey G., 11, 15
Wilno, 56, 79, 92, 211
Wilson, Woodrow, 211
Winter of 1979/1980, 301
Witos, Wincenty, 209
WOG, 300
Wójtowicz, Grzegorz, 5
Wojtyła, Karol (Pope John Paul), 274
Worcell, Stanislaw, 123
Working class, 288
World Bank, 271
World War I, 133, 263
World War II, 255
German settlement, 258

Wrocław, 92, 285, 286
Wybicki, Józef, 51

Y

Yalta political order, 321
Yalta Treaty, 263
Yanayev political coup in Russia, 322
Young Plan, 212

Z

Zamorski, Jan, 217
Zamoyski Code, 46

Zamoyski, Adam, 3
Zaolzie, 199
Żarnowiec, 304
Zarycki, Tomasz, 17
Zawadzki, Władysław, 177, 213, 214
Zdziechowski, Jerzy, 214, 244
Żeromsk, Stefan, 159
Zhang, Weying, 12
Zhivkov, Todor, 273
Zieleniewski, Ludwik, 179
Złoty, 102, 243, 308
ZSL, 323
Żurawicki, Seweryn, 6
Żyrardów, 138, 166, 239

Printed by Printforce, the Netherlands